PSEUDO-PETRARCH
THE LIVES OF THE POPES
AND EMPERORS

CHRONICA
DE LE VITE DE PONTE
FICI ET IMPERADORI RO,
mani, Composta per . M. Francesco Pe,
trarcha allaquale sono state aggiunte
qlle che da tèpi del Petrarcha
insino alla eta nostra
mancauano.

PSEUDO-PETRARCH
THE LIVES OF THE POPES
AND EMPERORS

Translated by Aldo S. Bernardo
and Reta A. Bernardo

Edited, with an Introduction,
by Tania Zampini

*

ITALICA PRESS
NEW YORK
2015

Translation Copyright © 2015 by Aldo S. Bernardo and Reta A. Bernardo
Introduction Copyright © 2015 by Tania Zampini

ITALICA PRESS, INC.
595 Main Street
New York, New York 10044
inquiries@italicapress.com

Italica Press Medieval & Renaissance Texts

All rights reserved. No part of this publication may be reproduced, stored in a retrieval system, or transmitted, in any form or by any means, electronic, mechanical, photocopying, recording or otherwise, without prior permission of Italica Press. For permission to reproduce selected portions for courses, please contact the Press at inquiries@italicapress.com.

Library of Congress Cataloging-in-Publication Data

Petrarca, Francesco, 1304-1374.
[Chronica de le vite de pontefici et imperadori Romani. English]
The Lives of the Popes and Emperors ; translated by Aldo S. Bernardo and Reta A. Bernardo ; edited, with an introduction, by Tania Zampini.
   pages cm. – (Medieval & Renaissance texts)
Includes bibliographical references and index.
ISBN 978-1-59910-253-5 (hardcover : alk. paper) – ISBN 978-1-59910-254-2 (pbk. : alk. paper) – ISBN 978-1-59910-252-8 (e-book)
 1. Petrarca, Francesco, 1304-1374–Translations into English. 2. Popes–Early works to 1800. 3. Emperors–Rome–Early works to 1800. 4. Holy Roman Empire–Kings and rulers Early works to 1800. I. Bernardo, Aldo S., translator. II. Bernardo, Reta A., translator. III. Zampini, Tania, editor. IV. Title.
PQ4499.C413 2015
851'.1–dc23
           2015001951

Cover art: Pope Pius II (Aeneas Silvius Piccolomini) and Emperor Frederick III from Hartmann Schedel, *The Nuremberg Chronicle (Liber Chronicarum)* (Nuremberg: Anton Koberger, 1493), fol. CCLXVIII verso.

FOR A COMPLETE LIST OF ITALICA PRESS TITLES
VISIT OUR WEB SITE AT:
WWW.ITALICAPRESS.COM

CONTENTS

Illustrations	VI
Translators' Preface	VII
Introduction	XI
Description and Genre	XI
Sources	XII
The Book as Artifact and Its History	XVII
Authorship	XXIV
Petrarch's *De viris illustribus*	XXV
Pseudo-Petrarch and the *Liber pontificalis* and	
De viris illustribus traditions	XXVIII
Conclusions	XXXV
Lives of the Popes and Emperors	1
Through the First Century	1
The Second Century	22
The Third Century	36
The Fourth Century	51
The Fifth Century	69
The Sixth Century	84
The Seventh Century	101
The Eighth Century	118
The Ninth Century	131
The Tenth Century	150
The Eleventh Century	163
The Twelfth Century	174
The Thirteenth Century	189
The Fourteenth Century	213
The Fifteenth Century	225
The Sixteenth Century	244
Select Bibliography	249
Index	253

*

ILLUSTRATIONS

Frontispiece. Title page of *Chronica de le vite de pontefici et imperadori Romani, Composta per M. Francesco Petrarcha, allaquale sono state aggiunte quelle che da tempi del Petrarcha insino alla età nostra mancauano.* Venice: Francesco Bindoni & Mapheo Pasini, 1534. II

All other images are taken from the woodcuts of Hartmann Schedel, *The Nuremberg Chronicle (Liber Chronicarum).* Nuremberg: Anton Koberger, 1493. Number 16, Pius III, following the practice of the *Nuremberg Chronicle's* use of repeated images for multiple popes or emperors, is a composite image, since the *Chronicle* ends before his pontificate.

1. Julius Caius Caesar, fol. XCIII — 2
2. Trajan, fol. CIX — 22
3. Zephyrinus, fol. CXIV verso — 36
4. Marcellus, fol. CXXVI verso — 51
5. Anastasius I, fol. CXXXIII verso — 69
6. Symmachus, fol. CXLII verso — 84
7. Phocas, fol. CXLIX — 101
8. John VI, fol. CLVII verso — 118
9. Charlemagne, fol. CLXVIII — 131
10. Romanus, fol. CLXXII verso — 150
11. John XVIII, fol. CLXXXI verso — 163
12. Paschal II, fol. CXCVI verso — 174
13. Otto IV, fol. CCVII — 189
14. Benedict XI, fol. CCXIX — 213
15. Rupert of Bavaria, fol. CCXXXVI — 225
16. Pius III — 244

*

TRANSLATORS' PREFACE

by Aldo S. Bernardo and Reta A. Bernardo

There is general agreement that this curious little book, *Chronica de le vite de pontefici et imperadori Romani*, is not the work of Petrarch despite the fact that the lengthy title does ascribe it to him. It is listed under "spurious works" in the Cornell Catalogue of the Petrarch Collection, but it nevertheless enjoyed a number of printings in the early Renaissance: Florence, 1478; Venice, 1507, 1526 and 1534.[1] The obvious reason for this popularity was Petrarch's reputation as a great historian of the eminent men of the ancient past and their accomplishments. In fact, his greatest work was considered his *De viris illustribus* — Latin biographies of the outstanding classical men of action. A work by him in Italian concentrating on popes and Roman emperors was therefore bound to attract great interest. Today copies may be found in at least eight American libraries: New York Public, University of Miami, Chicago, Cornell (5 copies, 2 of 1534), Indiana, Princeton, Washington (Seattle), and Yale.

The present translation is based on the edition of 1534. In octavo form it contains 120 leaves, has its title within an ornamental border, a colophon containing place of printing and printer, a vignette of Tobit, his dog and Angel Raphael on the versus of the last leaf, and an index of the names of the popes and emperors included. It is probably a reprint of the 1526 edition. Unfortunately, the many hands that participated in the preparation of the original led not only to considerable variations in the quality of the Italian, but to confusion and errors regarding the names and accomplishments of some of the popes and emperors. To assist with such moments we use brackets to indicate the accepted English form of names (e.g., Iulianus [Julian]; to provide clarification of the text (e.g. Pius [I]) and important corrections (e.g., the correct order of the popes and emperors).

All together the text contains 230 biographies of popes and 117 of emperors, including anti-popes and renegade emperors, as well as

---

1. The complete 1534 edition is available online at:
http://reader.digitale-sammlungen.de/de/fs1/object/display/bsb10188803_00001.html.

THE LIVES OF THE POPES AND EMPERORS

anecdotal accounts of unusual cosmic and human events. Aside from the exact length of time served by each pope, an interesting feature is the inclusion of the exact number of days the papacy remained vacant between popes. Each biography is listed in its chronological order, together with a date of service. Starting with the year 800 the biographies become increasingly short and eventually concentrate on the history of events — mostly deaths. There is even an account of a pope (not included in the regular order) who reigned for a few months until he turned out to be a woman. (See entry following Emperor 80.)

There are two breaks in the text, one after Pope 171 and the other after Pope 207. The first maintains that the text must be corrupt at this point because Petrarch would never have overlooked the victory of the Venetians over the emperor and his recent reinstatement of the pope. The second indicates that Petrarch's authorship ends at this point (1374: the year of Petrarch's death) and that the subsequent biographies were carefully added to have the text continue to the year 1534 (actually 1523).

The person or persons who mistakenly attributed these biographies to Petrarch actually adds to our grasp of the literary climate in Italy during the early sixteenth century. This may be seen even in the Proem to the book in which we find the presumed Petrarch defining what was later to be called the spirit of the Renaissance: "Since human minds desire to know the deeds of outstanding men of the past, certain writers describe at length the lives of such men. But because most men are impeded by various and diverse cares, they are unable to deal with so much material. And so, in order that even those who occupied with so many responsibilities might have some knowledge of things past, I have restricted this book to the lives of Pontiffs and Roman Emperors, carefully keeping in order the times in which they lived, how many years they lived...."

This work does indeed disseminate a great deal of information in brief fashion, but regrettably in an Italian which suffers from being so dense and condensed that it often requires intense historical and linguistic research to make sense of a statement. It nevertheless does serve the author's main goal of enlightening the minds of people too busy with their daily lives and chores to read extensive learned works in languages other then Italian. This certainly was part of the Renaissance spirit.

Editor's Note

The following introduction by Tania Zampini expands the Bernardo's philological preface with a more detailed analysis of the text, its authorship, cultural contexts and genre. The text of the *Lives of the Popes and Emperors* maintains the translation and the editorial approach laid out by the Bernardos in almost every respect. Exceptions include the following. We have divided the text into sixteen chapters by century. Within those we have used Arabic rather than Roman numerals for the papal and imperial numbers in the headers. We have kept annotation identifying the popes, emperors, other persons and historical places and events to a minimum, since these can be obtained through many online and printed sources. We have annotated the text to identify other historical persons and events or historical concepts, as appropriate. We have done so lightly. There were two reasons for our approach. The first is to not overwhelm or "correct" the text: it is, after all, a historical document of its time and not a modern reference work. It should therefore be read for what it reveals about sources used for these *Lives* and about the late medieval, early modern concepts of the ecclesiastical and imperial past. Secondly, our annotation provides enough information to disambiguate identifications and references for the curious reader who wants to take advantage of numerous resources readily available in both print and online.

The select bibliography presents both primary sources that occur repeatedly through sections of the text and secondary works of major importance. Other citations can be found in the notes throughout. For ready reference see Richard P. McBrien, *Lives of the Popes: The Pontiffs from St. Peter to John Paul II* (San Francisco: HarperCollins, 1997); or Eamon Duffy, *Saints and Sinners: A History of the Popes* (New Haven: Yale University Press, 2001). Ferdinand Gregorovius, *History of the*

THE LIVES OF THE POPES AND EMPERORS

City of the Rome in the Middle Ages, 8 vols. Annie Hamilton, trans. (London: George Bell & Sons, 1909-1912; rev. ed., with introduction by David S. Chambers, New York: Italica Press, 2000–2004), covers Roman events from the fifth into the early sixteenth century. The Roman *Liber Pontificalis* is a source for many of these papal biographies from the earliest through the ninth century. They have been translated by Raymond Davis in three volumes (Liverpool: Liverpool University Press, 1989–1995) and referred to here as *Liber Pontificalis* 1 (to A.D. 715), 2 (Eight-Century) and 3 (Ninth-Century). Biographies of Roman emperors are available in any number of reference works, monographs and popular histories both in print and online. We have annotated their entries only for clarification.

*

INTRODUCTION

by Tania Zampini

DESCRIPTION AND GENRE

Contained in eight libraries across the United States is a book in Italian, in the Tuscan vernacular, *Chronica de le vite de pontefici et imperadori Romani*, on the lives of 230 popes and 117 emperors from Julius Caesar to Pope Clement VII. Not much is known about this work beyond its title, which ascribes the majority of its composition to Petrarch — an attribution, for all intents and purposes, commonly held to be improbable. Still, it enjoyed a considerable amount of press and was printed once in Florence in Latin in 1478 and three more times in Venice in 1507, 1526 and 1534.[1] The latest of these editions, printed by Marchio Sessa in octavo form, is a little book of no more than 120 leaves, assumed to be a reprint of Gregorio di Gregorii's 1526 edition, which contained marginal rubrics to guide readers. A departure from both of these is the non-annotated 1507 version, edited by Jacomo de Pinci, printed by Francesco Bindoni and Maffeo Pasini, and held at the Newberry Library in Chicago. Over eighty printed copies of the Venetian editions are contained in Italian libraries from Padua to Soriano Calabro. The only substantial difference among them are their lengths: later editions feature biographies not found in earlier versions and likely added by the publishers themselves before going to print.

These Venetian printers provide a clue to understanding the use, if not dissemination, of the *Lives of the Popes and Emperors* and the intellectual milieu in which it might have circulated. Between 1530 and 1540, Bindoni and Pasini, in Venice, systematically (though not exclusively) promoted the publication of histories — both secular and ecclesiastical — of what we today call Italy. They typically addressed successions of wars throughout Italy and included both historical details specific to municipalities and ecclesiastical developments during

1. Eleven copies of the 1478 edition are held in special collections from Turin to Rome. The complete 1534 edition is available online at:
http://reader.digitale-sammlungen.de/de/fs1/object/display/bsb10188803_00001.html .

periods of political upheaval. A list of titles of such items of interest printed within those years include: *Lo assedio [et] impresa de Firenze : con tutte le cose successe : incominciando dal laudabile accordo del summo Po[n]tifice [et] la Cesarea maesta: et tutti li ordini [et] battaglie seguite* 1531, the *Guerre horrende de Italia : tutte le guerre de Italia : comenzando dala venuta di Re Carlo del mille quatroce[n]to nouantaquatro, fin al giorno presente* of 1534, the *Opusculo de trenta documenti del reuerendo padre Don Pietro da Luca canonico regulare: da essere obseruati da le persone che desiderano esser spirituale e veri Christiani* of 1539, and the *Historia de la guerra del Piamonte* of 1539.

The Marchio Sessa brothers and publishers increasingly focused their attention, instead, on moral philosophies; indeed, the Lives in many ways depart from a publication program that shifted from its interest in comedies and Dante's works on love (the *Convivio*) to a concern with moral integrity and its humanist links to classic culture (considering specifically Cicero's Latin epistles). These exemplars together are consistent, sometimes competing, but more often cooperating with trends in vernacular production and public interest of those years: Italy's national history as studied through the history of its wars (and European wars more generally), the development of the Church and the influence of classic culture. All three topics are also central to the *Lives of the Popes and Emperors* printed two decades earlier. Our discussion will therefore focus on two key, but interrelated questions: sources and authorship. These are bound together through an investigation of the book as an artifact and of its history.

SOURCES
Both ecclesiastical chronologies and the literary praise of illustrious men share in traditions that predate them by centuries and that continued to exist for years following their publication. Saint Jerome's *De viris illustribus* and Livy's *Decades* or *Roman History* provided the two models most essential to medieval and Renaissance thinkers and historiographers. Both are examples of texts embraced by the movement of early Renaissance humanism — or "the school of classical scholarship

INTRODUCTION

and ethical and aesthetic inquiry inaugurated by Petrarch in the 1340s, carried on by Boccaccio and Salutati in the last half of the fourteenth century, and further elaborated by Salutati's disciples in Florence in the first decades of the fifteenth century."[2] But as Eric Cochrane points out, they represent only one of what he terms history's "parents."[3] The other, and arguably much more prolific, is the pre-humanistic chronicle.

Chronicles were basically year-by-year accounts of local history, originally compiled by members of the clergy or, in Italy, often by members of the merchant class, frequently by professional notaries.[4] They were not intended to be works of literature and often grew out of, or alongside, a variety of compatible projects with similar goals that proliferated throughout Italy: diaries or *ricordanze* were family histories; urban annals were municipal accounts of wars often contextualized by references to momentous occasions throughout Europe. Although it was not uncommon for even smaller municipalities to commit their city's central events to writing, Italy's most representative and useful chronicles belong to its major urban centers: Venice,[5] Genoa,[6] Milan,[7]

---

2. Eric Cochrane, *Historians and Historiography in the Italian Renaissance* (Chicago: University of Chicago Press, 1981) 15.

3. Ibid.

4. For general overview see Gabrielle M. Spiegel, *The Past as Text: The Theory and Practice of Medieval Historiography* (Baltimore: Johns Hopkins University Press, 1997); and Deborah Mauskopf Deliyannis, ed., *Historiography in the Middle Ages* (Leiden: Brill, 2003), including Augusto Vasina, "Medieval Urban Historiography in Western Europe (1100–1500)," 317–52.

5. Gina Fasoli, "I fondamenti della storiografia veneziana," in Agostino Pertusi, ed., *La Storiografia veneziana fino al secolo XVI: Aspetti e problemi* (Florence: L.S. Olschki, 1970), 11–44; Antonio Lombardo, *Studi e ricerche dalla fonti medievali veneziane* (Rome: Il Centro di ricerca, 1982); John Melville-Jones, "Venetian History and Patrician Chroniclers," in *Chronicling History: Chroniclers and Historians in Medieval and Renaissance Italy*, ed. Sharon Dale, Allison Williams Lewin and Duane J. Osheim (University Park: Pennsylvania State University Press, 2007), 197–221.

6. See Giovanna Petti Balbi, *Caffaro e la cronachistica genovese* (Genoa: Tilgher, 1982); and John Dotson, "The Genoese Civic Annals: Caffaro and His Continuators," in Dale et al., *Chronicling History*, 55–85.

7. For example, Gary Ianziti, *Humanistic Historiography under the Sforzas: Politics and Propaganda in Fifteenth-Century Milan* (Oxford: Clarendon Press, 1988); and Paolo

Florence,[8] Rome[9] and Naples and its kingdom.[10] They enjoyed a particular proliferation in Tuscany during and after the Tuscan wars of the late thirteenth century. One need only consider the Villani family's chronicle of Florence ending in 1364 for a better understanding not only of the frequency but also of the importance attributed to chronicling history in a serious capacity.[11]

In many ways, these late medieval chronicles influenced sixteenth-century compilations of local history — Benedetto Varchi's *Storia Fiorentina* offers only one example. At the height of their popularity, furthermore, they all displayed variations on a functional formula that remained useful for later writers of local history: in addition to recounting wars and various political successions, most chronicles also contained bizarre anecdotal episodes and observations on cosmology or other natural events. Still, despite their zeal, chroniclers and annalists were not concerned with active authorship. Instead, they viewed writing as a passive activity and considered their responsibility as limited to the adequate (indeed, thorough) recording of historical events for the

---

Chiesa, ed., *Le cronache medievali di Milano* (Milan: Vita e Pensiero, 2001); Edward Coleman, "Lombard City Annals and the Social and Cultural History of Northern Italy," in Dale et al., *Chronicling History*, 1–27; and Sharon Dale, "Fourteenth-Century Lombard Chronicles, in Dale et al., *Chronicling History*, 171–95

8. Anna Maria Cabrini, *Un'idea di Firenze: Da Villani a Guicciardini* (Rome: Bulzoni, 2001).

9. See for example Gustav Seibt, *Anonimo romano: Scrivere la storia alle soglie del Rinascimento* (Rome: Viella, 2000).

10. See Marino Zabbia, *Notai-cronisti nel Mezzogiorno svevo-angioino: Il "Chronicon" di Domenico da Gravina* (Salerno: Laveglia, 1997); idem, *I notai e la cronachistica cittadina italiana nel Trecento* (Rome: ISIME, 1999); Fulvio Delle Donne, *Politica e letteratura nel Mezzogiorno medievale: La cronachistica dei secoli XII–XV* (Salerno: Carlone, 2001); Chiara De Caprio, *Scrivere la storia a Napoli tra Medioevo e prima età moderna: Tre studi* (Rome: Salerno, 2012). For Anglophone work see Samantha Kelly, *The* Cronaca di Partenope: *An Introduction to and Critical Edition of the First Vernacular History of Naples (c.1350)* (Leiden: Brill, 2011).

11. Giovanni Villani began writing the chronicle, which came to completion only posthumously by his brother and nephew. See Paula Clarke, "The Villani Chronicles" in Dale et al., *Chronicling History*, 113–43.

use of future generations and in so doing frequently borrowed wholesale from previous works.

While the Villani and other Florentine chroniclers certainly made moral judgments and linked events with reference to the wheel of fortune or fate,[12] it was not until humanism that historiography as a literary activity gained a distinct moral aspect. The central mandate of writing history for humanists was both educational and moral: histories should not only create a viable continuum between the ancient past and present arrived at through logic and deduction, but should also propose a model for the future by highlighting the valuable behaviors of admirable men and admonishing against the reprehensible acts of villainous ones. As such, they typically listed and expanded upon the lives of both secular figures (emperors) and religious figures (biblical characters and popes) to provide concrete examples of proper and improper human conduct. To this end, early humanist historiographers often wrote one of three different types of histories: biographies, local histories and universal histories, often drawing on earlier medieval traditions. Two subsets of the first type soon distinguished themselves in humanist circles: the writing of popes' lives — the medieval *Liber Pontificalis* tradition[13] — and the writing of emperors' lives, or the *De viris illustribus* tradition.

Humanist historiographers assembled their works in ways the earlier chroniclers did not; they framed their grand narratives thematically to entice readers to follow the examples set carefully for them. The duty of the humanist historiographer then was the proper (and perhaps subliminal) embedding of abstract ethical discourse into a text that was imitable on a practical level. As Cochrane has phrased it, "[humanist

---

12. See Louis Green, *Chronicle into History: An Essay on the Interpretation of History in Fourteenth-Century Chronicles* (Cambridge: Cambridge University Press, 1972).

13. The Roman *Liber Pontificalis* originally dated from c. 540 and was based on earlier compilations. See *The Book of Pontiffs* (Liber Pontificalis): *The Ancient Biographies of Nine Popes to AD 715*, trans. Raymond Davis (Liverpool: Liverpool University Press, 1989, rev. ed. 2010), XIII. Davis's translations are in three volumes and continue the *Liber* up to Pope Stephen V (d. 891).

historiography] therefore proposed, in an attractive literary garb, 'the example of the illustrious kings, nations, and men for the imitation... of posterity'."[14] This model of historiography remained current — and preferred — in Italy well into the sixteenth century and even among authors who in their other works squarely rejected the teachings and ideals of Renaissance humanism: notorious anti-humanist Lodovico Dolce adhered to this very practice in his early sixteenth-century recasting of Pedro Mexia's *Spanish Lives of All the Emperors*, also published in Venice numerous times between 1511 (with Giolito de' Ferrari) and 1610 (by Alessandro de' Vecchi) passing through the hands and publishing houses of Alessandro Griffio, Francesco Sansovino, Olivier Alberti, Girolamo Sansovino and Girolamo Scoto along the way.

Chief in the minds of humanist historiographers not only in accomplishment, but also in reputation, is Francesco Petrarch, who famously compiled the first, third and fourth of Livy's *Decades* into a single codex and who later penned his own *De viris illustribus* (or *Lives of Illustrious Men*) in several versions, the final of which was only brought to light posthumously.[15] It is most likely this later project that came to be associated with the later and vulgate *Lives of the Popes and Emperors* discussed here.[16] The stylistic differences between pseudo-Petrarch's *Lives* and Petrarch's *De viris illustribus*, however, as well as their separate focuses and publication history put into doubt the *Lives of the Popes and Emperors*' association with Petrarch. Examining the book first as an artifact and next as a text partaking of this larger and centuries-old trend, I will critically examine claims of Petrarch's authorship of the *Lives* and suggest other, more viable sources of inspiration for the

---

14. Cochrane 16.

15. See W. Braxton Ross, Jr., "Giovanni Colonna, Historian at Avignon," *Speculum* 45.4 (1970): 533–63.

16. On Petrarch's *De viris illustribus*, see Ronald G. Witt, "The Rebirth of the Romans as Models of Character," in *Petrarch: A Critical Guide to the Complete Works*, ed. Victoria Kirkham and Armando Maggi (Chicago: University of Chicago Press, 2009), 103–11.

present pseudo-Petrarch consistent with the text's structure, content and language.

The Book as Artifact and Its History

Examining the book as an object reveals a number of telling details about its use and the textual communities to which it might have appealed. The 1507 volume is essentially a pocketbook rather than a display book, desk book or reference volume. It is small, compact and light. It might have been easily transported even during travels abroad, if necessary. Like the 1526 and the 1534 editions, its title is contained in an elaborate border consistent with the major printing practices of first editions of the late fifteenth and early sixteenth centuries. The following pages include an index of popes and emperors' names and a woodblock image of Tobit, his dog and the Angel Raphael. These derive from the biblical Book of Tobit and its narrative of the latter's journey under angelic protection and is significant in the context of the heavy use of the Book of Tobit in liturgy: a theme central in the *Lives of the Popes and Emperors*.

This is the 1507 edition's only illustration, although it is more than likely that the first initial of the first *capitolo* was intended to be illustrated but was never completed. The others appear as capitals *(in capitalis)* and in bold. The printers' presence is seen in what is likely their own autograph at the book's close; no other evidence of it exists, either in the form of a printer's preface or in a note to readers. The 1534 edition by Melchiore Sessa does open, however, with a dedicatory letter from the editor, Nicolo Garanta, to "the reverent Monsignor Theodoro Pio," bishop of Venice's San Paolo diocese. Here Garanta discusses publishing this volume after the monsignor's visit to his bookstore in Venice, during which they both lamented the lack of satisfactory clarity and detail in books hitherto published dedicated to celebrating the lives of illustrious men. He also notes his addition of the lives that came after the death of Petrarch (its assumed author) and that Petrarch was unable to witness.

THE LIVES OF THE POPES AND EMPERORS

A look inside pseudo-Petrarch's densely written *Lives* reveals them, at least initially, to be a condensed history of the development of the Catholic Church, more specifically in Italy. They come as close to a literature of "Catholic national pride" as possible in an Italy that is not yet a nation. The earliest unbaptized emperors are implicitly evaluated on the strength of their character as it might be assessed by the Catholic Church — Julius Caesar is described as "moderate and divine," while Claudius is described as gluttonous and lecherous — and those living after Christ are almost always linked, at the end of their biographies, to the popes or religious figures that shared their tenure.[17] Pseudo-Petrarch also makes frequent mention of the martyrdom of various saints and the import of their relics for worship to different parts of Italy: under Pope Urban II, the spear used to pierce Christ crucified was found; under Pope Hilarius of Sardinia, Saint Mark's body was brought to Venice.[18] The popes, instead, are discussed mainly as a function of their concrete ability to develop the Catholic Church through the implementation of specific rules or religious rites: Pope Telesphore introduces and institutes the Lenten period; Pope Boniface makes concrete women's exclusion from the central functions of the holy liturgy.[19] As in the various versions of the medieval *Liber Pontificalis*, to which the *Lives* appears indebted, Roman events, buildings and personalities dominate much of the early sections of the book. Many of the Church accomplishments included are also representative of the Church's wealth, through architectural growth and the purchase of material goods for liturgical

17. This tendency grows stronger in the section of lives following the initial group up until 1371: Emperor Sigismund, King of Hungary, is described as "christianissimo e humile e divoto imperadore in modo che secondo la opinione di molti doppo la morte essere canonizato meritava" (MS Rome, Biblioteca Nazionale Centrale, 71.2.C.4, lxxxiii verso). See page 227 below.

18. "In questo anno anchora si trovò la lancia con la quale fu aperto il lato di Christo rivelandolo un religoso huomo che Andrea si chiamava" (MS Rome, BNC 71.2.C.4, lxv recto); "a suo tempo anchora il corpo di S. Marco fu portato in Vinegia, prospero equitanico etiandio in questi tempi fiori e per dottrine per miracoli fu chiaro" (MS Florence, Biblioteca Nazionale Centrale, Magl. 4.6.92, 40). See page 173 below.

19. "Ordinò che nessuna donna toccassi palla sacrata dello altare, o vero ponessi incensio" (MS Firenze, BNC, Magl. 4.6.92, 37v). See page 72 below.

INTRODUCTION

use. Pope Silvester ordered that the churches of Saints Peter and Paul be beautified and adorned with silver and gold and had the church of San Lorenzo built in Rome's Via Tiburtina.[20] Pope Innocent VI had a monastery for the Carthusian Order built in France, just as centuries before him, Pope Calixtus had ordered the construction of the church of Sta. Maria in Trastevere.[21] Just as frequent are the holy visions and miracles reported: Pope Deusdedit, kissing a leper, cured him of leprosy;[22] Pope Paschal I saw a vision of Saint Cecilia in the flames of a burning medieval neighborhood.[23]

By the late 1100s, when the line between Church and Empire becomes increasingly blurred in wider European politics, the lives of the popes come very much to look like the lives of the emperors. Both are praised for their prowess in battle and, during the Crusades period (which the book pushes back into the ninth century), for their ability to quash the foreigner, enemy both to their land and to their religion.[24]

---

20. "Fece anchora la chiesa del beato Lorenzo martyre nella via Tiburtina adornandola di molti bellissimi gradi, nella quale fece una casa dove pose il sacrato corpo ornato di marmo e di porfido chiudendola di sopra con oro purissimo e ordinovi un cancello e dinanzi da la grata una lucerna doro purissimo, e intorno al corpo uno adornamento dariento concerti dalphini artificisamente aconci e molti altri adornamenti nelle chiese fece" (ibid, 29r). See page 54 below.

21. "Costui fece la chiesa di Sancta Maria Transtevero. Et ordino le digiuna questro tempora e fece il cimiterio della Via Appia il quale fu chiamato di Calisto dove e sepolto grandissima multitudine di martyri." (MS Rome, BNC, 71.2.C.4, xvi verso); "fece fabricare nel regno di Francia presso a S. Andrea un monasterio dellordine Carthusiese dando a cotale ordine molti grandi privilegi. Fu iragione canonica excellente allultimo havendo sancatamente tradocto la vita simore e nel monaseterio dallui edificato fu sepolto" (ibid, lxxxi verso). See page 37 below.

22. MS Florence, BNC, Magl. 4.6.92, 52v. See page 104 below.

23. "Costui ardendo il borgo di Sanfogm [?] alla fiamma soppose e subito miraculosamente ne cadde il fuoco il qual poi lui rifece. A lui anchora la beata Vergine Cecilia apparedo vestito di dorate veste con Valeriano suo sposo, e con Tiburtio e Urbano e Lucio pontifici lo ringratio, conciosia che degli gli avessi una chiesa dentro nella città fabricato, doppoi gli rivelo dove i corpi predetti erano posti, i quali lui ritrovati nella detta chiesa con somma riverentia rispose." (ibid, 70r). See page 140 below.

24. The Catholic crusades are treated with inconsistent attention; greater emphasis is placed on the first, fourth, and fifth crusades and on the events leading up to each.

Indeed, by its last pages, war and the rise (and fall) of the Roman Empire emerge as themes just as fundamental to the *Lives* as the growth of the Church through its patriarchs. One might speculate that the depth of coverage owes as much to the varying value of the sources employed as to the author's particular interests.

What is more, the text lends itself to easy fragmentation, as sections of text differentiate themselves from those following or preceding them as much in tone as in selected content. The lives of Julius Caesar, Constantine I, Charlemagne and Frederick I receive unparalleled attention and are easily triple the length of any other biography; the history of the Tuscan wars exists as a concise cycle detached from the biographies surrounding it; the lives described between 1032 and 1277 seem more overtly preoccupied with anecdotes of strange occurrences than any others. Events around the Angevin conquest of Naples appear unusually well-informed. The personalities and conflicts of the Romagna and other areas of the emerging Papal States receive detailed attention. Events in Rome during the Renaissance papacy and the European wars of the late fifteenth and early sixteenth century also draw significant detail. Some places more than others rely on hearsay and popular belief in their narration of specific events, adopting specific verbal formulas to assist them.[25] There may, indeed, have been more than one author of pseudo-Petrarch's *Lives*; if there was not, its singular author, at the very least, was willing to sacrifice the consistency of his form to fit what he considered the needs of specific sections of text and the content of his borrowed sources.

Generally speaking, each chapter, like many others in both the *Liber Pontificalis* and *De viris illustribus* traditions, begins with the name of the pope or emperor being described, information about his birth, family, provenance and the period of his tenure — all standard formalities — before going on to address his most important accomplishments.

---

25. The text often includes speculative phrases like *"si legge che,"* and *"in questo tempo ancora, si legge"* to introduce second hand information that likely appears in a number of histories that inform it.

INTRODUCTION

The text itself, however, displays a number of properties more akin to the medieval chronicle than to the Renaissance humanist tradition. Among them is the frequent inclusion of supernatural events and cosmological oddities. Some are natural disasters in Europe at large: during a summer storm under Emperor Louis I's reign, a piece of ice six feet tall, fifteen wide, and two deep fell from the sky in France;[26] Pope Nicholas I's papacy witnessed a fire that ravaged most of Cologne;[27] the text elsewhere makes mention of a series of droughts and earthquakes in Italy, France, Syria and Damascus.[28] Others are medical anecdotes surrounding unnatural births. These include a pair of conjoined twins born under Pope Agapitus II,[29] a pig born with a human face,[30] a monster born with the torso of a man and the lower half of a dog[31] and a man who lived like a fish in the sea.[32] But the narration of these events occupies little space; relative to the rest of the text, the

---

26. "In questo tempo anchora inanzi al solstizio estivo sendo venuita gran tempesta cadde dal cielo, in Francia un pezzo di giaccio la larghezza del quale era di vi piedi, la lunghezza di xv laltezza di ii" (ibid 69v). See below, 139.

27. "Anchora si legge, che in Cologna i su la chiesa di S. Piero cadde una fulgura di fuoco, laquale in gran parte la rovinò, e fece molti huomini morire" (ibid 72v). See below, 145.

28. See below, 9. 14, 60, 87, 172, 178, 183, 192, 216.

29. See below, 156.

30. See below, 176.

31. See below, 178.

32. See below, 193. "Nel tempo delquale si legge, che in Guascogna nacque una femina dal bellico in su divisa lauqale haveva due capi e dua petti, con quattro braccia, et non faceva luna parte quello che laltra conciosia che talhora luna dormiva e laltra vegliava e spesso luna mangiava digiunando laltra e sendo vissuti a questo modo buono pezzo ne morì prima una sopravivendo laltra, laqual dipoi pel puzzo si morì" (ibid 77r); "in questo tempo una porca miracolosamente partorì un porcello il quale haveva la faccia humana" (MS Rome, BNC 71.2.C.4, lxv verso); "in hispagna nacque un mostro di dua corpi il quale nella parte dinanzi haveva la forma intera duno homo e la parte dirieto haveva di cane" (ibid lxvi recto); "leggesi anchora che in questi tempo fu uno huomo in Sicilia che si chiama Nicolao Pescie, il quale viveva in mare come pescie, ne poteva molto fuori dellacqua stare e molte cose a glijuomin de secreti del mare rivelo" (MS Florence, BNC Magl. 4.6.92, 93v).

lines devoted to such tangential observations are few and far between and may again point to their occurrence in the *Lives*' source materials.

Analyzing the feats and merits that the text chooses to privilege, however, a clearer picture emerges as to its overall aim and function. The *Lives*' author — or perhaps his printers in and after 1526 — adds rubrics in the margin to direct reading or perhaps to signal to readers not only the key issues to be found in the text itself, but the issues of central interest at the time. There are 216 in all in the 1534 edition. These rubrics all fall into one of the following categories: the first, and the largest, indicators of religious content (ecclesiastical ceremony, sacraments, developments of the liturgy, etc.), the next largest, names of the popes and emperors and their attributes, miraculous content (miracles and religious visions), followed by the mention of treatises and official events, references to "barbarian invasions," conversions of non-Catholic peoples and the growth of Catholicism beyond the Italian world. What does not fit in any of these categories constitutes the smallest category, "other," containing only nineteen of the 216 total rubrics.

Even just glossing over some of these marginal guides, however, two things about the *Lives* become clear: first, that its editors most likely aimed for its use as a book on Catholic virtues and both the expansion of Catholic practice in Italy and its importation to other countries; next that the *Lives* pivot on a fundamental "us" versus "them" dichotomy, pitting not only the Catholic Church against barbarians and heretics, but also pointing in turn to the infighting characteristic of the time at much more local levels in Rome, Florence, Milan, Venice and throughout the South. These civil wars are not addressed in any detail in the rubrics but are indeed central to the text they describe.

These rubrics also assist present-day readers in thinking about the book's intended public and purpose. It describes itself, in a proem also attributed to Petrarch (and just as unlikely his), as a condensed examination of the lives of certain illustrious men in chronological order, reduced for the modern (and busy) reader from more elaborate

INTRODUCTION

texts on the same subject. It also admits to fulfilling many of the typical chronicle's functions. Pseudo-Petrarch writes:

> In this book, I condensed the lives of the popes and Roman emperors, arranging them diligently in chronological order, and describing in which millennium both the popes and the emperors lived, how many years they lived, the particularities of their lives, and which worthy and saintly men also proliferated in those years. Nor have I left out the various ecclesiastical ceremonies developed, or the miraculous events, or other daily occurrences of the apostolic orders. In the end, I included everything that I deemed worthy of being remembered and that might be described concisely. For this reason, if readers consider my work to be of any use, not seeking within it the elegance of an ornate sermon, since the variety of the material covered precludes it, I don't doubt that they will commend my honest effort.[33]

Although not a university textbook, and lacking the marginal annotations characteristic of a carefully studied text, its concise prose suggests its at least secondary function as a didactic work.[34] Its compact form suggests an audience of laypeople with little time to consult larger, more exhaustive and more detailed histories of the Church and Empire, as is alluded to in the introductory proem. Its primary concern with Church developments points to an additional use by clergy as part of general Church teaching. Its humble format and

---

33. "Brievemente in questo libro ho ristrecto le vite de Pontefici e Imperadori Romani concordando con diligente ordine e tempi e descrivendo in che millesimo epontefici il papato e gli imperadori limperio pigiorono, quanti anni in quegli vissono, quale fussi la vita loro, che degni e sancti huomini in quali tempi fiorirono. Non ho anchora lasciate varie cerimonie da gli ecclesisastici trovate, ne miracoli advenuti, ne molte consuetudini dalla sedia apostolica ordinare. Alla fine nessuna cosa che degna di memoria mi sia paruta: e che brievemente si sia potuta toccare ho pretermesso. per laqual cosa se i lectori iutilità di questa mia opera diligentemente considerreanno, non ricercando lornato e elegante sermone conciosia che la varietà della material non lo richiede: non dubito che la mia [...] honesta faticha commenderanno" (MS Rome, BNC 71.2.C.4, ii recto). See page 1 below.

34. A copy of the 1507 edition held at the Biblioteca Nazionale Centrale di Roma reveals the hand of a later reader, who takes interest in the text's oblique mentions of the development of various chivalric orders (the Order of the Knights Templar). His notes were not used to compile the rubrics that appear in later editions, but demonstrate the text's accessibility to its audience.

non-illustrated first initial strongly suggest a middle-class audience of artisans and shopkeepers with basic knowledge of ecclesiastical history and the well-known illustrious figures of their times.

AUTHORSHIP

Thus far we have considered only the book's sources and its formal qualities, and links with Petrarch are tenuous at best and based solely on his strong positions on the practices of the Catholic Church of his time.[35] What is more, the text itself reveals inconsistencies with Petrarch's overall philosophical tendencies and preferences.[36] Indeed, given his humanistic sensibilities, it would have been quite unlikely for Petrarch to reduce in scope a project that seemed worthy not only of lengthy discussion but also of a dignified tone and of Latin composition. Furthermore, as Ugo Dotti points out in his introduction to *De viris illustribus,* the period in which Petrarch penned his catalogue of illustrious men is one in which his vitriol against the Church was particularly keen — and particularly felt. In fact, the purpose of his *De viris illustribus* was to react against his contemporary ecclesiastical milieu. Dotti writes:

> The text was likely written between 1352 and 1353, during the poet's last sojourn in Avignon — that is to say, the period during which he comes to consider the corruption of the Church unbearable. The Church was corrupt; humanity was infected. It became necessary to act, to bring back to righteousness a society that had long since been

---

35. His *Liber sine nomine* remains the most demonstrative collection of invectives against the Church, Church fathers, and contemporary Church practices. See *Petrarch's Book Without a Name,* trans. Norman P. Zaccour (Toronto: The Pontifical Institute of Medieval Studies, 1973); and, more recently, *Libro senza titolo,* ed. Laura Casarsa (Turin: N. Aragno, 2010).

36. Between the lives of Pope Alexander III and Pope Lucio III and in specific reference to the Venetian wars against the Empire, the 1534 edition reads: "Si deve credere che questa opera sia stata in alchun modo in questa parte corrotta. Conciosia chel Petrarcha non harebbe pretermessa la vittoria de Venitiani contra limperadore e sua restitutione del pontefice fatta per loro laquale tutti e veri scrittori hanno trattando l'historia di questi tempi commemorata" (88r). See page 184 below.

led astray even by its other guide, the Empire, and increasingly and dangerously lent itself to immoral practices.[37]

His overarching project in the *De viris illustribus* was, as Dotti continues, to:

> not only remember, but indeed almost to revive the great men of the past — and the men great in action, not thought. [This task] must have seemed no longer elusive to Petrarch, as an authentic and modern intellectual. In few words: Petrarch the historiographer, not unlike Petrarch the epistolographer, is also spurred on by this moral impulse and not only, therefore, by the need to begin presenting history through a more critical and humanistic lens.[38]

His project was intended not to glorify the Church or even to remind readers of its importance and influence over every aspect of daily life. It was written, rather, to exemplify the moral disposition to be followed among men not only associated with the Church but also as heirs to the larger pagan tradition that informs their behavior.

Petrarch's De viris illustribus

Objectively there is no reason to attribute even the Latin 1478 *Lives of the Popes and Emperors* to Petrarch or to believe that he could have written any part of it. The lives up until 1371 and just before his death in 1374 are presented under his presumed authorship; those that follow are said to have been added by an unattributed source.[39] But even in these earlier lives — which sometimes appear as much dissociated

---

37. Ugo Dotti, "Introduzione," *Gli Uomini Illustri: Vita di Giulio Cesare di Francesco Petrarca*, ed. Ugo Dotti (Turin: Einaudi, 2007), 9. For the most recent Anglophone work see Witt, "Rebirth of the Romans."

38. Ibid: "non solo ricordare, ma quasi riportare in vita i grandi del passato — e i grandi dell'azione, non quelli del pensiero — dovette sembrare a Petrarca, a questo autentico intellettuale moderno, un compito non più eludibile. In poche parole: il Petrarca storiografo — non diversamente dal Petrarca epistolografo — nasce anche da questo impulso morale e non soltanto dall'esigenza di cominciare a dare della storia una visione più critica e umanistica."

39. Inserted at this point in the text is a note from the editor affirming that, "Qui finiscono le vite de' pontefici et imperadori romani da messer Francesco Petrarcha composte. Seguitano le vite brievemente et con diligentia insino nel anno MDVII raccolte" (in the

from each other as they do from the lives added later — there is little evidence to suggest a connection with Petrarch. To a late fifteenth- or early sixteenth-century reader, however, the link may have been more plausible or, at the very least, more desirable.

From 1338 to 1343, in Vaucluse, Petrarch did set out to compile and expand on a list of lives of illustrious men. Originally his intention was to follow in a long tradition of similar biographical writings. As his preface (known as Preface B) makes clear, he projected a much more vast enterprise than he was ultimately able to produce. Between roughly 1341 and 1343, he composed in Latin the twenty-three lives that form what would later constitute the main corpus of the work. He then abandoned the work to favor other pursuits, including his long but never finished work on the *Africa* — an epic poem on the life of Scipio Africanus.[40] He picked up the *De viris* again, however, in 1351, working on it until 1353 with a mind to add to it twelve more biblical and mythical lives, which would not be considered part of the main corpus until centuries later.

It was only in the 1360s that Petrarch returned to his illustrious lives. Francesco da Carrara, his Paduan patron, had requested that he resume his work on the *De viris* to complement an artistic enterprise undertaken for the Sala dei Giganti in Padua.[41] Petrarch therefore penned a new preface (Preface A) in which he laid out the new terms and scope of his project: a collection of thirty-six biographies of some of the most illustrious men assembled specifically at da Carrara's request. Petrarch never lived to see his project brought to term. Not surprisingly,

---

1507 edition; the lives added in the 1526 and 1534 editions go up to 1523). See page 222 below.

40. For a detailed study of the various steps of composition of the *Africa*, see Gerhard Regn and Bernhard Huss, "The History of the *Africa* and the Renaissance Project," *Modern Language Notes* 124.1 (2009): 86–102. See also Simone Marchesi, "Petrarch's Philological Epic *(Africa)*," in Kirkham and Maggi, *Petrarch*, 113–130.

41. On the Sala dei Giganti and the tradition of illustrious men, see Theodor E. Mommsen, "Petrarch and the Decoration of the Sala Virorum Illustrium in Padua," *The Art Bulletin* 34.2 (1952): 95–116.

however, one of his many disciples, Lombardo de la Seta, personally saw to the completion of the work. To the original twenty-three lives as they were drafted between 1341 and 1343 he added the later-written life of Julius Caesar *(De gestis Cesaris)* and a supplement of twelve more lives up to the emperor Trajan, transcribing them alongside Petrarch's original lives in a manuscript now in the Bibliothèque nationale de France and bringing the work to its intended thirty-six chapters.[42] Under da Carrara's supervision, Lombardo de la Seta also assembled a compendium of the *De viris* consisting of its first fourteen lives, which usually circulated as supplement to the *De viris*. Despite its aristocratic patronage, Petrarch's *Lives* endured a difficult history. It was not until Pierre de Nolhac's work on the *De viris* that the existence of the twelve lives from Adam to Hercules, conceived from 1351 to 1353, came to light, resulting in a whole new round of literary interpretations and philological examinations.

How the text became so widely disseminated is something of a mystery. Here as elsewhere Petrarch was intent on keeping this literary activity to himself and to a small group of trusted friends — he never circulated either his first preface or the later preface that he redacted with his more specific project in mind with Francesco da Carrara's encouragement. The work may have acquired a degree of its fame through Lombardo de la Seta's initiative to complete it. This was an intentional and intelligent move on de la Seta's part who, quite rightly, would have wanted his name associated with Petrarch's, if not in print then at least in reputation. Regardless of the path of its rise to popularity, Petrarch's *De viris* in large part redefined the ancient tradition of praise of illustrious men and opened the door to other artistic media aspiring to the same end.[43]

---

42. Paris, BNF, MS Lat. 6069; see Francesco Petrarca, *De viris illustribus*, ed. Silvano Ferrone (Florence: Le Lettere, 2006).

43. See Christiane L. Joost-Gaugier, "The Early Beginnings of the Notion of 'Uomini Famosi' and the 'De viris illustribus' in the Greco-Roman Literary Tradition," *Artibus et Historiae* 3.6 (1982): 97–115.

THE LIVES OF THE POPES AND EMPERORS

We might get closer to understanding the link between Petrarch's *De viris illustribus* and pseudo-Petrarch's *Lives of the Popes and Emperors* by examining the fortune of the former in translated — Italian — form. In 1476 — just two years before the first printing of pseudo-Petrarch's *Lives of the Popes and Emperors* — Donato degli Albanzani's Italian translation of the *De viris illustribus* was set to print and, although badly translated and terribly corrupt, it circulated widely. It is not surprising, then, that in the hands of booksellers looking for more immediate profit and conscious of Petrarch's Italian-wide celebrity, pseudo-Petrarch's *Lives of the Popes and Emperors* might well be mistaken for — or marketed as — a draft of, an addition to or a different version of Petrarch's and de la Seta's *De viris illustribus*.

Pseudo-Petrarch and the Liber pontificalis and De viris illustribus traditions

But Pseudo-Petrarch's vernacular *Lives* look nothing like Petrarch's earlier Latin biographies. They have different starting points, different objectives, different styles and vastly different indices and tables of contents. Petrarch's *De viris illustribus* reads as a highly stylized praise of great men in truly Roman fashion and rhetoric. In fact, consistent with his overall poetic aesthetic and concerns, Petrarch's *De viris illustribus*, like his *Africa*, displays a clear preference for and preoccupation with "the Roman question": the Roman model of a republic, the grandness of the Golden Age of Rome and the nostalgia to return to this previous period of exceptional human achievement. Pseudo-Petrarch's *Lives of the Popes and Emperors* also concerns itself with the growth of the Roman Empire from Julius Caesar onward. But it also addresses various local histories without concern for recalling Rome's Golden Age or its revival. In addition, it takes part in a tradition of papal narratives from both the Middle Ages and of its own time, as espoused, for example, by humanists such as Bartolomeo Platina.

Platina wrote his *Vitæ Pontificum* or *Lives of the Popes* between 1469 and 1479, offering his 1474–75 manuscript to Sixtus IV who had urged him to compose it.⁴⁴ Its publication, then, was contemporaneous with the release of pseudo-Petrarch's first 1478 edition. Other examples of books on the lives of popes existed across Italy, spanning the centuries; but the most important proliferation of them occurred between the late fifteenth and early sixteenth centuries. Many, if not all of, such narratives might have drawn something of their style and still more of their content either directly from the Roman *Liber Pontificalis*, originally dating from c.540, continued by various compilers and eventually expanded between 1431 and 1464, or by using it as a point of reference.⁴⁵ At the very least, it seems clear, both in terms of style, and given the years in which the *Liber Pontificalis* received extensive enhancement, that the period between the mid-fifteenth to the early sixteenth century witnessed the development of a newly re-conceived literary genre. Comprehensive and portable, pocket-sized *(tascabile)* ecclesiastical and imperial histories were becoming increasingly user-friendly in the shift from Latin to vernacular lay reading communities.

But even Platina's *Lives* are an unlikely source of inspiration for pseudo-Petrarch's real author — or series of authors. Although pseudo-Petrarch shares with Platina's *Lives* an early attempt to reconcile Christianity with pagan antiquity, an occasional adherence to popular dictum, inclusion of supernatural events and important natural disasters, Platina's *Lives* remains distinct from it in its stylized narrative.⁴⁶ Platina's text is oriented more by narrated events and less by people; he includes no descriptions of the popes of which he writes or any of their personal attributes. His chapters are unconditioned by the strict formula purposely adopted in pseudo-Petrarch's *Lives* for their condensed presentation. Platina relies on a series of ancient sources not apparent in pseudo-Petrarch.⁴⁷ More importantly, he makes central to his

---

44. See most recently Platina, *Lives of the Popes*, trans. Anthony F. D'Elia, I Tatti Renaissance Library 30 (Cambridge, MA: Harvard University Press, 2008).

45. See above n. 13.

46. See also d'Elia, *Lives of the Popes*, "Introduction," ix–xxxi.

47. Ibid.

composition the link he wishes to draw between religious tradition and empire, often by way of comparison and to help the reader understand in imperial terms the importance of certain religious figures. Pseudo-Petrarch limits his examination of the interaction between papacy and empire to a reciprocal acknowledgment of the popes that lived under each emperor — and vice versa. With his *Vitae Pontificum*, Platina aims ostensibly to write a historical bible wherein theological teaching is only secondary to historical example. In other words, Platina writes a humanist history; pseudo-Petrarch more a medieval annal or chronicle. In addition, the *Lives'* favorable treatment of Paul II[48] — excoriated by Platina — indicates little direct influence or connection.

We must look elsewhere, then, for probable authors of pseudo-Petrarch's *Lives*. Writing in Petrarch's time in Avignon, and perhaps a key figure in introducing Petrarch to Livy's fourth Decade, Giovanni Colonna was a Dominican friar and author of both his own *De viris illustribus* and of his later history of the world, the *Mare historiarum*. W. Braxton Ross, Jr. outlines the main characteristics of these texts and their reception both in Colonna's lifetime and in subsequent generations.[49] Colonna's *De viris*, like his *Mare*, "apparently exercised little influence and has never been published except for brief excerpts" and are dissimilar both to Petrarch's *De viris illustribus* and to pseudo-Petrarch's *Lives*. Modeled more closely on Saint Jerome's *De viris illustribus*, the main content of Colonna's composition is focused on the lives of "writers and thinkers," ninety percent of whom "lived prior to A.D. 600, and nearly half [of whom] are pagan." His intention, as Ross sees it, is to "make the authors of an earlier age better known to his own time, to supply, as it were, a kind of fourteenth-century 'Oxford Companion' to ancient literature."[50]

Petrarch's intention in writing his *De viris illustribus* has already been discussed. Though the intention of its author is still debatable,

---

48. See below, 235–36.
49. "Giovanni Colonna," 539.
50. Ibid.

pseudo-Petrarch's *Lives* is a significant departure from Colonna's focus on the past in its interest in figures of recent history and, eventually, in current events.[51] It is unlikely, then, that Colonna's text should either have been translated into the Italian vernacular or that it had any direct effect on later writers of the same genre. Still, Colonna's little-known *De viris illustribus* points readers in the direction of other lesser-known texts more likely to have influenced pseudo-Petrarch and, because lesser known, less likely to have been recognized as direct influences on it.

The century following Colonna reveals perhaps the largest number of what might more properly be considered "exemplary" texts for pseudo-Petrarch's *Lives*.[52] Bartolomeo Scala, writing between 1450 and 1492 and chancellor of Florence for much of that time, provides one key for further investigation, not only for his links to Florence — a strong presence in pseudo-Petrarch as well — but for his style and presumed audience. As Alison Brown points out, "compared with Poliziano, [Scala] was not primarily a scholar, but a man of affairs who had to conform to common practice in his public writings."[53] In an important way this appeal to the growing educated middle class likens him to pseudo-Petrarch who also avoids, intentionally or not, the language of more erudite communities. But rather than the formation of the Church, Scala's primary concern was the governance of the state and "correct social behavior." As such, his early writings, all Latin, sustain his view of history as

---

51. It is more than likely, however, that the last cycle of sixteenth-century lives were added by a different author seeking to flesh out the original work and make it more marketable to a contemporary audience.

52. Influences on pseudo-Petrarch might not be limited to texts and books alone. As Joost-Gaugier points out, the topos of the glorification and remembrance of illustrious men is seen in art and architecture as well, and as early as Giotto (98). John R. Spencer discusses the presence and transmission of this topos in the world of coins and medals, pointing to Filarete, during his stay in Rome, as the most prominent example of this practice. See "Filarete, the Medallist of the Roman Emperors," *The Art Bulletin* 6.4 (1979): 550–61.

53. *Bartolomeo Scala, 1430–1497, Chancellor of Florence: The Humanist as Bureaucrat* (Princeton: Princeton University Press, 1979), 257.

"a reflection of the moral and political uncertainties of the present."[54] Although this tendency to leave the explicit study of religion out of his text places him at distinct odds with pseudo-Petrarch, Scala's *History of the Florentine People*, written in the mid-1480s, very likely coincided with the first printed edition of pseudo-Petrarch's *Lives*. If not reliant on each other, then, it seems plausible that Scala and pseudo-Petrarch should have been keenly aware of each other's projects and were likely writing for the same audience.

Another clue to the development of pseudo-Petrarch's content and prose is the work of Leonardo Bruni (1369-1444), chancellor of Florence. In addition to translating a number of Plutarch's *Lives*—another common source in the late-medieval and early Renaissance illustrious-men tradition — Bruni wrote both in Latin and in the Italian vernacular, on both (Florentine) history and on contemporary culture and, as Joost-Gaugier points out, "edited at least one collection of classical and early Christian *vite*."[55] In fact, after Petrarch, Bruni is most widely credited as the key proponent, and at times inventor, of the genre of such *vitae*. His *Historiae florentina populi* was composed around 1404 and within forty years was considered the property of the state. The work generated a series of other histories on the Florentine republic both within Bruni's lifetime and into the next century.[56] As the most canonical example of a work of civic humanism, it focused exclusively on the Florentines' efforts to remain faithful to a republican model despite the many internal and external conflicts complicating their politics from antiquity onward.[57] As such, it was not directly

---

54. Ibid, 301.

55. Joost-Gaugier, 97 n.3

56. See also Leonardo Bruni, *History of the Florentine People*, ed. and trans. James Hankins, I Tatti Renaissance Library 3 (Cambridge, MA: Harvard University Press, 2001), ix–xxi.

57. As Hankins explains, "Civic humanism in modern scholarship has come to stand for the view that, during the Italian Renaissance, there existed a powerful symbiosis between the republican traditions of city-states such as Florence and Venice, on the one hand, and that strain of Renaissance literary and intellectual life known as humanism, on the other.... In fifteenth-century terms civic humanism can be usefully identified with a literary and educational reform movement directed at the political classes of Italian city-states" (ix). It stated that

concerned with the Church. It was translated into the vernacular by Donato Acciaiuoli and printed in 1476 — just two years before pseudo-Petrarch's *Lives*.[58]

Also prominent during this time is another figure active on both ends of the humanist publication spectrum. Vespasiano da Bisticci began his career and achieved fame as a Florentine bookseller in the mid-fifteenth century. He quickly built the reputation for which he was eventually known: producing books in unique manuscripts for popes and Renaissance princes, such as Federico da Montefeltro, exquisitely bound and intended to be hallmark pieces of remarkable private collections. He single-handedly designed Cosimo de' Medici's Biblioteca Laurenziana and, employing a large number of copyists, produced the vast majority of its contents. He also later lent his services to Pope Nicholas V in the creation of the Vatican Library. In both these milieu and in a number of others with which he was famously associated, his most popular productions remained classical texts — both Latin and Greek — as well as theological documents and liturgical texts.

But in 1480, Vespasiano stepped away from the manufacture of luxury books. At this point he chose to turn his attention to writing, rather than producing, books. Most famous among his works, though not published until centuries later, is his *Lives of Illustrious Men of the Fifteenth Century*.[59] These were biographies of ecclesiastics and intellectuals with whom he had come into varying degrees of contact during his career. It was not until the nineteenth century that these *Lives*

"the best way to reform civic leaders [was] to train them in virtue and eloquence, and virtue and eloquence [were] best learned from prolonged study of the classical authors" (ix).

58. See *The Cambridge History of Italian Literature*, ed. Peter Brand and Lino Pertile (Cambridge: Cambridge University Press, 2001), 138.

59. Contained most famously in *The Vespasiano Memoirs*, translated by William George and Emily Waters and recently revisited and republished (Toronto: University of Toronto Press, 1997). See Harold S. Stone's review in *Libraries and Culture* 35.3 (2000): 475–76; and Anthony Grafton, *Commerce with the Classics: Ancient Books and Renaissance Readers* (Ann Arbor: University of Michigan Press, 1997).

were published and garnered much critical attention: 1839 saw the first complete critical edition. It is thus difficult to ascertain with any certainty what their fortune might have looked like in the immediate context of Vespasiano's lifetime. No doubt, the figures in his *Lives* still alive at the time of their composition would have known about his project and might have signed off on his representation of their personalities and religious or political importance. The extent to which other writers of his generation might have been familiar with his *Lives*, however, is still largely up for debate.

Hartmann Schedel's *Nuremberg Chronicle*,[60] for example, follows in much the same tradition, providing parallel lives of Roman popes and emperors — among many other events and personalities — and noting in both text and image celestial events such as eclipses, comets, bloody skies[61] and other natural disasters, prodigies and scandals, including Pope Joan (John of England),[62] the wonder of the Gascon co-joined women,[63] the story of Archbishop Hatto II of Mainz, eaten by mice,[64] the man with the head of a human and the rear of a dog.[65] Schedel had earned a medical degree from the University of Padua in 1466 and was well conversed in the Italian humanist movement of his time and collaborated with the German humanists of Nuremberg and other imperial centers. According to an inventory of 1498, Schedel's personal library contained 370 manuscripts and 670 printed books.[66]

60. *Liber Chronicarum* (Nuremberg: Anton Koberger, 1493). The complete German edition is available online at http://ora-web.swkk.de/digimo_online/digimo.entry?source=digimo.Digitalisat_anzeigen&a_id=4218 .

61. See below, 144, 155.

62. See below, 144.

63. See below, 155–66.

64. See below, 168–69.

65. See below, 178.

66. See Stephan Füssel, "Introduction," Hartmann Schedel, *Chronicle of the World: The Complete and Annotated Nuremberg Chronicle of 1493* (Cologne: Taschen, 2001), 8–14; and Catherine Kikuchi, "La bibliothèque de Hartmann Schedel a Nuremberg: Les apports de Venise a l'humanisme allemand et leurs limites," *Mélanges de l'École Française de Rome* 122.2 (2011): 379–91.

INTRODUCTION

Only about ten percent of Schedel's work is original, the rest are borrowings from a wide variety of sources, including Petrarch's *De viris illustribus*, Boccaccio's *De mulieribus claris*,[67] Platina, Flavio Biondo, Aeneas Silvius Piccolomini and Jacopo Filippo Foresti da Bergamo's *Supplementum chronicarum* (Venice, 1492). A study of these sources would also reveal much of the new lay interest in papal and imperial history at the prelude to the Reformation. Such possibilities provide another avenue of further research into the social contexts surrounding pseudo-Petrarch's *Lives*, an environment less and less concerned with appealing to elite classes and increasingly interested, instead, in reaching a broader public.

As the notes throughout the following text make clear, the author of the *Lives* also made use of a wide variety of sources, ranging from the Roman *Liber Pontificalis* to Villani's *Nuova Cronica*, from Suetonius to Einhard's *Life of Charlemagne*. What manuscripts or early printed editions were available to the author, and where, would be the subject of a detailed philological investigation and is not the purpose of our introduction. It remains an intriguing and important question. We can, however, underscore that the author did have a richness of sources readily at his disposal and made intense use of them, indicating the cultural sophistication required for even a popular compendium of this nature.

Conclusions

If readers take 1478 as an authoritative date of the first appearance of pseudo-Petrarch's *Lives of the Popes and Emperors*, they might correctly identify it primarily as a historical and secondarily as a didactic text for the educated middle class on the development of the Catholic Church at a time when that development was still a primary concern of historiographers. Indeed, the years from 1507 to 1600 witnessed not only the repeated reprinting and adaptation of Platina's *Lives*,

---

67. Both works are in a compendium along with collections of biographies by Jerome, Gennadius and Isidore of Seville, owned by Schedel and dated 1451, now in the Bayerische Staatsbibliothek, MS Clm 131.

but also a proliferation of other examinations of papal legacy from lengthy histories to local chronologies from both within and outside the Church.[68] Paolo Giovio's *Life of Leo X and Hadrian VI, Most Reverend Popes, and the Cardinal Pompeo Colonna* was published for the first time in Florence in 1549. Twelfth-century Abbott Joachim of Fiore's *Prophesies on the Lives of the Popes* followed in Vico in 1585. Antonio Ciccarelli's *Lives of the Popes* were printed three years later in Rome. A host of other authors contributed to this growing movement: Tommaso Costo, Vittorio Baldini and even the Confraternity of the Blessed Virgin at Santo Spirito in Florence were among them.

But pseudo-Petrarch's *Lives* and similar texts also participate in a more specific trend that grew stronger in the second half of the sixteenth century: the promotion of Catholic texts — and Catholic culture — in the face of the Protestant Reformation. The first reprint of the *Lives* appeared in 1526, nine years after Martin Luther posted his Ninety-Five Theses. By the third session of the council of Trent in 1563, ecclesiastical chronologies or celebrations of popes' lives, both by lay writers and by religious orders, were commonplace throughout Italy. Simon Lemieux sums up much of current consensus and argues that the development of the Catholic Church from 1500 to 1570 was not so much a reaction against Protestant reform as it was the mark of change already in place and expedited by the larger trends sweeping Europe. "What the Protestant Reformation did was act as a catalyst to the changes already taking place, giving them an added sense of energy. It also profoundly affected the nature and direction of these changes," he writes.[69] In this context, texts like pseudo-Petrarch's *Lives*, with their emphasis on the ongoing progress of the Catholic Church, speak not only to the preservation of Catholic values within Christendom, but

---

68. Over forty editions of Platina's *Lives* are currently found in various libraries across Italy, both in their original Latin and in Italian translations.

69. "Sixteenth-Century Catholicism: More Reaction than Reform," *History Review* 63 (March 2009): 43–47. On the Counter-Reformation, see also *The Counter-Reformation: The Essential Readings*, ed. David M. Luebke (Malden, MA: Blackwell, 1999).

also, in their didactic layout, to the Catholic Church's commitment to lay education, mostly by way of the Jesuit and other reform orders.[70]

That these texts eventually made their way into a mainstream textual community not through religious propagation but through secular publishers speaks to a shift in the production, marketing and manufacturing of ecclesiastical and historical chronologies in this pre-Tridentine atmosphere. Pseudo-Petrarch's *Lives* might have been conceived in a more elite literary tradition and for a higher literary class, but it was adapted both to the growing needs of the market and to the new medium of the press. In this transition from aristocratic to middle class, luxury manuscript to printed pocketbook, and amid an unending flourish of historical and ecclesiastical chronologies, associating this tiny book on the *Lives of the Popes and Emperors* with Petrarch would have been sound strategic marketing that likely would have guaranteed a greater number of readers. This new, active textual community also reached beyond the *Lives*' original composition and publication in the Tuscan vernacular. Given the number of Italian vernacular translations of other Latin texts in circulation between 1476 and 1480, it would have been all too easy to pass the *Lives* off as a previously unknown Petrarchan work in translation or the draft of a later and larger literary accomplishment.

Although the literary form of pseudo-Petrarch's *Lives* is not unique, its focus on issues of the Papal States, the Romagna and Florence — especially as affected by papal and imperial politics[71] — speaks to a text conceived in the new humanist book culture of Vespasiano

---

70. The text also makes explicit mention of Martin Luther twice, in the life of Leo X and in that of Clement VII (1523) who, it bears mentioning, is described as a good and peaceful pope: "nel pontificato suo fu molto molestato da Martino Luthero come anchor suo predecessori" (MS Florence, BNC, Magl. 4.6.92. 1534; Venezia, Melchiorre Sessa, 120r). See below, p. 248.

71. This might be borne out by the author's attention to the details of Cesare Borgia's activities in the Romagna and Papal States. Lorenzo de' Medici and his activities in Florence receive far less detail. On the other hand, Machiavelli showed the same interest in Cesare Borgia, and from a decidedly Florentine perspective.

da Bisticci's Florence, perhaps modeled on his *Lives*. Its author — whether in Rome, Florence or the Romagna — and its publisher were eager to establish it as an authoritative text — and a continuous historical narrative — for a new and broad textual community of lay readers concerned about issues of authority, legitimacy of rule and orthodoxy that coalesced around the unfolding development of papal and then secular rule in Central Italy. For modern readers, however, it provides both enthralling insight into the ecclesiastic propaganda of its time and is an impressive precursor of compositions in this same tradition to follow well into the next century.

*

A CHRONICLE OF THE LIVES OF THE PONTIFFS AND ROMAN EMPERORS COMPOSED BY MESSER FRANCESCO PETRARCH TO WHICH HAVE BEEN ADDED THOSE WHO WERE MISSING FROM THE TIME OF PETRARCH TO OUR OWN. 1534.

PROEM BY MESSER FRANCESCO PETRARCH FOR THE BOOK ON THE EMPERORS AND PONTIFFS

Since human minds naturally desire to know the deeds of outstanding men of the past, certain writers describe at length the lives of such men. But because most men are impeded by various and diverse cares, they are unable to deal with so much material. And so, in order that even those who are occupied with so many responsibilities might have some knowledge of things past, I have restricted this book to the lives of pontiffs and Roman emperors, carefully keeping in order the times in which they lived, describing in what century the pontiffs occupied the papacy and the emperors the empire, how many years they lived, what their lives were like, and when worthy and holy men flourished. Nor have I overlooked the various ceremonies practiced by the churchmen, the miracles performed or the many customs followed by the Apostolic See. Finally, I have omitted nothing that seemed to me worthy of remembrance and that could be handled briefly. For this reason, if readers were to consider carefully the usefulness of this book of mine, seeking not ornate and eloquent language (since the variety of the matter does not require it), I have no doubt that they would commend my useful and sincere labor. Wishing to benefit many, I have briefly and carefully included here the lives of Roman emperors and pontiffs from the beginning to our own time.

HERE BEGIN THE LIVES OF THE ROMAN PONTIFFS AND EMPERORS
COMPOSED BY MESSER FRANCESCO PETRARCH

Caius iulius cesar

LIFE OF GAIUS JULIUS CAESAR,
DICTATOR[1]

Gaius Julius Caesar,[2] dictator, after whom all the emperors are called Caesar, was born of the family of the Iulii, which received its beginnings from the goddess Venus as follows. Having had an affair with Anchises, a citizen of Ilium, a city in Troy, she gave birth to Aeneas who, after the ruin of his fatherland, came to Italy with his son, Ascanius, from whom subsequently the noble family of the Iulii descended. But his maternal origin (as he himself testifies) derived from Ancus Marcius, king of the Romans. Thus his paternal origin came from gods and his maternal one from kings. One morning in Pisa, his father who was called Caesar, suddenly died while putting on his shoes from no apparent cause, leaving [the young] Caesar who was sixteen years old.

Subsequently he enjoyed many honors and held many offices; and while being a quaestor in Spain, it so happened that while in Gades[3] he saw in the temple of Hercules a picture of Alexander the Great, king of Macedonia, which he gazed upon with great sighs inasmuch as he was the age when Alexander had conquered the entire world. For this reason, convinced that he had not done anything worthy of remembrance, and having dreamed the following night of having had an affair with his mother, he interpreted this as meaning that he would have the world in his power and keeping, inasmuch as his mother whom

1. The sources for this biography could be any number of contemporary Renaissance works of history or more directly any of the classical histories and lives known during the period. See Introduction, XII–XVII, XXVII–XXXV.

2. 100–44 B.C.

3. Cadiz.

he seemed to have subdued could only mean the earth, the mother and keeper of all things. Thereupon he returned to Rome and undertook many projects that made him famous and won him many offices.

Among these was his being made consul with Bibulus and running affairs as he pleased without the approval of his running mate. When the nobles began resisting him, he joined Pompey the Great (to whom he later gave his daughter, Iulia, as a gift after he had her leave Servilius Caepio whom he first had her marry) and Marcus Crassus, both of whom were leading citizens in those days. He made an agreement with them that nothing would be done in the republic that would be displeasing to any of the three. After that he did as he pleased to such an extent that having once been contradicted by Cato he had him dismissed from the Curia and imprisoned. After the consulship he was given the administration of Gaul where he ruled for nine years and fought some very great battles. He was the first Roman to dare fight the Germani who lived beyond the Rhine, subjecting them to great routs. Later he fought the English,[4] who previously had been unknown to the Roman people, defeated and subjugated them.

When he was persecuted in Rome by his adversaries, he organized an army in an attempt to take over the government (as many believe). (He would say that if one must violate justice, one must do so in order to rule, but he must observe piety in other matters.) He subsequently went to Rome, after having pursued Pompey — from whom he had distanced himself — into Macedonia and sided with the Senate, saying he was fighting in the name of the fatherland. He drove Pompey to Pharsalia and defeated him after he had fled to Alexandria where he was killed by Achillas and Pothinus by order of King Ptolemy. When this news reached Caesar, knowing that Ptolemy was making similar plans for him, he engaged him in battle and defeated him. Then, having passed into Syria and Pontus, within five days after his arrival and within four hours after landing, he overcame Pharnaces, son of Mithridates. Proceeding then to Africa, he defeated Scipio and

4. That is, the Britons.

King Iuba. In Spain he defeated the sons of Pompey. As a result of all these victories he enjoyed five triumphs after his return to Rome. The first and most outstanding triumph was for Gaul, the second for Alexandria, the third for Pontus, the fourth for Africa and the last for Spain. He was very liberal toward his soldiers and his people, assigning to them certain lands and giving each one a certain sum of money. Besides this, he sponsored various games for the people.

Turning then to the condition of the republic, he readjusted the calendar year by having it conform to the course of the sun. He was a lustful man since we read that he seduced many Roman noblewomen, and even had affairs with many queens, among whom was Cleopatra, queen of Alexandria, with whom he had a son named Caesarion. He was also greedy, accepting a great deal of money from officials, and often sacking cities and castles during a war, more often for the thrill of looting than because of mistakes made by his men. He took many treasures from temples in Gaul that resulted in his becoming very wealthy. Nevertheless, he was kind and likeable, and was not vengeful for wrongs done to him, making short shrift of personal hatreds. Similarly, after the civil wars he was moderate and forgiving toward those whom he had overcome and defeated.

He was of large stature and fair complexion, handsome, with a striking build, but his mouth was rather large, his eyes dark and lively, and he enjoyed good health, except that in later life he twice contracted the dread disease because of his activities.[5] He was very moderate in his daily life and extremely devout, so that Cato would say that Caesar soberly damaged the republic. Very eloquent, he left behind many works he composed, among which was the commentary on his wars.[6]

His wife was Cornelia, daughter of Cinna, by whom he had Iulia. He then married Pompeia whom he left because he thought she had committed adultery with Clodius [Publius Clodius Pulcher]. He

5. While this is usually taken to mean cancer in the modern world, it appears to have meant epilepsy for classical writers. See Plutarch, *Caesar* 17, 45, 60; and Suetonius, *Julius* 45.
6. *Commentarii de bello gallico*

thereupon took as his wife Calpurnia, daughter of Lucius Piso. He had no other children from any of them, but there appeared in his will Gaius Octavius, his grand-nephew whom he had adopted and about whom we will speak below. But many things brought serious censure upon him.

In addition to the dictatorship that he had assumed in perpetuity, and to the title he took from the empire, he also wished to be called Father of the Country. And beyond his title of King and the fact that he had the month of July, which used to be called Quintilis, named after himself, he also agreed to have a seat of gold placed in the Senate for him, and enjoyed many other honors that were considered superhuman. For these reasons and because they thought that he would grab the kingdom, the citizens Brutus and Cassius, along with many other conspirators, killed him in Pompey's Curia when he was fifty-six, wounding him twenty-four times. The people took his death so seriously that they rushed with torches to the homes of Brutus and Cassius and could barely be stopped from killing them. Then he was declared a god after a comet appeared, which was thought to be Caesar's soul being received in heaven, during the games that Octavius Augustus, whom he had adopted, held in his honor for seven days.

Octavius Augustus, First Roman Emperor

Octavius Augustus,[7] Roman emperor, son of Octavius of the Octavian family from Veletrae in ancient times and of Atia, daughter of Maccius Balbus and of Iulia, sister of Gaius Caesar, dictator, was born in Rome on September 13 near a place called Capita Bubula, where he was made a sacrarius. At the time of his birth, Marcus Tullius Cicero and Antonius were consuls. He was raised near Veletrae and at first given the name of Thurinus, but later, he was called Gaius Caesar because of Caesar, brother of his grandmother on his mother's side. Many wanted him to be called Romulus after the founder of the city of Rome. Numacius Plancus succeeded in having him called Augustus,

---

7. Emperor 27 B.C.–A.D. 14.

which means venerable. From then on, all subsequent emperors were called Augustus.

He ruled first with Mark Antony and later with Marcus Lepidus for some twelve years. Finally, he ruled alone for forty-four years, so that all together he ruled, either alone or with someone else, for fifty-six years. He conducted five civil wars in Modena, Perugia, Philippi, Sicilia and Actium. Being victorious in these wars, he fought against the Dalmatae and the Cantabri, subduing Cantabria, Aquitania, Pannonia and Dalmatia, together with all of Illyria in addition to Rhaetia and the Vindelici and the Salassi; and he pushed the Germani back beyond the Elbe River. After the Suebi and the Sugambri surrendered to him, he led them into Gaul and made them settle near the Rhine River.

After these wars he enjoyed a triumph three times — the first for Dalmatia, the second for Asia, the last for Alexandria where he defeated Mark Antony. He beautified the city of Rome, which had been subject to flooding and fires, by so rebuilding it that he rightly took pride in the fact that he had inherited it in brick and left it in marble.[8] He also built many beautiful structures: the Forum with the temple of Mars, where he built a portico with a library containing Greek and Latin works, the temple of Jupiter on the Capitoline and many other buildings. In his day, he also encouraged the construction of many beautiful wonders, such as the building of the temple of the Pantheon by his son-in-law, Marcus Agrippa. It was dedicated to the mother of all gods and today is known as Sta. Maria Rotonda, about which we will speak below, since it was donated to the Catholics. He made corrections to the calendar that had been set by his father Caesar because certain portions of the year had become confusing. He had the month that had previously been known as Sextilis changed to August after himself.

He hated being called "sir," considering it a kind of curse. Many say that he avoided it because the first great sire, Christ, had been born. In governing he ruled the empire with great peace and behaved so

8. A quote attributed to Augustus by Suetonius, *Augustus* 28.3.

pleasingly and kindly toward his people that the public, together with the Senate, hailed him as the father of the country. While he was still alive, they showered him with divine honors as though he were a god.

He took several wives. The first was Claudia whom he repudiated prior to the marriage. The second was Scribonia whom, after having had a daughter, Iulia, by her, he likewise left because of the perversity of her ways. The last was Livia Drusilla who was married to Tiberius Nero and was pregnant by him; he had her leave Tiberius while she was still pregnant. He took her and truly loved her, but had no children by her. He adopted (her son) Tiberius as his stepson after the deaths of Gaius and Lucius, his nephews, whom he had earlier adopted.

His way of life was rather lascivious and lustful, taking great delight in molesting virgins; it is said that even in this he used his wife as a go-between. Otherwise, he ruled the empire so outstandingly and peacefully that many kings readily offered him their friendship. Finally he died of natural causes in Nola, a city in Campania, at the age of seventy-six, having ruled the empire for thirty-five days less than fifty-six years. He was buried in a very beautiful tomb between the Via Flaminia and the bank of the Tiber.

It was during his reign that that fine and outstanding light of eloquence, Marcus Tullius Cicero, the distinguished orator, was killed by Popilius, a soldier; that Ovidius Naso, a poet from Sulmona, was born; that Sallust, the renowned historiographer, died in Rome; that the Mantuan Virgil, a truly excellent poet, died in Brindisi and his remains were taken to Naples and buried outside the city; and that the Venutian poet, Horace, also died a natural death. It was also during this period that Mark Antony, a Roman citizen, and Cleopatra, queen of Alexandria, ended their own lives while battling against their Augustus, Antony with a dagger and Cleopatra with serpents clinging to her breasts; and that Plancus Munatius, an outstanding orator and disciple of Cicero, while ruling Gaul, built the city that today is called Lyons.

In the forty-second year of Augustus's reign, the sun darkened and the moon's course changed, according to the Romans, when the Redeemer of humanity, Jesus Christ, was born in Bethlehem of a virgin mother, [Mary] wife of Joseph. From the time of Adam to this child's birth five thousand one hundred and ninety-nine years and nine months had passed.[9] And from the time that the noble city of Rome was built, seven hundred and fifty-two years had passed. After His birth there was a very great and universal peace throughout the entire world. But we will not deal with His life, since it would be a long and arduous task, and we would be going beyond what we intended.

TIBERIUS (EMPEROR 2), A.D. 15

The Roman emperor, Tiberius,[10] son of Tiberius Nero and Livia Drusilla, was born in Rome on November 16. As we stated above, he was adopted by Augustus. He was so daring and persistent in war that, fighting patiently with the Rhaetii, the Vindelici, the Pannonii and the Germani, he subdued the Alpine people, the Breuni and the Dalmatae. He brought forty thousand Germani to Gaul settling them near the Rhine River where he provided them with quarters. Afterwards he conquered all of Illyria, which had rebelled against the Romans.

At the beginning of his reign he managed to conceal some of his abominable and very serious vices. Later on, he recklessly indulged in every kind of intemperance, cruelty and unbridled lust with males and females in forbidden places and at forbidden times. He did not spare even his grandchildren, close friends and relatives from suffering every kind of death. He finally withdrew to the island of Capri, located opposite Naples, where he indulged his every wickedness in various ways with unbridled appetite and evil will.[11]

---

9. According to biblical reckoning.
10. A.D. 14–37.
11. As recounted in Suetonius, *Tiberius* 42–45.

Yet he was widely read both in Greek and in Latin and composed several works. Finally he died near Misenum at the villa of Lucullus.[12] Some say that he died from fevers, others say that he was poisoned, while still others assert that, weakened by illness, he was smothered by a feather mattress. He was seventy-eight years old when he died, having ruled for twenty-three years. He left no structures worthy of remembrance, except for a temple dedicated to his father Augustus.

In his day Ovidius Naso[13] of Sulmona, an outstanding poet, died in exile after Augustus sent him to Greece. Also in his time Christ was baptized by John the Baptist who had begun to preach a baptism of repentance in the thirty-first year of our Lord and in the eighteenth year of his reign.

On March 25, a Friday, Jesus Christ was crucified by the Jews at the time when Pontius Pilate ruled over Judea. And from the beginning of the world until the crucifixion of Christ five thousand two hundred and thirty-two years had passed. One reads that at this time, at the sixth hour of the day, there was such a great darkening of the sun that stars could be seen, and in Bithynia there was such a strong earthquake that many houses were destroyed, while in many other places were heard great commotion and outcries at the hour of Christ's suffering. Josephus, the masterful writer of Jewish history, in dealing with Christ and rendering favorable testimony about Him, recounts at some length many things about His Passion.

During this same period Stephen[14] was stoned on the third of August, Saint John preached near the Jordan, and Saul, a persecutor of Christians, was converted to the faith of Christ and was thereafter called Paul. After Pontius Pilate had been accused of doing many things against Tiberius, he was sent with Herod, who had caused John's death, to Vienne where he killed himself by his own hand because of the many sufferings he had had to endure.

12. In Naples, now Castel dell'Ovo.
13. 20 March 43 B.C.–A.D. 17/18
14. St. Stephen Protomartyr.

Tiberius ruled for five years after the Passion of Christ.

Peter, First Pontiff, A.D. 35

Saint Peter, the son of John from the province of Galilee in the region of Bethsaida and the brother of Andrew, held the clerical chair in the East for four years and celebrated the first mass in the year thirty-nine, saying only the Our Father. Then he went to Antioch where he held the chair for nearly seven years. Later, at the time of the Emperor Claudius, in the year forty-five of the Lord, he came to Rome and there held the pontificate and ruled over Holy Church for twenty-five years, seven months and eight days, preaching a faith of salvation. He brought honor to the Church with his many outstanding virtues. While there, he wrote two epistles that are considered canonical and gave his approval to the gospel of Mark. He ordained in the month of December three bishops and ten priests, as well as seven deacons, and sent Apollinaris to Ravenna, which at that time was a very famous city, and he sent Syrus to Pavia. He also sent his interpreter Mark, after he had written his Gospel in Italy and Aquileia, to Egypt where he founded the first church in Alexandria. In addition, he sent many disciples to various cities in Gaul, such as Saints Savinianus, Potentianus, Altinus, Martial, who, according to some, totaled six hundred seventy-two disciples in all, and many others he sent to various places and cities in Gaul and elsewhere.

Furthermore, in Rome he consecrated Linus and Cletus as bishops who served always with priestly concern the faithful of Rome as well as newcomers while he concentrated on prayers and sermons. He also entrusted to blessed Clement the care of the see since he had declared him his successor, saying that "just as by my Lord Jesus Christ I was given the power to bind and unbind, so I commit it to you and make you the arbiter of all the Churches of God and of all ecclesiastical acts and overseer of all prayers and sermons."

He was then martyred with Paul during Nero's reign thirty-eight years after the Passion of Christ.[15] At the same time in Egypt, one reads, there appeared a phoenix, a bird of which only one its species can be found throughout the world. It had appeared in Arabia seven hundred years earlier; it is said to live for five hundred years and is reborn after burning in its nest. Its size is the same as an eagle; it has a crested head and a neck of a splendid golden color, a purple back and a red tail.

GAIUS CALIGULA (EMPEROR 3), A.D. 40

Gaius Caligula,[16] Roman emperor, the nephew of Tiberius Caesar, was born to Germanicus, Drusus's son and Tiberius's brother, and ruled in Rome for three years, ten months and eight days. He was deeply entangled in lecherous affairs, even to the point of laying with his sisters whom he then condemned to exile.[17] He also abused many other Roman noblewomen. He was very cruel, having his friends die by means of long and varied tortures. Once when he asked someone who had been recalled from exile what he used to do there, he replied, "I prayed every day that Tiberius would die, hoping that during your reign you would allow me to return to my country." Fearing that those whom he had exiled would be thinking the same thing, he had them all killed.

Furthermore, he was very arrogant, raising himself to the level of the gods and wishing to be worshiped no differently than they were. He deeply loved Caesonia who was known neither for her morals nor her beauty, but was given to reckless and blind lust. She preferred referring to him as a monster rather than as a man. Ultimately, he was killed in his palace at the age of twenty-nine by his own men who inflicted thirty wounds on him. During this period, the Apostle Matthew wrote his gospel.

---

15. Died c.A.D. 64.
16. Emperor A.D. 37–41.
17. See Suetonius, *Caligula* 24.

THE LIVES OF THE POPES AND EMPERORS

CLAUDIUS (EMPEROR 4), A.D. 44

Emperor Claudius,[18] a grandson of Tiberius and Drusus's son, reigned in Rome for thirteen years, eight months and twenty-four days. According to some he ruled for twenty-four years. He was deeply involved in affairs with women, but stayed away from men. He embellished Rome with many beautiful buildings, doing so more for beauty than necessity. He fought against the English [Angles], adding to the empire some islands named the Orkneys. He greatly loved his libertine friends to whom he gave expensive gifts. Nor was he a useless emperor, since he did kill his wife, Messalina, who was so uncontrollably lustful that she would secretly expose herself to everyone and then fall into such venereal madness that, like a prostitute in a wolf's den, she would publicly give unbridled rein to her lust and though exhausted would depart unsatisfied.[19]

Claudius was also unrestrained in his eating and drinking habits no matter where he was. Once when he heard that someone at a banquet had tried to hold back his wind out of shame and had died, he decreed that this should be allowed at all banquets.[20] Finally at the age of forty-four he was poisoned with mushrooms by his wife, Agrippina, Nero's mother.[21] After his death he was declared a god.

It is written that during that period St. Peter met with Simon Magus in Rome, and Mark the Evangelist preached about the great works of Christ in Alexandria and wrote his gospel. Also at that time there was great discord in Jerusalem, and it is written that in a desperate attempt to escape through the gates, thirty thousand Jews perished. During the reign of Claudius there was also a widespread famine, and the grammarian Polemon[22] became famous.

---

18. Emperor A.D. 41–54.
19. See Tacitus, *Annals* XI.
20. Suetonius, *Claudius* 32.
21. Suetonius, *Claudius* 44.2.
22. Rhemmius Polemon (also spelled Polaemon), Lucan's teacher.

NERO (EMPEROR 5), A.D. 58

Emperor Nero[23] was Domitius's son of the ancient family of the Domitii. He ruled in Rome for thirteen years, eight months and nineteen days. He was adopted by Claudius because of the flatteries of his mother, Agrippina, who was married to Claudius. He was outrageous in every imaginable way. His parties would last from midday to midnight. He spent profusely, taking great delight in doing so, and recklessly wasted an incredible amount from the treasury. He would fish with golden nets that he would control with silk lines. He had his horse shod with golden shoes and would make countless, extravagant purchases. He never wore any clothes more than twice. He was especially extravagant in constructing buildings, owning a palace whose size, appearance and ornamentation were marvelous to behold.

But it was especially in lechery that he sought new, unusual and cruel thrills. Besides corrupting many noblewomen and indulging in many other lustful pursuits, he took it upon himself to change one of his servants, named Sporus, into a woman by cutting off his testicles, keeping him as a wife according to a custom of the time. Infected throughout his body, he dressed as a woman and married one of his servants named Doryphorus, mimicking virgins on their first night with a husband. He also lay with his sister and his mother, whom he had killed, reverting once again to his sick ways.[24]

He took great delight in song, shamelessly wasting funds on this activity beyond imperial custom. Finally, in his endless cruelty he was inferior to no one, having a great number of senators murdered. And he quarreled with all the good citizens and had many of them mercilessly killed. Nor did he spare his immediate relatives, for he had his brother and his wife as well as her mother and aunt killed.

He possessed many women. The first was Octavia whom he rejected and often thought of strangling, but then, with the false accusation of adultery, he had killed. The second was Poppaea Sabina whom

23. Emperor A.D. 54–68.
24. Suetonius, *Nero* 28–29.

he loved very much, but nevertheless he killed her with a kick even though she was pregnant. The last one was Statilia Messalina, whose husband Taurus, at that time a consul, he had torn to pieces so that he could have her as a mistress. Finally, he spared none of his relatives or friends from death.[25]

He even had Seneca[26] killed, the great philosopher who had been his teacher, as well as Lucan[27] from Cordoba, an outstanding poet and Seneca's nephew. To make certain that he had indulged in every kind of wickedness, he set fire to a large area of Rome because he was bored with its old buildings and ugly, winding roads. He also wanted to see a conflagration like Troy's and did not allow anyone to fight the flames as he stood singing in a very tall tower named the Tower of Maecenas.[28] Finally, abandoned by all the people because of his mad and horrible vices, he took refuge in a villa four miles from Rome, and there, to avoid falling alive into his enemies' hands, killed himself with a dagger. He was thirty-two years old. With him ended the offspring of the Caesars. He was the first to have Christians persecuted.

In his day the famous poet Persius of Luna died, and Statius of Naples[29] became well-known. We also read that during his reign there was a powerful earthquake and darkening of the sun. Judea rebelled against the Romans, and Nero sent Vespasian against it. Also during his reign, Paul came, as can be read in the Acts of the Apostles,[30] from Judea to Rome because of his special status, and took a lodging outside the city where he then converted to the faith many people swayed by his words. His way of life proved attractive to the Romans both because of his behavior and because of his marvelous sanctity. It is written that

25. Suetonius, *Nero* 35–36.

26. Circa 4 B.C.–A.D. 65. Author of moral essays and tragedies.

27. A.D. 3 November 39–30 April 65, author of the *Pharsalia*. See *Lucan*, ed. Charles Tesoriero, Frances Muecke, Tamara Neal (Oxford: Oxford University Press, 2010).

28. Suetonius, *Nero* 38.

29. Circa 45 A.D.–c.96, author of the *Silvae* and the *Achilleid*.

30. Acts 28.

many members of Nero's family and of other Roman families would seek him out. Among these was Seneca, Nero's teacher, who was very friendly toward him, and they often exchanged letters since they could not converse. And when St. Paul said in Nero's presence that the world would come to an end in fire, Nero ordered that he be ejected from the city with all his followers. These were his disciples, holy and good men, such as Titus, Timothy, Trophimus, Onesimus and many others whom he sent to preach to various parts of the world.

In the sixth year of his reign, James, the cousin of Christ, whom everyone called "the just," was stoned by the Jews and then killed with a club; and Mark the Evangelist died. Flavius Josephus[31] was attacked and taken prisoner by the Romans and, having been condemned to die, proclaimed before his end what Nero ought to do and how Vespasian ought to rule. Pope Gelasius [I][32] writes about Peter's pontificate and death, saying that the Roman Church is above all other churches in the world, not because of conciliar approval but through the evangelical voice of our Lord Jesus Christ who said that she was the mistress of all other churches, and then added "You are Peter and upon this rock I shall build my church."[33] Peter was given the Apostle Paul as companion since both lived at the same time and not in different eras, as the cursed heretics would have it. They were in Rome under the Emperor Nero in the last year of his reign, fighting for the faith against Simon Magus.[34] Both were crowned with martyrdom thirty-eight years after the Passion of Christ. Peter was crucified on the Vatican Hill on the Via Aurelia near Nero's palace and was buried there. Paul was beheaded at the saline waters on the road to Ostia.[35] This is how they were martyred and sanctified.

---

31. A.D. 37–c.100. Author of *The Jewish War* and *Antiquities of the Jews*.
32. Author of letters and several spurious works attributed to him.
33. See Matthew 16:13-20, Mark 8:27–30 and Luke 9:18–20.
34. Acts 8:9–24.
35. At Tre Fontane or Abbatia trium fontium ad Aquas Salvias.

The church of Rome then took precedence over all other churches in the world because of the apostles' virtues, their corporeal remains and their venerable victories, even though the church of Antioch was first in time. It is written concerning the apostles' remains that, at the time of Pope Cornelius, the Greeks stole their remains in order to take them to Greece, but a voice was heard from pagan idols yelling loudly, "Help, O Romans, for your gods are being taken away." Since the faithful thought that this referred to the apostles' remains and the infidels to their gods, both groups banded together. When the Greeks in their flight saw this, they threw the corpses in a sewer at the catacombs, but both were later retrieved by Pope St. Cornelius. Since there was some doubt as to whose remains they were, the faithful through prayer and fasting received a divine reply, namely that the larger bones were the preacher's and smaller ones the fisherman's. Whence it is said that Pope St. Silvester then weighed them with carefully adjusted scales, and after building a church for each of them he solemnly placed the bones of each in the one consecrated to him. Let this suffice regarding the apostles and their remains.

LINUS (POPE 2), A.D. 71[36]

The Italian Linus from the region of Tuscany, the son of Scolaius, began his pontificate during Nero's time and remained pope for eleven years, three months and thirteen days. Concurring with an order from St. Peter, he decreed that women should have their heads covered when entering a church.[37] He was crowned a martyr during the time of Vespasian on the twenty-third of September, and buried in the Vatican [cemetery] next to St. Peter.

---

36. A.D. 67–76 in the official Vatican list.

37. The Roman *Liber Pontificalis* is a source for many of these papal biographies from the earliest through the ninth century. They have been translated in 3 vols. by Raymond Davis (Liverpool: Liverpool University Press, 1989–1995) and referred to here as *Liber Pontificalis* 1 (to A.D. 715), 2 (Eighth-Century Popes), and 3 (Ninth-Century Popes). See *Liber Pontificalis* 1.2, Davis 1:2.

GALBA (EMPEROR 6), A.D. 71

Galba[38] the elder, born of the noble house of the Sulpitii, ruled over the Roman Empire for seven months. He was given to vice and illicit lust, and finally was killed in the [Roman] Forum by Otho's soldiers. He lived for twenty-three years.

Those who have carefully studied the See of the Roman Church say that Linus and Cletus, about whom we shall speak later on, did not sit as pontiffs or popes but as aides of the apostles. During his lifetime, St. Peter made them focus on ecclesiastical affairs while he concentrated on sermons and speeches. And therefore, endowed with so much authority, they deserved to be placed among those listed as pontiffs, although St. Peter chose as his successor Clement who should be listed below St. Peter. Finally after St. Linus had expelled demons and resuscitated the dead, performed miracles and baptized many people, he freed from a demon the daughter of a man named Saturnus who had kept her imprisoned. Because he believed that these miracles were performed by means of incantations, Saturnus had Linus decapitated after many painful tortures.[39] His body was buried in the Vatican [cemetery] although later it was taken by Gregory, bishop of Ostia, with the greatest clerical solemnity to the church of San Lorenzo. In the days of the above-named Galba, Titus and Vespasian destroyed Jerusalem,[40] removed all the treasures from the Temple and brought them to Rome where they were placed in the Temple of Peace.

OTHO (EMPEROR 7), [N.D.]

Otho,[41] son of a Roman knight, ruled the Roman Empire for ninety-five days. Finally, after having been defeated by Vitellius, he killed himself with a dagger. He lived for fifty-eight years.

---

38. Emperor A.D. 68–69.
39. Platina, *Lives of the Popes*, ed. d'Elia, 38–41.
40. A.D. 70.
41. Emperor A.D. 69.

VITELLIUS (EMPEROR 8), [N.D.]

Vitellius,[42] born into the noble family of the Vitellii, ruled the Roman Empire for eight months. He was addicted to gluttony and finally was killed by an angry populace. He lived for fifty-seven years.

VESPASIAN (EMPEROR 9), A.D. 72

Vespasianus [Vespasian],[43] a member of the Flavian family, ruled the Roman Empire for nine years, eleven months and twenty-two days, but according to others he ruled for eight months and ten days. As emperor he was useful to the state and loved by the Senate and the Roman people. He died of digestive problems; feeling death's approach he sat up and said, "Ought the emperor exit from the world lying on the ground?",[44] whereupon he stood up and died. He was sent by Claudius to Romania and England at different times and twice engaged the enemy in battle, adding some very powerful peoples to the empire. He lived for sixty-nine years and one month; some say three months and seven days.

TITUS (EMPEROR 10), A.D. 81

The Emperor Titus,[45] Vespasian's son, ruled the Roman Empire for three years and thirteen days; according to others he ruled for two years, two months, and twenty days. He destroyed Jerusalem where, by fighting or starvation, he killed hundreds of thousands of Jews not counting those who were sold, numbering about a hundred thousand. At Eastertime these were all gathered in the city where they were attacked.

He was so outstanding in every virtue that he was called the treasure and refinement of the human race. Those he defeated in war and in battle he left in the same condition as he found them. He was so courteous that he never denied a request. He would say that no one should

---

42. Emperor A.D. 69.

43. Emperor A.D. 69–79.

44. Suetonius, *Vespasian* 24; Dio Cassius, *Roman History* 66.1. Often translated as, "An emperor should die on his feet."

45. Emperor A.D. 79–81.

leave the emperor feeling sad, and once during a meal recalling that on a given day in the past he had done nothing for anyone, he made that memorable and praiseworthy remark, "I have lost a day, dear friends."[46] He was also literate, learned in Greek and Latin. And although his father had been virtuous, he still surpassed him by far. He died of fevers, and the public took his death badly with many tears and lamentations. He lived for forty-one years, although some say forty.

CLETUS (POPE 3), A.D. 82[47]

Cletus, born in Rome in the district called the Vicus Patricius, the son of [A]melianus, held the pontificate for eleven years, one month and eleven days. The Church was left leaderless for eleven days before the pontiff was elected. At the bidding of St. Peter, he ordained in the month of December twenty-six priests in the city of Rome. At the time of this pontificate Emperor Titus died and was buried near his father; and after his death there was so much grieving in Rome that it seemed everyone was in tears. Cletus was crowned with martyrdom and his body buried in the Vatican [cemetery] near the remains of St. Peter on the twenty-third of February.

DOMITIAN (EMPEROR 11), A.D. 85

Emperor Domitian,[48] Titus's brother and Vespasian's son, ruled the Roman Empire for thirteen years, five months and two days, although some say he ruled for fifteen years. In the first years he was very temperate, but he soon fell into serious vices and became deeply involved in activities that erased the merits of his father and brother. He killed the Gentiles in the Senate and sent many into exile; he ordered that he be addressed as "sir" and "god," and did not allow any statue of himself to be erected on the Capitoline unless made of gold or silver.[49] He killed his closest cousins. Following in Nero's footsteps, he brought about the

---

46. Suetonius, *Titus* 8.
47. A.D. 76–88 in the Vatican list.
48. Emperor A.D. 81–96.
49. Suetonius, *Domitian* 13.

second persecution of Christians. Although he was Vespasian's son and Titus's brother, he imitated none of their outstanding works; rather he resembled Nero and Caligula. It is also said that he sent St. John the Evangelist into exile on an island called Patmos, and ordered that all Jews descended from David be killed so that none would remain who were descendants of the royal progeny. Finally, he was killed in his room by his ministers and in his forty-fifth year buried with dishonor.

CLEMENT I (POPE 4), A.D. 93[50]

Clemens [Clement I] was born in Rome in the district of the Caelian Hill. He was the son of Faustin[us], and held the pontificate for nine years, three months and ten days. The Church was left leaderless for thirty-one days. He wrote many books on the Christian religion, and had the Church divided into seven notarial regions, each of which was to document the martyrs of that area. He scheduled two ordinations in the month of December including ten priests, two deacons and fifteen bishops for various places.[51]

Although he was chosen by St. Peter to be his successor, we nevertheless found Linus and Cletus listed before him, and so he was first by choice after St. Peter, but third in the listing. He once wrote in a letter to James[52] that Simon Peter "anticipating the end of his life appeared before me as I stood with a group of friends, and taking me by the hand he said, 'My brothers, I am ordering that this Clement be bishop of Rome, inasmuch as he has been a companion to me under all circumstances from start to finish.' And as I threw myself at his feet and expressed my desire to avoid the honor of the See, he replied, 'You flee from the See because you fear the danger of sin, but rest assured that you would be committing a worse sin, since you can help the people of God who seem to be caught in the storm which you flee, thinking more of yourself than the common welfare.'" At this time during

---

50. A.D. 88–97 in the Vatican list.

51. See *Liber Pontificalis* 4.1–4, Davis 1:2–3; and Introduction above, XXVII–XXXV.

52. Clement was the author of one genuine letter, to the Christians of Corinth. Several others were attributed to him in the Middle Ages.

Emperor Domitian's reign according to Dionysius the Areopagite, St. Lucius, a disciple of St. Peter, was declared a martyr, whom along with his companions the pontiff had assembled to send to Gaul.

NERVA (EMPEROR 12), A.D. 98

Nerva[53] from Narni ruled as Roman emperor for one year and four months. He was noble, honest and modest in governing and ruling the empire. He was easy-going and friendly to everyone. With the approval of the Senate he condemned what Domitian had done. Having no sons, he displayed outstanding virtue by adopting Trajan. Ultimately, his life ended in a natural death at the age of twenty-two.[54]

*

---

53. Emperor A.D. 96–98.
54. Actually sixty-six.

THE SECOND CENTURY

Traianus

TRAJAN (EMPEROR 13), A.D. 100
Emperor Traianus [Trajan],[1] of the Aelii family from Spain, ruled the Romans for nineteen years and seven months. He was a generous and peaceful emperor, extremely just and clement, very friendly towards all. Asked by someone why he was so friendly and welcoming with everyone, he replied that the emperor should behave toward individuals as they wish him to be. He was likewise outstanding in battle. After conquests in Africa, he went to Babylon and later on to the Indian frontier where he built beautiful ships in order to plunder their borders. He expanded the Roman Empire as far as the Orient, and was accepted and well liked by the Romans as well as by all the provinces. He strengthened and extended the empire that had become very weak. Finally he died of a stomach ailment near Selinus, a city in Syria, as he was returning from Persia. He lived for forty-four years, nine months and three days. His remains were placed in a golden urn and deposited in the Forum under a column a hundred feet tall.

During his reign Pope Clement was declared a saint and crowned a martyr. His body had lain a long time in the sea near Kherson where he had been thrown with a millstone around his neck during his exile. But after many years, his body was washed ashore by the waves and found, and then in Pope Nicholas's time brought to Rome where it was placed with the greatest solemnity by the pontiff and the Roman people in the church of St. Clement.[2] A few days later, St. Cyril was buried there for whom Jesus Christ performed many miracles.

1. Emperor A.D. 98–117.
2. This story is related in Jacobus de Voragine, *The Golden Legend: Readings on the Saints,* trans. William Granger Ryan, 2 vols. (Princeton, NJ: Princeton University Press, 1993), 2:170.

THE SECOND CENTURY

In these days St. Ignatius,[3] a disciple of St. John the Evangelist and bishop of Antioch, also died. One reads about him that, upon encountering Emperor Trajan, who was returning from his victories after threatening the Christians, he confessed to being a Christian and was led in chains to Rome, and not long afterwards he was crowned with martyrdom. Jesus Christ then performed a great miracle in his honor: after his heart had been removed from his body and divided into many parts, the name of Christ was written in golden letters on each part.

Emperor Traianus [Trajan] Eustachius[4] also flourished at this time. At first known as Placidus, he had been a very fine officer under Trajan. But it is said that after having a vision of Christ on the cross, he converted and was baptized along with his wife and children to the Catholic faith. Likewise at this time the temple of the Pantheon, of which we have spoken above, was struck by lightning and partially burned. It was rebuilt not long afterwards. We also read that Pliny,[5] a writer of natural history, was able to temper the emperor's cruelty toward the Christians, by writing to him that no evil could be found in them except that they refused to worship idols but instead adored and worshiped Christ by rising during the night before daybreak to say their offices and to sing praise. As a result Trajan later issued an edict that Christians should not be hunted down but punished when the occasion arose. Also during Trajan's day, Simeon, son of Cleophas and bishop of Jerusalem, was crucified, and Galen,[6] the doctor, who was born in Bergamo, became famous.

---

3. Ignatius of Antioch, c. A.D. 35/50–98/117. Author of several letters of basic importance to the development of Christianity.

4. The author's meaning here is unclear. This refers to Trajan himself. See n. 5.

5. Pliny the Younger, Gaius Plinius Caecilius Secundus, A.D. 61–c.113. Governor of Bithynia and author of a famous letter of A.D. 112 to Trajan seeking policy guidance on the persecution of Christians.

6. Aelius Galenus, c.A.D. 129–c.215, author of several Greek works on medicine that would become known to the medieval West through their Arabic translation.

THE LIVES OF THE POPES AND EMPERORS

ANACLETUS (POPE 5), A.D. 102

Anacletus,[7] from the city of Athens in Greece and the son of Nocho [Antiochus], held the pontificate for nine years, two months and ten days. The Church was without a pontiff for thirteen days. He was ordained a priest by St. Peter the Apostle. In the month of December Anacletus ordained in various locations ten priests, three deacons and six bishops, and he also built a place where bishops were to be buried. He decreed that no cleric should have long hair or beard. In his history Eusebius says that Anacletus and Cletus were one and the same,[8] but Pope Damasus maintains in his *Chronicles of Roman Pontiffs*, which he wrote to Jerome,[9] that they were two different popes, saying that Cletus was Roman and Anacletus Greek. Not only in this instance but in many others does the history of Eusebius differ from those of this saintly pontiff. Through his epistle he warned the faithful that priests should be honored more than other men, saying that because they sacrificed themselves for God everyone must esteem and honor them. He also wished that at the sacrifice priests should have witnesses present, especially bishops, so as prove that they have offered a perfect sacrifice to God. He died on the twelfth of July and was buried near St. Peter.

EVARISTUS (POPE 6), A.D. 131

Evaristus,[10] a Greek with a Jewish father from the city of Bethlehem, held the pontificate for eleven years, seven months and two days. The Church was without a pontiff for eighteen days. He ordered priests and deacons to protect the bishop who preached on behalf of the truth so that he would not be erroneously defamed by those who envied him and so that the word of God would not be maligned. He also ordered that matrimony be first widely proclaimed by the parents and then

---

7. The official Vatican list names Evaristus (A.D. 95–105) as the fifth pope. This may be a confusion with (Ana)Cletus above.

8. See Eusebius, *Ecclesiastical History* III.13.

9. Pope Damasus's correspondence with Saint Jerome was purported to be the basis of the first *Liber Pontificalis*. See Davis, *Book of Pontiffs* 1:xiii.

10. There is great uncertainty over the life and pontificate of Evaristus, but he is dated A.D. 97–105 as fifth in the official Vatican list.

solemnly by the holy priest. He ordained fifteen priests, two deacons and fifteen bishops. Finally he was a victim of Trajan's persecutions, declared a martyr and buried in the Vatican [cemetery] near St. Peter.

HADRIAN (EMPEROR 14), A.D. 119

Emperor Hadrianus [Hadrian],[11] born to a cousin of Trajan, and adopted by Trajan as his son, whose ancestors were in Italy in Scipio's time, ruled the Roman Empire for twenty years and eleven months. He was a man of profound learning and amazing eloquence and expanded the empire to the Euphrates River. He defeated the Jews during their second rebellion and rebuilt Jerusalem where people other than Jews had remained, changing its name to Aelia.[12] He was outstanding in everything and enacted many good laws. He had a column bearing his name erected in Rome, and although he was Trajan's relative, he envied his fame and returned to the Persians three eastern provinces acquired by Trajan. These were Syria, Mesopotamia and Armenia, and he wanted to do the same even with Dacia. This seemed unwise to his friends, so they stopped him because Trajan had sent people from throughout the Roman Empire to work and live in the lands of Dacia.

He enjoyed peace throughout his rule, was very learned in Greek and Latin, extremely wise, and an observer of military discipline. He also promulgated laws for the Athenians who had requested them. He died near Baia at the age of seventy-two years and eight months. Many maintain that he lived ninety-two years. In his day lived the heretic Basilide.

ALEXANDER I (POPE 7), A.D. 121

Alexander,[13] born in Rome and the son of Alexander from the Capitoline district, held the pontificate for eight years, five months and two days. The Church was without a pontiff for thirty-five days. He decreed that holy water be blessed with salt and then distributed to

---

11. Emperor A.D. 117–138.
12. In A.D. 135.
13. Pope 6, A.D. 105–115 in the official Vatican list.

people's homes. Later on, he was imprisoned under Emperor Hadrian, when Hermes was prefect of Rome; thinking he enjoyed the emperor's support, he had ordained priests and the deacon Theodolus, all of whom were declared martyrs along with Pope Alexander and many others. Alexander was then buried on Via Nomentana, and later moved to the church of Sta. Sabina. In memory of the Passion of Christ, he added to the sacred words the following: "On the day before He suffered He said, 'This is My body.'" He also declared that holy water at the Mass be mixed with the wine to designate the unity of Christ and of the Church, and that the host be made by Zimus, maintaining that the rounder it was the better. He also ordained in the month of December six priests, two deacons and five bishops.

SIXTUS I (POPE 8), A.D. 129

Xystus[14] [Sixtus I], born in Rome, a shepherd's son from the district of Via Lata, held the pontificate for ten years, four months and twenty-one days. The Church was without a pontiff for two months. He decreed that in the Mass one should say, "*Sanctus, sanctus, sanctus, Dominus Deus Sabaoth,* etc." and that sacred objects on the altar should be touched only by the celebrants. He was later beheaded outside the Appian Gate where Christ appeared to St. Peter, saying to him, "Where are you going?" and he replied, "I come to Rome to be crucified once again."[15] He was buried in the Vatican [cemetery] near St. Peter.

In his day, because the persecutions of Christians had become so cruel that very few could be found who wished to be called Christian, the Christians of Gaul sent a request that someone be sent to them who could rekindle the lamp of the Christian faith that was almost spent. And so the pontiff sent Bishop Petrinus, who was born in Rome, accompanied by many Christians. Many of those converts to the faith were declared martyrs there. He also ruled that the communion cloth should be not of silk but of the finest uncolored linen, and that women

---

14. Pope 7, A.D. 115–125 in the official Vatican list.
15. That is, at the church of Domine Quo Vadis on the Via Appia.

THE SECOND CENTURY

were not to touch the sacred vessels on the altar. He mandated too that any bishop reported to the Apostolic See was not to be welcomed in the bishop's residence at home without a papal letter. In the month of December he performed three separate ordinations of eleven priests, four deacons and four bishops.

At this time when Hadrian was emperor, Jerusalem was rebuilt, and it was ordered that no Jew was to enter the city. The place where Christ underwent his Passion, which was located outside [the city], was relocated inside. Since Hadrian was called Aelius, he wanted Jerusalem to be called Aelia, as we said above in speaking of his life. Under Hadrian, the saintly virgin Serafina suffered persecution. Being from Antioch, she was staying with Olinia, a very fine lady, known as Sabina, and who had earlier converted her with her teaching. Because St. Sabina was accused of having gathered and buried the remains of St. Serafina, she too was crowned with martyrdom.

During this period flourished Aquila who was born in Pontus and was a prolific interpreter of the Mosaic law. It is also said that during Hadrian's rule no one could condemn Christians without proof or testimony of their having sinned. It is said that in the same period the Christian liturgy was celebrated according to the Greek custom in the eastern church, having previously been in Hebrew.

TELESPHORUS (POPE 9[16]), A.D. 139

Telesphorus,[17] a Greek, held the pontificate for eleven years, three months and twenty-two days. The Church was without a pontiff for eight days. In his day, Emperor Hadrian died in Campania. Telesphorus ruled that fasting be observed for seven weeks before Easter, that no Mass be sung before terce, that the angelic hymn be sung before the holy sacrifice, and that at Christ's birth three Masses be sung including the hymn *"Gloria in excelsis Deo."* At his death he was crowned a martyr and buried in the Vatican [cemetery] near St. Peter.

---

16. Text reads "Pope XI."
17. Pope 8, A.D. 125–136 in the official Vatican list.

He ordered that the seven-week fast be observed especially by the clergy, saying that the clerical life must be different from lay practices; thus there should be a difference in the fasting for the seven weeks, with clergy abstaining from meats and other delicacies. He ordered three Masses at Christmastime, the first at midnight at the rooster's crowing when Christ deigned to be born in Bethlehem; the second between day and night when Christ was adored by the shepherds; the third during daytime when the brilliance of our Lord Jesus Christ shines upon us — that is to say, upon our rebirth. During the month of December he performed three separate ordinations of twelve priests, nine deacons and fourteen bishops.

Antoninus Pius (Emperor 15), A.D. 138[18]

Antoninus Pius,[19] with his children Aurelius and Lucius, ruled the Roman Empire for twenty-two years, four months and one day; some say twenty-three years. He was Hadrian's son-in-law as well as his adopted son; he was handsome, very intelligent and eloquent, as well as very modest and kind. It is said that he issued an order revoking the census debt that Octavian had ordered in every locality. As a result he was given the title of Pius. It is also said that he was liked by Christians, and ran the government so humanely and so smoothly that he was worthy of the title of Pius. He used to say, "As far as discipline goes, I would prefer to save one citizen than to kill a thousand men."[20] He died in his sleep at the age of seventy from the fevers while asleep in a villa about eleven miles outside the city. His body was taken to Rome and consecrated among the gods, like Romulus.

In his day, Galen the doctor from Pergamum was still alive, as was Iustinus who condensed the histories of Pompeius Trogus the Spaniard who had written the history of Rome from King Ninus of the Assyrians

---

18. Text reads "A.D. 111."
19. Emperor A.D. 138–161.
20. See *Historia Augusta,* Antoninus Pius 9.10

down to the reign of Caesar.[21] He divided them into forty-four books and sent them to Antoninus Pius. The heretics Valentinus and Martionus also lived during this period.

HYGINUS (POPE 10), A.D. 140[22]

Hyginus,[23] a Greek philosopher born in Athens, held the pontificate for four years, two months and seven days. The Church was without a pontiff for three days. He systematized the clergy by assigning them to various ranks. He performed four separate ordinations consisting of fifteen priests, five deacons and six bishops. He also ordered that the person who baptized someone in the baptismal font should be considered the equivalent of a mother and a father in order to confirm and proclaim the faith. In addition, he decided that no metropolitan official except the pope could hear any charge against a bishop within his province, nor could he be condemned without the charge being considered in the presence of other bishops of his province. Finally he was declared a martyr and buried near St. Peter.

PIUS I (POPE 11), A.D. 154

The Italian Pius [I][24] from the city of Aquileia, the son of Rufinus, held the pontificate for eleven years, four months and sixteen days. The Church was without a pope for fourteen days. During his papacy, Hermes[25] composed the book in which he states that Christ's Resurrection should be celebrated on a Sunday. Pius ruled that the heretic who was descended from the Jews be accepted and baptized. In the month of December he ordained nineteen priests, twenty-one deacons and twelve bishops.

---

21. Justin condenses Pompeius Trogus's expansive work, *Historiae Philippicae et totius mundi origines et terrae situs*, into his own *Historiarum Philippicarum libri XLIV* (n.d.).

22. Text reads "A.D. 40."

23. Pope 9, A.D. 136–140 in the official Vatican list.

24. Pope 10, A.D. 140–155 in the official Vatican list.

25. Perhaps St. Hermes, martyr, d.120. This may be the Hermes associated with the *Shepherd of Hermes,* a contemporary visionary text, often part of the early Christian biblical canon. Hermes is thought by some scholars to be the brother of Pius I.

In his time Bishop Polycarp of Ephesus,[26] a disciple of John the Evangelist, came to Rome and saved many from the heresy that had corrupted them through the teaching of Valentinus and Martionis. As for Hermes who was mentioned above, Pope Pius wrote a letter, saying that in those days an angel of God in shepherd's dress appeared to Hermes, a doctor of the faith and of scripture, with the command that Easter be celebrated on Sunday, something which, the pope added, "we announce with apostolic authority."[27]

MARCUS AURELIUS (EMPEROR 16), A.D. 162

Marcus [Aurelius][28] Antonius Verus [Antoninus], son-in-law of Antoninus Pius, ruled the Roman Empire for nineteen years and ten days. But he ruled together with Lucius Aurelius, his brother, for eleven years. These two brothers were the first to be called Augustus.

Antoninus was an excellent emperor, wisely enduring the vices of his brother, Lucius. He was very learned in Latin and Greek as well as a very fine philosopher with no peers in piety. He was extremely austere, so much so that nowhere is it written that he ever changed expression. He was also unmatched in modesty and treated his subjects leniently; and he triumphed over the Parthians and Persians. He was a man of such virtue that he would have been called happy were it not for his wife Faustina and his son Commodus.

Finally, he died of fever in Pannonia at the age of sixty-one. In his day Christians suffered their fifth persecution, and Pope Pius was crowned with martyrdom and buried in the Vatican [cemetery] beside St. Peter. St. Justin, bishop of Vienne, and St. Fortius, bishop of Lyons, were martyred in Asia together with a very large multitude, while St. Polycarp, along with thirteen others from Philadelphia, was martyred in Gaul. In his day there was an author from the mountains who wrote about the heretics Catafrigius and Zizanus.

26. Polycarp of Smyrna, A.D. 80–167.

27. The version in the *Liber Pontificalis* 11.2–3 is somewhat different. See Davis 1:5.

28. Emperor A.D. 161–169 (with Lucius Verus), 169–177 (alone), 177–March 180 (with Commodus).

THE SECOND CENTURY

ANICETUS (POPE 12), A.D. 165[29]

Anicetus,[30] born in Syria, the son of Ioannes Vicus, held the pontificate for nine years, three months and four days. The Church was without a pontiff for fifteen days. He ruled that clergy should not have long hair or a long beard, but should have a round tonsure. He also ruled that a bishop should be consecrated by no less than three bishops because the apostles observed such a custom and that at an archbishop's ordination all the bishops of his province be present since they will be expected to obey him. He ordered too that if a bishop has a difference with his archbishop, they must settle their differences at the apostolic seat of their primate. He also ruled that no archbishop should be called primate or patriarch, except those who control large cities or patriarchies, and that the others should be called metropolitans. In the month of December he ordained priests, deacons and twelve bishops.

SOTER (POPE 13), A.D. 175

Soterius [Soter],[31] born in Campania, the son of Concordius from the city of Fondi, held the pontificate for nine years, three months and twenty-one days. The papacy was vacant for thirty-one days. He ruled that no nun could touch the holy patent nor burn incense in church, and that every nun wear a veil. He also decreed that a wife is legitimate only when blessed by a priest and given in marriage by several relatives and parents. This he did to end the many perils that occur in matrimony.[32]

At this time lived the historian Hegesippus,[33] as well as the two holy virgins Potentiana and Prossedia. While burying martyrs' remains, Prossedia would pray to God that he call her to himself, and having

---

29. Text reads "A.D. 65."

30. Pope 11, A.D. 155–166 in the official Vatican list.

31. Pope 12, A.D. 166–175 in the official Vatican list.

32. The biases of these sections indicate a clerical source that the later compiler — lay or clerical — did not choose to alter.

33. c. A.D. 110–c. April 7, 180. Church chronicler, Jewish convert, and author of the *Hypomnemata*.

been heard by him, she died in the eternal peace of Christ. At this time too, the Emperor Marcus [Aurelius] waged great battles against the Gergani, the Scoti and the Sarmatae. Because he lacked funds for the troops and wished not to hurt any of them, he sold his gold and silver vessels and all his wife's jewelry as well as many other valuables, in an attempt not to anger the Senate and the provinces. Once he was victorious, he not only bought back those items but gave a tribute to all the provinces. When later he died in Pannonia, he was greatly mourned, taken to Rome and consecrated among the gods.

COMMODUS (EMPEROR 17), A.D. 181

Commodus,[34] the son of Antonius Verus [Marcus Aurelius], ruled the Roman Empire for seventeen years, was inimical to his father's virtues and very prone to lechery. He was nevertheless successful in his battles against the Normans.[35] He strove to have the month of September called Commodus after himself, but since he was troublesome to everyone, he was strangled without anyone being troubled about it.

In his time, a lightning bolt struck the Capitoline, burning the library and several surrounding buildings. Pope Soter was martyred and buried in Vatican grounds near St. Peter. In his day arose the Catafrigian heretics named after Frigia, the city where they originated, who held that the Holy Spirit was not given to the apostles. Theodosius from Ephesus, known as the third interpreter, lived at this time, as did Hermes, bishop of Lyons, who was famed for his learning.

ELEUTHERIUS[36] (POPE 14), A.D. 183

The Greek Soterius [Eleutherius], the son of [A]bindius from Nicopolis, held the pontificate for fifteen years, six months and five days. The Church was without a pope for six days. He received letters

---

34. Emperor A.D. 180–192.

35. The text reads "Normanni." It is not clear what is meant here.

36. There is some confusion here with the previous pope, Soter. This is pope 13, A.D. 175–189 in the official Vatican list.

THE SECOND CENTURY

from King Lucius of England[37] who wished to become a Christian by papal decree. The pontiff sent him two religious, Fridian and Damian, who baptized him together with all his people. There were at that time in England twenty-seven idolatrous pontiffs who supposedly were Flemish. In exchange for these pagans, the holy men ordained bishops and archbishops. In his day Bishop Apollonaris flourished as did Dionysius, bishop of Corinth. This holy pontiff ruled that no pope could be removed from office without being formally accused, reasoning that our Lord Christ knew that Judas was a traitor and a thief, yet because he had not been accused by all the apostles, he maintained the dignity of his office. He forbade that the final sentence be made public only in the presence of the accuser. He also declared that no food could be refused by faithful Christians.

In his day Emperor Commodus was strangled and, after his death, was considered the enemy of the human species. It is also said that at this time Philippus, a Roman, was sent by the emperor as prefect to Alexandria. It is said of him that his daughter named Eugenia,[38] dressed as a man, secretly left him and had herself baptized using the name Eugenius. Somewhat later, he was elected abbot. Since he was attractive, a woman called Melantia, upon seeing him, fell deeply in love with him, but because he would not yield, she was moved to despair and discredited him saying that Eugenius wanted to force her. As a result, he and all the other monks were disgraced. When the news spread throughout the city, it came to the attention of the prefect who captured them and condemned them to death. Eugenia was about to be tortured, when, tearing off her clothes before the prefect, she revealed that she was a woman. Whereupon the prefect recognized her as his daughter and received her with great joy as did all the people. After being baptized, Melantia, who had brought disgrace upon everyone, was struck by lightning and killed. At the end of his life, Soterius

---

37. The *Liber Pontificalis* 14.2, Davis 1:6 is the origin of this legend that was later popularized by Bede. His existence may be the result of a scribal error.

38. St. Eugenia of Rome, d. c. A.D. 258. The story is amplified in Jacobus de Voragine's *Golden Legend* under Protus and Hyacinthus.

[Eleutherius] was declared a martyr and buried in the church of St. Peter [Vatican cemetery].

PERTINAX HELVIUS (EMPEROR 18), A.D. 194

Pertinax Helvius[39] ruled the Roman Empire for six months and twenty-five days. Being the son of a libertine, he was considered of lowly birth, but noble with respect to uprightness and behavior. He was declared emperor by order of the Senate, which then requested that he call his wife Augusta and his son Caesar. He refused, answering, "It is enough that I rule against my will."[40] He was reputed to be somewhat greedy, but was loved by the people and hated by the soldiers who had Julianus kill him in his room at the age of seventy-one. In his day lived Symmachus IV, the interpreter, as did Bishop Narcissus of Jerusalem, Tertullian of Africa and Origen, the great scholar in Alexandria.

DIDIUS JULIANUS (EMPEROR 19), [N.D.]

Didius Iulianus [Julianus],[41] son of Iulianus the great jurist, whose ancestors were from Milan, ruled the Roman Empire for two months. He was very greedy and lived a shameful life, and because the people hated him, he was stripped of the empire by authority of the Senate and killed in his palace at the age of forty-six years and four months.

SEVERUS (EMPEROR 20), [N.D.]

[Septimius] Severus,[42] born in Africa at a castle near Leptis in the province of Tripolis, ruled the Roman Empire for seventeen years — some say eighteen or nineteen. He was a powerful man and waged many wars, conquering the Parthians and the Arabs, and subjecting many other people to the Roman Empire. His last battle was in England. He was very daring and renowned in warfare. He was horrible to the Senate and the Roman people, but loved by his troops because he paid them better than any other commander. Concerning this situation, he told

---

39. Emperor 1 January 193–28 March 193.
40. See *Historia Augusta*, Pertinax 13.
41. Emperor 28 March–1 June 193.
42. Emperor A.D. 193–211.

the Senate that he ought never to have been born or that he should never die.[43] In honor of Pertinax, whom Julianus had killed, he wished to be called Pertinax. In the end, he died in England at the age of eighty-nine.

Upon his death he left so many supplies that the city had enough for seven years. Finally, he was the last emperor from Africa in whose honor an arch can be seen even today in Rome. During his time the sixth persecution of Christians took place, in which many saints from many provinces were killed. Leonidas, Origen's father, was decapitated. As a result Origen was left at a young age with six brothers and a widowed mother. Since he was learned in grammar at sixteen, he taught school and was able to support his entire family.

VICTOR I (POPE 15), A.D. 199.

Victor,[44] born in Africa and the son of Felix, held the pontificate for ten years, two months and ten days. The Church was without a pontiff for twelve days. He decreed that the Easter Resurrection always be celebrated on Sunday. When priests inquired regarding the end of Eastertide, he summoned a council that was held in Alexandria.[45] This pontiff, as well as Patriarch Narcissus of Jerusalem, Bishop Theophilus of Caesarea and Bishop Reticius of Lyon, participated in it. The council ruled that Easter always be celebrated on the Sunday following the fourteenth moon in the month of April until the twenty-first moon because many bishops in Asia and the East were celebrating the Jewish Easter [Passover]. He also decreed that every man must be baptized in a river or fountain or sea, thereby clarifying the Christian ritual. Finally he was given the martyr's crown and buried in the Vatican cemetery in the church of St. Peter on the eighteenth of July.[46] In December he ordained twelve priests, deacons and bishops.

*

43. *Historia Augusta,* Septimius Severus 18.7.
44. Pope 14, A.D. 189–198.
45. See *Liber Pontificalis* 15.3, Davis 1:6.
46. There is no evidence either of his martyrdom or of his burial in the Vatican. His feast day is July 28.

THE THIRD CENTURY

Zepherinus

ZEPHRYNUS (POPE 16), A.D. 208

The Roman Zephrynus[1] held the pontificate for nine years, six months and ten days. The Church was without a pontiff for six days. He decreed that all faithful Christians from the age of twelve receive communion on the day of the Christ's Resurrection, and that all altar vessels be either of metal or glass if they could not be made of gold or silver. At this time, Bishop Alexander of Cappadocia went to Jerusalem on pilgrimage while Bishop Narcissus was still living. He also ruled that neither patriarchs nor primates nor metropolitans could pass sentence on an accused bishop without prior apostolic approval, and that the ordination of priests and of Levites[2] take place at solemnly ordained times in the presence of many good and selected men.

BASSIANUS (EMPEROR 21), A.D. 212

Bassianus,[3] son of Severus, called [M. Aurelius] Antoninus Caracalla from a kind of garment that he created upon succeeding his father, ruled the Romans for seven years less twenty days. He was more vulgar and much more lustful than his father. He had the jurist Papinianus killed because he reproached him for having taken his stepmother Iulia as his wife. He was a truly terrible emperor, and eventually was killed at the age of forty-three near the city of Carrhae by the Prefect Macrinus.[4] In his day Pope Zephyrinus died and was buried in the cemetery of Callixtus on the Via Appia.

---

1. Pope 15, A.D. 199–217 in the official Vatican list.
2. Young priests.
3. Emperor A.D. 198–211 (with Severus); 209–4 February 211 (with Severus and Geta); February–December 211 (with Geta); December 211–8 April 217 (alone).
4. During the Roman war with Parthia.

THE THIRD CENTURY

CALLIXTUS I (POPE 17), A.D. 218

The Roman Callistus [Callixtus I],[5] son of Demetrius, held the pontificate for five years, two months and ten days. The Church was without a pontiff for six days. He built the church of Sta. Maria in Trastevere. He instituted the four seasonal fasts and built the cemetery on the Via Appia called the cemetery of Callixtus where a large number of martyrs are buried. He himself was crowned with martyrdom. In his day Emperor Caracalla died.[6]

MACRINUS (EMPEROR 22), A.D. 219

After Bassianus [Caracalla] was killed, Macrinus[7] the prefect was made emperor and ruled the empire for one year and twenty-eight days. He was a very cowardly man, very vicious and cruel. Finally, he and his son were killed because of envy near Antioch by [Narius Avibus Bassianus] Elagabalus.

ELAGABALUS (EMPEROR 23), A.D. 220

Marcus Aurelius Antoninus [Narius Avibus Bassianus] Elagabalus[8] ruled the Roman Empire for three years, or rather four years. He was considered the son of Antoninus Caracalla and a very vulgar prostitute named Semiramia [Soaemias], at whose instigation he did many indecent things and did not try to avoid lechery of any kind in his disgusting life.[9] He gave an oration dedicated to this prostitute that may still be seen in our day. Finally he and his mother Semiramia died in Rome during a soldiers' uprising and were thrown into a sewer full of excrement.[10] In his day one finds the sixth accord at Nicopoli, and during his reign rose a generation of heretics that were called Sebellians.

---

5. Pope 16, A.D. 217–222.
6. On 8 April 217.
7. Emperor A.D. 217–218.
8. Emperor A.D. 218–222.
9. See Cassius Dio, *Roman History* LXXX; and the *Historia Augusta*, Elagabalus.
10. *Historia Augusta*, Elagabalus 17.

Pope Callixtus was crowned with martyrdom and buried in a cemetery that then was named after him.

URBAN I (POPE 18), A.D. 223

Urbanus [Urban I],[11] born in Rome and the son of Pontianus from the Via Lata district, held the pontificate for eleven years, ten months and thirteen days. The Church was without a pontiff for thirty days. He was of noble descent and also most noble in virtue, and was considered outstanding in abstinence and chastity. He decreed that vessels used in the divine mystery be of gold and silver. He was responsible for many conversions, among whom was Valerianus, a very fine man and husband of St. Cecilia, both of whom were crowned with martyrdom. In the month of December he ordained eight priests, deacons and bishops, and he strongly condemned the persecution of Christians. Often he was sent from Rome into exile.

ALEXANDER SEVERUS (EMPEROR 24), A.D. 223

Alexander [Severus],[12] son of Varius and Mamaea, a truly Christian woman, and cousin of [Narius Avibus Bassianus] Elagabalus, ruled Rome for eighteen years. He was given the title of Caesar by the people and Augustus by the Senate. He was very demanding with regard to military discipline and brilliantly defeated the Persians. He was extremely popular and skillfully administered the republic with his advisor Vipianus who had an outstanding legal mind. Ultimately, he was killed by Maximin's troops in Mainz, a city in Gaul. He lived for thirty-eight years, three months and seven days. His death greatly displeased the people. In his day, Pope Urban [I] was secretly brought back by the faithful, but he was taken prisoner during a baptismal service and decapitated.

At this time Origen[13] excelled above all others in knowledge and conduct, aside from the apostles. He composed a great number of works

11. Pope 17, A.D. 222–230.
12. Emperor A.D. 222–235.
13. Origen of Alexandria, theologian, 184/185–253/254.

THE THIRD CENTURY

on different subjects, without counting his letters to various people. A proverb about him was popular, which said that his life was like his learning. In fact, he did not lie in bed or wear socks or eat meat or drink wine, as one reads in Ecclesiastes.[14] And although he was very learned and led a very holy life, he nevertheless was accused of many errors for which great scholars forgive him, for example Eusebius of Caesarea and Rufinus, a priest from Aquileia, in writing to Jerome. Many say that, after his death, heretics introduced many serious errors into his writings in order to obscure his brilliant learning. At this time St. Hippolytus was the bishop of Porto.

PONTIAN (POPE 19), A.D. 232

Pontianus [Pontian],[15] born in Rome and the son of Calpurnius, held the pontificate for five years, two months and one day. The Church was without a pontiff for ten days. He was sent into exile to Sardinia, and was there crowned with martyrdom. St. Fabian then took his body to Rome and buried it in the cemetery of Callixtus. This pontiff, it is said, was succeeded by Syriacus who held the pontificate for one year and three months. But because he had been elected contrary to the clergy's will, substituting himself for Pope Anterus, and had brought with him many virgins whom he had baptized in Rome and had left with Agrippina, he is not listed in the *Book of Pontiffs*[16] since many believe that he kept virgins not for devotion but for pleasure. Nevertheless, according to the *Book of Virgins*, he was martyred along with all of them.

MAXIMINUS (EMPEROR 25), A.D. 236

Maximinus [Thrax, Maximin],[17] born in the Thracian region of a barbarian father and mother, ruled the Roman Empire for three years. Without the Senate's approval, he was made emperor by the soldiers

14. A very loose paraphrase of 2:24, 9:7–10.
15. Pope 18, A.D. 230–235.
16. He is in the Roman *Liber Pontificalis* 19, Davis 1:7–8.
17. Emperor A.D. 235–238

and given the title of Augustus. Of large stature, he was very strong and proud, rough and arrogant. For this reason the soldiers chose another emperor in Africa called Gordian, an old and serious man. But soon Maximin had him killed and with his son attacked the Romans. Then the Senate chose three emperors to combat him: Pupienus, Albinus and the younger Gordian, grandson of Gordian. Sometime after that, Maximin and his son were killed by soldiers in Aquileia, but some say that he was killed by Pupienus. He defeated the Parthians and the German tribes and was a terrible persecutor of Christians.

ANTERUS (POPE 20), A.D. 237

The Greek Anterus[18] held the pontificate for three years, one month, and nineteen days. The Church was without a pontiff for thirteen days. He ruled that bishops could move from see to see, and he had the deeds of martyrs carefully written down and required that they be registered. He also created a bishop for the city of Fondi[19] in the month of December.

GORDIAN III (EMPEROR 26), A.D. 239

The Emperor Gordianus [Gordian III][20] ruled the Roman Empire for six years less twenty days. He was given the title of Augustus by the Senate, as were Pupienus and Albinus, who after ruling for two years were slain in a soldiers' mutiny, and he was left as the lone ruler of the empire. He was an amiable and gracious young man. He fought with the Persians and defeated them. While fighting in the East on the advice of his father-in-law Misitheus, a very prudent man, he was killed by soldiers through the deception of Phillip of Arabia. A tomb was built for him near the Euphrates, although his bones were sent to Rome. At this time Pope Anterus was crowned with martyrdom and buried in the cemetery of Callixtus. During Gordian's reign one

---

18. Pope 19, A.D. 235–236.
19. In current day Lazio, between Rome and Naples.
20. Emperor A.D. 238–244.

THE THIRD CENTURY

also reads that a dove was involved in the papal election by lighting on Fabian's head, but others say this happened to Zephyrinus.

FABIAN (POPE 21), A.D. 240

Fabianus [Fabian],[21] a Roman from the district of Monte Celio and the son of Fabius, held the pontificate for twelve years, two months and six days. The Church was without a pontiff for seven days. Following the death of Pope [Anterus], he returned from abroad and, during the electoral process, a white dove descended from heaven and lit on his head. This was considered to be an intervention manifesting the divine will, and he was elected pontiff. Subsequently he ordained seven bishops who, after carefully investigating the martyrs' deeds, were expected to give the results to notaries. He also ruled that once a year during the Lord's Supper, confirmation should be performed and celebrated. Finally, he was crowned with martyrdom and buried in the cemetery of Callixtus. In his day, the well-known heretic Novatian came from Africa.

PHILLIP OF ARABIA (EMPEROR 27), A.D. 245

Phillippus [Phillip] of Arabia,[22] the first Christian emperor, ruled the Roman Empire with his son Phillip for seven years. He was very arrogant in ruling and did nothing worthy of praise. In the end both were killed, the father in Verona and the son in Rome, in a military uprising through the instigation of Decius.

One reads that in his day one thousand years had elapsed since the founding of Rome. As a result, to celebrate that event the Romans organized a great feast and special solemnities where certain games were played called "theatrical" that lasted three days and three nights, with the populace remaining awake to view them.[23]

---

21. Pope 20, A.D. 236–250.
22. Emperor A.D. 244–249.
23. The Ludi Saeculares of April 248.

THE LIVES OF THE POPES AND EMPERORS

CORNELIUS (POPE 22), A.D. 252

The Roman Cornelius,[24] son of Iustinus, held the pontificate for three years, two months and ten days. The Church was without a pontiff for twenty-six days. Cornelius ruled that a priest could take an oath under certain conditions if he wished. He also, at the behest of St. Lucina, had the bodies of Saints Peter and Paul the Apostle removed from the catacombs. They buried St. Paul on the Via Ostia and St. Peter near the place where he was crucified, on Vatican Hill in the temple of Apollo in Nero's Palace. Finally Cornelius was crowned with martyrdom under Emperor Decius.

We must here note, so that we may better be understood in the future, that anyone may be called Augustus and Caesar, but not vice-versa since one is called Caesar by the ruler or by the army, but Augustus by confirmation of the Senate.

DECIUS (EMPEROR 28), A.D. 252

Decius,[25] born in Bubalia in lower Pannonia,[26] ruled the Roman Empire for two years and four months. He was a man of military talent, but with a great hatred for the poor. He was responsible for the seventh persecution of Christians whom he persecuted ruthlessly because of his hatred for the two Christian emperors named Phillip that he had killed. In the end some barbarians killed him and his son whom he had made Caesar. In his day lived St. Antony,[27] the first monastic father in Egypt.

GALLUS HOSTILIANUS AND VOLUSIAN (EMPERORS 29), A.D. 254

Gallus Hostilianus [Trebonianus] together with his son Volusianus ruled over the Romans for two years.[28] In his time there arose the Novatian heresy known as Novatiana that denied repentance for sins.

24. Pope 21, A.D. 251–253.
25. Emperor A.D. 249–251.
26. Present-day southeast and central Europe.
27. Anthony of Egypt, or the Great, c.251–356.
28. Co-emperors A.D. 251–253.

THE THIRD CENTURY

Novatian,[29] a priest under Cyprian, came to Rome and disseminated this heresy. And there flourished St. Cyprian,[30] bishop of Carthage, and in addition there was widespread persecution of Christians.

LUCIUS I (POPE 23), A.D. 255

The Roman Lucius [I],[31] son of Porphyrius, held the pontificate for three years, three months and three days. The Church was without a pontiff for thirty-five days. He ruled that two priests and three deacons could not leave their bishop because of some kind of error. He also appointed Stephen as archdeacon for the entire Church while he attended the Passion. He also announced three ordinations in December of seven priests, deacons and bishops. Finally he was beheaded under Emperor Valerian.

VALERIAN AND GALLIENUS (EMPERORS 30), A.D. 256

Valerianus [Valerian],[32] with his son Gallienus, ruled the Roman Empire for fifteen years. He was given the title of Augustus by the army, which also pleased the Senate, since he was a nobleman, outstanding in knowledge and eloquence. But he proved to be the most unsuccessful emperor of all because, while fighting in Mesopotamia, he was captured by Sapor, king of the Persians. The emperor suffered a miserable old age due to him because he was forced to use his shoulders to help the king mount his horse.[33] He was a very ruthless persecutor of the Christians. In his day the Goths sacked Greece, Macedonia, Asia and the Pontus, and Pope Lucius was beheaded, St. Cyprian was killed, and it is believed that St. Paul, the first hermit, entered a hermitage.

---

29. c.200–258.

30. Early Christian writer, 200–September 14, 258.

31. Pope 22, A.D. 253–254.

32. Emperor A.D. 253–260.

33. Shapur I, the Great, 240/42–270/72. The incident, after the battle of Edessa in 260, is recorded in Eutropius, *Abridgement of Roman History* 9.7.

He reigned for six years, after which his son Gallienus,[34] who had been given the title of Augustus by the Senate, took over the empire. He devoted himself to lustful activities, and even allowed the German tribes to advance as far as Ravenna. After the Alemanni had defeated the Gauls in Italy and the Roman Republic was greatly weakened, Egypt, Syria, Rhaetia, Noricum and Pannonia rebelled against the Romans. Nevertheless, he was a very fine poet, and eventually died in Milan. In his day Cyprian, first a rhetorician and later a bishop, was crowned with martyrdom.

STEPHEN I (POPE 24), A.D. 258
The Roman Stephanus [Stephen I],[35] son of Iulianus, held the pontificate for four years, three months and twenty-five days. He ruled that clergy and young priests use only silk vestments in church. Then, after converting many Gentiles and burying many martyrs, he was himself crowned with martyrdom. In his day there were widespread persecutions of Christians.

SIXTUS II (POPE 25), A.D. 257[36]
Xystus [Sixtus] II,[37] born in Greece, held the pontificate for two years, eleven months and six days. The Church was without a pontiff for thirty-five days. He ruled that the Mass be celebrated on an altar and nowhere else, something which in those days was not always observed. Finally, he was beheaded with Agapitus. They were accompanied in their martyrdom by St. Lawrence, Hippolytus and many others.

DIONYSIUS (POPE 26), A.D. 265
The monk Dionysius,[38] whose background is unknown, held the pontificate for two years, three months and one day. The Church was

---

34. Emperor A.D. 253–260 with Valerian; 260 with Saloninus; 260–268 alone.
35. Pope 23, A.D. 254–257.
36. Text reads "222."
37. Pope 24, A.D. 257–258.
38. Pope 25, A.D. 260–268.

THE THIRD CENTURY

without a pontiff for eight days. He assigned churches to priests and set up parishes and dioceses.

Felix I (Pope 27[39]), A.D. 267

The Roman Felix [I],[40] son of Constantinus from the Capitoline district, held the pontificate for two years, nine months and twenty-seven days. The Church was without a pontiff for three days. He ruled that Masses be celebrated in memory of the martyrs and had a church built on the Via Aurelia a mile from Rome.[41] When later he was crowned with martyrdom, he was buried there.

Eutychian (Pope 28), A.D. 270

Eutychianus [Eutychian],[42] son of Martinus from the Tusculan city of Luna,[43] held the pontificate for eight years, ten months and four days. The Church was without a pontiff for eleven days. He ruled that wheat be blessed on the altar; and his charity was such that with his own hands he buried some three hundred forty-two martyrs in various places. At his death he was crowned with martyrdom. In his day Emperor Gallienus died through the conspiring of Aurelian.

Claudius II (Emperor 31), A.D. 271

Emperor Claudius II[44] ruled the Roman Empire for one year and nine months. He was elected by will of the Senate, and it is said that he possessed the finest qualities of all the emperors. He did battle with the Goths, and after defeating them, a golden shield in the Curia and a golden statue on the Capitoline were placed there in his honor. Finally he died in Smyrna. After his death, his brother Quintillus, an excellent man, took over the empire, but had held it for just seventeen days when he died in Aquileia.

---

39. Text reads "xxvi."
40. Pope 26, A.D. 269–274.
41. From *Liber Pontificalis* 27.2b, Davis 1:11.
42. Pope 27, A.D. 275–283.
43. In present-day Liguria, on the gulf of Spezia.
44. Emperor A.D. 268–270.

THE LIVES OF THE POPES AND EMPERORS

AURELIAN (EMPEROR 32), A.D. 273

Aurelianus [Aurelian],[45] born of barbarian parents in Dacia, ruled the Roman Empire for five years and six months. He was a very strong and skilled in all kinds of warfare, and thus was in charge of many wars in the Orient. He fought the Goths and defeated them. Nevertheless, he was not tolerant, which is the primary virtue that a ruler must possess. He enlarged the city walls of Rome, making them stronger and more attractive than any others before or after.[46]

Upon his return from Gaul, he began to persecute harshly the Christians among whom was St. Columba, killed along with many others. In his day, Pope Eutychian was crowned with martyrdom and buried in the cemetery of Callixtus on the Via Appia. Near Antioch he defeated Zenobia,[47] a brave lady who had conquered Syria in an incredible fashion. He then led her in triumph before his chariot, bound with many golden chains. It is said that he was the first in Rome to wear a crown adorned with various gems as well as the first to order the people to eat pork. He had a city in Gaul, Aurelia,[48] named after him. It is also said that after his persecution of the Christians he was struck by lightning, although he did not die. He also built the temple of the Sun in which he placed many gold and silver ornaments. In the end, between Constantinople and Heraclea, he died as a result of a plot by his servant, and was then consecrated as a god.

TACITUS (EMPEROR 33), A.D. 278

Emperor Tacitus[49] ruled the Roman Empire for six months. A good and serious consul and elder, he was made emperor with the widespread consent of the military and the people. He was temperate and sober, and loved to read. He did nothing outstanding because of the brevity of his tenure.

45. Emperor A.D. 270–275.
46. These are the Aurelian Walls of Rome, which still stand.
47. Queen of Palmyra in Syria, 240–c.275.
48. Orléans.
49. Emperor A.D. 275–276.

THE THIRD CENTURY

FLORIANUS (EMPEROR 34), [276]

Emperor Florianus[50] ruled the Roman Empire for eighty-nine days. He was Tacitus's brother and very akin to him. After his brother's death he took control of the empire. Later he was killed at the hands of the military.

CAIUS (POPE 29), A.D. 278

Caius [Gaius],[51] born in Dalmatia in Diocletian's time and the son of Gaius, held the pontificate for eleven years, three months and eight days. The Church was without a pontiff for eleven days. He decreed that the Church hierarchy would be as follows: subdeacon, deacon, priest and above all bishop.

In his day the heretic Mani,[52] who was born in Persia, became well known. Possessing a subtle mind but crude in his behavior, he maintained that there were two basic life principles, one of light and the other of darkness; and he would argue his position so subtly that he left many followers victims of the same error. This pontiff ordered that pagan heretics could not bring accusations against Christians or serve as witnesses against them. He also ruled that no man should presume to accuse a bishop or any other prelate or cleric before a secular judge. In addition, he ordered that the deeds of martyrs be recorded in the diaconate regions. He also wrote an epistle against heretics on the Incarnation of the Son of God upon which the Catholic faith rests.

PROBUS (EMPEROR 35), A.D. 279

Probus,[53] born in Pannonia in a city named Sirmium, ruled the Roman Empire for six years and four months. He was a truly good man, and by agreement of all the people was made emperor. He freed Gaul from the barbarians. Finally, he was killed by his troops near

---

50. Emperor A.D. 276.
51. Pope 28, A.D. 283–296.
52. c.216–274.
53. Emperor A.D. 276–282.

Sirmium[54] because he had driven them to exhaustion in battle. It was in his day that the bestial heresy of Manichaeism began.

CARUS (EMPEROR 36), A.D. 286

The Roman Carus,[55] according to some from Milan, others from Illyria, and still others from Narbonne, ruled the Roman Empire for three years. He was neither a good nor a bad ruler. After capturing the city of Carrhae, then destroying the Parthian regions and pitching his camp across the Tigris River, he died when struck by an arrow. He had two sons whom he named as Caesars. The younger son, Numerian, a great orator and poet without equal in his day, was killed at the hands of his father-in-law, [Arrius] Aper. His other son, Carinus,[56] was very corrupt and was defeated and killed by Diocletian.

DIOCLETIAN (EMPEROR 37), A.D. 289

Diocletianus [Diocletian],[57] born in Dalmatia and a chancellor's son, ruled the Roman Empire for twenty years. He was a magnanimous and prudent man who ruled alone with tolerance.[58] Because of the very troublesome wars that had erupted, he appointed Maximian as a partner with the title of Augustus, having first made him a Caesar. Later he chose Constantius, father of the great Constantine, and Galerius, and made them Caesars. Constantius, the son of Eutropius and Claudius's daughter, took as his wife Theodora, Herculeus's stepdaughter, by whom he had six children. Galerius took Valeria, Diocletian's daughter, but both were forced to leave them.

Diocletian was responsible for widespread persecutions of Christians, burning their sacred books, destroying their churches and killing their prelates and any others they found. It was the worst slaying of Christians that ever took place at any time. Diocletian in the west

---

54. In Pannonia, in September/October 282.
55. Emperor A.D. 282–283.
56. Emperor A.D. 282–285.
57. Emperor A.D. 284–305.
58. It is difficult to reconcile this statement with his history of persecution narrated below.

and Maximian in the east caused the slaughter of an infinite multitude. Among them was Pope Marcellinus who was crowned as a martyr.

Finally when Diocletian grew old, he retired after many victories to private life in Salonae, a city in Dalmatia, while Maximian retired to Milan. Diocletian was the first to have his robes and boots decorated with gems, while all the other rulers simply used purple robes. In the end he poisoned himself at the age of sixty-eight. In his day, sixty thousand Germans were killed by Constantius Caesar at Longre.

MARCELLINUS (POPE 30), A.D. 289

The Roman Marcellinus,[59] son of Projectus from the Capitoline district, held the pontificate for seven years, six months and twenty-five days. The Church was without a pontiff for seven years, five months and twenty-five days as a result of Diocletian's persecutions. Emperor Diocletian forced him to worship idols with incense. Later after a formal council was convened, he repented in the presence of one hundred eighty bishops and, sprinkling his head with ashes and wearing a sackcloth, did penance, admitting that he had gravely sinned. When later he went to the emperor to acknowledge his error, the enraged emperor had him beheaded.[60]

One can read that when Marcellinus submitted to the council and to the bishops' judgment, saying that he was ready to obey their wishes, the bishops replied that it was improper for anyone to pass judgment on the high pontiff. They added, "You have denied Christ, but even after your master, St. Peter, denied him, none of the apostles dared to judge him. But Peter, going outside and recognizing his error, repented fully and cried bitterly. So you, as he himself had done, are judging your sin with your own mouth." Then St. Marcellinus replied, "I admit to having been prone to the sin of idolatry, and I excommunicate whoever buries my body." Weeping in this manner, he went to the emperor and

---

59. Pope 29, A.D. 296–304.
60. There is no evidence that Marcellinus was martyred. Instead, he was either deposed or voluntarily abdicated as a result of his act of obedience to Diocletian's decree.

confessed to being a Christian. And that is how he was condemned to decapitation.[61]

After his death, his body remained in the square for some thirty days as an example to Christians, and after thirty days without being buried, the Apostle Peter appeared in a vision to St. Marcellus who had succeeded to the pontificate. Peter said to him, "I am the prince of the apostles. Why don't you bury my body," meaning Marcellinus's body. Then he added, "Whoever humbles himself will be exalted, and he humbled himself greatly, judging himself unworthy of burial. Therefore, go and bury him alongside me so that he not share his burial with those whose grace I have justified."

At that time in Spain, near Valencia, St. Vincent[62] was martyred. Following the Saracen invasion, his remains were taken to Provence to a place called Castres; the preaching friars now have his holy body. In that persecution were killed and martyred the virgin Anastasia, Vincent of Spain, Vitus and Modestus, St. Blaise bishop, George of Cappadocia, Sebastian, Agnes, Barbara, Lucia, Humilianus, Gervaise and Protasius, the virgin Agatha and Grifogono.[63] Likewise suffering such persecution were Cosmas and Damian born on the same day as one flesh and spirit. At that time too, the Christian city of Phrygia[64] was so heavily besieged that those inside could not escape, and the city was burned with everyone in it. In England almost all Christians were accepted.[65]

*

61. See *Liber Pontificalis* 30.3, Davis 1:12, which lacks the details of these quotations.

62. Vincent of Saragossa, also known as Vincent Martyr, Vincent of Huesca or Vincent the Deacon. Martyred c.304 during Diocletian's persecution.

63. Identity unclear.

64. This could be a misreading for the province of Phrygia, divided under Diocletian.

65. This cryptic sentence could be a reference to the more moderate acceptance of Christians who had lapsed under Diocletian's persecution, as opposed to the Donatists of North Africa, who refused to readmit lapsed Christians into the fold. Eusebius, *Historia Ecclesiastica* 8.13.13; *Vita Constantini* 1.13; and *De Martyribus Palestinae* 13.12 seems to indicate that British Christians fared far better under Constantius's handling of the persecution.

THE FOURTH CENTURY

Marcellus

Marcellus (Pope 31), A.D. 304

The Roman Marcellus,[1] from the district of Via Lata[2] and the son of Benedictus, held the pontificate for five years, seven months and twenty-one days. The Church was without a pontiff for thirty days. He ordained twenty-five cardinals to administer baptism, penance and the burial of martyrs. In his day Emperor Diocletian died of poisoning and Maxentius was designated emperor. He ordered Marcellus to offer sacrifice to the idols, and upon his refusal had him assigned to a stable to care for the animals. Upon seeing how shamefully he was being treated, some clerics secretly freed him. Whereupon Maxentius had St. Lucia's house, which the Christians had converted into a church, turned into a stable, and there he locked him [Marcellus] up to care for the animals. Dressed in sackcloth, he led a miserable life and died.[3] Later he was buried on Via Salaria.[4]

Constantius and Galerius (Emperors 38), A.D. 309

Constantius[5] and Galerius,[6] Caesars who were later elevated to the rank of Augustus, divided the empire between them. Since Constantius preferred Gaul and Spain, the other provinces were given to Galerius. Constantius was the son of Eutropius, a Roman nobleman of

1. Pope 30, A.D. 308–309 in the official Vatican list.

2. Now known as the Via del Corso, running through the center of the city. It is the continuation of the ancient Via Flaminia.

3. See *Liber Pontificalis* 31.4–5, Davis 1:12–13. Maxentius exiled him from Rome due to his severity in dealing with formerly lapsed Christians.

4. At the church of St. Priscilla.

5. Constantius Chlorus, emperor A.D. 293–306, 305–306 with Galerius.

6. Caesar 293–305, Augustus 305–308.

outstanding constancy, although many say he was from England where he subsequently died. He left a son named Constantine who was born to Helena, presumably the daughter of the king of England, whom he had taken as his concubine. But with Galerius ruling in Illyria, the troops made Maxentius, Maximian's son, ruler in Rome. Against him Galerius sent a certain Severus[7] who besieged Rome with an incredible force. However, because his own men betrayed him, he was defeated and killed as he fled. Consequently, Maxentius was confirmed as ruler and became an extremely cruel tyrant. Under him, St. Catherine[8] was crowned with martyrdom for her faith in Christ. But after the numerous evils he had perpetrated against the Christians, Galerius was wracked by a terrible disease just as he was preparing to go to Italy. The continuous expelling of worms[9] caused him to be overcome with exhaustion, and he committed suicide after ruling for only two years.

Eusebius (Pope 32), A.D. 310

Eusebius,[10] born in Greece and son of a doctor named Ioannes, held the pontificate for two years and twenty-five days. The Church was without a pontiff for seven days. This was during the reign of Constantine to whom the sign of the cross appeared in the heavens as he confronted Maxentius. When Eusebius discovered heretics in the city, he placed his hands upon them,[11] which brought about a reconciliation. In the month of December he ordained fourteen priests, deacons and bishops.

Constantine the Great (Emperor 39), A.D. 311

Constantine the Great, son of Constantius and Helena, ruled over the Roman Empire for thirty years and ten months [306–337]. Resplendent in every virtue he was begged by the Senate and the Roman people to free its citizens from Maxentius's slavery. Joining Licinius, who was

---

7. Flavius Valerius Severus, Caesar in west 305–306, Augustus in west 306–307.

8. Catherine of Alexandria, feast day November 25.

9. Probably a bowel cancer. See Eusebius, *Historia Ecclesiae* 352–56; Lactantius, *De Mortibus Persecutorem*, 33.

10. Pope 31, April–August 309/10 in the official Vatican list.

11. That is, he blessed them.

THE FOURTH CENTURY

ruling in Spain, Constantine went with great pomp from Gaul to Rome in order to attack Maxentius who, after very intense fighting, drowned in the Tiber.[12] Whereupon, with much acclamation and much joy, Constantine was welcomed into the city by the Romans. Later when Licinius rebelled against him, he had him killed.

Then he was baptized by Pope Silvester. With great predilection for the Church of Rome, he endorsed the Christian religion and donated all the western territory to St. Peter and his successors. He ordered that the Roman Church should take preference above all others throughout the world. Finally, he moved the (seat of the) empire to Byzantium, a city in Greece that later was named Constantinople after him,[13] and there made plans for war against the Persians, who unexpectedly surrendered to him. His life ended at the age of seventy-six. During this time the Arian heresy arose, as well as the Donatist heresy, started by a certain Donatus,[14] which assigned gradations to the persons of the Trinity. We shall deal with further matters concerning Constantine in the life of Silvester.

MILTIADES (POPE 33), A.D. 311

The African Miltiades [Melchiades][15] held the pontificate for three years, six months and seven days. The papacy was vacant for sixteen days. He ruled that no one should fast on Sunday or Thursday since the pagans celebrate those days. He also ordained in the month of December priests, deacons and eleven bishops.

SILVESTER I (POPE 34), A.D. 315

The Roman Silvester [I],[16] son of Rufinus, held the pontificate for twenty-three years, ten months and eleven days. The Church was without

---

12. At the battle of the Milvian Bridge outside Rome, 28 October 312.

13. These are all elements of the medieval legend of the Donation of Constantine. See Lorenzo Valla, *On the Donation of Constantine*, trans. G.W. Bowersock (Cambridge, MA: Harvard University Press, 2007).

14. Bishop of Carthage from A.D. 313 and primate of North Africa. At the council of Arles 314 he was condemned and exiled to Gaul, where he died.

15. Pope 32, A.D. 311–314.

16. Pope 33, A.D. 314–335. See also n. 13.

leadership for fifteen days. At his summons the council of Nicaea convened with three hundred eighteen Catholic bishops who defined the Catholic faith and issued many decrees. He lived in the days of Emperor Constantine who, having been stricken with leprosy, was suddenly cleansed and cured after being baptized by Silvester. As a result, Constantine gave permission to Christians to meet and pray freely.[17] He converted the Lateran Palace to the church of San Salvatore[18] where one reads that he too wanted to be involved in its founding, stating that it be the mother of all churches in the world. He ordered that churches be erected in the name of Peter and Paul that he then had adorned with much gold and silver. Whereupon, he had their bodies, still in wonderful condition, placed in very expensive cases five feet long on each side and on each placed a cross of gold weighing one hundred fifty pounds as well as many other beautiful ornaments. He also built the church of San Lorenzo [St. Lawrence the Martyr] on the Via Tiburtina and used many beautiful decorations, including a case adorned with marble and porphyry where he placed the holy remains, covering its lid with the purest gold. In addition, he included a grated portal with a lantern of pure gold, and around the corpse a silver ornament depicting artfully sculpted dolphins. He added extensive decoration to other churches.[19]

Later, as we mentioned above in his biography, following his donation to Peter and his successors of all the western kingdoms and whatever he possessed on this side of the sea, Constantine placed the imperial crown on St. Silvester's head and personally led the horse he was riding. Then, having exalted and enlarged the Roman Church and having enriched it to the best of his ability, he transferred his empire to Constantinople[20] and there, as many tried to maintain, he was

17. This story appears in Jacobus de Voragine's *Golden Legend*, ed. Ryan, 1:62–71.
18. Referred to elsewhere in the text as the "Constantinian basilica," or St. Peter's.
19. These are detailed in the *Liber Pontificalis* 34.9–33, Davis 1:15–25.
20. All elements of the Donation of Constantine legend. This story is in neither the *Liber Pontificalis* nor the *Golden Legend* but appears in the twelfth-century *Mirabilia Urbis Romae* II.8. See *The Marvels of Rome. Mirabilia Urbis Romae,* ed. and trans. Francis Morgan Nichols, 2nd ed. Eileen Gardiner (New York: Italica Press, 1986), 29–30.

THE FOURTH CENTURY

rebaptized by Bishop Eusebius of Nicomedia, since in the meantime he had been converted to the Arian doctrine.[21] This is untrue inasmuch as St. Gregory, while speaking with Mauritius, referred to Constantine as being of happy memory, while his life was found to be in good order, and the Western Church includes Constantine among the saints, celebrating him with a feast day on the twenty-first of May. In his commentary on the fourteenth psalm, St. Ambrose says of him that, after Christ, Constantine was most deserving of merit because he was the first emperor to bequeath to rulers the paths of faith and devotion. It does not appear realistic that he had scorned his baptism by having himself rebaptized after having been cured of leprosy.[22] But it is true that many infidels claimed about him that he had indeed been rebaptized. This was true of his son, Constantius, although many others say this of his brother, Constantius.

After Constantine's conversion Pope Silvester suffered much grief at the hands of the Jews who, after he had restored the Torah, had all converted along with Empress Helena. Subsequently many others were baptized after he had cleansed the city of Rome of the dragon's plague that it is said had daily killed many men with its breath. After praying to God with the sign of the cross, Silvester was able to capture and imprison it.[23] This holy pontiff also ruled that no layperson could curse clergy and that deacons were to wear the dalmatic. He also ordered that the blessed sacrament on the altar not be celebrated on silk or

---

21. Heresy named after the Christian priest Arius of Alexandria (c.250–336), who held that Christ the Son was not co-eternal with the Father but created by the Father. His belief was condemned at the council of Nicaea in 325 and again at the first council of Constantinople in 381. Arianism attracted many imperial families and many among the elite of the Germanic peoples.

22. Doubts about the veracity of the Donation legend were forcefully stated by Lorenzo Valla in 1439/40. See above n. 13.

23. Another well-known Roman legend, painted for example by Maso del Banco c.1340 in the Bardi di Vernio Chapel of Sta. Croce, Florence. Silvester and Helena's disputation with the Jewish doctors takes up most of his life in the *Golden Legend*. As here, the episode is followed by the story of the dragon. See Ryan edition, 65–71.

THE LIVES OF THE POPES AND EMPERORS

colored cloth but on cloth of pure linen, just as the body of our Lord Jesus Christ was wrapped in a linen shroud in his tomb.

In Silvester's time, many people believed in Christ, and the people from the Tiburtine district converted thanks to a Christian woman whom they had taken prisoner. Likewise, Christ was preached in India. In these days St. Antony [Abbot][24] became famous as the father and abbot to many monks; St. Jerome carefully recorded his life and deeds in his *Life of the Holy Fathers*.[25] Also at this time Helena, Constantine's mother, dressed in religious habit, went to Jerusalem where she assembled the Jews, and by threatening them found the cross of Christ that she was seeking. In those times lived St. Nicholas, bishop of Myra, and Eusebius of Caesarea who wrote the history of the Church. In the month of December Pope Silvester ordained in various places fifty-two priests, twenty-six deacons and sixty-five bishops.

MARCUS (POPE 35), A.D. 338

The Roman Marcus [Mark],[26] son of Priscus, held the pontificate for two years, seven months and twenty days. The Church lacked a leader for twenty days. He ruled that the bishop of Ostia install the pope and that the bishop carry an honorary banner to promote greater honor. In the month of December he ordained twenty-seven priests, deacons and bishops.

JULIUS I (POPE 36), A.D. 339

The Roman Iulius [Julius I],[27] son of Rusticus, held the pontificate for fifteen years, two months and six days. The Church was without a leader for twenty-five days. He affirmed that clergy are not subject to any secular

---

24. Anthony the Great, or of Egypt, (c. A.D. 251–356).

25. Jerome lived c. 347–420 and was a foundational writer and theologian of the Christian tradition. His works included the Latin Vulgate Bible and biographical and hagiographical writing, among them his *Vitae Patrum* and *De viris illustribus*. See Saint Jerome, *The Lives of Illustrious Men*, ed. Thomas P. Halton (Washington, DC: Catholic University of America Press, 1999); and Jean Steinmann, *Saint Jerome and His Times* (Notre Dame, IN: Fides Publishers, 1959).

26. Pope 34, January–October 336.

27. Pope 35, A.D. 337–352.

THE FOURTH CENTURY

agreement outside the Church. In his day a second council was held in Nicaea with one hundred eighteen bishops who condemned the Arian heresy that maintained that the Son was inferior to the Father.[28] He endured many difficulties and was exiled for ten months. Subsequently he returned to the Apostolic See with great pomp.

In his day Anastasius [Athanasius of Alexandria], St. Paphnutius, Epiphanius and St. John Chrysostom became known, the latter of whom was called St. John of the Golden Mouth, in addition to many other hermits and saints, such as Sisoes, pastor and abbot, and Maximinus. At that time, the Emperor Constantine died in Nicomedia,[29] and just before his death the famous comet appeared.

CONSTANTINUS AND CONSTANS (EMPERORS 40), A.D. 361

Constantinus [Constantine II],[30] Constantius and Constans, brothers and sons of Constantine the Great, ruled the Roman Empire for twenty-three years. When Constantine died, the brothers Constans and Constantius ruled the empire. Constans was a bad man and an Arian who, after harshly persecuting Christians and fighting many battles with the Persians, became so intolerable that he was killed after an eighteen-year reign; whereupon Constantius alone gained the empire. He was a temperate and likeable man, although he did follow the Arian sect and persecuted Christians throughout the world. Trusting in his assistance, Arius went to Constantinople in order to fight the faithful, and while in the marketplace of Constantius he was forced to take his leave in order to defecate. While purging his stomach, he died as his insides gushed forth.[31]

---

28. This was actually the first council of Nicaea in 325. During Julius's reign and controversy with the Eastern church, major councils were held at Constantinople in 336 and Sardica in 343, which he convened but did not attend.

29. At Achyron on 22 May 337.

30. March 317–337, Caesar in the West; 337–340, co-emperor with Constantius II and Constans, over Gaul, Hispania and Britannia; 340 rival with Constans.

31. This story is related in chapter 28 of the *Ecclesiastical Histories* by Socrates Scholasticus and Sozomenus.

During Constantius's reign the grammarian [Aelius] Donatus became well known as Jerome's preceptor, St. Antony Abbot passed away, and the remains of St. Andrew and St. Luke the Evangelist were transported to Constantinople. Among his many persecutions of the faithful, Constantius exiled Athanasius of Alexandria, a defender of the faith, who had welcomed St. Maximin at the Tiber with the creed of the Catholic faith that begins, "Whoever wishes to be saved must above all profess the Catholic faith, etc." He then banished Stephen from Vercellae and Hilary from Poitiers, both of whom were later recalled; Dionysius from Milan and Paulinus from Trier died in exile.[32]

Finally, after proclaiming his grandson Julian as Caesar, Constantius sent him to Gaul where he became so arrogant that he tried to take over the kingdom of Italy since the emperor was delayed by the war against the Parthians. When he returned, he was killed at the age of forty-five after ruling only six years. In his day the anthropomorphic heresy[33] began.

LIBERIUS (POPE 37), A.D. 353

The Roman Liberius[34] from the district of Via Lata, the son of Leguscus [Augustus], held the pontificate for fifteen years, seven months and three days. The papacy was without a leader for twenty-five days. He lived at the time of Constantius, son of the great Constantine, by whom he was sent into exile because he would not accept the Arian faith. As a result, the Roman clergy and priests made pontiff a priest named Felix [II, antipope], who was a venerable and religious man. Felix convened a council and, upon finding two Arian priests named Ursatius and Valens, friends of Emperor Constantius and in agreement with him in adopting the Arian faith, expelled them from the council and condemned them in the presence of one hundred forty-eight bishops. But the bishops were extremely angry with Felix and

32. All early Christian saints.

33. Audianism, espoused by the fourth-century Syrian Audius. It held that God had a human form.

34. Pope 36, A.D. 352–366.

THE FOURTH CENTURY

begged Constantius to recall Liberius from exile because they wanted to get rid of Felix.[35]

And this is why Liberius, after being recalled from exile, consented by imperial order to accept the faithless heresy of Arius. Because of this, Constantius became reconciled with the Arian heresy, with Ursatius and Valens and expelled Felix from the papacy, who was a Catholic and religious man. He then returned the pontifical see to Liberius who had accepted the heresy. Thus, for six years the treacherous Liberius assumed by force the leadership of the church of St. Peter and later the churches of San Paolo and San Lorenzo.[36] Meanwhile after St. Felix was removed from the pontificate, he retired to a small property of his and there he remained.

Subsequently there were so many persecutions against the faithful that they were not allowed either in the churches or in the baths, and many clerics who were against Liberius were martyred. Among those killed was the priest Eusebius who had openly demonstrated that Liberius was a hopeless heretic. Nevertheless, in the month of December Liberius ordained priests, deacons and eighteen bishops. Felix's years of service are included in those of Liberius.

JULIAN (EMPEROR 41), A.D. 364

Emperor Iulianus [Julian],[37] grandson of the great Constantine, ruled over the Roman Empire for one year and six months. He was called "the Apostate" because he revealed his great hatred for the faithful after Constantine [II] left the Catholic faith and because, although a cleric before becoming emperor, he became a pagan and a cultivator of idols.[38] He was a literate man, eloquent and memorable, desirous of glory, but he was nevertheless ungrateful to Constantius and treacherous to the

---

35. See *Liber Pontificalis* 37.2–4, Davis 1:27.

36. All three in Rome.

37. Caesar A.D. 355–360, Augustus 360–361, sole Augustus 361–363.

38. Julian attempted to revive the religion and culture of pagan Rome. See Adrian Murdoch, *The Last Pagan: Julian the Apostate and the Death of the Ancient World* (Stroud: Sutton, 2003).

faith. Julian became emperor in the following manner: learned in secular and ecclesiastical writings and, having abandoned the faith and the monastic life, he was made Caesar by Constantine and sent to Gaul where fighting gloriously he conquered many people. This caused him to become arrogant and to rise up against Constantius upon whose death he was made emperor.

When he subsequently began persecuting Christians and coaxing them first out of love and then by force to worship idols, he issued many orders against them. And he proclaimed an infinite number of martyrs, among whom were Saints John and Paul, servants of Constantius, the son of the great Constantine, along with the deacon Cyril and many others. In addition he gave permission to rebuild the temple of Jerusalem to the Jews who then gathered from various places to initiate the project with great vigor.[39] But once the foundations were set, a great and horrible earthquake occurred one night, and when boulders from great heights became loose, the entire project was largely ruined, and the plans had to be abandoned. A large flame also appeared from heaven that burned a great portion of the building and the builders as well. As a result, those who ran away because of their fear of what was happening offered themselves to Christ.[40] But so that they might believe that this had not happened by chance but purposely and by divine will, there appeared on the following night the sign of the cross on their clothing.

Julian then proceeded to attack the Persians and, passing near Cappadocia and Caesarea, he said many shameful things about St. Basil, the bishop of that city. When God also threatened many Christians who were there, Basil saw in a dream while praying and fasting with them the Blessed Virgin Mary who ordered that vengeance be exacted against Julian, something that happened not much later. And so, while fighting against the Persians, Julian was wounded and died at the age of thirty-two.

39. In 363. For this episode see Ammianus Marcellinus, *Res Gestae* 23.1.2–3.
40. See Ammianus Marcellinus, *Res Gestae* 23.1.2–3.

THE FOURTH CENTURY

At this time St. Martin [of Tours] died after leaving the military, and Pope Julius I who had shortly before, after many tribulations, been sent into exile returned with great glory to the church of St. Peter. He then built two churches, one in the marketplace, the other near St. Valentinus on Via Flaminia. Following a holy life, he was buried in the cemetery of Callixtus, three miles from Rome.

JOVIAN (EMPEROR 42), A.D. 365

Iovianus [Jovian],[41] a native of Pannonia, ruled the Roman Empire for seven months, but according to others for one year. Handsome, with a happy disposition, knowledgeable and large, he was made emperor by the army two days after Julian's death, but he declared that as a Christian he could not rule over pagans, indicating that he wished to renounce the position. Thereupon the army declared that "just as we deserted the name of Christ because of Julian, so do we wish to become Christians with you." Having heard this, Jovian accepted the imperial scepter and signed a peace with the Persians.[42] He quickly saw to it that privileges were restored to the Christians and closed the pagan temples. Then at the age of thirty-three he died. According to Sextus Rufus[43] four hundred seven years elapsed from the beginning of the rule of Octavian to that of Jovian, with which we agree.

VALENTINIAN I (EMPEROR 43),[44] A.D. 366

The Emperor Valentinianus [Valentinian I],[45] born in Pannonia, ruled the Roman Empire with his brother Valens for eleven years. He was a good man, prudent and handsome, as well as a strong Christian and very like Hadrian and Aurelian. While campaigning under Emperor Julian, he was ordered by him that, though a Christian, he either worship the idols or surrender his military command.

---

41. Emperor A.D. 363–364.
42. See Ammianus Marcellinus, *Res Gestae* 25.5–10.
43. Author of the *Breviarium rerum gestarum populi Romani* completed c.379.
44. Text reads "XLII."
45. Emperor 26 February–28 March 364, emperor of the West 364–375.

Unwilling to abandon his faith in Christ, he departed from the emperor. After the deaths of Julian and Jovian, he was made emperor. Then with marvelous speed, after conquering the people of Saxony[46] on an Ocean island, he subjected them to Roman rule. Later on, after giving his son Gratian together with his brother, Valens, the title of Augustus, and after many wars, he died of a sudden bleeding problem. He was fifty-five years old. One reads that in his day so much hail mixed with rain fell that it killed whomever it struck. Hilary of Poitiers died, and some seventy thousand Burgundians reached the banks of the Rhine, something that had never happened before. Also in his day, upon the death of Auxentius, Ambrose was consecrated as bishop of Milan.

Felix II [anti-pope] (Pope 38), a.d. 369
Felix II [anti-pope],[47] born in Rome and the son of Anastasius, held the pontificate for one year and four days. The Church was without leadership for thirty-eight days. He was a strict Catholic and ruled that every bishop summoned to a council was expected to attend. He was declared a martyr on the twenty-ninth of July. In the month of December he ordained priests, deacons and nineteen bishops.

Damasus I (Pope 39), a.d. 370
Damasus [I],[48] born in Spain and the son of Antonius, held the pontificate for eighteen years, three months and eleven days. The Church was without a leader for thirty-one days. A man of great intellect, he composed many poems and produced many other works. In his time lived St. Jerome who, in writing many things about religious practices, composed these two verses: "Glory be to the Father and the Son and to the Holy Spirit. This is how it was in the beginning and is now and ever shall be world without end."[49] The pontiff also ruled that

---

46. The text reads "Sansogna."
47. See above under Pope Liberius.
48. Pope 37, a.d. 366–384.
49. This is the *Gloria Patri* or Lesser Doxology, with different readings in various traditions. There is no evidence that Jerome composed it.

THE FOURTH CENTURY

the psalms be sung day and night and that the clergy be set apart in the choir as they solemnly sing the Divine Office.

In those days in India there flourished Josephat, the king's son who had become a hermit, and Barlaam[50] who had converted him, as well as Apollinaris of Antioch, an outstanding teacher of sacred scripture who trained St. Jerome with great reverence in sound doctrine and learning. Also at this time St. Ambrose was installed as a bishop and Emperor Valentinian died, while in Italy nearly everyone converted to the correct and true faith of Christ.

There also lived in those days Basil of Caesarea and Gregory Nazianzen who were schoolmates in Athens, as well as Peconius[51] the abbot in Egypt. Monks likewise flourished in hermitages, namely the two Macarii, the two Pauls, Isidore, Moses and Heclide. At this time Jerome corrected the Psalter, because it was corrupt, with seventy-two modifications that were sung in all the churches and also composed some new ones. For this reason Pope Damasus, at his request, ordered that they be sung in Gallic churches, which is why the Psalter is called Gallic by the Gauls and Psalter by the Romans. Later Damasus also decreed that after the singing of the Psalms be sung those verses that he had composed, namely "Glory to the Father, etc." Ambrose also composed a new way to sing the Antiphon.

This pope was accused of adultery, but following the convening of a council of forty-four bishops he was absolved. They condemned Concordius and Callixtus who had accused him. At this time too in Constantinople[52] was held a council consisting of 150 holy fathers

---

50. The medieval legend of Barlaam and Josephat ultimately had its roots in the story of the Buddha. A version appeared in John Damascene. See *Barlaam and Ioasaph*, ed. David M. Lang, trans. G.R. Woodward and Harold Mattingly (Cambridge, MA: Loeb Classical Library, W. Heinemann; 1967). For a medieval version see Gui de Cambrai, *Barlaam and Josaphat: A Christian Tale of the Buddha*, trans. Peggy McCracken (New York: Penguin Books, 2014). See also an edition printed at Augsburg by Günther Zainer, c.1476.

51. Pachomius (c.292–348) is meant.

52. The first council of Constantinople in 381.

where Donatus the Macedonian,[53] who denied that the Holy Spirit was God, was present. But with subtle reasoning it was proven that the Holy Spirit was consubstantial and equal to the Father and the Son. This resulted in the Credo that is recited in the Latin rite.

VALENS (EMPEROR 44),[54] A.D. 377

Valens,[55] Valentinian's brother, together with Gratian, Valentinian's son, ruled the Roman Empire for three years and administered Rome in a dignified and excellent manner. But since Valens was an Arian he persecuted the Catholic Christians ruthlessly, something he had tried to do while his brother was alive. He then ordered the monks to take up arms if they did not wish to be punished and also sent many religious into exile. Eventually he repented and recalled them. Later while fighting in Thrace with the Goths, he was routed and, after losing his besieged army, took refuge in a certain house where he was burned alive by the inhabitants.[56] In his day St. Ambrose lived as bishop of Milan as well as St. Jerome, Augustine, Photinus and Eunonius while Apollinaris and the heretics[57] spread their wicked heresy through their preaching.

GRATIAN (EMPEROR 45), A.D. 381[58]

Emperor Gratianus [Gratian],[59] after his uncle's death, ruled the Roman Empire with his brother Valentinian [II] for six years. He was a great and faithful man and a Catholic and successfully fought against the Alemanni in Gaul near the castrum of Argentoratum[60]

---

53. Perhaps Donatus of Evorea (d. 387).

54. Text reads "XLIII." Eastern emperor A.D. 364–378.

55. Emperor in the East A.D. 364–375, with his brother Valentinian I in the West; emperor in the East 375–378, with Gratian and Valentinian II as emperors of the West.

56. At the battle of Adrianople, 9 August 378. This account is from Ammianus Marcellinus, *Res Gestae*, 31.13.14-16.

57. Most likely the Arians.

58. Text reads "481."

59. Senior Augustus of the whole empire with his brother 9 August 378–19 January 379; 379–383 senior Augustus in the West with his brother.

60. Strasbourg, established by the Romans as a military camp by 12 B.C.

THE FOURTH CENTURY

because he had much respect for the good and true faith of Christ. He enjoyed a great victory in a battle where it is written that more than thirty thousand died. Since a large part of Italy was still sympathetic to the Arian faith, he then succeeded in freeing most of the country from Arius's evil teaching and wickedness. Then, seeing that many people were hostile toward the Roman Empire, he appointed as emperor in the East his brother Theodosius who was distinguished in the martial arts. Although only thirty-three years old, he defeated three times the Tartars[61] who had rebelled against the Roman Empire, and he went to Constantinople as victor with many others who joined him. Finally while fighting against a certain Maximus who had taken over the empire in England, Gratian was killed near Lugdunum.[62] In his day Bishop Martin [of Tours] became famous in Gaul, while Priscilian spread his heresy, and the poet Ausonius flourished.

VALENTINIAN II AND THEODOSIUS (EMPERORS 46), A.D. 387
Valentinianus [Valentinian II],[63] Gratian's second brother, ruled the Roman Empire with his brother Theodosius[64] for eight years, Valentinian in the West and Theodosius in the East. After Valentinian had been expelled from Gaul by the tyrant Maximus, Theodosius with a small contingent successfully did battle with him. Even though Maximus had a powerful and large army, Theodosius still defeated and captured him near Aquileia and had him decapitated. He then returned the empire in the West to his brother who not much later, according to many, was strangled near Vienne through the deceit of Arbogastes.[65] Others say that he hung himself.

And so Theodosius remained in charge of the empire, and after ruling with his brothers for thirteen years, he subsequently ruled the empires of the East and the West for three years. He was an excellent man

---

61. Probably Alans and Huns.
62. Lyons on 25 August 383.
63. Emperor of West A.D. 375–392.
64. Emperor in the East A.D. 379–392; of whole empire 392–395.
65. Zosimus, *Historia nova* IV.53.

and a devout Christian like Trajan from whom he was descended. As a result, St. Ambrose praises him at great length since he expelled the Arians from Milan. Later Theodosius fought against Eugenius who was usurping the empire in Gaul. Consulting first with Ioannes the Anchorite, famous in those days, Theodosius predicted his own victory and placed his trust in the power of Christ by invoking his name with sincere prayers. He then descended the Alps and attacked Eugenius,[66] and when a great windstorm arose accompanied by a very powerful rainstorm, he defeated and killed him with a minimum loss of troops.

In his day, because there were many arguments between Jews and pagans, Theodosius tore down the temples with their idols. St. Jerome was at the time enjoying great honor in Bethlehem where he translated the Old Testament. Ambrose died after Honorius, and Arsenius became famous in Rome where, after he became a monk after being a senator, he lived in a hermitage for some forty years. Pope St. Damasus died at the age of eighty. Augustine was converted, although he had been a Manichean against the true faith of Christ, and made bishop of Hippo. The council of Constantinople was held with 150 holy fathers, in which all heretics were condemned. Priscilian was cut in pieces, and also at this time the head of St. John the Baptist was taken to Constantinople to a place seven miles outside the city.

Theodosius was endowed with so many virtues that even his enemies loved him. As a result, with his encouragement many people left their mistaken paths and their idols and converted to the Christian faith. Finally, at the age of fifty he died happily in Milan leaving behind, with the title of Augustus, his sons Arcadius and Honorius.

---

66. At the battle of Frigidus in September 394.

THE FOURTH CENTURY

SIRICIUS (POPE 40), A.D. 388

The Roman Siricius,[67] the son of Tiburtius, held the pontificate for fifteen years, eleven months and twenty-five days. The Church was without a leader for twenty days. He decreed that the Manichean heretics could not converse with the faithful and that if anyone of that sect were to convert and to desire to return to the Church, he could not be received unless he were connected with some monastery or order for life, thin from fasting and prayers and put to every type of test. Only then could he receive the Eucharist.

During his time the council of Constantinople,[68] composed of three hundred fifty bishops, was held, which attacked Macedomus and Eudosius. At that time also, Paula, a Roman woman of the high nobility, went to Jerusalem with her daughter Eustochium.[69] One also reads that in a castle named Emous was born a child so divided from the navel up that he had two chests and two heads, each having its own characteristics. Yet they lived for some time; one died before the other who survived for another four days. At this time Rufinus, a priest from Aquileia, became well known, and Theodosius died in Milan; that same year his body was taken to Constantinople. In the month of December Siricius ordained thirty-one priests, sixteen deacons and thirty-four bishops. Also in this period St. Jerome translated the Bible from Hebrew into Latin.

ARCADIUS AND HONORIUS (EMPERORS 47), A.D. 396

The brothers Arcadius[70] and Honorius[71] succeeded their father Theodosius and ruled the Roman Empire for thirteen years. Arcadius ruled in the East and Honorius in the West; they were good emperors,

---

67. Pope 38, A.D. 384–399.

68. First council of Constantinople, in 381.

69. On Paula and Eustochium, their friendship with Jerome and travels to the Holy Land see, *The Letter of Paula and Eustochium to Marcella about the Holy Places, 386 A.D.* trans. Aubrey Stewart, ed. C.W. Wilson (London: Palestine Pilgrims' Text Society, 1889).

70. Augustus under Theodosius 383–395, emperor in the East A.D. 395–408.

71. Emperor in the West A.D. 393–423.

doing nothing to degrade their father's name. In the tenth year of their rule, Alaric and Radagaisus, Gothic chiefs, went to Italy with a large number of barbarians with the intent of occupying Rome. But the Romans fought with them, and Radagaisus with many thousands of troops was overcome and defeated in Tuscia by Stilicho,[72] Theodosius' son-in-law, who was famous in his day. Radagaisus himself and a large number of his followers died from hunger and cold, and the survivors were captured, taken to Rome and sold like animals. In the end, Arcadius died in Constantinople, leaving his son Theodosius [II] as emperor in the East.

At that time Bishop Donatus of Arezzo[73] became well known as a man venerable both for his virtue and for the miracles he performed, as did Bishop Zephyrinus who, upon confronting in his town a huge dragon that was attacking the entire region, killed it by spitting in its mouth.[74] He then wanted to burn it so that its stench would not trouble or poison those areas, and so with eight pairs of oxen he took it with difficulty to a place to be burnt. Also in that period were found the bodies of the prophets, Abachum [Achab] and Michaeas. Ioannes of Constantinople and Theophilus of Alexandria, both outstanding bishops, also were well known. They had great differences between them, and for a time Ioannes remained in exile. Under these emperors, the Vandals and the Alans crossed the Rhine and went into Gaul. It was also then that the tyrant Constantinus ruled in England, the poet Claudianus lived in Rome, and Bishop Martin of Tours died at the age of eighty-one after holding office for twenty-six years.

*

---

72. At Pollentia on 6 April 402.
73. Martyred on 7 August 362.
74. Unable to identify this story.

THE FIFTH CENTURY

ANASTASIUS I (POPE[1] 41), A.D. 404
The Roman Anastasius,[2] son of Masinus, held the pontificate for three years and ten days. The Church was without a leader for twenty-one days. He ruled that any one who lacked a bodily part should not become a cleric, and that, when the scripture was read, priests should not sit but remain standing, while others bowed. He also decreed that no cleric from abroad should be received without a letter from his bishop since at that time the Manicheans[3] were in Rome. In the month of December he also ordained thirty priests, thirteen deacons and fifty-four bishops.

INNOCENT I (POPE 42), A.D. 407

Innocentius [Innocent I],[4] born in Albano and the son of Innocentius, held the pontificate for fifteen years and twenty days. He decreed that there should be fasting on Saturday, since Christ lay in his tomb on Saturday while his disciples fasted. He also put the Church in order and issued rules for monasteries and for Jews and pagans. In addition, he condemned many heretics. He ruled that anyone born of a Christian woman who had somehow been impregnated must be

---

1. Text reads "Emperor."
2. Pope 39, A.D. 399–401.
3. Gnostic religion that was founded by the prophet Mani (Manichaeus or Manes) (c.216–276 A.D.) in the Persian Sassanian Empire. Manicheans believed in dualistic cosmology describing the struggle between a good, spiritual world of light, and an evil, material world of darkness. It was known in the Roman Empire by c.280. See *Liber Pontificalis* 41.2, Davis 1:30.
4. Pope 40, A.D. 401–417.

baptized, which was condemned by Pelagius.⁵ It is also said that he excommunicated Emperor Arcadius who had agreed with his wife Eusebia that St. John Chrysostom⁶ should be expelled from the church in Constantinople because of a sermon he had delivered against her. Besides this, he ruled that the kiss of peace be given at Mass and that the oil blessed by the bishop be used on the infirm, and not just on priests but on all Christians.

Since the heretic Pelagius was in England at that time, Innocent condemned him to death for his wicked heresy, which maintained that man could be saved without God's grace and that each person could stand on his merits and on his personal will and justice. Pelagius furthermore affirmed that children were born without original sin. Innocent also condemned Celestinus and Iulianus who agreed with the false beliefs of Pelagius. In the month of December he ordained thirty priests, twelve deacons and fifty-four bishops.

In his day St. Alexius became famous in Rome and Radagaisus,⁷ king of the Goths, was imprisoned in Tuscia by the Fiesolani where together with many thousands of men he was condemned to death. Later the rest were all dispersed with a portion of them captured and shamefully sold. During Innocent's pontificate, Arsenius became well known, and after having served the emperor for forty years, became a monk and ended his life in a hermitage.

HONORIUS (EMPEROR 48), A.D. 410

Emperor Honorius,⁸ who had already ruled with his brother Arcadius for twelve years, then ruled the Roman Empire for fifteen with Theodosius the Younger, Arcadius' son. In their day Alaric, king of the [Visi]goths, captured and sacked Rome with much violence, having first ordered that all who fled into churches, especially

---

5. Bishop Pelagius (354–c.430) taught that humanity was free of original sin and that free will and works were enough to guarantee salvation. See *Liber Pontificalis* 42.2, Davis 1:30.

6. Circa 349–407. Archbishop of Constantinople and early Church Father.

7. Died 23 August 406 after unsuccessful siege of Florence.

8. Emperor in the West A.D. 393–423.

THE FIFTH CENTURY

into St. Peter's and San Paolo, be spared.[9] The Vandals and the Alans captured Spain, and in the same period the heretic Pelagius preached his false doctrine against God's grace. Against him a council of one hundred fourteen bishops was held at Carthage[10] where his heresy was attacked and condemned.

Also during their reign, Bishop Cyril of Alexandria became well known. Attalus was later made emperor in Rome and, after being deprived of the empire shortly thereafter, he joined the Goths. Constantinus, even though a tyrant, was defeated and captured near the castle of Arelate[11] by Constantius and Ulfilas, officers under Honorius whose son was ruling alone in Spain and was killed by his friend Gerontius. Alaric, king of the Goths, after leaving Rome to go to Apulia, passed into Africa by way of Calabria and there died suddenly, which caused the Goths to make king his relative Atawulf who, one reads, returned to Rome and burned and destroyed whatever had remained of the city. He then went and occupied Gaul.

One also reads that at this time Heraclianus came from Africa with many thousands of men and ships and was defeated by Constantius whom Honorius had made commander. Heraclianus barely survived the battle, escaped to Carthage in the one remaining ship and died there not long afterward. And at that time, through Constantius's orders and support, heretics returned from Africa and made peace with the Church. St. Augustine, bishop of Hippo in the province of Africa and of the city of Tagaste, became very famous because of his divine eloquence, and Jerome passed on from the present life at the age of ninety-one in the year 419 of our Lord.[12] In Honorius' time, although there were many wars, they nevertheless were waged and settled with little or no shedding of blood. All of this happened because of the emperor's goodness that he demonstrated to all the people. When he

9. 24 August 410.
10. 1 May 418.
11. Arles.
12. Died 30 September 420.

was told that the rebels were not being killed, he replied, "Would that God would make it possible to bring back to life all those who have died." In his day also Pope Innocent [I] died and was buried on the twenty-eighth day of July. Finally, Honorius died childless in Rome.

ZOSIMUS (POPE 43), A.D. 422

The Greek Zosimus[13] held the pontificate for one year, three months and two days. The Church was without a leader for eleven days. He ruled that the candle be blessed on Holy Saturday and that no servant could be a cleric and that no cleric could serve at table except under unusual circumstances. He also ordained in the month of December ten priests, three deacons and eight bishops.

BONIFACE I (POPE 44), A.D. 423

The Roman Bonifacius [Boniface I],[14] son of the priest Iucundus, held the pontificate for three years, eight months and seven days. The Church was without a leader for nine days. But in the eighth month and fifteenth day of his papacy, there was dissension among the clerics, and Eulalius was declared pope. On hearing this, Placidia Augusta,[15] who was in Ravenna with her son Valentinian, informed the emperor who was in Milan. As a result of Honorius's advice and intervention, both popes resigned and the bishops, with the emperor's aid, drove Eulalius into the countryside and retained Boniface as pope. Subsequently, he ruled that no woman could touch the sacred altar cloths or prepare the incense, and that neither a servant nor anyone obligated to the court could become a cleric.[16]

In his day, Emperor Honorius died, leaving the Roman Empire at peace. He was buried near the church of St. Peter. By custom and

---

13. Pope 41, A.D. 417–418.

14. Pope 42, A.D. 418–422.

15. Daughter of the Roman Emperor Theodosius I, half-sister of Emperor Honorius, and regent for Emperor Valentinian III, her son, 423–437.

16. For the above see *Liber Pontificalis* 44.1–5, Davis 1:32–33.

THE FIFTH CENTURY

religion he was similar to his father, Theodosius. At his death he left no children.

THEODOSIUS AND VALENTINIAN III (EMPERORS 49), A.D. 425
Theodosius [II],[17] the younger son of Arcadius, ruled the Eastern Empire alone for twenty-six years. In his second year he made his aunt, Placidia, empress of the East, and also Valentinianus [Valentinian III], his son-in-law and cousin, co-ruler. In his day the Vandals with their king, Genseric, left Spain and, crossing over into Africa, captured and ravaged Carthage[18] where they stained the faith with the Arian heresy. Bishop Nestorius[19] of Constantinople spread his dreadful heresy by preaching against our faith and maintaining that Christ was only human. A council at Ephesus was convened against this heresy.[20] Also at this time the devil, appearing in Crete in the form of Moses, promised the Jews to lead them to the promised land, causing many of them to drown.[21] Those who survived then converted to the Christian faith.

St. Augustine, bishop of Hippo, died at seventy-six years old,[22] after twenty-nine years as a bishop, while still writing against the apostate Julian. Eutychius, the heretical archimandrite, was condemned following the council in Constantinople under Bishop Flavian.[23] Later, with the approval of Dioscorus of Alexandria and Theodosius, a second council was held in Ephesus[24] which freed Eutychius with the help of a great number of monks and troops. But Leo [I], the Roman pontiff,

---

17. Emperor A.D. 408–450, with his sister Aelia Pulcheria regent 408–416.

18. Genseric was king of the Alans and Vandals from 428 to 477. He seized Carthage on 19 October 439.

19. Archbishop of Constantinople from 10 April 428 until August 431, he taught that Mary, as the mother of Jesus, was not truly the mother of God.

20. First council of Ephesus in 431.

21. The story appears in both Socrates, *Historia Ecclesiastica,* 7.38; and John of Nikiû, *Chronicle,* 86.1–11.

22. On 28 August 430.

23. Patriarch of Constantinople, 446–449. The council was held in 448. It grappled with the Nestorian doctrine of Mary.

24. In 449.

nullified everything and through his ambassadors deposed Dioscoros of Alexandria.

At that time Attila was sacking all of Italy, but after receiving messengers from Pope St. Leo, stopped the plundering despite his cruelty and, having made peace, went to live beyond the Danube.[25] Finally, Emperor Theodosius [II] died in Constantinople.[26] One reads that at that time it was decided that the feast of St. Peter in Chains be held on a particular day. And [Galla] Placidia, while voyaging by sea to Italy, swore to build a temple to St. John the Evangelist that later she had built in Ravenna.[27]

Celestine I (Pope 45), a.d. 427

Coelestinus [Celestine I],[28] born in Campania, held the pontificate for eight years, ten months and twenty-three days. The Church was without a leader for twenty-one days. He decreed that the Psalms of David be sung with an antiphon before the Consecration since at that time only the scriptures were read.[29] He sent Patricius to Spain to convert the people, Bishop Germanus[30] to England so that he might cleanse it of the Pelagian stain, and Bishop Palladius to Scotland[31] whose people he converted.

Sixtus III (Pope 46), a.d. 436

The Roman Xystus [Sixtus III][32] from the district of Celio Monte[33] and the son of Priscus, held the pontificate for thirteen years and nineteen days. The Church was without a leader for twenty-two days. A

---

25. Attila met Leo in 452 near Mantua. He died in 453.
26. 28 July 450.
27. The Mausoleum of Galla Placidia (392–27 November 450).
28. Pope 43, a.d. 422–432.
29. See *Liber Pontificalis* 45.1, Davis 1:33.
30. Germanus of Auxerre, c.378–c.448.
31. This may refer to Palladius, first bishop of Ireland, c.408–c.461.
32. Pope 44, a.d. 432–440.
33. In Rome.

THE FIFTH CENTURY

year and seven months into his pontificate, someone named Bassus[34] made accusations against him. This caused Emperor Valentinian [III] to summon a council and together with a large number of bishops he had Pope Sixtus investigated. Not finding any basis for the false accusation by Bassus, the pope was absolved and Bassus condemned. Thus, the emperor banished Bassus and gave all his possessions and goods to Holy Church. When he died within three months, the pope who did not want to show anger personally bathed his body with spices before burial.[35] He ruled that no cleric be ordained in another parish. We also read that he built the church of Sta. Maria Maggiore[36] that is called *ad praesepe*.[37] In addition, he adorned many churches with gold and silver and donated many of his collections to the poor. He ordained Petrus as bishop of Ravenna.

MARCIAN AND VALENTINIAN III (EMPERORS[38] 50), A.D. 451

Emperors Martianus [Marcian][39] and Valentinianus [Valentinian III][40] ruled for seven years. At the beginning of their reign the fourth council of Chalcedon[41] with six hundred thirty bishops was held, which condemned the heresy of Abbot Eutychius of Constantinople, as well as that of Bishop Dioscoros of Alexandria and Nestorius, thereby strengthening the Christian faith. Whereupon the pope composed a letter against the heretics' deception and a similar one to Marcian and his wife in which he laid out the entire Christian faith. He also sent many other letters to Flavian, bishop of Constantinople,

34. Anicius Auchenius Bassus (consul 431).

35. From *Liber Pontificalis* 46.1–2, Davis 1:34.

36. One of the seven major basilicas in Rome, Sixtus's founding of the church, based on a legendary snow miracle, was an affirmation of Mary as mother of God and a rebuff to the Nestorians.

37. *Ad presepe* refers to the relics of Jesus's manger, collected under Pope Theodore I (640–649). The name predates the snow miracle story.

38. Text reads "Pope."

39. Emperor in the East A.D. 450–457.

40. Emperor in the West A.D. 425–455.

41. 8 October–1 November 451.

among which was one of great clarity on the Incarnation of Jesus Christ that condemned the Eutychian heresy.[42]

Finally, Valentinian died in Rome in Campus Martius through the deception of [Petronius] Maximus and Heraclitus.[43] Maximus proceeded to make himself emperor, but later when Genseric, king of the Vandals, was about to enter Rome, Maximus was cut into pieces by the Romans and thrown into the Tiber. After Genseric had entered Rome, he dealt with the situation as he pleased and imprisoned the emperor's daughter and wife. When he was about to set fire to the city, his mind was so changed by Pope Leo's pleas that he went to Nola and Capua, which he captured and burned and had the men imprisoned in Africa.[44]

Also in Marcian's days, Theodoric, king of the Goths,[45] entered Spain with a great army, St. Geneviève became famous in Paris,[46] and eleven thousand virgins in Cologne were martyred by the Huns. St. Paulinus, bishop of Nola,[47] used all his possessions to ransom prisoners and then offered himself in an attempt to recover a widow's son who had been captured and taken to Africa. St. Gregory wrote about this in his *Dialogues*.[48] In the end, Marcian died in Constantinople through his men's treachery, and Leo was made emperor there. Also at this time, Bishop Epiphanius of Ticino, a man famous for his sanctity, became well known.

Leo I (Pope 47), A.D. 454

The Tusculan Leo [I],[49] son of Quintianus, held the pontificate twenty-one years, one month and thirteen days. The Church was

42. Also discussed under Theodosius and Valentinian III, above, p. 73.
43. He was assassinated on 16 March 455.
44. For these events see Priscus, *The Fragmentary History*, trans. John Given, (Merchantville, NJ: Evolution Books, 2014), 125–29.
45. King of the Visigoths, 418–451.
46. The patron saint of Paris, c.420–c.510.
47. c.354–22 June 431.
48. 3.1.
49. Leo the Great, pope 45, A.D. 440–461.

THE FIFTH CENTURY

without a leader for eight days. He was a doctor and decreed that the *"Sanctum Sacrificium"* and the *"Immaculatam Hostiam"* be said before the Consecration.[50] He also ruled that a nun could not take the veil if she were not proven a virgin.

In his day was held the general council of Chalcedon[51] at the church of St. Euphemia that was attended by two hundred fifty-six bishops. There were four hundred eight who registered but were unable to attend in person; also present was Martianus Augustus because of his love of the Catholic faith. They all espoused the Catholic faith, affirming that there were two natures in Christ and two wills, one divine and one human. Consequently, the emperor and his wife, Pulcherria Augusta, affirmed their faith before the council. With the bishops' approval, he sent her to Pope St. Leo in Rome with the condemnation of all the heretics. Later on, the pontiff wrote many notable letters against all the heresies.

At that time, following the death of Attila, king of the Huns, his brother, King Bleda, went to Italy with a very large army to attack the besieged city of Aquileia and captured it.[52] He also seized and destroyed many other cities such as Verona, Vicenza, Bergamo, Brescia and Milan. In order to avoid his doing something similar to Rome, Pope Leo personally went to him on the banks of the Po where he was living and somehow persuaded him not only to spare Rome but also all of Italy. When the barbarians marveled at how the king, contrary to his custom, had received the pope so honorably and then listened to him, he replied to many of them that a frightening figure had appeared to him in a dream threatening his death if he did not listen to the pope's pleas. As a result, he quickly departed from Italy, and after returning to Pannonia, died there. At this time the German Lupus and Fulgentius, both bishops, became well known.

---

50. See *Liber Pontificalis* 47.8, Davis 1:37; Platina, *Lives*, ed. d'Elia, 256–64.
51. See also above, Theodosius and Valentinian III, p. 73.
52. These events belong to the biography of Attila.

THE LIVES OF THE POPES AND EMPERORS

LEO THE ELDER (EMPEROR 51), A.D. 458

Leo the Elder,[53] together with his son Leo,[54] ruled in the East for seventeen years at the time when the Acephalian heresy[55] arose in opposition to the council that had been held in Chalcedon. It was so called because the movement's founder and leader could not be found; because of it many in the East suffered. At this time died Majorian, who was ruler in the East for four years. After him [Libius] Severus was made emperor at Ravenna and died in Rome four years later.

HILARIUS (POPE 48), A.D. 465

Hilarius,[56] born in Sardinia, held the pontificate for six years, three months and ten days. The Church was without a leader for ten days. He ruled that a pope could not appoint someone to succeed him, and chose the monastery of San Lorenzo[57] where he wished to be buried beside the body of the martyr.

One reads that at this time in England there ruled King Arthur who through his goodness and kindness was able to win control of Gaul, Flanders, Dacia and many islands. Having been mortally wounded in a battle, he fled to care for his wounds, and his whereabouts or how he died could not be ascertained by the English.[58] During this time, Emperor Leo took to Constantinople all the paintings that he found in Rome and there burned them.[59] Also in his day St. Mark's remains

---

53. Leo I the Thracian, 457–474.

54. Leo II, 18 January 474–17 November 474.

55. Also known as the Haesitantes.

56. Pope 46, A.D. 461–468.

57. San Lorenzo fuori le Mura in Rome.

58. The Arthurian legend was extremely popular in Italy from at least the thirteenth century onward, and versions circulated in many manuscripts and printed editions. For a good introduction see Edmund G. Gardner, *Arthurian Legend in Italian Literature* (New York: E.P. Dutton, 1930).

59. The author here confuses Leo I with Leo III the Isaurian (717–741), a proponent of Iconoclasm, which rejected all images of divinity.

THE FIFTH CENTURY

were taken to Venice, and Prosper of Aquitaine[60] became famous for his learning and his miracles.

SIMPLICIUS (POPE 49), A.D. 471
Simplicius of Tibur[61] held the pontificate for fifteen years, one month and seven days. The Church was without a leader for six days. He built the church of Sto. Stefano[62] near that of San Lorenzo. He ruled that seven priests a week should be on duty at the churches of St. Peter and San Paolo so that those wishing to repent and be baptized could be accommodated. He organized groups of priests who were to be appropriately divided: the first group at St. Peter's, the second at San Paolo, the third at San Lorenzo, the fourth at St. John Lateran and the fifth at Sta. Maria Maggiore.[63]

One reads[64] that at this time in England Merlin was born to a nun, daughter of the king of Moesia, who maintained that she had never slept with anyone, but that one night an attractive man appeared to her, kissed her many times and then reappeared at regular intervals; this started the rumor that she had been impregnated by the devil. At this time one also finds that the heretic, Peter of Alexandria, was condemned by Pope Simplicius after being accused by Bishop Accius of Constantinople. Finally, Simplicius died and was buried in the Vatican grounds near St. Peter. At this time there also lived Bishop Mamertus of Vienne, who instituted fasting before the Ascension.

---

60. c.390–c.455.
61. Pope 47, A.D. 468–483.
62. Sto. Stefano Rotondo on the Caelian Hill.
63. From *Liber Pontificalis* 49.1–2, Davis 1:40. This was probably a reference to the beginning of the naming of the Roman cardinal churches.
64. The story appears in Geoffrey of Monmouth's *Historia Regum Britanniae*, written c.1136.

ZENO I (EMPEROR 52), A.D. 475

Zeno [I],[65] Emperor Leo's son-in-law, ruled in the East for seventeen years. After [Leo] Augustus had sent him to Italy, he made him emperor of the East. When Zeno was searching for Leo, the [grand]son of Leo Augustus, in order to kill him, his mother, Adriana Augusta, substituted a look-alike for her son Leo and, having kept him in hiding, made him a cleric so that he lived until the time of Emperor Justin.[66] Not much later Basiliscus with his son Marcus illegally seized the empire and expelled Zeno to Isauria where he had been born. Twenty months later, leading a very large army, Zeno returned to Constantinople, and after defeating and capturing Basiliscus with his wife and children, Zeno had them live out their lives in a miserable exile.[67]

One also reads that, having made peace with the Goths, Zeno held as hostage Theodoric, the Gothic king's son whom he had sent to Italy at thirteen years of age with his troops against Odoacer, king of the Torcilinghi [Heruli or Ostrogoths], who having overcome Augustulus, emperor in the East,[68] occupied Italy. Whereupon Theodoric overcame and defeated him in a battle near Aquileia. Odoacer fled with a few men to Rome and, since the people refused to receive him, went on to Ravenna. There Theodoric again defeated him, peacefully took control of everything, and took as his wife the daughter of the king of Africa. But being affected by the Arian heresy, he closed many churches in Sardinia and sent their bishops into exile.

Also at this time the Saxons occupied the island of England after many cruel battles. Finally, Zeno who was also stained by the Eutychian heresy died in Constantinople. After his death Anastasius promised

65. Emperor A.D. 474–491, with a period of exile January 475 to August 476.

66. The story seems to confuse the identity of Leo's first surviving son, whose legitimacy might be questioned.

67. See Evagrius Scholasticus, *Historia Ecclesiae*, book 3.

68. This is Romulus Augustulus, last Roman emperor of the West (31 October 475–4 September 476), placed on the throne by his father Orestes. Odoacer's deposition of Romulus had traditionally marked the end of the empire and the beginning of the Middle Ages. See Jordanes, *Getica sive De origine actibusque Gothorum* XLVI.242–43.

Bishop Euthymius of Constantinople not to resist the Roman faith and was then made emperor, but he did not keep that promise. Also in Zeno's time were found the remains of St. Barnabas, holding in his hand the gospel of Matthew in Hebrew.[69]

FELIX III (POPE 50), A.D. 486

The Roman Felix III[70] held the pontificate eight years, eleven months and nineteen days. The Church was without a leader for five days. He built the church of Sant'Agapito[71] next to the church of San Lorenzo and decreed that churches be consecrated by a bishop. He also sent St. Germanus with many others to England to quell the Pelagian heresy. Upon receiving news from Greece that the heretic Peter of Alexandria had been recalled by Acacius, Felix condemned both Acacius and Peter. Three years later, having received a report from Emperor Zeno that Acacius had repented, he sent Bishops Mesenus and Vitalis to Constantinople, and ordered them, if they found that Acacius had fallen into the same error as Peter without repenting, to condemn him once again. When they arrived in Constantinople, they were corrupted by money and did nothing the pope had ordered, but upon their return to Rome, the pope summoned a council that found them guilty and condemned them.[72] When Mesenus admitted his error, the council imposed a period of repentance upon him. At this time King Honorius of the Vandals, Genseric's son, greatly persecuted Catholics during his stay in Africa. Also at this time Fulgentius became famous for his faith and outstanding knowledge, and the Roman Boethius became prominent in philosophy.

---

69. The Hebrew version of Matthew is an old tradition that goes back to Eusebius, *Ecclesiastical History* 3.39.14-17, but the earliest manuscripts are in Greek.

70. Pope 48, A.D. 483-492.

71. From *Liber Pontificalis* 50.1, Davis 1:40-41. This, instead, must be the church of Sant'Agata dei Goti, now on Via Mazzarino, built for the Arian Goths by Ricimer c.460. It is near the churches of San Lorenzo in Fonte and San Lorenzo in Panisperna.

72. From *Liber Pontificalis* 50.2-4, Davis 1:41, This began the Acacian Schism, which lasted from 484 to 519 and anticipated the great Christian schism between Western and Orthodox churches.

Anastasius I (Emperor 53), A.D. 491

Anastasius [I Dicorus],[73] Emperor Zeno's son-in-law, ruled for twenty-seven years. Following the council of Chalcedon, he tried in every way to persecute, afflict and banish the council's defenders. In his day when a certain man called Barba, who was stained by the Arian error, wanted to baptize another man in the name of the Father through his Son and in the Holy Ghost, the water suddenly disappeared from the vase, which then broke. Upon seeing this, the person being baptized ran to the Catholic Church and was baptized in the usual way.[74] At this time large numbers of people from Egypt and Alexandria were so influenced by unclean spirits that they were chewing on their hands, but an angel who appeared to certain ones said that this was happening because they were impugning the teachings reached by the council of Chalcedon. As a result, some people repented and were healed of such madness.[75]

With Anastasius widely persecuting the Christians, many ills befell his city when large numbers of Prasians[76] rose up against him and burned a large portion of the city. His comrade Vitalianus, in an attack against Constantinople with a large number of men, begged Anastasius to declare peace. The emperor swore to absolve and revoke all accusations against those whom he had condemned and exiled as defenders of the council of Chalcedon. Finally he died, having been struck by lightning in his palace, and was later buried without the usual ceremonies. In that same period near Carthage a certain man named Olympius, a follower of the Arian heresy who was cursing the Trinity while in a bath, was burned by three visible bolts of fire sent by an angel. Bishop Fulgentius was killed for his faith.

---

73. Emperor A.D. 491–518.
74. We have been unable to identify the source of this story.
75. We have been unable to identify the source of this story.
76. Herodotus 1.82 mentions the Prasians of Prasíeis, who were conquered by Sparta. This might be a textual error for the Sassanid Persians, against whom Anastasius fought from 502 to 506.

THE FIFTH CENTURY

GELASIUS I (POPE 51), A.D. 494

Gelasius [I],[77] born in Africa and the son of Valerianus, held the pontificate for four years, eight months and eighteen days. The Church was without a leader for seven days. He managed to have Manichean writings burned at the entrance of Sta. Maria[78] and ordered that Manicheans be exiled. He recalled Bishop Mesenus, who had been condemned, and returned him to his former see, and freed Rome from hunger. When once again stories circulated about Peter and Acacius doing great harm, he held a council and, sending for information throughout the Orient, he condemned Peter and Acacius in perpetuity if they did not repent satisfactorily. He also delivered many sermons and composed hymns in the style of St. Ambrose, such as "*Uere dignum et iustum est,* etc.," which were to be sung before Mass. In his day Cassiodorus,[79] a noble and outstanding man from Ravenna, became famous.

ANASTASIUS II (POPE 52), A.D. 499

Anastasius III [II],[80] born in Rome, held the pontificate for one year, eleven months and twenty-four days. The Church was without a leader for seven days. He decreed that under no circumstances was a cleric to avoid saying the hours and the offices as well as the Mass. Because he wanted to recall Acacius, many clerics rebelled and prevented him from doing so. Subsequently he was struck by divine judgment while in the bathroom and died a miserable death, after spewing his intestines.[81]

*

---

77. Pope 49, A.D. 492–496.
78. Sta. Maria Maggiore. See *Liber Pontificalis* 51, Davis 1:41.
79. Flavius Magnus Aurelius Cassiodorus Senator (c.485–c.585).
80. Pope 50, A.D. 496–498.
81. The *Liber Pontificalis* 52.2, Davis 1:42 records only that "he was struck down by God's will."

THE SIXTH CENTURY

Simachus

SYMMACHUS (POPE 53), A.D. 501
Symmachus,[1] born in Sardinia, held the pontificate for fifteen years, seven months and seventeen days. The Church was without a leader for seven days. He was elected and installed in one day along with someone called Laurentius, Symmachus in the basilica of Constantine[2] and Laurentius in the church of Sta. Maria Maggiore. Because of this the clergy broke with the Senate, some siding with one and some with the other. Then, in order to restore peace and quiet amid such discord, both candidates went to Ravenna before King Theodoric in order to have him decide who ought to have been chosen pope. Whereupon Symmachus was selected and then, after consultation, he made Laurentius bishop of Nuceria out of pity.

After some time the pope was accused by some clergy and especially by Senators Faustus and Probinus; they had false witnesses sent to King Theodoric who secretly had Laurentius recalled. Then at the request of the Apostolic See for an emissary, the king sent Bishop Petrus from the city of Altinum. But Symmachus assembled a council of one hundred sixteen bishops who cleared and absolved him of the false accusation. Whereupon Petrus and Bishop Laurentius of Nuceria were condemned because, while the pope was still alive, they had attacked the Apostolic See. As a result, Symmachus was reaffirmed as pontiff. But Faustus and Probinus together with others began to fight within the city and killed many clerics and soldiers, among whom were the priests, Dignissimus and Gordianus. St. Symmachus, excercising

1. Pope 51, A.D. 498–514.
2. St. Peter's Basilica. See *Liber Pontificalis* 53.2–5, Davis 1:43–44.

his pastoral authority, expelled and banished the Manicheans that he found in the city and burned all their paintings and writings. He ruled that the *"Gloria in excelsis Deo"* be said every Sunday and all feast days for the martyrs.

At this time King Thrasamund of the Vandals, Genseric's second son, who was persecuting the Christians and favoring the Arians, closed Catholic churches and exiled many bishops to Sardinia. Also at this time flourished Boethius[3] who had been banished by King Theodoric of Italy; he wrote many important books, and along with many other Catholics he was killed by Theodoric in Pavia where his tomb can be seen. Finally, in this period King Sigismund of Burgundy[4] built a monastery in honor of St. Maurice and his companions, decorating it with beautiful and valuable ornaments. St. Remigius also gained fame as well as the abbot St. Quirentius, St. Lodogonius and St. Arnulfus.

HORMISDAS (POPE 54), A.D. 516

Hormisdus [Hormisdas][5] from the city of Frosinone in Campania, the son of Iustus, held the pontificate for nine years and seventeen days. The Church was without a leader for six days. He stressed formation of the clergy, having them instructed and trained in the Psalms. Moved by compassion, he absolved the Greeks and allowed them once again to be communicants because they had been excommunicated by Bishop Peter of Alexandria and Acacius.

He sent ambassadors to Emperor Anastasius with the request that he abstain from the Eutychian heresy and profess the Catholic apostolic faith. Not wanting to do so, the emperor tried to corrupt the ambassadors with money, but having failed to do so, he put them under his soldiers' command with the order that they not be allowed to enter any city. They, however, secretly sent letters concerning the faith to every city they passed, and many from these cities went to Constantinople.

---

3. Roman philosopher, senator, consul and *magister officiorum*, c.480–524/25, author of *The Consolation of Philosophy* and other works.

4. King 516–524.

5. Pope 52, A.D. 514–523.

The emperor answered the pope, saying among other things that he wanted to command and not be commanded, but then he died by the will of God, struck by lightning.

As a result the Catholic Iustinus [Justin] took command of the empire and, desiring to make peace with the Church, sent outstanding and noble ambassadors to the pope. The pontiff in turn sent apostolic ambassadors to the emperor whom he received courteously with a large multitude meeting them outside the city. They thus became friends. At this time the Barba incident occurred, which we treated above. Finally, after distributing many alms to the poor and leaving many ornaments to the Church, Hormisdas died and was buried in the church of St. Peter.

JUSTIN I (EMPEROR 54), A.D. 519

Iustinus [Justin I][6] the Elder ruled for nine years. A believer in the council of Chalcedon, he condemned the Acephalian heresy because he was the grandson of Eusimia, a Christian and the wife of a certain Catholic who had been a supporter of the council. He sent Pope Hormisdas to Constantinople together with St. Germanus, bishop of Capua, and many other holy persons in order to recall the bishops whom Anastasius had banned and to win the friendship of the emperor, who received them honorably and, zealous for the Catholic faith, vigorously fought to eliminate the heretics in its name. Later, convinced by senators' pleas and against his will, he made his nephew Iustinianus [Justinian] Caesar, who assumed the empire after him.

JOHN I (POPE 55), A.D. 525

The Tuscan Ioannes [John I],[7] the son of Constans, held the pontificate for two years, seven months and eighteen days. The Church was without a leader for three days. In his day the most Christian emperor, Justin, decreed that all heretical churches should be consecrated to the faith of Christ. When the Arian Theodoric, king of Italy, heard this,

6. Emperor A.D. 518–527.
7. Pope 53, A.D. 523–526.

THE SIXTH CENTURY

he sent for Pope John and other Catholics while he was in Ravenna and sent them to Constantinople to Emperor Justin, warning him that if he did not return churches to the Arian heretics, he would have all the Christians in Italy killed either by fire or by the sword, and would lay waste to all of Italy. The emissaries were honorably received by Justin when he went out some fifteen miles to meet them along with a very large multitude and with all the clergy, carrying lit torches and a cross. The Greeks at that time said that no ambassadors or vicars of Peter had ever been received with such honor since the days of Constantine and St. Silvester. The emperor paid homage in a prone position to the pontiff who then tearfully begged him to take pity on Italy. What he sought was granted and thus Italy was set free.

Later the emperor was crowned by the pope and expressed his great pleasure at having received Peter's blessing. Upon the pope's return, King Theodoric thought that the pope and the others who had accompanied him to Constantinople had taken too long, and fearing Emperor Justin's anger he sent [the pope] to Ravenna to die. There he had the pope placed under strict guard. After many afflictions, the pope passed away, but the others who also had been placed under guard killed themselves. He also had Symmachus, an excellent man and Boethius's father-in-law, killed.

Closely upon these cruel acts, there followed divine judgment and vengeance against Theodoric, for suddenly he died. At this time King Hilderic of the Vandals,[8] Thrasamund's son, who was born to a daughter of Emperor Valentinian, who in turn was taken prisoner when Rome was captured by the Vandals, abandoned his father's error and converted to the Catholic faith. The bishop, St. Remigius, baptized Clovis,[9] king of the Franks, who was the first of that line to become a Christian. And also at this time all the beauty of Antioch

---

8. King of the North African Vandals 523–530.
9. c.466–c.511. He was baptized on Christmas Day, 496.

was destroyed by an earthquake, and St. Brigid died in Scotland.[10] Leonard was also baptized by Remigius and became well known for his holiness.

Felix III (Pope 56), A.D. 527

Felix [III],[11] born in Samnium, held the pontificate for four years and thirteen days. The Church was without a leader for three days. He decreed that the sick be anointed with holy oil before death, and he excommunicated the patriarch of Constantinople. At this time King Alaric of the Goths, having first ruled in Italy for a long time, died and was succeeded by Queen Amalasuntha, his mother. After she was strangled, Theodahad succeeded her.

Justinian I (Emperor 55), A.D. 528

Iustinianus [Justinian I],[12] the son of a sister of Emperor Justin, ruled the empire for thirty-eight years. He passed many laws and abridged the legal codes, the *Digest*[13] and many other laws. In his day Belisarius,[14] a Roman patrician, scored a great victory against the Persians, and later was sent by Justinian from Judea to Africa where he destroyed the Vandals. Arator, an admirable poet, became famous as well as the grammarian Priscian. There were also great numbers of deaths in Constantinople.[15] At this time too lived St. Benedict[16] with his monks in the monastery of Monte Cassino, following the disciplined and unusual life he had previously led as a hermit. The remains of St. Antony were found and transported to Alexandria to the church of St. John the Baptist.

---

10. This is Brigid of Kildare, c.451–525. Once again the text confuses Scotland and Ireland.

11. Pope 54, A.D. 526–530. Actually the fourth Felix, including the antipope Felix II in 355.

12. Emperor A.D. 527–565.

13. In the *Corpus Iuris Civilis*.

14. c.500–565.

15. The Justinianic plague. See Lester K. Little, ed., *Plague and the End of Antiquity: The Pandemic of* 541–750 (New York: Cambridge University Press, 2006).

16. Benedict of Nursia, c.480–c.545.

THE SIXTH CENTURY

BONIFACE II (POPE 57), A.D. 531

The Roman Bonifacius [Boniface] II[17] held the pontificate for two years and thirty-six days. The Church was without a leader for two months and twenty-five days. He was ordained pontiff together with Dioscorus [of Alexandria], creating a schism between the Senate and the clergy, but a little later Dioscorus died. Boniface remained pontiff and ruled that clerics be separated from the laity during the singing of Mass.

JOHN II (POPE 58), A.D. 533

The Roman Ioannes [John] II,[18] from the district of Monte Caelio, was originally named Mercurius and held the pontificate for two years, four months and six days. The Church was without a leader for six days. In his day flourished St. Benedict together with his disciple Maurus.

AGAPITUS I (POPE 59), A.D. 535

The Roman Agapitus [I][19] held the pontificate for one year, three months and eighteen days. The Church was without a leader for one year and nineteen days. He was sent by Theodahad,[20] king of the Goths, to Emperor Justin[ian] in Constantinople who was very angry with him because of Queen Amalasuntha's death; he was sent to reinstate Theodahad and reconcile him with the emperor. Upon the pope's arrival he was received by the emperor with great joy.

At the time in Constantinople there was a heretical bishop, Anthimus. In order to test the pope's seriousness,[21] the emperor said, "Dear pontiff, either you consent to this [bishop] or I will have you sent into exile." To this the pope happily answered, "As a sinner I thought I was coming to Emperor Justinian, a most Christian ruler, but now I

---

17. Pope 55, A.D. 530–532.
18. Pope 56, A.D. 533–535.
19. Pope 57, A.D. 535–536.
20. King 534–536. The text reads "Theoderic."
21. For this episode see *Liber Pontificalis* 56.2–5, Davis 1:51–52.

have found a heretic. Nevertheless I in no way fear your threats. And so that you may know that you are not fit for the Christian religion, know that the bishop you prefer [does not] accept two natures in Christ." Then he had Anthimus summoned who would not to admit to any error or agree with him, and so the pope, after charging him with many faults, condemned him. For this reason the emperor, in harmony with the Apostolic See, humbled himself and did reverence to the pope. Then, following Anthimus' banishment, the pontiff installed a bishop named Lenna.[22] Furthermore, after obtaining what he wanted from the emperor, he suddenly died in Constantinople, and his body was taken to Rome. He ordained four deacons and eleven bishops, and also decreed that processions be held on Sundays.

SILVERIUS (POPE 60), A.D. 539

Silverius,[23] born in Campania, held the pontificate for three years. The Church was without a leader for one year. He was appointed bishop by Theodahad, the tyrant of the Goths, without consultation or decree, in an attempt to corrupt the clergy with money and with the threat of death for any who did not consent. Not long after Theodahad's death, Witiges[24] was made king of the Goths. Within a few months he set up a camp near Rome and set siege to the city because Belisarius was there whom Emperor Justinian had sent against him.[25] For one year he continued such a siege that no one could enter or exit, and there was so much famine in the city according to accounts that mothers ate their own children.

At this time Vigilius was a deacon in Constantinople, residing in the palace. Theodora Augusta, the emperor's lady, complained about the manner in which the heretic Anthimus had been condemned and agreed with Vigilius that were he to become pope he would reinstate

22. The *Liber Pontificalis* reads "Menas."
23. Pope 58, A.D. 536–537.
24. Vitiges, king of the Ostrogoths in Italy, 536–540.
25. The siege of Rome, 537–538, during the Gothic Wars. See Procopius, *De Bello Gothico* I.

Anthimus. Thus, in writing to Silverius, she said through the deacon, "O Pontiff, either come to us or reinstate Anthimus."[26] The pope replied that he would never free him since he had been justly condemned as a heretic. Whereupon she indignantly wrote to Belisarius that either he replace the pope, using some pretext, or send him to her and make Vigilius pope because he had promised to reinstate Anthimus. Upon hearing this Belisarius said, "I shall do as ordered, but be careful of them since they will have to justify everything before God." Having thereupon gathered some false witnesses who said that Pope Silverius intended to send letters to Asinarius, king of the Goths, and wanted to open the city gates to him, he exiled him to the island of Pontia [Pandataria] where he suffered a miserable death. In his day Bishop Arcolanus of Perugia was beheaded by the king of the Goths.

VIGILIUS (POPE 61), A.D. 541

The Roman Vigilius[27] held the pontificate for seventeen years, six months and twenty-seven days. The Church was without a leader for four months and five days. In his day Belisarius, the Roman patrician, fought against Witiges, king of the Goths, defeating him and freeing the city of Rome from their siege. The size of the Roman Empire increased surprisingly both in the East and in the West, and although Emperor Justinian was very occupied with legislation, he still enjoyed many victories because of the above-mentioned Belisarius who fought in many territories.

After his stupendous victory against the Persians, Belisarius proceeded against the Vandals in Africa. And after having conquered many other peoples and retaking Carthage [...], he went on to Sicily and then to Naples. But since the Neapolitans refused to welcome him because of the Goths who were in the city, he lay siege and within a few days captured it. Not only did he behave cruelly against the Goths, but he also killed every Neapolitan citizen, male and female, big and small, treating them all in the same fashion. He pardoned no one and took all

26. See a more detailed version in *Liber Pontificalis* 60.6–7, Davis 1:53–54.
27. Pope 59, A.D. 537–555.

the goods and treasure from their temples.[28] As he approached Rome, the Goths who were inside left the city gates open at night and fled toward Ravenna. There having joined battle with Belisarius, they were again defeated and their king Witiges captured. When the battle was over, Belisarius took the king and with great fanfare led him to prison in Constantinople.

At this time too Cassiodorus, the senator from Ravenna, became well known; later on he became a monk, famous for his knowledge and eloquence. Also at this time in a Sicilian city, the archdeacon Theophilus joined the enemy of the human race by denying Christ and his mother, thereby obtaining the honors he desired. After recognizing his great error, he regained a clear conscience with tears and mortifications, and after completing a harsh penance with the aid of the Virgin Mary he obtained grace and forgiveness.

Empress Theodora, through whom Vigilius had become pope, sent him a request to keep his promise and recall the heretic Anthimus. The pope replied that he would not do so because, even though he had knowingly made the promise, he now as vicar of the apostle Peter would never reinstate a heretic who had been condemned by St. Agapitus and Silverius, his predecessors. Then the emperor and empress wrote to Rome that Vigilius, having successfully deposed Silverius, must come to them. After he had been captured in the church of Sta. Cecilia and led to the shore to be put on a ship, the Romans requested that Vigilius bless them. After the blessing, the ship set sail, and they began throwing rocks and sticks at him, saying, "May hunger and death accompany you, for you have done evil to the Romans, and may you encounter evil where you are going." When he reached Sicily, he was left there for the month of December to ordain priests and deacons. Setting sail on the vigil of our Lord Jesus Christ, he later arrived in Constantinople where the emperor, as well as the empress, did what they could to have him recall Anthimus. When he

28. *Liber Pontificalis* 60.3, Davis 1:52–53. A very different account from that of Procopius, *De Bello Gothico* V–VI.15.

refused to do so under any conditions, a rope was tied around his neck and he was dragged throughout the city. Subsequently he was jailed and given bread to eat and water to drink. Whereupon he himself confessed that they were doing to him what he deserved.

At this time, the Goths with their king Totila recaptured Rome, but soon afterwards left the city because of their worry about Belisarius, Emperor Justinian's general. But when the emperor realized that the Goths were still sacking all of Italy, he sent the Roman Narses[29] who killed the king and his soldiers. The Romans begged Narses to join them in appealing to the emperor to reinstate the pope along with the many other clerics whom he had banished. When this was done, while returning, Vigilius died of gallstones in Sicily, and his remains were then taken to Rome.

One reads that at this time there was a council against the heretics who believed that Holy Mary had only given birth to a man, and not God and man. At this time also Bishop Theodorus of Nicaea died and was buried with great honors by the king of Sicily. St. Remigius also died. He had presided over the church of France for seventy-two years.[30]

PELAGIUS I (POPE 62), A.D. 558

The Roman Pelagius[31] held the pontificate for four years, ten months and fourteen days. The Church was without a leader for two months and twenty-six days. Since no bishops were willing to install him as pope, Ioannes from Perugia and Bonus from Sorrento, both bishops, together with the priest Andrea from Ostia did so, but the clergy, the wise men and nobility did not wish to obey him, saying that he was involved in the painful events surrounding Pope Vigilius. Whereupon he came to St. Peter's holding the scriptures and the cross over his head and made excuses for himself by maintaining that he had not

---

29. Born 478, Byzantine commander c. 538–573.
30. The text reads "days."
31. Pope 60, A.D. 556–561.

participated in the Vigilius matter, thereby satisfying the general public. He then added, "I want you all, together with me, to establish and confirm that no one may become bishop or take another office through gifts and promises since this would be considered simony, whereas he who does God's holy work and leads a good and holy life according to scripture is learned and erudite."[32]

In his day, because of the many casualties in Constantinople, Pelagius ordered that the feast of the Purification of the Virgin Mary be celebrated. St. Brendan became well known in Scotland while the bones of St. Stephen, the first martyr, were transported to Rome and placed with those of St. Lawrence. Also at this time under Emperor Justinian, the Jews and Saracens, having gathered all the Christians living in the city of Caesarea in Palestine, killed them all. When he heard this, the emperor sent to Palestine a person named Adalmatius who took great vengeance upon them. Also at this time St. Euphrasia became well known in Paris.

JOHN III (POPE 63), A.D. 562.
The Roman Ioannes [John] III,[33] son of Anastasius, held the pontificate for twelve years, eleven months and twenty-six days. The Church was without a leader ten months and twelve days. He enlarged and repaired the cemeteries of the holy martyrs.[34] In his day flourished [Venantius] Fortunatus,[35] a most eloquent poet who wrote the biography of St. Martin[36] and later was made bishop of Poitiers. St. Maurus, a disciple of St. Benedict, went from Italy to Gaul, where he lived a good life and then died near Paris, where he was buried. Emperor Justinian died peacefully,[37] after having built a magnificent

---

32. *Liber Pontificalis* 62.2, Davis 1:58.
33. Pope 61, A.D. 561–574.
34. Which catacombs are meant is unclear.
35. A.D. c.530–c.605.
36. The *Vita Sancti Martini* of Martin of Tours.
37. On 14 November 565.

church to the glory of God in Constantinople[38] and the churches of San Vitale and Sant'Apollinare in Ravenna. St. Germanus, bishop of Paris, finished the course of his life[39] and was buried there; one reads about him that because of his merit the time of his death was revealed to him. Archbishop Agnellus of Ravenna became well known, as did the monk Cassiodorus. A famous comet also appeared at that time.

JUSTIN THE YOUNGER (EMPEROR 56), A.D. 566

Iustinus [Justin II] the Younger,[40] the son of Vigilantia who was Emperor Justinian's sister, assumed the scepter and ruled for eleven years as widespread peace prevailed among the people. At this time the Roman patrician Narses, who was concerned about the victories by the Gothic king and frightened by the threats of the emperor and of Empress Sophia, to whom he had been falsely accused because of envy, asked the Lombards to come to Italy. Even though they were from Pannonia, Narses became so friendly with their king Alboin and then with his successor Rotumnius that they loved each other like brothers. Thus allied, they took counsel on how to occupy the kingdom of Italy, and after successfully taking what they had planned, they occupied the kingdom and separated it from the kingdoms of Constantinople.[41] Whence, from that time was established the kingdom of Italy by the Lombards who then expelled the peoples of Milan, Cremona, Brescia and Bergamo and began inhabiting those areas for the first time. The Lombards used to dress in a unique way, wearing long vestments made primarily of linen with stockings hanging down to the heels, tied on both sides with belts. Many kings succeeded Rotumnius, among whom were Grimwald and his son Romuald who was lord of the Samnites.[42]

38. Hagia Sophia.
39. Germanus of Paris, c.496–28 May 576.
40. Emperor A.D. 565–574.
41. See Paul the Deacon, *History of the Lombards*, book 2.
42. That is, of the Lombard duchies of Benevento and the South.

At this time, even though the Lombards were baptized, they still worshiped idols, especially the serpent idol. St. Barbarus, bishop of Benevento, later saved them from this error by converting the gold with which the serpent was made into chalices. There later succeeded to power King Astolf,[43] whom Pepin,[44] king of France, attacked at the pope's summons. At the time of Romuald, the remains of St. Bartholomew were brought first to Lipari from India and then to Benevento. At this time also, Pope John III died after completing the church of the Apostles Philip and James,[45] and was buried in St. Peter's. In addition, the Armenians were converted to the Christian faith, and Justin died after conferring the title of Caesar on Tiberius.

BENEDICT I (POPE 64), A.D. 575

The Roman Benedictus [Benedict I],[46] the son of Bonifacius, held the pontificate for four years, one month and twenty-nine days. The Church was without a leader for three months and four days. In his day, Justin [II] ruled the empire. He was a Catholic and would have enjoyed greater peace were it not for his wife, since his stepfather Narses created no trouble for him, despite becoming greatly feared because of his many victories after taking the emperor's leave. But when he abandoned the faith, many people turned against him, which resulted in him to have to wage many battles. At this time, after the Lombards had conquered all of Italy and besieged Rome, causing much famine and many deaths, the pope died of grief and distress and was buried in St. Peter's. The church of San Severo outside of Ravenna was built.

---

43. King of the Lombards, 749–756.
44. Pepin the Younger, or the Short, c.714–September 24, 768.
45. Now the church of Santi Dodici Apostoli.
46. Pope 62, A.D. 575–579.

THE SIXTH CENTURY

TIBERIUS II CONSTANTINE (EMPEROR[47] 57), A.D. 577

Emperor Tiberius [II Constantine][48] ruled for six years. He was a very devout Christian and very merciful to the poor, giving them a good portion of his riches. In his day the Goths, who were heretical pagans, converted to Christianity. Also at this time the Christians were divided into many groups and often fought continuously among themselves causing great destruction. Tiberius finally died, after giving one of his daughters to Maurice, the leader of his troops, and after making him emperor.

PELAGIUS II (POPE 65), A.D. 580

The Roman Pelagius [II][49] held the pontificate for ten years, two months and ten days. The Church was without a leader for three months and twenty-five days. He was installed as pope without the emperor's knowledge inasmuch as the city was under siege by the Lombards. At this time there were terrible rains with winds and hail that were followed by widespread destruction.[50] Also at this time St. Gregory[51] was sent to Constantinople at the request of Bishop Leandro of Campania, and there composed books on morals.

MAURICE (EMPEROR 58), A.D. 583

Emperor Maurice [I Tiberius][52] ruled for twenty years. He was a devout Catholic and extremely valuable to the empire for having fought the Lombards in the second year of his rule after leading the Franks into Italy. In that battle both sides suffered great losses. He subsequently proclaimed his son Caesar who was later made emperor with him. In his day Recared, king of the Goths, became Christian along with his entire people. Later, fighting against the Franks, he and Claudius,

---

47. Text reads "Pope."
48. Emperor A.D. 574–582.
49. Pope 63, A.D. 579–590.
50. *Liber Pontificalis* 65.1, Davis 1:59.
51. Pope Gregory the I, the Great. Among his works is the *Moralia*.
52. Emperor A.D. 582–602.

THE LIVES OF THE POPES AND EMPERORS

his army commander, miraculously defeated forty thousand Frankish troops with three hundred men.[53] In his day there was held near Toledo a very famous council comprised of seventy-two bishops that condemned the Arian and all other heresies.[54] Maurice also fought the Persian king who later, after the declaration of peace, became a Christian together with him.

At that time there were such widespread and devastating tides that everyone said that [Noah's] flood had returned. Because of these high tides the Tiber became so swollen that, after streaming through the city of Rome, it flooded a great portion of the countryside dragging along many animals, including serpents and the like. After the flood they became so rotten and spoiled that the air became polluted, causing widespread deaths unlike anything anyone had ever heard of in the past. As a result many homes remained vacant because of the very large numbers of deaths, among whom was the pope. At the same time a woman gave birth to a child without eyes or hands or legs, and had from his hips down something like a fish tail.[55] Finally, Maurice and his children were killed by Phocas with the aid of his troops.

GREGORY I (POPE 66), A.D. 590

The Roman Gregorius [Gregory I],[56] the son of Gordianus, held the pontificate for thirteen years, six months and ten days. The Church was without a leader for five months and eighteen days. He was a teacher and a doctor, and while an archdeacon was elected pope with Emperor Maurice's consent. He was a prudent pope and a scholar of divine scripture, very easy-going and kind. He composed about forty homilies, expounded on the books of Job and Ezekiel, and also composed a work entitled *[The] Dialogues*, along with many others. He

---

53. The source of this story is unclear.
54. The third council of Toledo, 583, which also imposed restrictions upon Jews.
55. Most of these details are found in Paul the Deacon, *History of the Lombards* III.24; see also Jacobus de Voragine, *Golden Legend*, Life of St. (Pope) Gregory, ed. Ryan, 1:171–84, at 173.
56. Pope 64, A.D. 590–604. The *Liber Pontificalis* 66, Davis 1:60, is by contrast quite brief in its discussion of Gregory. There are many sound, modern biographies.

THE SIXTH CENTURY

made his home a monastery for which he was deservedly called an angel on earth since he led a holy life. Gregory had the heads and members of all the statues representing idols cut off so that by eliminating the root of heresy he might more fully exalt the victory of Christian virtue.[57] He also added these words to the Mass: *"Dies que nostros in tua pace disponat."* Daily he had Mass and the Office celebrated at the tombs of the Apostles Peter and Paul, and also ordered litanies known as the Seven Forms be recited to mitigate God's anger. They are called the seven forms for the following reason: firstly, all the clerics would chant them; secondly, the abbots and monks; thirdly, the abbesses with their congregations; fourthly, all the children; fifthly, the laity; sixthly, the widows; and seventhly, married and unmarried women.

He was also the first pontiff to begin to use, in signing his letters, the words "servant of the servants of God," something that was subsequently continued by other pontiffs. At this time in Josephat, not far from Jerusalem, were found the vestments of Christ by Bishop Gregory of Antioch, together with Bishop Thomas of Jerusalem. This pontiff also sent the monk Augustine to Anglo-Saxon England[58] to have the people return to the faith of Christ since many years earlier they had been converted by papal emissaries.

At this time also such a serious disagreement arose between this pontiff and Emperor Maurice that, following many accusations and curses by the emperor against St. Gregory, he even threatened to kill him. For this reason in the city of Rome on a particular day there appeared a man dressed as a monk who, wandering through the city with a bare knife in hand, yelled that his knife would kill the emperor that same year. Upon hearing this, Maurice truly repented of the wrongs he had committed against the pontiff and humbly prayed to God, causing

---

57. This appears in the twelfth-century *De mirabilibus Urbis Romae* by Master Gregory. See John Osborn, ed. (Toronto: University of Toronto Press, 1987), 22–23, 48–51. See also Tilmann Buddensieg, "Gregory the Great, the Destroyer of Pagan Idols: The History of a Medieval Legend concerning the Decline of Ancient Art and Literature," *Journal of the Warburg and Courtauld Institutes* 28 (1965): 44–65.

58. Augustine of Canterbury, d.26 May 604. Canterbury's first archbishop from 597.

many others also to pray for him that the threat directed against him be retracted. Not long afterwards, on a certain night as he slept, he seemed to hear a voice from heaven saying things such as this: "Do you want me to pardon you here or in the other world?" To which the emperor replied: "O God, lover of the wretched, visit my punishment upon me so that you might forgive me in the other world."[59]

Although Gregory was virtuous in his way of life and conduct and learned in knowledge, he still suffered so many abominations and curses after his death that his holy and praiseworthy books would have been burned, had it not been for his deacon Petrus. While he was still pope, Emperor Maurice in the East ordered his troops to commit thefts and rapes without making restitution as was the custom. As a result, they directed their anger against him and, electing Phocas as their lord, made him emperor. When Maurice heard this, he fled to an island where he, his wife and two children were killed. He was the first Greek emperor to rule the empire.

At this time also through the deceit of the Lombard king, Agilulf,[60] Padua was burned down, and its citizens went to live in Ravenna, Cremona and Mantua. The people of Anglia[61] were converted to the faith of Christ. On the feast day of St. Gervasius and Protasius, peace was declared between the Romans and the Lombards. Theudelinda, queen of the Lombards, had a church built near Modena in honor of St. John the Baptist.[62]

*

---

59. This story can be found in Jacobus de Voragine, *Golden Legend*, Life of St. (Pope) Gregory, ed. Ryan, 1:171–84, at 177–78.

60. King 591–616.

61. The mission of Augustine of Canterbury to the Angles or English.

62. See Paul the Deacon, *History of the Lombards* III.21.

THE SEVENTH CENTURY

Phoca

PHOCAS (EMPEROR 59), A.D. 603

Emperor Phocas[1] ruled the empire for eight years. He was made emperor because of disagreements between the troops and Emperor Maurice whom he killed along with many others. In his day when the Persians marched against the Romans, many violent battles were fought in which the Romans, by fighting ferociously, succeeded in overpowering the Persians and winning the victory. Having been defeated and overrun as far as the Euphrates River, the Persians lost many eastern provinces as well as Jerusalem.[2] At this time the Venetians also engaged in battle with peoples from the East causing many casualties on both sides.[3]

SABINIAN (POPE 67), A.D. 604

The Tuscan Sabinianus [Sabinian][4] held the pontificate for one year, five months and eight days. The Church was without a leader for eleven months and twenty-six days. He decreed that churches announce the times of the Office by pealing the bells. Sabinian spoke ill of and cursed St. Gregory, the previous pope, accusing him of being too generous in giving away the goods of the Church; he was thereby forced to beg for alms and able to give very little to the poor. Three times St. Gregory appeared to him and reproved him harshly for this. Nevertheless, by continuing to do this and with no concern about

---

1. Emperor A.D. 602–610.
2. The situation was actually much the reverse, with Phocas losing all these territories to the Persian Sassanid King Khosrau (Chosroes) II. Emperor Heraclius recovered them, only to see the rise of the Muslims and their conquests of both the Roman East and Persia.
3. The sense of this passage is unclear. Venice did not emerge as a city-state until the mid-eight century.
4. Pope 65, A.D. 604–606.

this reproof, one evening he was beaten so badly that he died not long afterwards.[5]

BONIFACE III (POPE 68), A.D. 606

The Roman Bonifacius [Boniface] III[6] held the pontificate for eight months and twenty-two days. The Church was without a leader for ten months and seven days. In his day, when Phocas was emperor, Boniface entreated him to have the see of Constantinople, which was the principal one, be subject to the see of Rome, and that the one in Constantinople cease calling itself with so much arrogance the primary one. Consequently, the church of Rome was pronounced the grand lady and mother of all churches. He decreed that, as long as a pope was living as well as a bishop of any other city, no one should be allowed to discuss a bishopric, and that on the third day following a pontiff's death, after gathering the clergy and other children of the Church, an election was to be held fairly and freely according to God's will. He also decreed together with a council of thirty-two bishops and a great many priests and clergy that each church have the freedom to choose its own priest under the threat of excommunication.

BONIFACE IV (POPE 69), A.D. 607

Bonifacius [Boniface] IV,[7] born in Marsi and the son of Ioannes who was a doctor, held the pontificate for six years, seven months and thirteen days. The Church was without a leader for six months and twenty-five days. He, together with many faithful Christians, begged Phocas, who was emperor at the time, to donate the temple of the Pantheon to him; Marcus Agrippa, the father-in-law of Octavius Augustus and the first Roman emperor (as we said above) had it built and consecrated it to Cybele who was considered the mother of all the gods. Following a request from Phocas, he and all the people, on the kalends of November, dedicated and consecrated the temple to Mary ever-virgin and all the

---

5. This story appears in the *Golden Legend*, St. Gregory, ed. Ryan, 1:181.
6. Pope 66, 19 February–12 November 607.
7. Pope 67, A.D. 608–615.

THE SEVENTH CENTURY

martyrs; today it is called Sta. Maria Rotonda.[8] Boniface decreed that on that day the pope solemnly chant the Mass, that the Virgin Mary and all the heavenly holy spirits and other saints be venerated and honored, and that the entire Christian community solemnly honor them annually on that day. He decreed too that on the next day, the second of November, throughout all the churches of Christendom the Office and the Passion be celebrated for all those who had passed on from the present life and were undergoing the sufferings of purgatory.

In his day Priscus, Emperor Phocas' brother, no longer wished to support his brother's rule and sent a message to Heraclius in Africa asking him to attack Phocas. With a great fleet and strong, daring followers, Heraclius defeated and killed Phocas.

HERACLIUS (EMPEROR 60), A.D. 611

Emperor Heraclius[9] ruled for thirty-one years. In his day Sisebut, king of the Goths,[10] fought the Romans in Spain, and in that battle the Roman troops were defeated and driven out. Subsequently Sisibut had Jews in his kingdom baptized after they had converted to the Christian faith, but after his death Suintila, a most glorious king, succeeded to the throne. He did battle with the Romans for the last time, and then seized control of all of Spain. Also in Heraclius's day, the Persians captured Syria, Egypt and many other provinces.

DEUSDEDIT I (POPE 70), A.D. 613

The Roman Adeodatus [Deusdedit] I,[11] son of the subdeacon Stephanus, held the pontificate for three years and twenty-three days. The Church was without a leader for one month and sixteen days. He loved the clergy and greatly enriched it. In his day there were so many cases of scabies that all who died of it were unrecognizable. One also

---

8. In 609. This name of the church is a Roman usage and indicates a familiarity with Roman topography and sources.
9. Emperor A.D. 610–641.
10. Visigothic king of Spain, 612–620/21.
11. Pope 68, A.D. 615–618.

reads that once, after the pope kissed a leper, the leper was suddenly cleansed and cured of his illness.[12] In his day when Heraclius was emperor, Chosroes [II] ruled as king of Persia, and he conquered a large part of the Roman holdings and, after destroying Jerusalem, burned the holy places and captured many Christians together with Patriarch Zachariah. Furthermore he took possession of the wood of the Holy Cross and took it to Persia along with prisoners.[13]

BONIFACE V (POPE 71), A.D. 616

Bonifacius [Boniface] V,[14] born in Campania, held the pontificate for five years. The Church was without a leader for thirteen days. He decreed that thieves be excommunicated and that no one except priests should carry the relics of saints. In his day the king of Persia was baptized in Constantinople.

HONORIUS I (POPE 72), A.D. 621

Honorius I,[15] born in Campania, held the pontificate for twelve years, eleven months and seventeen days. The Church was without a leader for seven months and twenty-eight days. He decreed that litanies be sung in St. Peter's every Saturday and taught many precepts to the clergy; he was also very compassionate toward the poor, giving them a great deal of alms. At this time the monk St. Anastasius[16] was declared a martyr, about whom it is written that he devoted much time to the art of necromancy in his youth. But later, having been taught the Christian faith by some Christians, he hastened to go to Jerusalem where he was baptized with great devotion and became a monk. After

---

12. *Liber Pontificalis* 70.3, Davis 1:61.

13. Just the opposite is true: Heraclius inflicted a series of definitive defeats on the Persians and ended the war triumphant in 629, recovering Jerusalem and the relic of the True Cross. The wars exhausted both Romans and Persians, however. By 644, the newly unified Muslims had conquered the Persian Empire and were to seize much of the Eastern Roman Empire.

14. Pope 69, A.D. 619–625.

15. Pope 70, A.D. 625–638.

16. Anastasius the Persian, a Zoroastrian in his youth, d.22 January 628.

THE SEVENTH CENTURY

his capture by the Saracens, he was martyred following much torture. A monk who was ill donned his cape and was immediately cured. His venerable remains were taken to Rome by Emperor Heraclius and placed in saline fluid at the monastery of San Paolo. This pontiff adorned many churches with gold and silver, among which were the churches of St. Peter and San Paolo which, after adorning them with many ornaments, he had covered with copper. He also built on Via Aurelia the church of St. Agnes[17] where the sacred body of St. Paul reposes as well as the remains of other martyrs.[18]

One also reads that at this time King Chosroes of Persia was defeated by Emperor Heraclius. This enabled the emperor to free Zachariah and all the other Christians whom Chosroes had imprisoned, along with the wood of the most holy Cross, which Chosroes had also seized at the same time and which the emperor now returned triumphantly to Jerusalem. It was later decreed that every year the Cross be celebrated and that this be called "the Exaltation."

In this same period it is also written that Muhammad, the Saracen prophet who was very learned in the science of magic, was in Arabia.[19] Also at this time Bishop Isidore of Spain,[20] the successor to St. Leander and a very learned man, wrote a book entitled *Etymologies* and histories from the time of Jerome until his own death that became well known. St. Gall,[21] the abbot and disciple of the German St. Columbanus, also became well known. In the fifteenth year of Heraclius's reign, the Saracens, who were usually under the control of the king of Persia, were conquered by the emperor. At that time too died Muhammad who it is said was succeeded by Albior.[22] Also

---

17. This is the basilica of Sant'Agnese fuori le Mura, on the Via Nomentana, correctly located in the *Liber Pontificalis* 72.3, Davis 1:62.

18. St. Paul is buried, appropriately, in the basilica of San Paolo fuori le Mura.

19. See above, n. 13.

20. Isidore of Seville, c.560–4 April 636.

21. Lived c.550–c.646.

22. Abu-Bakr, c.573–23 August 634.

in those days the emperor waged war with the Saracens and, fearing defeat, had the wood of the cross of Christ taken from Jerusalem to Constantinople. Much later, in 1247, a portion of the same cross, at the request of King Louis of France, was very secretly transported to Paris.

Finally Pope Honorius died and was buried in St. Peter's. He ordained three priests, deacons and eighty-one bishops.

SEVERINUS (POPE 73), A.D. 635

The Roman Severinus[23] held the pontificate for eleven months and four days. The Church was without a leader for four months and twenty-nine days. In his day the bishopric at the Lateran was sacked after the pope's election by Mauritius the cartularius[24] and the patrician Isacius. In this sacriligious event, the soldiers and the Roman populace, from the most to the least important, participated and sent into exile the primates of the Church, there being no one to offer resistance. A great portion of the loot was sent to Emperor Heraclius. Severinus was a holy and kind pontiff, a great lover of the poor and great supporter of the Church, winning for it many passionate adherents.

JOHN IV (POPE 74), A.D. 637

Ioannes [John] IV,[25] born in Dalmatia, held the pontificate for three years, eight months and nine days. The Church was without a leader for one month and thirteen days. Using his wealth, he was able to purchase the release of many thousand men who were held in slavery in Dalmatia and Istria. He also returned to Rome from Dalmatia and Istria the relics of the martyrs Vincentius, Anastasia and many other saints, placing them near the fountains of the Lateran in the oratory of John the Baptist.

---

23. Pope 71, 28 May–2 August 640.

24. A *cartularius* was a high-ranking office, of the same rank as *dux* or *comes*, probably having to do with official documents, perhaps akin to a military legal advisor or chancellor. A far more detailed account appears in the *Liber Pontificalis* 75.1–2, Davis 1:65.

25. Pope 72, A.D. 640–642.

THE SEVENTH CENTURY

At this time the Saracens who had rebelled against the emperor destroyed Jerusalem and captured Antioch while Heraclius was ill and had become deaf. Later he died, stained with the Manichean heresy that denied there were two wills in Christ. Previously the emperor had taken the wood of the cross to Jerusalem, staying with the patriarch of the acolytes who were beginning to falter in the faith. The acolytes are Christians whom St. James had converted to the Catholic faith, but had become feeble in that faith since they believed that Christ was not God because he was born of a virgin, died, was reborn and went to heaven.

Also at this time, the kingdom of Persia that Heraclius had earlier conquered was once again captured by the Saracens with the help of the Arabs. When their king, named Hormuzd [IV],[26] had been driven out and Silebrido,[27] king of the Goths, had taken many cities in Spain held by Romans, the Roman Empire began to collapse everywhere from this time onward without ever recovering its pristine dignity and reputation. Finally John died and was buried in St. Peter's.

THEODORE I (POPE 75, A.D. 641

The Greek Theodorus [Theodore I][28] from the city of Jerusalem held the pontificate for six years, five months and nineteen days. The Church was without a leader for three [...]. He reaffirmed that candles be blessed on Holy Saturday and composed a book on penance. In his day the cartularius Mauritius, having been involved in a sacrilegious attack on the Lateran, was captured and beheaded.

At this time also Pyrrhus [I], who had been patriarch of Constantinople, went from Africa to Rome and offered a booklet to the Apostolic See in the presence of the clergy and people. In the book he condemned all those things that had been done or said by him or by his followers against the Church of Christ. Pope [Theodore] had

---

26. King of the Sasanian Empire, 579–590.
27. Probably Sisebut, king 612–662. See above, p. 103 n.10.
28. Pope 73, A.D. 642–649.

a seat placed for him near the altar, honoring him as a priest of the royal city. But later on, the pope changed his mind and, with the clergy agreeing, placed Pyrrhus under excommunication in the church of St. Peter the Apostle, and as a result Pyrrhus returned to the eastern regions.[29] Also at this time, Patriarch Paulus [II][30] of the same see of Constantinople not only preached his evil and heretical doctrine, but openly persecuted the Catholic faith, condemning even the ambassadors sent to correct his errors, to the point of having some beaten and others put in prison. Finally he was condemned in perpetuity by the pope who had many times summoned him to Rome and warned him to abstain from such error.

CONSTANTINE III HERACLIUS (EMPEROR 61), A.D. 642

Constantine [III Heraclius],[31] third son of Heraclius, ruled the empire for twenty-nine years. He was a terrible emperor and an enemy of the Christians. In agreement with Patriarch Paulus [II], Constantine ordered that a certain man named Typus[32] warn the people that they should not believe in a Christ with two wills and two natures, one divine and one human. When they refused to accept this heresy, he exiled many of them and subjected many others to torments and punishments. In his day, with the greatness of Rome already considerably weakened, the Saracens weakened it still further with the conquest of Africa. Furthermore, during his reign the son of the king of England[33] left his kingdom and the royal life to become a hermit.

One also reads that at this time Edradius, an Augustinian bishop, went to Rome in order to beg the pope for Gregory's books on morals[34] because he wanted to transcribe them, but because the pope took his time, the bishop remained in the city for a long period. Later on,

29. See *Liber Pontificalis* 75.3, Davis 1:65–66.

30. A.D. 641–653.

31. Emperor 612–641.

32. A misnomer: "*Typus*" is a Byzantine imperial decree.

33. This might refer to Sigeberht of East Anglia, king c.629–c.634.

34. *Moralia in Job*.

while meditating one night in St. Peter's there appeared to him Saints Peter and Paul with a great following of Roman pontiffs, and in this vision there was such a lightning bolt that he nearly died. Then St. Peter said to him, "I am the first bishop of this See, and these are all my successors." St. Gregory then came forth a little from the multitude of followers to say, "I am Gregory for whom so many have labored, but you will not depart without hope." Then this bishop asked him if St. Augustine were also among them; and he replied that Augustine was in a higher place. Having said this, they all disappeared. And that same night an angel of God appeared to him and showed him the case containing the book he was seeking. When all of this was told to the pope, the bishop obtained what he wanted and was held in great veneration by all.[35] Finally Constantine died in Siracusa because of discord among his own people.

MARTIN I (POPE 76), A.D. 647

The Tuscan Martinus [Martin I][36] held the pontificate for six years, one month and twenty-six days. The Church was without a leader for one month. In his day, after Bishop Paulus [II] of Constantinople had used the *Typus* to persuade others to err against the Catholic faith, he destroyed and ruined an altar of the Holy See that had been consecrated in Placidia's home, forbidding any of our people to offer sacrifice there or take the sacrament of communion. And warning the Christian laity along with many religious to avoid falling into such error, he exiled some and had others beaten. For this reason, Pope Martin summoned a council of one hundred and five bishops that condemned Paulus along with Pyrrhus and Sergius. But then the emperor, having appointed Olympius the exarch of Italy, ordered that anyone who did not accept the *Typus* as previously ordered by Paulus be condemned, even were he officially the pope.

---

35. We have not identified the source of this story.
36. Pope 74, A.D. 649–654. The events related below are recorded in greater detail in *Liber Pontificalis* 76.1–8, Davis 1:66–69.

When Olympius learned that all the bishops were gathered with the pope in Rome and realized that he could not accomplish by force what he had been told to do, he ordered that the pope be killed treacherously by one of his servants while receiving communion on the vigil of Christ's birth in the church of Sta. Maria ad Praesepe.[37] But Christ, the pope's defender, did not abandon him and caused the servant who was to commit the murder to lose his sight. Unable to accomplish the mission, Olympius made peace with the Church and begged the pope's absolution. He then went to Sicily to fight the Saracens, where he lost a good portion of the Roman army, fell ill and died. And so the emperor sent other envoys to Rome who, finding the pope in the church of the Savior, led him out, but when the pope refused to obey, they sent him into exile to a place named Kherson where he led a holy life until he died.

EUGENIUS I (POPE 77), A.D. 653

The Roman Eugenius [I][38] from the Aventine district held the pontificate for two years, eight months and twenty-four days. The Church was without a leader for one month and nineteen days. From his youth he was a good cleric. When he was later made pontiff, he was kind, loving and outstanding in sanctity.

VITALIAN (POPE 78), A.D. 656

Vitalianus [Vitalian],[39] born in Campania in the region of Signia, held the pontificate for fourteen years and six months. The Church was without a leader for two months and twelve days. He composed hymns for the Roman church and tuned all the organs. He also sent ambassadors to the emperor[40] in Constantinople as was the custom, informing him that he had been made pope. The ambassadors were received with honor and once again received from the emperor all the

---

37. Sta. Maria Maggiore.
38. Pope 75, A.D. 654–657.
39. Pope 76, A.D. 657–672.
40. Constans II.

THE SEVENTH CENTURY

privileges granted to the Church. They were sent back once again with many gifts to present to the pope at St. Peter's.

Not long afterward, the emperor left Constantinople[41] with a large fleet and came to Italy in an attempt to free it from Lombard control. Having arrived in the vicinity of Benevento, he fought with Romuald who was their leader at the time, but he made little progress because Romuald's father Grimwald, king of the Lombards, offered help. He thereupon turned toward Rome from which the pope traveled many miles to meet him, and accompanied by all the people of Rome he received him with great honor, taking him to St. Peter's and many other churches. After remaining there for some twelve days, the emperor departed and went to Sicily where he greatly harmed the people and was killed in the soldiers' baths. After his death one of his Armenian knights was made emperor whose name was Maxentius. A little later, the emperor's son, Constans [Constantine IV], after already assuming the office, arrived with his fleet and killed Maxentius and all those involved in his father's murder.

At this time, the leader of the Saracens rebuilt the temple in Jerusalem[42] that was said to have been built by Vespasian. In the same period,[43] a Frankish army that was returning from Provence landed near the Lombards, and when they advanced toward them King Grimwald faked defeat and fled, leaving behind pavilions without men that were full of provisions and many other things. Believing the Lombards had fled, the Franks carelessly raced to the pavilions and found great abundance, especially wine, which they loved, and so they drank their fill as was their custom and, overcome by sleep, forgot about the enemy. Whereupon Grimoald with his troops found them dulled with wine and sleep and attacked them, killing nearly everyone.

---

41. Paul the Deacon, *History of the Lombards* V.6–7.

42. The Dome of the Rock, built under Umayyad Caliph Abd al-Malik and completed in A.D. 691.

43. Paul the Deacon, *History of the Lombards* V.5.

Finally Vitalian died and was buried in the church of St. Peter. He ordained four priests and twenty-seven bishops. Among these he ordained for the English city named Canterbury a Greek named Theodore[44] who at the time was a monk and later wrote a book that included all kinds of sins and which is mentioned in the *Decretals*.[45] He also ordained the Roman Martinus as bishop of Ferrara after declaring it a city.[46]

CONSTANTINE IV (EMPEROR 62), A.D. 671

Constantine IV,[47] Emperor Constans' son, ruled the empire for eighteen years. He was a Catholic emperor, faithful and admired by Christians for his temperate living. When ruling he always followed the advice of wise men, and made peace with the Arabs who inhabited Damascus. He rebuilt many churches that at the time of Heraclius, his grandfather, were all in bad shape, and severely persecuted the heretical Manicheans who had been defended by many previous emperors. In an attempt to refute their false belief, he held a world council in Constantinople[48] attended by one hundred fifty bishops. It affirmed the belief that there were two wills in Christ as redeemer and two natures, divine and human.

In his day the Saracens captured Sicily, and after despoiling and robbing it of all its riches, they departed. Also during his rule, after Grimwald, king of the Beneventans, had had his blood drawn, the vein from which the blood was drawn ruptured a few days later because of fatigue. When the bleeding failed to stop, he sought aid from doctors who caused his death. With the excuse that they were stopping the blood flow, they applied poisonous medication to the wound.[49] At that time too, the wife of the king of Persia, named Cesarea, went

44. Theodore of Tarsus, or Canterbury, 602–19 September 690.
45. A book of canon law, first collected officially under Pope Gregory IX in 1230.
46. That is, a *civitas*, from late antiquity the seat of a bishop.
47. Emperor A.D. 668–685.
48. Third council of Constantinople, 680.
49. Paul the Deacon, *History of the Lombards* V.33.

to Constantinople with some faithful Persians and was received with great honor by the emperor and baptized. But when her husband who searched for her everywhere after her secret departure finally found her and insisted that she return, she refused unless he were first baptized. As a result, the king with a large retinue went to Constantinople, where the emperor received him kindly, and was devoutly baptized in Christ's name. Finally, being persecuted by his own men, Constantine fled into his palace from which he was thrown to his death.

ADEODATUS II (POPE 79), A.D. 672[50]

The Roman Adeodatus II[51] who was raised from monk to pope held the pontificate for four years, two months and five days. The Church was without a leader for four months and fifteen days. He was a very kind and easygoing person, welcoming everyone cordially, and never refusing to receive anyone whether famous or not, whether lofty or humble, he sent them away satisfied and grateful. In his day the remains of St. Benedict and of St. Scolastica were taken from Monte Cassino to Ferrara.

DONUS (POPE 80), A.D. 675

The Roman Donus,[52] the son of Martius, held the pontificate for one year, five months and ten days. The Church was without a leader for two months and five days. He decorated and repaired the area facing St. Peter's that is called Paradise.[53] In his day the church of Ravenna, which had become arrogant and had rebelled against the church of Rome, was once again subjected to the Roman see.

AGATHO (POPE 81), A.D. 675

The Sicilian Agatho,[54] the son of Franciscus, held the pontificate for two years, six months and four days. The Church was without a leader

---

50. Text reads "621." We have re-ordered this entry into chronological order.
51. Pope 77, A.D. 672–676.
52. Pope 78, A.D. 676–678.
53. That is, the atrium of the Old St. Peter's.
54. Pope 79, A.D. 678–681.

for one year, seven months and five days. At this time Archbishop Theodore of Ravenna rejoined the Apostolic See after being separated for many years. Also celebrated under Agatho's papacy was the council in Constantinople[55] that included the pope's ambassadors, at which Bishop Macarius of Antioch was condemned and exiled to Rome, together with all his followers. At the hour when they were exiled and cursed, so many spider webs were seen falling onto the people that it was shocking.[56] Theophonius was ordained bishop in Macarius's place. So many praises were heaped on the apostolic ambassadors that Bishop Ioannes of Porto had public masses celebrated in the church of Hagia Sophia in the presence of the emperor and the entire populace.

LEO II (POPE 82), A.D. 681

The Sicilian Leo II,[57] son of Paulus, held the pontificate for one year, nine months and twenty-seven days. The Church was without a leader for twenty-two days. He was made pope by three bishops, Andrea of Ostia, Ioannes of Porto and Placentinus. He decreed that during Mass [the sign of] peace be given to faithful Christians and that the *Agnus Dei* be said. He was a very subtle orator in his preaching about the Divinity, and learned in Greek and Latin. He was a great lover of the poor, favoring them and helping them with every means and care. In his time the church of Ravenna once again recognized the authority of the church of Rome according to the ancient custom.

BENEDICT II (POPE 83), A.D. 683

The Roman Benedictus [Benedict] II[58] held the pontificate for one year, ten months and twenty-two days. The Church was without a leader for three months and fifteen days. He received the emperor's stamp of approval and decreed that, as soon as someone is elected to the Apostolic See, he should be installed as pontiff without delay; this was

55. Third council of Constantinople, 7 November 680–16 September 681.
56. This detail probably comes from the *Liber Pontificalis* 81.12, Davis 1:75, which offers a day-by-day account of the council.
57. Pope 80, A.D. 682–683.
58. Pope 81, A.D. 684–685.

not done previously, but instead the emperor's consent was sought after the election. He ordained twelve bishops.

JOHN V (POPE 84), A.D. 685
Ioannes [John] V,[59] born in Syria, held the pontificate for two years and eight months. The Church was without a leader for two months and eighteen days. He was named and installed pope by the same three bishops who had elected his predecessor, Leo.

CONON (POPE 85), A.D. 688
Conon,[60] born of a Thracian father, was raised in Sicily and held the pontificate for one year. The Church was without a leader for one month and eighteen days. He was made pontiff over two other men since some preferred a certain Petrus and others a certain Theodore. But the wiser priests and clerics, thinking that creating a schism was not a good thing, turned to Conon and proclaimed him pontiff. He led a holy and praiseworthy life. In his day the Catholic emperor, Constantine [IV], died[61] and the priest Bede[62] became well known.

JUSTINIAN II (EMPEROR 63), A.D. 689
The Emperor Iustinianus [Justinian] II[63] succeeded his father as emperor and ruled the empire for ten years. He battled the Saracens in Africa for a long time by land and by sea and freed it from them. A good emperor, liberal and wise, very useful to the empire that was greatly expanded under him, he promulgated many good laws and especially honored ecclesiastical authority. In his day the extremely holy priest Bede became famous, and St. Columbanus came to Vienne in Burgundy. Finally, through the actions of Leo[64] who later took over the

---

59. Pope 82, A.D. 685–686.

60. Pope 83, A.D. 686–687.

61. On 14 September 685.

62. The Venerable Bede, 672/73–26 May 735, a monk at Jarrow and author of the *Ecclesiastical History of the English People*, a major source for the early history of Britain. To Bede is attributed the first use of *Anno Domini* (A.D.) in chronology.

63. Emperor A.D. 685–695, 705–711.

64. Leontius, 695–698.

empire, Justinian was stripped of the empire, which he later recovered, as we will show below.

SERGIUS I (POPE 86), A.D. 689

Sergius [I],[65] born in Syria and the son of Tiberius, held the pontificate for nine years, eight months and twenty-two days. The Church was without a leader for one month and twenty days. Before being elected pope, two others had been formally elected in a contentious way, but later they turned to St. Sergius. In his day Emperor Justinian [II] held a council[66] in his imperial city where some innovations against the faith arose, which he sent to the pope for his approval, but the pope preferred to die rather than approve them. This he did with the help of God so that he overcame the threats and disloyalty surrounding him. He installed Damian as archbishop of Ravenna and also Archbishop Hercoald[67] and Clement[68] from Frisia. He also upheld that at Mass the *"Agnus Dei qui tollis peccata mundi"* be sung three times at the breaking of the [bread of the] body of our Lord. In his day, St. Galganus along with his followers from the region of Gaul were martyred. Finally, Sergius, having lived a praiseworthy life, died and was buried in the church of St. Peter.

LEO, ANTIPOPE (POPE 87), A.D. 699

The Roman Leo, son of the deacon Nicolaus, held the pontificate for two years and eleven months. He is not numbered among the popes because he was elected by the Roman noblemen without the consent of the clergy. In his day died St. Lambert, a bishop, and Africa was once again occupied by the Saracens.

---

65. Pope 84, A.D. 687–701.
66. The Trullan Council of 692.
67. Berhtwald, archbishop of Canterbury, d.731.
68. Willibrord, c.658–7 November 739, first bishop of Utrecht.

THE SEVENTH CENTURY

LEONTIUS II (EMPEROR 64), A.D. 699

Leo[ntius] II[69] took over the empire as a tyrant after having driven out Justinian [II]. He ruled for two years after which Tiberius [Apsimar] drove him from the empire by means of various attacks and exiled him to Kherson where he came to a wretched end while Tiberius seized and occupied the empire. In his day there was a wide rift in the Church because the clergy in Aquileia refused to accept what had been decided at the general council of Constantinople by Justinian I and promulgated by Pope Vigilius. The pope resolved and defused the situation.

*

---

69. Emperor A.D. 695–698.

THE EIGHTH CENTURY

Johannes vi

John VI (Pope 87), A.D. 701

Ioannes [John] VI,[1] born in Greece, held the pontificate for three years, two months and twelve days. The Church was without a leader for one month and eighteen days. When the Romans fought the Greeks,[2] he freed them from the hands of the Greeks because they were losing, and later, again during a similar battle, when the Greeks proved inadequate, he freed them from the hands of the Romans and liberated many other prisoners with prayers and payment from the Lombards. In his day the excellent priest Bede became well known in Anglia [England].

Tiberius III (Emperor 65), A.D. 701

Tiberius [III],[3] also called Apsimar, rebelled against Emperor Leontius and exiled him from the empire, thus taking possession of it for six years. In his day Gisulf, duke of Benevento, sacked Italy,[4] and Pope John [VI] was martyred[5] and buried in the catacomb of St. Sebastian. There was also a council that met in Aquileia[6] against Theodore in which it was affirmed that Blessed Mary be called the Mother of God.

---

1. Pope 85, A.D. 701–705.
2. Perhaps a reference to the wars between the Lombards of Benevento and Byzantine Greeks for control of the area that would become part of the Papal States in the later Middle Ages.
3. Emperor A.D. 698–705.
4. Gisulf I, 689–706. A reference to his depredations in the Campania of Naples and Rome.
5. There is no basis for this martyrdom story.
6. In 698, also known as the synod of Pavia.

THE EIGHTH CENTURY

JOHN VII (POPE 88), A.D. 704
Ioannes [John] VII,[7] born in Greece and the son of Gregory, held the pontificate for two years, seven months and seventeen days. The Church was without a leader for three months. Wise and eloquent, he is said to have built the oratory of St. Mary in the church of St. Peter the Apostle where he was buried before the altar. He ordained nineteen bishops.

SISINNIUS (POPE 89), A.D. 707
Sisinnius,[8] born in Syria, held the pontificate for twenty days. The Church was without a leader for two months. He was a wise pontiff, but he was in bad health because of gluttony and died suddenly. He consecrated a bishop of Corsica. At this time Tiberius [III, Apsimar] was emperor and had earlier stripped Justinian [II] of the empire, exiling him to Kherson. Justinian tried to include Pope Sisinnius in a conspiracy to recover the empire, but failing to win the pope's support he fled to the prince of Turkey to whom he gave his sister as a wife. Aided by the prince, he recovered the empire and captured Leontius who had stripped him of it. In the meantime Tiberius, who had driven Leontius out and retaken the empire, took great vengeance on him and on all his enemies.

JUSTINIAN II (EMPEROR 66), A.D. 707
Justinianus II[9] [Rhinotmetus] was restored as emperor and ruled for six years. He ordered the destruction of Kherson where he had been exiled. Assembling a great naval force, he besieged and stormed it, killing large numbers of people and pardoning only the children and the women.

---

7. Pope 86, A.D. 705–707.
8. Pope 87, 15 January–4 February 708.
9. The Text reads "III."

THE LIVES OF THE POPES AND EMPERORS

CONSTANTINE (POPE 90), A.D. 707

Constantinus [Constantine],[10] born in Syria, held the pontificate for seven years and fifteen days. The Church was without a leader for forty days. He summoned Emperor Justinian [II] to Constantinople where he received him royally by sending his son with Patriarch Cyrus and all the nobility seven miles to meet him. Then the emperor, after being crowned by him, kissed his feet. As a result there was a great festival because of the prince's humility and the pope's glory and exaltation. Later on Sunday, during the celebration of Mass when the pope offered him communion with his own hands, the emperor begged him humbly on his knees to pray for his sins. Later the pope conferred all the privileges of the Roman Church upon him. In this period the heretic Philippicus came to Constantinople and with his son took over the empire upon Emperor Justinian's death.

PHILIPPICUS [BARDANES] (EMPEROR 67), A.D. 713

Emperor Philippicus [Bardanes][11] ruled the empire for seventeen months. With his son he killed Justinian [II] and took over the empire. Since he was a heretic and the Romans refused to obey him, a great war broke out between them. Were it not that the pontiff intervened, a large number would have died. Philippicus sent letters against the faith to Pope Constantine, letters that the pope scorned. Instead, in the portico of St. Peter he had scenes painted depicting the accomplishments of the six universal councils, while the emperor had all the sacred paintings of Christians destroyed. Finally he was driven from the empire by Anastasius [II] and had his eyes plucked out.

ANASTASIUS II (EMPEROR 68), A.D. 715

Emperor Anastasius [II][12] Orthodox ruled for three years after Philippicus had been stripped of the empire. He wrote letters to the pope and sent ambassadors to him, showing that he possessed the

10. Pope 88, A.D. 708–715.
11. Emperor A.D. 711–713.
12. Emperor A.D. 713–715.

THE EIGHTH CENTURY

holy faith. As a result, he was joyfully acclaimed by the pope and the Romans. Later when Theodosius [III] rebelled against him and deposed him as emperor, he became a priest. In his day, Pepin[13] died after having a child named Charles Martel by one of his concubines named Alpaida.

GREGORY II (POPE 91), A.D. 715

The Roman Gregorius [Gregory] II[14] held the pontificate for sixteen years, eight months and twenty-two days. The Church was without a leader for thirty-five days. He ordered that on the fifth day of Lent there must be fasting and Masses sung. He also converted the German people to the Catholic faith of Christ through Bishop Boniface of Mainz,[15] who later was martyred. In his day the ruling king of the Lombards, having been warned by the bishop, returned certain lands that he had taken from St. Peter's. Later when the Lombards had taken certain lands near Cumae and refused to release them at the papal command, the pontiff wrote to Duke Giovanni of Naples and Theodotto, deacon and rector of the army, asking that they have the king return the lands. They then killed more that three hundred Lombards and captured around five hundred whom they took back with them.[16]

At this time also the Saracens attacked Spain, but were defeated by the Franks who fought against them. In addition, [Emperor] Leo [III], who ruled during this period, wanted to have the pope killed, but the Romans who had made peace with the Lombards saved him. The same emperor burned paintings of Christ and of the saints, and sent into exile many who did not obey him.[17] During this time, the Greek St. Egidius became well known as did the Bishop Albinus [Alcuin of York] and the priest Bede.

13. Pepin of Herstal, Frankish mayor of the palace, 680–16 December 714.

14. Pope 89, A.D. 715–731.

15. Wynfrith, d.754.

16. This is a famous event in Neapolitan history and took place in 715. See *Liber Pontificalis* 91.7, Davis 2:7.

17. As part of the first Iconoclast period with the Eastern church, 730–787.

THE LIVES OF THE POPES AND EMPERORS

Theodosius III (Emperor 69), A.D. 718

Theodosius III[18] ruled the empire for one year. He led a rebellion against Anastasius near Nicaea and defeated him, and after deposing him as emperor, he forced him to become a priest. He was a kind and popular emperor, ruling the empire with great integrity. During his reign there was such great flooding of the Tiber in Rome that much of the city was under water.

Leo III, the Isaurian (Emperor 70), A.D. 719

The Isaurian Leo III[19] ruled the empire for twenty-five years. He made his son Constantine [V] a partner in the empire. A persecutor of Christians, he brought from Rome to Constantinople paintings of the saints that he then had burned. In his day for about three years the Saracens besieged Constantinople where a great number died because of hunger and pestilence.[20] Eventually, after their departure, the Saracens were shipwrecked at sea, but they then went on to Sardinia where the relics of St. Augustine were and completely destroyed it. When Liutprand, king of the Lombards, heard this, he sent an ambassador to search for the relics. When they were found, he had them taken with great reverence to Pavia and there laid them to rest in the church of St. Peter the Apostle.[21]

During Leo's reign Charles Martel,[22] father of the young Pepin of the house of France, crossed the Rhine, defeated the Alamanni and subdued many other peoples as far as the Danube, after subjugating Burgundy, Frisia and many other places. Also in that period, the Saracens with large numbers of troops occupied Spain and later sought to capture Aquitania and Provence, but Charles engaged them in battle and overcame them. In that battle[23] great numbers from both

18. Emperor A.D. 715–717.
19. Emperor A.D. 717–741.
20. From 717 to 718.
21. San Pietro in Ciel d'Oro.
22. Lived c.688–22 October 741, ruler of Francia from 718.
23. Of Tours, or Poitiers, October 732.

sides perished. Also at that time Pope Gregory II died after distributing many things to monasteries and to the clergy. He was buried in St. Peter's.

GREGORY III (POPE 92), A.D. 731

Gregorius [Gregory] III,[24] born in Syria, held the pontificate for ten years, eight months and fourteen days. The Church was without a leader for twenty days. He added the following to the Secret of the Mass: *"Ut in conspectum divinae maiestatis tuae, etc."* He also had all of Italy abandon its loyalty to Emperor Leo [III], a heretic and destroyer of images of Christ and of the saints. He also created an archbishopric in Vienne, and then, when the Lombards with their king Liutprand besieged Rome,[25] Gregory sent the confessional key of St. Peter by sea to Charles, Pepin's father, begging him to free the church of Rome from the Lombards who after their departure had besieged Ravenna and then had gone on to destroy Faenza.

ZACHARY (POPE 93), A.D. 741

The Greek Zacharias [Zachary][26] held the pontificate for ten years, four months and fourteen days. The Church was without a leader for eleven days. He translated the *Dialogues* of St. Gregory from Latin into Greek, thereby making them available to the Greeks. He also made peace with Liutprand, king of the Lombards, who went to Rome and offered many gifts to St. Peter's, and at his urging, Zachary consecrated a bishop. Then, upon Liutprand's death,[27] he was succeeded by Ratchis[28] who stopped the siege of Perugia at the pope's request. As a result the pontiff received the city within the dominion of St.

---

24. Pope 90, A.D. 731–741.

25. In 738.

26. Pope 91, A.D. 741–752.

27. In 744.

28. Liutprand was succeeded by his nephew Hildeprand, associated king from 735, but supplanted by Ratchis in 744.

Peter.[29] Not long afterwards, Ratchis renounced the world, together with his wife and children, and was accepted as a monk by Zachary. Ratchis was succeeded by his brother, Aistulf. At this time the body of St. Mary Magdalen was moved by Count Gerard of Burgundy to Zela, although many Italians say that she was buried on an island in the Lake of St. Cristina [Bolsena].

CONSTANTINE V (EMPEROR 71), A.D. 743

Constantinus [Constantine] V,[30] the son of Leo [III], ruled the Roman Empire for twenty-five years. More malicious and cruel than his father in persecuting Christians, he practiced magic arts in which he wasted much time. This caused many to leave the Catholic faith with those arts and with the consent of Anastasius, who had unworthily been made patriarch of Constantinople by his father, Leo, when he had replaced Germanos who would not agree to his error.

At this time Charles [Carloman], Pepin's brother and the eldest son of Charles Martel, king of the Franks, who had succeeded him as ruler, went to Rome, renounced the world upon the advice of Pope Zachary, and became a monk at the monastery of Monte Cassino. After Childeric [III] had assumed the throne, Pepin wrote to the pope asking him who was more worthy of being called king, the one who simply possesses the noble title or the one who has the responsibility of governing. The pope replied that he should be called king who was most useful in governing the kingdom. As a result Childeric was deposed after a short rule and Pepin was declared king of the Franks.[31] At this time also, Aistulf, the king of the Lombards, who was ruling in Pavia, was burdening Italy with taxes, and Duke Anselm, his wife's brother, had withdrawn from the world and become a monk. He built a monastery with his riches near Modena named after the apostles and

---

29. The first expansion of papal territories outside the duchy of Rome and the beginning of the Papal States.

30. Emperor A.D. 741–775.

31. Ruled from 751 to 24 September 768, replacing the Merovingian with the Carolingian dynasty.

later had the remains of Pope St. Silvester transported to Rome. At this time also the venerable priest Bede[32] passed away.

STEPHEN II (POPE 94), A.D. 751

The Roman Stephanus [Stephen] II,[33] son of Constantinus, held the pontificate for five years and twenty-eight days. The Church was without a leader for thirty-five days. Along with him was also elected another Stephen who died within two days. This Stephen was installed [as pope].

At this time Aistulf, king of the Lombards, had begun to devastate Italy, sacking and burning many places. As a result, Pope Stephen, who was unable to make him halt the warfare through ambassadors or to pacify him by any other means, had Pepin, the king of the Franks, write to Aistulf. The pope then personally went to Pepin in Gaul, who received him very cordially, to ask that he liberate Italy. This is why Pepin, after raising an army, went to Italy to do battle with Aistulf and to besiege him in Pavia,[34] which resulted in Aistulf reaching an agreement bringing peace to the Romans with the king and the pope. After Pepin's departure, Aistulf, who was not a Christian, broke the agreement, followed the pope to Rome and besieged him. Thereupon the pope again sent ambassadors to Pepin who found him in Marseilles and informed him of what had happened. So Pepin returned again and besieged Aistulf, leading to new agreements with him to return all that he had taken from the Church. Not long after Aistulf's death,[35] Desiderius was made king of the Lombards.[36]

During Stephen's pontificate, the remains of St. Vitus were taken from Rome to France by Falcondus, abbot of St. Denis. Also at this time he [Desiderius] ordered Emperor Constantine to destroy all

32. On 26 May 735.
33. Pope 92, A.D. 752–757.
34. Pavia was the Lombard capital. These events took place in 754.
35. In 756.
36. King 756–774.

images and conducted much persecution against the Christians. In the last year of his pontificate Stephen transferred the empire from the Romans to the Franks[37] who began to rule under the imperial banners but without any coronation. We shall deal with this later, below, with Charlemagne who was the first to be crowned by Leo III.

Paul I (Pope 95), A.D. 756

The Roman Paulus [Paul I],[38] the son of Constantinus and Pope Stephen's brother, held the pontificate for ten years and one month. The Church was without a leader for one year and one month. He was elected pope together with the archdeacon Theophilas. Nevertheless, by overcoming Theophilas he gained the pontificate. He decreed that Masses be said before tierce and before noon during Lent. He was a humble, forgiving pontiff and loved the poor. At this time, in Scythia the sea froze to such a degree that the ice was more than thirty cubits thick, and there was tremendous frost in many other regions.

Constantine II (Pope 96), A.D. 767

The Roman Constantinus [Constantine] II [antipope], held the pontificate for one year. A layman, he was quickly made a priest and through the force and malice of astute, evil and powerful men under his brother Ottone [Totona], duke of Nepi, he gained the papacy, thus causing great scandal and tribulation to the church of God. One reads that the faithful plucked out his eyes and stripped him of the pontificate.

Stephen III (Pope 97), A.D. 768

Stephanus [Stephen] III,[39] born in Sicily, held the pontificate three years, five months and twenty-seven days. The Church was without a leader for nine days. He summoned a council, gathering in Rome the clerics of Gaul and Italy, which undid everything that Constantine II

---

37. The concept of the *translatio imperii*.
38. Pope 93, A.D. 757–767.
39. Pope 94, A.D. 768–772.

had done except baptism. He also nullified Constantine's decrees. At this time Pepin, the king of the Franks, died in 759.⁴⁰

LEO IV THE KHAZAR (EMPEROR 72), A.D. 769

Leo IV the Khazar,⁴¹ the son of Constantine whom he succeeded, ruled for five years. Being feeble-minded, he demanded a crown depicting a consecrated church, which he wore on his head. Not long afterward he caught a very serious fever and died.

HADRIAN I (POPE 98), A.D. 772

The Roman Hadrianus [Adrian I],⁴² the son of Theodorus from the district around Via Lata, held the pontificate for thirteen years, ten months and seventeen days. The Church was without a leader for twenty days. In his day, because Desiderius, king of the Lombards, sacked places near Rome with fire and arms, the pope wrote to Charlemagne, king of the Franks,⁴³ asking him to come to Italy in order to help the Church, but if he refused, he would be excommunicated. Upset that he was unable to convince Desiderius to return what he had taken from the Church, Charlemagne himself came with an army to Pavia where the Lombards fled from fear.⁴⁴ There he captured King Desiderius with his wife Hidalgari, and after sending them to Gaul, he took over the Lombard kingdom. Later, he went to Rome where he was received with honor by the pope and returned to the Church all that had been taken from it, giving what had been taken in either direction as far as the island of Corsica and the Italian border as well as all that belonged to Ravenna up to Benevento.⁴⁵ But many write that Charlemagne, after leaving some of his army in Pavia, went

40. 24 September 768.
41. Emperor A.D. 775–780.
42. Pope 95, A.D. 772–795.
43. From 768 to 28 January 814.
44. In 774.
45. The text reads "Buonconvento," in Tuscany, but Benevento was then a major Lombard duchy and a point of contention in the developing Papal States. This reading appears several times throughout the *Lives*.

to Rome before he attacked the city and captured Desiderius. We will deal with this below.

The pope then summoned a council in Rome of one hundred fifty-four bishops that gave Charlemagne the power and authority to elect a pope, to govern the Apostolic See, and to select the archbishops for the provinces under his jurisdiction. He also convened the seventh council of Constantinople consisting of three hundred bishops.

This pontiff also rebuilt the church of Sant'Anastasio ad Aquas Salvias,[46] which had burned down. In addition, he rebuilt the city walls of Rome and built beautiful towers as well as the great metal doors of St. Peter's. At this time the holy abbot Egidius became famous to whom Charlemagne confessed his sins. Likewise famous at this time were two very close friends, Amelius and Amicus, who in the battle with the Lombards perished near Mortara.[47] In addition, in 784 the imperial emblems were conferred upon Charlemagne, and he assumed the office of emperor, even though he had not yet been crowned.

Constantine VI (Emperor 73), A.D. 774

Constantinus [Constantine VI],[48] son of Leo [III], ruled for ten years with his mother, Empress Irene [Sarantapechaina].[49] Later he came to scorn his mother and dismissed her from the empire. He ruled for only seven years because she, urged on by female anger, took over the empire, and after having him blinded, she ruled with his son Leo for three years. At this time, the sun was so darkened that it did not appear for several days, and many said that this happened because the mother had blinded the son. As a result, Irene also had her grandsons blinded in order to rule with greater security.

---

46. On the Via Ostiense near Tre Fontane.
47. In Lombardy. The church of San Lorenzo there contains portraits of the two saints. They are also pictured in Hartmann Schedel, *The Nuremberg Chronicle* (Nuremberg: Anton Koberger, 1493), fol. CLXIV verso, as children of Pepin II, of Herstal, king of France.
48. Emperor A.D. 776–797.
49. Regent A.D. 780–797, empress 797–802.

THE EIGHTH CENTURY

TAURITIUS (EMPEROR 74), A.D. 794

Tauritius,[50] the son of Queen Irene, ruled the empire of Constantinople for two years and was succeeded by Nicephorus [I].

LEO III (POPE 99), A.D. 796

The Roman Leo III[51] held the pontificate for twenty years, five months and sixteen days. The Church was without a leader for ten days. He was arrested in front of the monastery of San Silvestro built by Pope Paul [I] and had his eyes and tongue ripped out, but not long afterward (as church writers report) through the grace of God, he recovered his sight and his speech.[52] He then left Rome and went to Gaul to Charlemagne who cordially received him and offered him many of his bishops and dukes to accompany him back to Rome in order to restore him to the Apostolic See as he deserved. A short time later Charlemagne followed him to Rome, wreaking vengeance on the pope's enemies and clearing him of the charges that had been leveled against him. Then on Christmas Day in 902 [800] A.D., Leo crowned Charlemagne with the imperial crown, in whose honor were sung the following lauds, "May God grant the most pious and peace-loving Charles, the crowned emperor, a long life and victory." Whereupon Charlemagne made his son Charles [the Younger] king of the Franks[53] and offered many beautiful gifts to St. Peter's. He also renewed and increased all the privileges of the Roman Church.

This pontiff built a portico to St. Peter's and once again repaired the city walls to guard against Saracen attacks; this is why part of the city is called Leonine.[54] He also decreed that the litanies discovered earlier by Bishop Marineto of Vienne be chanted three days before the

---

50. This is probably Staurakios, son of Nicephorus and emperor 26 July–2 October, 811.

51. Pope 96, A.D. 795–816.

52. Recounted in the *Liber Pontificalis* 98.11–14, Davis 2:184–87.

53. c.772–4 December 811.

54. The historic Leonine Walls around the Vatican were built by Leo IV after the Saracen sack of St. Peter's in 846.

Ascension of the Lord, and he declared that on Mondays the pope and other clerics process with songs and hymns from the church of Sta. Maria ad Presepe[55] to the church of San Salvatore, which is called Constantinian,[56] on Tuesdays from the church of Sta. Sabina to the church of San Paolo [fuori le Mura], and on Wednesdays from the church of [Sta. Croce in] Gerusalemme to the church of San Lorenzo fuori le Mura.[57]

NICEPHORUS I (EMPEROR 75), A.D. 796

Nicephorus [I],[58] who succeeded Tauritius, ruled the empire in Constantinople for five years. During the time of his reign, the Eastern Empire nearly collapsed. He was a very greedy emperor and hurt many because of it. Michael succeeded him as emperor.

*

---

55. Sta. Maria Maggiore.
56. The "Constantinian basilica" usually refers to St. Peter's.
57. This mention of the Roman processionals is for the Rogation days.
58. Emperor A.D. 802–811.

THE NINTH CENTURY

CHARLES, KING OF THE FRANKS (CHARLEMAGNE) (EMPEROR 76), A.D. 802

Charles, king of the Franks,[1] who was called Great [Charlemagne] because of his outstanding virtues, was crowned with the imperial crown by Pope Leo [III], with the unanimous approval of the Senate and the people.[2] He ruled the Western Empire of Rome for thirteen years. But since we have above dealt with his father Pepin and his outstanding achievements, we will deal with Charlemagne at greater length, so that readers might better grasp the outstanding deeds of his life.

After Pepin had driven out Childeric [III], king of the Franks, with the approval of the Roman pontiff and the Franks, he ruled for fifteen years. Upon his death, his kingdom was equally divided between two sons who succeeded him, Charlemagne and Carloman. Not long after Carloman's death, the kingdom reverted to Charlemagne who first battled the Aquitanians. Aquitania is partly in Gaul and, according to ancient opinion, extends from the Garonne River to the Pyrenees and to that part of the ocean that faces toward Spain between the sunset and the north. Pepin had first conquered the Aquitanians and their duke Vaisardo [Waifar], but after his death a powerful man named Unuldo [Hunoldus] caused them to rebel.

---

1. Most of the following account is taken, in close order of narration, from Einhard's *Life of Charlemagne*.
2. On Christmas Day, 800.

Whereupon Charlemagne attacked and defeated him and, when he fled to Loup who ruled over Gascony, pursued him there. When the army stopped some distance away, he sent ambassadors to determine whether Loup would surrender one or the other to him. Upon reaching an agreement, Charlemagne returned to his kingdom.

Later on, when ambassadors were sent to him by Pope Adrian whom Desiderius, king of the Lombards, had angered, Charlemagne was unable through the ambassadors to calm down Desiderius concerning the pope, so he crossed the Alps after calling up an army and set up camp near Turin. This was the place where it is said that the Carthaginian Hannibal stopped after crossing the Alps. And there, learning that King Desiderius had encamped near Vercelli, he went to that territory where he engaged him in battle. Since the Frankish army was superior in bravery and skill, even though smaller in number, the Lombards were defeated. Whereupon Desiderius, with those who remained, went to Pavia, the capital city of his kingdom. Charlemagne followed him and, unable to capture the city, besieged it; and leaving part of his army there, he turned with his other troops against those living across the Po. When many of their cities learned of his reputation, they surrendered to him, and many voluntarily joined him, among whom were his brother Carloman's sons, who after their father's death, following their mother's daring advice, had fled to King Desiderius. Charlemagne received them kindly and accepted them as his own sons for the future. Wishing furthermore to go and visit the pope and to see the very famous church of St. Peter (as many do), he went to Rome and there was cordially received by Pope Adrian. Some days later, he left and returned to Pavia where the Lombards surrendered after a siege of six months.[3] He then captured King Desiderius with his wife and children and sent them to Gaul. At this time, because the seat of the Roman Empire was moved to Constantinople, Italy began to breathe again after having been occupied by barbarians, first by the Goths, then

---

3. These events took place in 773/774.

at different times by the Huns, the Vandals, the Heruli and finally by the Lombards.

Charlemagne defeated all the cities that had rebelled against the pope and returned to the Apostolic See the towns of Benevento[4] and Spoleto. For this action the pope after consultation rewarded him with many great privileges. Once the situation was calm in Italy, he returned to Gaul to the war with Saxony that he had begun two years before going to Italy, which in the meantime was waged carefully through his subordinates. The people of Saxony were the most bellicose in Germany, wherefore Charlemagne fought with them first at Onegiomonte [Osneng Hill], called Theomille [Theotmel] by the inhabitants. He fought them a second time near the Hasa River where the Saxons surrendered to him after a complete defeat.[5] He ordered them to accept the Christian faith after abandoning their false gods. Then he had ten thousand men along with their women and children go to Gaul.

Charlemagne waged war almost exclusively for this reason — so that his power would increase the Christian religion and faith. When the barbarians who were powerful enemies of the Christians oppressed Spain, Charlemagne turned back, quickly crossed the Pyrenees in order to free it and arrived at the enemy lines where many cities voluntarily surrendered. When Augusta[6] and Pamplona,[7] perhaps the wealthiest of the cities, refused to surrender, they were taken by force and sacked: one was leveled, the other had its walls destroyed. This led to other cities surrendering to him. And thus nearly all of Spain fell under Frankish rule, and Charlemagne had them accept our faith and our laws.

After returning with his army to Gaul through the Pyrenees he accidentally fell into an ambush by the Gascons and suffered a great rout

4. The text reads "Buonconvento," which is in the province of Siena.
5. Their king Widukind finally submitted in 785.
6. This is most likely Caesaraugusta or modern Zaragoza.
7. First in 778, finally by 806.

at the enemy's hands, losing many worthy men among whom were Anselm and Eggihard, outstanding leaders in battle. Many still say that Roland, a man of outstanding strength and a son of Charlemagne's sister, died there. This is the same Roland whose strength is renowned throughout the world.[8] But the people of Gascony did not long rejoice over this rout because a short time later Charlemagne defeated them and imposed on them the appropriate punishments for their deceitful treachery. At this time he also defeated the Bretons, and later Arichis, duke of Benevento[9] who was planning a war against the pope. Once again Charlemagne went with his army into Italy and, stopping in Capua, he threatened Arichis and the troops from Benevento[10] who then sent their sons as hostages and swore to him that they would remain faithful to the Church.

While this was occurring in Italy, Charlemagne had taken control of Tassilo, duke of Bavaria, who had been moved by the urgings of his wife, the daughter of King Desiderius of the Lombards, whom Charlemagne had defeated and was holding prisoner. She then joined the men who inhabited the western part of Bavaria but, having turned back, was secretly preparing to wage war. When Charlemagne learned of this, he went with his army to the Bavarian border and from his camp near the river Lech, which divides the Bavarians from the Germans, sent ambassadors to Tassilo suggesting that he surrender. Frightened by this, Tassilo deliberated as to whether to obey him and then sent to him many hostages, including his son Theodo.

At this time the Obrotrites,[11] considered as allied by the Franks, were being harassed by the Wiltzes[12] and turned to Charlemagne for

8. The Basque attack on Charlemagne's rear guard at the pass of Roncesvalles is the origin of the story told in *The Song of Roland*.

9. The text reads "Buonconvento." Arichis II was Lombard duke of Benevento 758–26 August 787.

10. The text reads "Bonconvento."

11. A confederation of West Slavic peoples on the Baltic. This account is taken from Einhard's *Life of Charlemagne* 12.

12. A Slavic people.

THE NINTH CENTURY

help. They inhabit the German confines near a gulf of the [Baltic] sea that extends about one hundred miles from west to east, around which the Normans and other barbaric tribes lived.[13] For that reason, Charlemagne went there with his army and freed his allies from the enemy incursions. After this was finished, he considered waging war against the Huns who had helped his enemies. The Huns were once from Scythia and lived in the Maeotine Marshes. Later on, after gathering a large number of men, they went to Pannonia and settled there. Against them, therefore, Charlemagne fought and after eight years overcame them, but not without great losses on both sides since two outstanding leaders of the Franks, Henic [Eric] and Gerold, were killed.

Later Charlemagne returned to Gaul with many valuable spoils taken from the enemy, and upon hearing that Adelchis, son of King Desiderius of the Lombards, was trying to retake the paternal kingdom (he had fled to Greece before the storming of Pavia), he went to confront him and defeated him. He then defeated the Bohemians and subsequently the Northmen with their king Gudfred,[14] who had subjugated the Obrotrites. With their ships, they had been preying upon the shores of Germany and Gaul, threatening to take Frisia and Saxony and then to advance rapidly into Aachen[15] where King Charlemagne resided. Charlemagne did not have much trouble with that war because in a short time he killed their king, Gudfred, and they surrendered.

In the meantime, after the Romans had driven Pope Leo [III] from the city and Charlemagne learned of it, he quickly organized an army and went to Italy where, straightening out the disagreements and punishing the guilty, he reinstated the pontiff in the city with great pomp. Because of this he was called Augustus for his merits and his good works for the Christian faith with the overwhelming consent of the

---

13. That is the Baltic litoral, from where the Vikings came. This war took place in 789.
14. Danish Viking king c.804–810.
15. Or Aix-la-Chapelle. The text reads "Aquisgranna."

people and the Senate, which bestowed upon him the imperial title and dignity.[16] At this time, the grandeur of the great empire which it had lost for more than three hundred years, returned to the West because of Charlemagne's outstanding virtue since, after Constantine left Rome to live in the East, it was customary for the empire to be so divided that the empire in Constantinople was called the Eastern Empire and the other the Western Empire. Earlier, after the barbarians had ruined Italy, from the time of Odoacer, the barbarian king who defeated Augustulus, emperor in the West (as we saw above in the life of Emperor Zeno), the Western Empire had ceased to exist down to the time of Charlemagne. Then Charlemagne, king of the Franks and emperor of the Romans, in returning to Gaul and passing through Florence, which the Goths had nearly completely ruined, enclosed the city with new walls and many beautiful decorations.

It is also written that, since barbarians had occupied Jerusalem causing great damage, Charlemagne was moved by Emperor Constantine's pleas and went with his army to liberate it, returning it to the Christians. Later, he went to Constantinople and was received with great joy by Emperor Constantine who wished to present him with many gifts, but he scorned all such things and accepted only sacred gifts, such as a part of Christ's Crown of Thorns, a nail from the Passion and a part of the Cross, as well as the Holy Shroud. He then left to Rome a shift of the Virgin Mary and an arm of St. Simeon. If this is all true,[17] it must have happened some time before Pope Leo [III] came to return them. All these wars, fought during the forty-seven years in which he ruled, caused the kingdom to grow immensely. But let this be enough about his wars.

Of large stature with a wide chest and shoulders, Charlemagne had large and lively eyes, a rather large nose and a long beard, and on feast days he wore a robe interwoven with gold and carried a sword

16. On Christmas Day, 800.

17. These details do not appear in Einhard's *Life* but in the *Le Pèlerinage de Charlemagne*, a *chanson de geste* composed c.1140. The author of the *Lives* here casts doubt on these legendary exploits.

THE NINTH CENTURY

decorated with various gems.[18] He was very respectful toward his father, Pepin, before he died, as well as toward his mother, Bertrada, who long outlived Pepin and treated Charlemagne with kindness. Above all else, he cultivated the faith of Christ, encouraging bishops to destroy temples to the gods, and he himself built in Aachen, the seat of the empire, a church to St. Mary, which he had adorned with striking marble columns and much gold and silver.[19] He also built other structures among which was a bridge on the Rhine near Mainz[20] where the river's width exceeded five hundred feet, as well as many other buildings and churches in various places and in different cities. Such splendor did not lack the ornamentation of Latin and Greek lettering since he had had as his teacher Albinus who was also known as Alcuin,[21] a very learned man and a great philosopher, whose works it is said inspired Charlemagne to found the University of Paris.

Charlemagne had by his wife Hildelgarde, who was born near Seur of noble lineage, three sons, Charles [the Younger], Pepin[22], and Louis, and just as many daughters, Hrotrud, Bertrada, and Gisila. But in the eighth year of his reign Pepin, after conquering Florence, died in Milan where his son Bernhard replaced him. And in the ninth year, [his son] Charles died, leaving Louis.[23] In the eleventh year of his reign, with the general consent of the people, he conferred the title of Augustus upon Louis and made him a partner in the empire. Not much later, having gone hunting as was his custom, Charlemagne returned home with a slight fever, and having developed a pain in his side, died on 14 January at the age of seventy-two in the year 815. His body was placed in the church in Aachen[24] built by him and was

18. From Einhard, *Life* 22–23.
19. This is the famous cathedral of Aachen.
20. See Einhard, *Life* 17.
21. Alcuin of York, c.735–19 May 804. Northumbrian scholar, ecclesiastic, poet and Carolingian court official. See Einhard, *Life* 25.
22. King of the Lombards, April 770/3–8 July 810.
23. Louis I, the Pious, b.778, emperor 814–840.
24. The text reads "Aquisgranni"

buried with full honors. On his monument was placed a golden arch that included his portrait with the epitaph: "Here lies the body of Charlemagne, the most Christian Roman Emperor."[25]

Three years before his death he wrote a will,[26] dividing his gold and silver vases as well as his other beautiful treasures into three parts. He left two parts to twenty-one cities under his rule, called metropolitan by the Greeks, and to their bishops to help repair churches and aid the poor. The third part he left to his sons, nephews and servants. There were among his treasures three silver tables and one large one of gold. The one with the image of Constantinople he sent to St. Peter's in Rome; the second on which Rome was sculpted he donated to the church in Ravenna; and the third he left to his children together with the gold one. This is what we have learned about Charlemagne, although we have gone beyond what we promised. Nevertheless, considering the size of the benefices that he increasingly donated to our religion, we hope that we may be excused for our unusual length that is much less than he deserved.

MICHAEL I RHANGABE (EMPEROR 77), A.D. 811[27]

Emperor Michael [I Rhangabe][28] ruled the empire in Constantinople for one year. He was a good Catholic, likeable and popular, and tried to appease those harmed by Nicephorus's greed. He very seriously sought to destroy enemies of the Christian religion. He was succeeded by Leo. But let us now pass on to Charlemagne,[29] who at this time was crowned by Pope Leo, after having administered for many years previously the Roman Empire.

LOUIS I (EMPEROR 78), A.D. 815

Ludovico [Louis],[30] Charlemagne's son, succeeded his father and ruled for twenty-five years. He was a good emperor and imitated his

25. Einhard, *Life* 31.

26. Einhard, *Life* 33.

27. Text reads "801." He would actually have been emperor 76 in the original sequence.

28. Emperor A.D. 811–813.

29. This sentence is out of sequence. Charlemagne was discussed above, pp. 131–38.

30. See n. 20 above.

THE NINTH CENTURY

father's virtues. He had three sons, namely Lothair [I], Pepin and Lewis: he gave Lothair, the first-born, the title of Augustus and entrusted the rule of Italy to him; he made Pepin king of Aquitania, and Lewis, the third-born, king and prince of Germany and Bavaria. Later Louis attacked Brittany[31] and there defeated the enemy with fire and sword, devastating the country. Louis's sons were tempted by many nobles through whose malice, according to accounts, he was stripped of most of the empire after the people abandoned him. But not much later, the people and his sons recognized their serious error, sought his pardon and returned him to the imperial throne with great honor.

One also finds that the emperor in Constantinople sent him the books of St. Dionysius *On the Angelic Hierarchies*.[32] In his day the bones of the martyr St. Vitus were transferred from Paris to a monastery in Saxony, which greatly upset the Franks. During his rule one also reads that the twelve-year old girl, having received the body of Christ from the priest at Easter, took no food or drink, except for bread and water for six months; she then lived for a period of three years without eating.[33] At this time too, before the summer solstice, during a strong storm in Gaul, there fell from the sky a block of ice measuring six feet wide, fifteen feet long and two feet in height. In Louis' day, the Normans[34] fought with cruelty against the Franks.

STEPHEN IV (POPE 100), A.D. 816

The Roman Stephanus [Stephen] IV,[35] son of Iulius, held the pontificate for eight months. The Church was without a leader for two months. He went to Gaul where he was graciously received by Emperor Louis[36] from whom he obtained what he wanted, i.e., he was able to

---

31. In 818.
32. Pseudo-Dionysius the Areopagite, author of *The Celestial Hierarchy*, among other works.
33. This story also appears in the ninth-century Royal Frankish Annals *(Annales regni francorum)*, sub anno 825.
34. That is, the Vikings, from whom the Normans of Normandy descended.
35. Pope 97, A.D. 816–817.
36. At Rheims in October 816.

bring back to Rome with him many of those who had offended Pope Leo [III] and had been in exile there. After he died, he was buried in the church of St. Peter with honor. In his day, Bishop Theophilus of Orléans found this verse on Palm Sunday: *"Gloria, laus, et honor tibi fit rex Christe, etc."*[37]

PASCHAL I (POPE 101), A.D. 817

The Roman Paschalis [Paschal I][38] held the pontificate for seven years, ten months and seventeen days. The Church was without a leader for four days. When the Saxon borgo was on fire, he fought the flames and suddenly the fire miraculously subsided, something which he did once again.[39] Also, when the virgin Cecilia appeared to him[40] dressed in golden garments with her spouse Valerianus and Tiburtius, along with the pontiffs Urban and Lucius, he rendered thanks to her for allowing him to build in the city a church in their honor.[41] She later revealed to him where these saints' remains were located, which were originally thought to have been taken by Aistulf[42]; he found and buried them with the greatest reverence in this church. He also built an altar in front of St. Peter's tomb near the bronze doors where St. Sixtus had formerly been laid to rest. He also redid the hospital of San Pellegrino.[43]

EUGENIUS II (POPE 102), A.D. 824

The Roman Eugenius [Eugene] II[44] held the pontificate for four years. The Church was without a leader for three days. He redid and restored the church of Sta. Sabina where he had been a priest, and also freed

---

37. All glory, laud and honor, / To thee, Redeemer, King.

38. Pope 98, A.D. 817–824.

39. See the *Liber Pontificalis* 100.7, Davis 3:8–9. This is the English borgo or the Schola Saxonum on the banks of the Tiber near the Vatican.

40. For a more detailed version of the story see *Liber Pontificalis* 100.15–17, Davis 3:15–18.

41. This story is related in the Roman Breviary.

42. Duke of Friuli c.744, king of Lombards c.749, duke of Spoleto c.751.

43. Founded by Leo III in 800, originally San Pellegrino in Naumachia, at Castel Sant'Angelo.

44. Pope 99, A.D. 824–827.

THE NINTH CENTURY

many Romans who were prisoners in Gaul. Finally he was martyred by the laity and buried in the Vatican [cemetery].

VALENTINUS (POPE 103), A.D. 828
The Roman Valentinus [Valentine][45] held the pontificate for sixty days. The Church was without a leader for three days.

GREGORY IV (POPE 104[46]), A.D. 828
The Roman Gregorius [Gregory] IV[47] held the pontificate for sixteen years. The Church was without a leader for fifteen days. He renovated the city of Ostia and named it after himself, Gregoriopolis.[48] He decreed that the feast of All Saints be held on November 1st and that on the following day be celebrated the feast of All Souls. In addition, he transferred St. Gregory's remains and ordered monks to participate in the service.

During this period, because of the great discord among powerful and pernicious Christians, the sultan in Babylon was sent for; he then went to Italy with a multitude of Saracens, laid siege to Rome and captured it. After entering the city and despoiling St. Peter's, he made it a stable for his horses,[49] and furthermore sacked all of Tuscany, Apulia and Sicily. But not much later, Count Guido and Emperor Louis with a large Frankish force went against the sultan, drove out the Saracens with much bloodshed and freed Italy. Also at this time King Bernhard of Italy, the son of Pepin who was Charlemagne's son,[50] organized a conspiracy against Emperor Louis in which he was blinded and killed. And Barbanus, a doctor and outstanding poet, became abbot at the monastery of Fondi.

---

45. Pope 100, August–September 827.
46. Text reads "103."
47. Pope 101, 827–844.
48. This was a fortress at Ostia built against Saracen raids.
49. This took place in August 846, during the pontificate of Sergius II.
50. Louis I's nephew, king of the Lombards 810–818.

LOTHAIR (EMPEROR 79), A.D. 840

Lotteri [Lothair],[51] Emperor Louis's son, ruled for fifteen years. He was crowned by Pope Sergius [II] who then made his son, Louis, king of the Lombards. But his brothers, Charles [the Bald] and Lewis [the German], were unable to accept patiently that Lothair alone would rule the empire and, organizing an army, they waged a great war against him with numerous casualties on both sides. And when the forces on both sides became weakened they agreed on the following conditions for peace[52]: Louis would gain control of Germany, Charles France, and Lothair Italy and the part of France that was called Lotharingia [Lorraine] after him and over which he ruled most peacefully. But before they arrived at an accord, the news of their discord reached the Saracens in Africa, and many other nations rose up to impede their rule, which they successfully defended.

In his day the Normans and Saxons entered Gaul from opposite directions, destroyed it largely with fire and sword and sacked it. One also reads that in the ninth year of Lothair's reign the body of St. Helena, Constantine's mother, who had been buried in Rome, was transferred to Gaul. Finally Lothair left the empire to his sons and renounced the active life to become a monk.[53]

SERGIUS II (POPE 105), A.D. 844

The Roman Sergius II[54] held the pontificate for three years. The Church was without a leader for two months and fifteen days. Having earlier been called "Hogs' Mouth," his name was changed and thenceforth the custom of all popes taking an appropriate name continued. The deacon Ioannes was named pope with him but then repudiated, and Sergius was elected pope. Emperor Lothair sent his son Louis to the pope in the company of many bishops and abbots with the request that he confirm him as the king of the Lombards.

51. Emperor A.D. 817–855.
52. The treaty of Verdun, in August 843.
53. He entered the monastery at Prüm on 23 September 855.
54. Pope 102, A.D. 844–847.

THE NINTH CENTURY

LEO IV (POPE 106), A.D. 847

The Roman Leo IV[55] held the pontificate for eight years, three months and six days. The Church was without a leader for six days. He was named pope without the emperor's knowledge. He was very learned in scripture, attending assiduously to his preaching and performing many miracles in everyone's presence. An example of this happened when a basilisk near the church of Sta. Lucia was killing many people with his breath, and he caused its death with the sign of the Cross after directing an efficacious prayer to God.[56] Another example occurred when he extinguished a fire with the sign of the Cross when a town of the Saxons and the Lombards was aflame.[57] He decreed that the week of the martyrs be declared a feast.

In his day as the Saracens were leaving Rome, which they had largely destroyed, having burned St. Peter's along with other beautiful churches, Leo pursued them as far as Ostia,[58] and when they then fled on the high seas, they were shipwrecked, causing many of their spoils to be washed ashore. Once back in Rome, he rebuilt all the churches and places that had been destroyed and burned by the Saracens,[59] and in addition composed this sermon: *"Deus cuius dextera beatum Petrum etc."*[60] It was to this pope also that the king of England offered tribute by giving a certain sum of money for each house, something that can be seen to this day.[61]

LOUIS II, BALBA (EMPEROR 80), A.D. 855

Louis [II][62] Balba, Lothair's son who succeeded his father, ruled for twenty-one years. In his day when the Normans sacked Aquitania they

---

55. Pope 103, A.D. 847–855.

56. See *Liber Pontificalis* 105.18, Davis 3:117–18.

57. See *Liber Pontificalis* 105.20, Davis 3:119.

58. The battle of Ostia, in 849. See *Liber Pontificalis* 105.48–54, Davis 3:132–34.

59. The origins of the Leonine City and walls around the Vatican, built 848–852. See *Liber Pontificalis* 105.55–72, Davis 3:134–42.

60. See *Liber Pontificalis* 105.73, Davis 3:142.

61. Origins of Peter's Pence.

62. Emperor A.D. 844–875.

killed Duke Arnulf with all his followers, and then went to England, sacking it in the same way and killing Edmund,[63] their very Christian king. In his day the remains of Pope St. Urban and the Tiburtine martyrs[64] were transferred to the church of San Germano. Also during his reign John Scotus,[65] very learned as a scholar of sacred scripture, became famous. At Emperor Louis's request he translated from Greek into Latin the books of St. Dionysius *On the Angelic Hierarchies*.

JOHN OF ENGLAND [ANTI-POPE, POPE JOAN], A.D. 855
Ioannes [John] of England [anti-pope] occupied the pontificate for two years, five months and four days. The Church was without a leader for one month. He is not placed in the listing of popes since, according to what one reads, he was a woman. During his teenage years a lover took him to Athens dressed as a boy, and there he studied various sciences and became very learned. Later, upon coming to Rome, he became so famous that everyone considered him outstanding and conferred upon him the supreme honor of the papacy. Subsequently the truth was discovered.[66]

In his day, in the city of Brescia, it miraculously rained blood[67] for three days and three nights, while in Gaul there appeared incredible locusts with six wings, six feet and very hard teeth that amazingly were able to fly through the air. Then they all drowned in the British sea and their remains were washed ashore by the waves so that they infected the air, causing the deaths of many people.

63. Edmund, king of East Anglia, killed by the Vikings on 20 November 869.

64. Symphorosa and her seven sons, martyred in Tivoli c.138. Their relics were moved to the church of Sant'Angelo in Pescheria in 752.

65. Johannes Scotus Eriugena, c.815–c.877, translated and wrote commentary on the work of pseudo-Dionysius the Areopagite, including the *Celestial Hierarchies*.

66. This is the legend of Pope Joan, also described in the *Nuremberg Chronicle*, fol. CLXIX verso as "John of England." See Alain Boureau, *The Myth of Pope Joan* (Chicago: University of Chicago Press, 2001).

67. Instances of "blood rain" (rain tinged red by suspended dust) have been recorded by Homer, Plutarch, Livy and Pliny. This incident is also recorded in Brescia during the reign of Louis II in the *Nuremberg Chronicle*, fol. CLXXI recto.

THE NINTH CENTURY

BENEDICT III (POPE 107), A.D. 857
The Roman Benedictus [Benedict] III[68] occupied the pontificate for two years and five months. The Church was without a leader for sixteen days. Among his good works was the repair of the portico leading to San Paolo [fuori le Mura] as well as the one that goes to San Lorenzo [fuori le Mura]. In his day Charles, Emperor Louis's son, was overcome by a demon in the presence of all; he later confessed that it had happened because he had conspired against his father.[69]

NICHOLAS I (POPE[70] 108), A.D. 859
The Roman Nicholaus [Nicholas I][71] occupied the pontificate eight years, two months and twenty days. He was a very holy pope and after the great Pope Gregory [I] the most outstanding occupant of the Apostolic See. He approved the anointing of Emperor Louis and blessed him in his homily. In his day St. Cyril[72] flourished who was considered like an apostle. He brought the remains of St. Clement from Kherson to Rome where the pope and people of Rome solemnly put him to rest in the church of San Clemente. Also at this time one reads that in Cologne lightning struck the church of St. Peter, destroying most of it and killing many people. Finally, having lived a virtuous life Nicholas died and was buried in the church of St. Peter.

ADRIAN II (POPE 109), A.D. 868
The Roman Adrianus [Adrian] II[73] occupied the pontificate for five years and two days. He was a good and a most virtuous pontiff. In his day the king of France[74] left secular life and entered religious life

---

68. Pope 104, A.D. 855–858.
69. This is the "Vision of Charles the Fat," the son of Lewis the German. See Eileen Gardiner, trans and ed., *Visions of Heaven and Hell before Dante* (New York: Italica Press, 1989), 129–33.
70. Text reads "Emperor."
71. Pope 105, A.D. 858–867.
72. Of Cyril and Methodius, c.827–14 February 869.
73. Pope 106, A.D. 867–872.
74. This is probably Carloman (848–c.877), son of Charles the Bald.

as a monk. His son assumed the throne, but later failed to follow the Christian religion, preferring the beliefs of the Gentiles. His father abandoned the monk's habit, dug out his son's eyes and deprived him of the kingdom. Later he decided to give it to his other son, and returned to the life of a monk.

JOHN VIII (POPE 110), A.D 872

Ioannes [John] VIII[75] occupied the pontificate for eleven years and two days. In his day, while on their rampage through Italy, the Saracens destroyed and burned the monastery of St. Benedict on Monte Cassino,[76] but shortly thereafter they were driven from Italy. Emperor Charles II sent many gifts to Rome for the pope and repaired many damaged churches using his own wealth. At this time John, a deacon in the Roman church, who had first written a life of Gregory, became famous,[77] and his remains together with an arm of St. Leo were taken to Sermona.

CHARLES II, THE BALD (EMPEROR 81), A.D. 872

Emperor Charles II,[78] called the Bald, son of Louis I and Lothair's brother, ruled for five years. First he went to Rome and, having reconciled with Pope John [VIII] in order to gain backing from the Romans, was made emperor. Immediately he declared war against Lewis [II] and took over the empire. He built many monasteries in Gaul and Italy and restored many others; among these he built the monastery of St. Cornelius in Gaul, around which he started building ramparts like those in Constantinople, and named it Carlopoli. But then he wished to return from France to Italy, but was killed by a Jew named Zedekiah, named like the poison.[79]

---

75. Pope 107, A.D. 872–882. John VIII (872–882), Marinus (882–884) and Hadrian III (884–885) have no entries in the *Liber Pontificalis*. See Davis 3:296.

76. In 883.

77. John the Deacon, d. before 882.

78. Emperor A.D. 840–877.

79. He died while crossing the Alps at Mont Cenis, on 6 October 877. He body was said to have immediately started to decompose. Zedekiah was his physician. This story is likely from Flavius Josephus' *Sequel to the History of the Jews* 9.

THE NINTH CENTURY

CHARLES III, THE FAT (EMPEROR 82[80]), A.D. 881

Charles [III], called the Simple [Fat],[81] the son of Charles the Bald, was crowned by Pope John VIII and ruled for twelve years. He governed Gaul and Germany with great peace and tranquillity. At this time the Danes and the Normans went with their King Rollo[82] into the region today called Normandy, sacking and destroying many cities. The people then sent for help to Emperor Charles who, having mustered a great army, confronted them and fought a fierce battle. But not much later they reached an accord[83] and declared peace as follows: that they be allowed to inhabit the area called Normandy, and furthermore that Emperor Charles give one of his daughters as wife to the king. Thus they become friends, and the king was baptized not long after, becoming Christian with the name of Robert. He was the first Norman prince to acquire Apulia.[84] Also at this time the Hungarians went from Scythia to Pannonia and occupied it after they drove out the Amerii, Attila's descendants.

MARINUS (POPE 111), A.D. 883

Marinus I[85] held the pontificate for seventeen months. The Church was without a leader for two days.

ADRIAN III (POPE 112), A.D. 884[86]

The Roman Hadrianus IV [Adrian III][87] held the pontificate for fourteen months. He ruled that the emperor must not interfere in a pope's election. In his day, the Romans were overcome and defeated

---

80. Text reads "72."
81. Emperor A.D. 881–888.
82. c.846–c.932.
83. In the treaty of Saint-Clair-sur-Epte of 911.
84. There is confusion here as to the later Normans of the Guiscard family.
85. Pope 108, A.D. 882–884.
86. Text reads "984."
87. Pope 109, A.D. 884–885.

in their battle with the Gauls, losing about five thousand men in the fighting.[88]

STEPHEN V (POPE 113), A.D. 885[89]

The Roman Stephanus VI [Stephen V],[90] son of Hadrianus from Via Lata, held the pontificate for seven years and nine days. The Church was without a leader for five days. In his day, St. Martin's remains were moved to the church of Saint-Germain[91] for fear of the Normans who, after joining forces with troops from Dacia, had sacked all of Gaul and destroyed it with fire and sword. This is why in those days there were awesome miracles that resulted in the healing of many people stricken with various serious diseases.

FORMOSUS (POPE 114), A.D. 892[92]

Formosus,[93] bishop of Porto, was elected pope and held the pontificate for six years and seven months. The Church was without a leader for two days. Because he feared Pope John [VIII], he left the bishopric of Porto. Later when they recalled him, he refused to return and was excommunicated and demoted, but not much later he was pardoned by Pope Marinus, John's successor. As a result he not only returned to Rome but also assumed the dignity of the papacy. He restored and repaired many paintings that had been damaged in the church of St. Peter and also did many other worthy things.

ARNULF (EMPEROR 83), A.D. 893

Arnolfo [Arnulf][94] ruled for ten years, but was never crowned emperor. He fought the Normans, who had sacked and occupied Lorraine in France and many other places, and conquered them by means of

---

88. This event is not identifiable.
89. Text reads "985."
90. Pope 110, A.D. 885–891.
91. Perhaps Saint-Germain-des-Prés in Paris, founded in the sixth century.
92. Text reads "992."
93. Pope 111, A.D. 891–896.
94. Emperor A.D. 896–899.

THE NINTH CENTURY

wide-ranging attacks. Later he contracted a strange disease in which large numbers of lice issued from his skin and then devoured him to death.[95]

BONIFACE VI (POPE 115), A.D. 898
Bonifacius [Boniface] VI,[96] born in Tuscia, held the pontificate for fifteen days.

STEPHEN VI (POPE 116), A.D. 898
The Roman Stephanus [Stephen] VI[97] held the pontificate for three years and three months. The papacy was vacant for three days. He summoned a council and annulled everything done by Pope Formosus by whom he had earlier been made bishop of Anagni. He also had Formosus' body stripped of its pontifical garments and dressed in secular clothing He then cut two fingers from his right hand and ordered that his body be thrown into the Tiber.[98]

*

---

95. *Morbus pediculosis*, an infestation of lice under the eyelid.
96. Pope 112, April 896.
97. Pope 113, A.D. 896–897.
98. This is the infamous Cadaver Synod held at the Lateran in January 897. The event is described by Liutprand of Cremona, *Antapodosis* 1.30.

THE TENTH CENTURY

Romanus

ROMANUS (POPE 117), A.D. 901
Romanus,[1] born in Rome, held the pontificate for three months and twenty-two days. At his death he was buried in the church of St. Peter.

THEODORE II (POPE 118), [N.D.]
The Roman Theodorus [Theodore] II[2] held the pontificate for twenty days.

JOHN IX (POPE 119), [N.D.]
Ioannes [John] IX,[3] who became pope while still a monk, held the pontificate for two years and twenty-five days. He summoned to Ravenna a council of many bishops in order to reaffirm the ordinations that had been performed by Pope Formosus. The council decreed that anything done by Pope Stephen [VI] against Formosus be annulled and that the truth concerning Formosus be made known.

BENEDICT IV (POPE 120), A.D. 903
The Roman Benedictus [Benedict] IV[4] held the pontificate four years and two months. The Church was without a leader for six days.

LOUIS III (EMPEROR 84), A.D. 903
Louis III,[5] Arnulf's son, succeeded his father and ruled for five years. After several years he was driven from the kingdom of France by Hugues the Great of Burgundy who then ruled after him for a while. But then Louis regained the throne, and because of his stubbornness

1. Pope 114, August–November 897.
2. Pope 115, November–December 897.
3. Pope 116, A.D. 898–900.
4. Pope 117, A.D. 900–903.
5. Emperor A.D. 901–905.

the empire was removed from the descendants of Charles and the Franks and so divided that some controlled Italy, others France and still others Germany, but without the imperial crown. This division continued until the Saxon Otto I, who recaptured the regions of the empire and once again began ruling over them all. Finally, after having driven out Berengar, who was then ruling in Italy, Louis was captured and blinded in Verona, and Berengar was restored as ruler.

Leo V (Pope 121[6]), A.D. 907

The Roman Leo V[7] held the pontificate for forty days before he was seized by one of his priests, Christopher,[8] put in prison and deposed as pope. Christopher was pope for seven months before Sergius, but he too was deposed, put in prison and died as a monk.

Sergius III (Pope 122), [N.D.]

The Roman Sergius III,[9] son of Benedictus, held the pontificate for seven years, two months and sixteen days. The papacy was vacant for seven days. He had the church of the Lateran, which was in ruins, rebuilt from its very foundations. He went to France, and with the aid of the French he captured and imprisoned Christopher who had seized the papacy. Later on, he had the remains of Pope Formosus removed from his sepulcher, cut off the head and threw the body into the Tiber.[10] Not long afterwards, the body was found by some fishermen and brought to Rome where it was placed in church of St. Peter.

Berengar I (Emperor 85), A.D. 908

Berlinghieri [Berengar I],[11] without the title of Augustus, ruled in Italy for four years. He was skilled in arms and bravely fought many battles.

---

6. Text reads "LXXI."

7. Pope 118, July–September 903.

8. He was likely Roman and held the papacy, many consider illegitimately, from October 903 to January 904 when he was deposed by Theophylact, count of Tusculum.

9. Pope 119, A.D. 904–911.

10. At a synod that reaffirmed the Cadaver Synod of 897.

11. Emperor A.D. 915–924.

THE LIVES OF THE POPES AND EMPERORS

In his day Count William of Burgundy founded the monastery of Cluny.[12]

CONRAD I (EMPEROR 86), A.D. 912
The German Churrado [Conrad I][13] ruled the empire in Germany for seven years, but he is not listed among the emperors because he did not have the formal imperial blessing nor was he called Augustus. In his day, invading Saracens heavily sacked Sicily, Apulia and nearly all of Italy. Before dying, Conrad scorned his sons because he had little regard for them and wanted to be succeeded as ruler by his adversary Henry, son of Duke Otto of the Saxons, who was a good man.

BERENGAR II (EMPEROR 87), [N.D.]
Berlinghieri [Berengar] I ruled as emperor in Italy[14] while Conrad governed in Germany, and although not crowned he ruled for three years.

ANASTASIUS III (POPE 123), A.D. 914
Anastasius III,[15] born in Rome, held the pontificate for two years and ten days.

LANDO (POPE 124), A.D. 916
The Roman Lando,[16] the son of Ioannes, held the pontificate for six months and three days. The Church was without a leader for twenty-one days.

JOHN X (POPE 125[17]), A.D. 918
The Roman Ioannes [John] X,[18] son of Pope Sergius, held the pontificate for thirteen years and two months. Previously he had been bishop of Ravenna but then was deposed by the people; nevertheless he later

12. Founded by William I, duke of Aquitaine, in 910.
13. Emperor A.D. 911–918.
14. King of Italy 915–924.
15. Pope 120, A.D. 911–913.
16. Pope 121, A.D. 913–914.
17. Text reads "CXXXV."
18. Pope 122, A.D. 914–928.

attained the papal office. In his day the Saracens were overcome and defeated by the Romans with the aid of Marquis Alberic,[19] and ousted from Apulia that they were occupying.[20] But later, as a result of a disagreement between the marquis and the people, the marquis brought to Italy the Hungarians who occupied Pannonia, and once there they completely sacked it.[21]

Henry I of Saxony (Emperor 88), A.D. 919

Henry [I][22] of Saxony, Otto's son, ruled in Germany for fourteen years, but he was never crowned emperor by the pope. In his day Duke Spitigneo of Bohemia[23] converted to the true faith of Christ and then ruled justly and religiously. He was succeeded by his son, Wenceslaus,[24] who was outstanding in justice and holiness. Because of his very holy and honorable life, Wenceslaus was hated by his brother [Boleslav the Cruel] who had him cut to pieces. Soon afterward, out of vengeance, Emperor Otto declared war against the brother and defeated him by slaughtering his people and destroying all of Bohemia.

Leo VI (Pope 126), A.D. 930

The Roman Leo VI[25] occupied the pontificate for six months and two days. The Church was without a leader for ten days.

Stephen VII (Pope 127), A.D. 930

The Roman Stephanus [Stephen] VII[26] occupied the pontificate two years and twenty-two days. The Church was without a leader for two days.

---

19. Alberic I, duke of Spoleto, 896 and 900–c.920.
20. At the battle of the Garigliano in June 915.
21. Alberic was murdered in Orte c.925.
22. Emperor A.D. 919–936.
23. Vratislaus I.
24. Duke 921–935.
25. Pope 123, May–December 928.
26. Pope 124, A.D. 928–931.

Berengar III (Emperor 89), A.D. 931

Emperor Berlinghieri [Berengar] III,[27] though not crowned, ruled in Italy for seven years. During his time there was great discord throughout Italy.

John XI (Pope 128[28]), A.D. 932

The Roman Ioannes [John] XI[29] occupied the pontificate for three years, ten months and five days. One reads that, during his first year, in the city of Genoa there appeared a fountain where much blood flowed; this was interpreted as meaning that a great defeat would occur there.[30] In fact, not long after, the Saracens with a large fleet went to Genoa and captured it, despoiling it of men and every treasure.[31] At this time in France Hugues the Great[32] ruled with much violence. It was from him that the French [Capetian] kings of today are descended.

Leo VII (Pope 129[33]), A.D. 936

The Roman Leo VII[34] occupied the pontificate for three years and six months. The Church was without a leader for one day.

Lothair II (Emperor 90), A.D. 938[35]

Emperor Lothair II[36] ruled in Italy for two years but was never crowned. In his day the sun darkened, becoming the color of blood, and a few days later there were widespread deaths.[37]

27. King of Italy 950–961.
28. Text reads "CXXXVIII."
29. Pope 125, A.D. 931–935.
30. This story also appears in Platina's *Lives of the Popes*, ed. d'Elia, 154.
31. In 934/935. See Jacobus de Voragine, *Cronaca di Genova dalle origini al MCCXCVII.*
32. Hugh the Great, 898–16 June 956. His son, Hugh Capet, succeeded the last Carolingian king in 987.
33. Text reads "CXXXIX."
34. Pope 126, A.D. 936–939.
35. Text reads "638."
36. King of Lotharingia 855–869.
37. Christian scripture frequently describes solar and lunar eclipses — darkened or blood-red suns, moons, and stars — as omens of death. See especially Joel 2:10, 30–31; Acts

THE TENTH CENTURY

STEPHEN VIII (POPE 130), A.D. 949
Stephanus IX [Stephen VIII],[38] of German descent, held the pontificate for four years, four months and fifteen days. One reads that some Romans ripped out his tongue.

BERENGAR IV (EMPEROR 91), A.D. 940
Berlinghieri [Berengar] IV, together with his son Adalbert,[39] ruled Italy for fourteen years. Ruling with harshness, he seized and imprisoned Davilda [Adelaid] who had been Emperor Lothair's wife.[40] Not long afterward the German Otto [I] went to Italy with a powerful force and drove out Berengar, freeing Empress Adelaid from prison and taking her as his wife with a festive celebration in Pavia during Christmastide.[41] With Otto's consent Berengar was given Lombardy, but soon after was driven out by Otto because ambassadors of the church of Rome and other princes had revealed his terrible deeds to him. After Berengar's expulsion he went to Rome and was received with honor by the pope and the Romans and crowned emperor.[42]

MARINUS II (POPE 131), A.D. 942
The Roman Marinus III [II][43] held the pontificate for two years, six months and ten days.

AGAPITUS II (POPE 132), A.D. 945
The Roman Agapitus II[44] occupied the pontificate for eight years and six months. One reads that in his day a girl born in Gascony was divided in two from the navel upwards and had two heads and two

---

2:20; Revelation 6:12; Matthew 24:29. The *Nuremberg Chronicle* presents three illustrations of bloody skies on fol. CXCVIII recto just before discussing Lothair II.

38. Pope 127, A.D. 939–942.
39. The text reads "Alberic."
40. These details belong to the life of Berengar II.
41. In 951.
42. On 2 February 962.
43. Pope 128, A.D. 942–946.
44. Pope 129, A.D. 946–955.

chests with four arms. No part of her did what the other did, so that when one slept the other was awake, and often one would eat while the other did not. Having lived in this manner for some time, one part of her died while the other remained alive, which subsequently died of the stench.[45] At this time also died Odo I, abbot of the monastery of Cluny.[46]

JOHN XII (POPE 133), A.D. 954

The Roman Ioannes [John] XII[47] from the district of Via Lata held the pontificate for eight years and twenty-five days. He was the son of Prince Alberic [II] who, as a powerful man in Rome, had organized the Roman nobles and elites and made them swear that after Pope Agapitus's death they would elect his son Ottaviano.[48] This was done and he was given the name John. In his day Emperor Otto of Saxony went to Italy, was received magnificently in Rome and crowned with the imperial crown for having helped the Church; he thereupon gave many gifts to the Church. Eventually John was stripped of the papacy because of his immoral life.

OTTO I (EMPEROR 92), A.D. 955

Otto I,[49] the son of Henry [I], descended from the Saxons, ruled for thirteen years over the Western empire. He was the first emperor from Germany, and Italian rule came to an end until the present day. A wise emperor, he was expert in arms and victorious in many wars. He then went to Rome where he was magnificently and honorably received by the pope, the clergy and the people. He was crowned emperor with much support, and after giving many gifts to the Church and pacifying Italy, he returned to Saxony with his wife by whom he had a son

---

45. The *Nuremberg Chronicle* discusses and illustrates this Gascon wonder on fol. CLXXXII verso.
46. On 18 November 942.
47. Pope 130, A.D. 955–964.
48. Scion of the powerful Roman Theophylact family and the counts of Tusculum.
49. Emperor A.D. 962–973.

THE TENTH CENTURY

named Otto [II] who succeeded him. And there he ruled with the greatest justice and died.[50]

BENEDICT V (POPE 134), A.D. 962

The Roman Benedictus [Benedict] V[51] held the pontificate for two months and five days. He became pope in the following manner. After John [XII] had been deposed because of his evil life, the clergy elected someone named Leo [VIII] in the presence of Emperor Otto [I] who was in Rome at the time. As soon as Otto departed from Rome they deposed Leo, replacing him with Benedict. For this reason the emperor returned and besieged Rome, causing the Romans to place Leo once again in the Apostolic See. Afterward they seized Benedict and handed him over to the emperor who took him to Saxony and there had him suffer a miserable death.

LEO VIII (POPE 135), A.D. 964

Leo VIII[52] occupied the pontificate for seventeen months and two days. He was elected pope in the emperor's presence after John was deposed. Having later been deposed by the Romans who had chosen Benedict as pope, he was once again reinstated as pope (as we said above) after the emperor besieged Rome and decreed that no one could become pope without imperial consent because of the Romans' malice.

JOHN XIII (POPE 136), A.D. 964

Ioannes [John] XIII,[53] born in Narni, held the pontificate for eight years and thirteen days. He was seized by Piero, the prefect of Rome[54] who, after having held him prisoner, sent him to Campania. Within a short time John returned to Rome where he took revenge on his enemies with Emperor Otto's support.

---

50. On 7 May 973.
51. Pope 132, 22 May–23 June 964.
52. Pope 131, A.D. 963–965.
53. Pope 133, A.D. 965–972.
54. On 16 December 965. Piero was the son of Alberic III Theophylact of Tusculum.

THE LIVES OF THE POPES AND EMPERORS

Otto II (Emperor 93[55]), A.D. 967

Emperor Otto II, the son of Otto I, ruled the empire for thirty-one years. He was skillful and brave in battle. He went to Rome and gave an elaborate banquet for the nobles, many of whom were considered unpatriotic, so while they were eating he had them seized and beheaded. He then went to Benevento,[56] besieged and captured it, and then took the remains of St. Bartholomew the Apostle to his country. But he returned to Rome and placed the relics on an island where he then died, thus leaving them there.[57] In his day St. Adalbert,[58] a bishop, became well known. He was from Bohemia, and later baptized St. Stephen, king of Hungary. Finally, while preaching in Poland, he was crowned with martyrdom for his faith.

Benedict VI (Pope 137), A.D. 972

The Roman Benedictus [Benedict] VI[59] held the pontificate for eighteen months. He was imprisoned in Castel Sant'Angelo and strangled.

Donus II (Pope 138), A.D. 973

The Roman Donus II[60] held the pontificate for one year, six months and one day.

Pope CXXXX, A.D. 980[61]

Boniface VII [Anti-pope] (Pope 139[62]), A.D. 973

Bonifacius [Boniface] VII [anti-pope] held the pontificate for forty-two days.

---

55. Text reads "XCII."

56. The text reads "Buonconvento."

57. That is, in the church of San Bartolomeo all'Isola, actually founded by Otto III and initially dedicated to St. Adalbert of Prague. See also below, p. 163.

58. Adalbert of Prague, c.956–23 April 997.

59. Pope 134, A.D. 973–974.

60. Not official. His existence is due to a misreading of *"Domnus"* in the *Codex Estensis*.

61. Textual error.

62. Text reads "CXXXVIII." He appears in no formal list. For this antipope see Gregorovius, *History* 3:384–86.

THE TENTH CENTURY

BENEDICT VII (POPE 140), A.D. 975

The Roman Benedictus [Benedict] VII[63] occupied the pontificate for nine years and six months. In his day Archbishop Rudolph of Rheims, an honorable man from the house of Charlemagne whom King Hugh of France envied, was deposed from the archbishopric and his place taken by the necromancer, Gerbert,[64] who in turn was deposed by the papal legate; the archbishopric was returned to Rodolph. But some time later this Gerbert (as we will show) was elected pope and took the name of Silvester II. Also at this time died Hugh,[65] the first French king of the royal family that is still ruling today.[66] He was succeeded as king by his son Robert [II] who lived a holy life and reigned happily for thirty-four years.

JOHN XIV (POPE 141), A.D. 985

Ioannes [John] XIV[67] held the pontificate for eight months and two days. After he was harshly besieged in Castel Sant'Angelo [in Rome], he was buried there.

JOHN XV (POPE 142), A.D. 986

The Roman Ioannes [John] XV[68] held the pontificate for four months.

JOHN XVI [ANTIPOPE] (POPE 143), [N.D.]

The Roman Iohannes [XVI, antipope] held the pontificate for ten years, seven months and ten days. In his day the Saracens sacked Calabria when Emperor Otto tried to confront them, but he was

---

63. Pope 135, A.D. 974–983.

64. Gerbert d'Aurillac, archbishop of Rheims in 989. His reputation derived from his knowledge of the sciences of his day.

65. Died 24 October 996.

66. Charles IV (d.1328) was the last Capetian king of France. The throne then passed to the Valois dynasty. It is uncertain whether this reference can be used as a dating element for the original compilation of the *Lives* or whether it was deliberately inserted to bolster claims for Petrarch's authorship.

67. Pope 136, A.D. 983–984.

68. Pope 137, A.D. 985–996.

overcome and defeated.[69] In that battle many Christians were killed, causing the emperor to flee under the cover of secrecy to Sicily. With the aid of a Sicilian bishop he then returned to Rome. Also at this time St. Edward, king of England,[70] was killed by his stepmother, according to what one reads. Later he was credited with many miracles.

GREGORY V (POPE 144), A.D. 996

Gregorius [Gregory] V,[71] born in Saxony, held the pontificate for two years and six months. His given name was Bruno [of Carinthia] and through the assistance and demands of Emperor Otto [III] was elected Roman pontiff; later Otto went to Rome to crown him. At that time in Rome there was a powerful man, the consul Crescentius, who drove Gregory from the papacy and substituted in his place John, a Greek bishop from Piacenza and a very wealthy man. For this reason, Otto returned to Rome and besieged Crescentius in Castel Sant'Angelo where he had fled. He later had him arrested and beheaded, and even blinded the pontiff who succeeded Gregory, after which he returned to Saxony.

OTTO III (EMPEROR 94), A.D. 998

Otto III, the son of Otto II, ruled the western empire for twelve years. Because of his courage and tenacity he was called the "wonder of the world."[72] He went to Rome and was crowned by Gregory V. He returned to Saxony, but soon after returned to Rome when Pope Gregory was deposed by Crescentius. Otto gouged out the eyes of John the Greek who (as we said above) had replaced Gregory as pope, and after settling matters in Italy he returned to Saxony.

---

69. At the battle of Capo Colonna in Calabria on 14 July 982.

70. Edward the Martyr, king 975–18 March 978. There were many suspects in his assassination, and the sources vary in assigning guilt.

71. Pope 138, A.D. 996–999.

72. Otto was emperor 996–1002. The title, "wonder of the world" (*stupor mundi*), is more usually attributed to Emperor Frederick II.

THE TENTH CENTURY

JOHN XVII (POPE 145), A.D. 998

Ioannes [John] XVII,[73] born in Greece, held the pontificate for ten months and four days. Because John was bishop of Piacenza, the Roman Crescentius made him pope after Gregory V had been deposed. But then he was deposed and blinded by Otto III, as we have indicated.

SILVESTER II (POPE 146), A.D. 999

Silvester II,[74] born in France, held the pontificate for three years, one month and eight days. His given name was Gerbert [d'Aurillac], and he was a Florentine monk[75] and necromancer.[76] He was so learned in doctrine that it is written among his disciples were Emperor Otto and King Robert [II] of France, a holy man. He was also previously bishop of Rheims and then of Ravenna. It is written about him that, having surrendered to the devil,[77] he was successful in all his endeavors, even attaining the papacy. But then when he tried to learn how long he would live, he was told "until he celebrated Mass in Jerusalem." As a result he confidently determined never to set sail, but it so happened that one day he celebrated Mass in a place in Rome called Jerusalem.[78] When he realized this and recognized the deceits of demons, he repented, sought God's mercy and ordered that the bodily members with which he had served the demons be forcibly cut off and thrown away. Later, after his death, he was taken up by divine mercy to perpetual blessedness (as was seen by several miracles).

---

73. Pope 140, June–December 1003. The *Lives* has mis-ordered John XVII with Silvester II.

74. Pope 139, A.D. 999–1003.

75. The text here is corrupt, Gerbert was French.

76. See above under Benedict VII.

77. This is the story of the demon Meridiana embodied in the talking bronze head of Silvester's making and is recounted in Walter Map, *De nugis curialium* IV.11.

78. That is, the basilica of Sta. Croce in Gerusalemme.

THE LIVES OF THE POPES AND EMPERORS

In his day Emperor Otto had his wife burned after her false accusation against a man for having wanted to have an affair with her.[79] And at this time, the Saracens besieged Capua.

*

---

79. Otto III never married. Otto II's wife, the Byzantine princess Theophanu, accompanied him on all his travels. However, her high culture and foreign ways gave rise to many slanders, including Peter Damian's assertion that she had an affair with a Greek monk. After Otto II's death on 7 December 983, she was empress regent from May 985 until her death in 991.

THE ELEVENTH CENTURY

Johannes xviij.

JOHN XVIII (POPE 147), A.D. 1002
Ioannes [John] XVIII[1] held the pontificate for five months and fifteen days. The papacy was vacant for nineteen days.

JOHN XVIII (POPE 148), A.D. 1002
Ioannes XIX [John XVIII][2] held the pontificate for five years and four months. In his day King Robert [II] of France[3] thrived; he was a wise and holy man, outstanding in his devotion to the Christian religion, so devout that even after assuming the throne he sang the Divine Office with the friars. Once while besieging a castle on the feast of St. Damian, he left what he was doing to participate in the Divine Office and celebrate the feast day by singing the *Agnus Dei, etc.* Later he miraculously took the castle.

SERGIUS IV (POPE 149), A.D. 1008
Sergius IV,[4] born in Rome, held the pontificate for two years, eight months and two days. The Church was without a leader for seven days. He led a very holy, honest and religious life. In his day Emperor Otto [III] went to Poland to visit the remains of St. Adalbert [of Prague] from which he took an arm to Rome where he placed it on an island in the church of San Bartolomeo.[5] Shortly thereafter he died after beginning many renovations to the palace that had belonged to Emperor Julian. Because of this, he became very unpopular among the Romans.[6]

---

1. Textual error. See the following entry.
2. Pope 141, A.D. 1003–1009.
3. King 996–20 July 1031, called "the Pious."
4. Pope 142, A.D. 1009–1012.
5. San Bartolomeo all'Isola on the Tiber Island. See also above, p. 158.
6. The Romans revolted against the pope's Crescentii patrons. He may have been murdered at the time.

THE LIVES OF THE POPES AND EMPERORS

At this time appeared a moon the color of blood, and the empire was without leadership for several years.

HENRY II (EMPEROR 95), A.D. 1010

Henry Claude [Henry II],[7] son of Otto II, ruled the empire for twelve years and six months, but the empire had been without a leader for several years. As duke of Bavaria, he was unanimously elected emperor by all the princes. He waged many battles in Germany, Bohemia and Italy. He had a sister named Galla whom he gave as wife to King Stephen of Hungary, who was still a Gentile; as a result, Stephen and the Hungarian people converted to the Christian faith. Because of his outstanding virtues, he was baptized by Bishop Albert of Poland who was born in Bohemia. One also reads that Henry and his lady Renaganda [Kunigunde][8] dedicated themselves to perpetual virginity.

BENEDICT VIII (POPE 150), A.D. 1022

Benedictus [Benedict] VIII,[9] born in Tuscany and the son of Gregorio, held the pontificate for eighteen years, eleven months and eleven days. The papacy was without a leader for one year. Later he was deposed as pontiff and another substituted in his place; this caused great discord in Rome. At this time, the Saracens occupied the Holy Land. King Robert [II] of France, a holy man, died and was succeeded by his son Henry [I].

CONRAD II (EMPEROR 96), A.D. 1030

Conrad I [II],[10] French duke and the grandson of Henry [II] the Elder, was made emperor, succeeding him, and ruled for twenty years. At first, the empire was without a leader after Henry's death for nearly three years. He made and enacted many laws, among which, in the hope of maintaining a peaceful empire, he decreed a specific punishment for insurgents. As a result when Count

---

7. Emperor A.D. 1014–1024.
8. Circa 975–3 March 1040. Roman Catholic saint and patroness of Luxembourg.
9. Pope 143, A.D. 1012–1024.
10. Emperor A.D. 1027–1039.

Lapondo was reported to him as an insurgent, Lapondo fled out of fear and hid in a forest with his pregnant wife. But one day when Emperor Conrad was hunting, he was separated from the others and caught by darkness; he then happened upon Lapondo's house who welcomed him warmly. Since Lapondo's wife had given birth to a boy, he learned in a dream that the boy would become his son-in-law and succeed him as ruler. Whereupon, upon awakening, he returned to his hunting party and ordered that they take the boy, kill him and bring him his heart. They kidnapped the boy, but moved by pity, did not kill him and left him in the forest. Upon returning to the emperor they gave him an animal's heart and said that they had obeyed his command. Later on, the crying boy was found by a hunter who raised him in the fine arts. Finally after it became known whose son he was, he became the emperor's son-in-law, later succeeded him and was called Henry.[11]

JOHN XIX (POPE 151), A.D. 1031

The Roman Ioannes XX [John XIX],[12] son of Gregory, held the pontificate for nine years. The papacy was without a leader for four days. He fought a very serious war with the Romans. In his day died Emeric, son of King Stephen of Hungary,[13] who with his lady had vowed perpetual virginity; for them God performed many different miracles to reflect their sanctity. Also at this time could be seen running across the sun's sphere a kind of fiery beam of amazing size.

---

11. This story may be a conflation of the history of Adalbero of Eppenstein (980–29 November 1039), duke of Carinthia and margrave of Verona from 1011/12 until 1035 when he was deposed by Conrad, and folklore elements common to many medieval romances and *chansons de geste*.

12. Pope 144, A.D. 1024–1032.

13. Emeric, last surviving son of Stephen, first king of Hungary 1000/1001–1038. According to Emeric's *Legenda*, he and his wife, an Eastern princess whose identity is disputed, took oaths of chastity.

THE LIVES OF THE POPES AND EMPERORS

BENEDICT IX (POPE 152), A.D. 1041

The Tusculan Benedictus [Benedict] IX,[14] the son of Henry, held the pontificate for seven years. He was driven from the papacy and succeeded by the bishop of Sabina who took the name of Silvester [III]. A short while later, he too was driven from the papacy and the Apostolic See was given to Giovanni, archpriest of San Giovanni a Porta Latina with the name of Gregory VI. Not much can be read about Benedict who appeared in a vision as a strange animal figure to a man giving evidence of Benedict's bad life and fitting punishment. In his day St. Gerard, a bishop, was crowned with martyrdom in England.[15]

SILVESTER III (POPE 153), A.D. 1048

Silvester III,[16] bishop of Sabina, was elected pope and held the pontificate for fifty-six days.

GREGORY VI (POPE 154), A.D. 1049

Gregorius [Gregory] VI,[17] archpriest of San Giovanni a Porta Latina, originally named Giovanni, was elected pope and held the pontificate for two years, seven months and three days. He fought many battles, the last one with the Emperor Henry [III]. As one can read,[18] he was a good and holy pontiff, perceiving little or no value in the papacy because of his predecessors' negligence and infighting; they had done nothing about the predators in many different areas who were robbing those coming to Rome to make offerings or for other reasons. Consequently, because people were unable to come to Rome, the pope at first warned the robbers to cease stealing, and when this did not happen, he excommunicated them. When they then refused to obey him, he organized an army and attacked them, killing some of them and causing others to

---

14. Pope 145, A.D. 1032–1048, with interruptions.

15. More likely the Italian Saint Gerard Sagredo, bishop of Chonad (Hungary), martyred in Hungary (in one account, in Budapest) in 1046.

16. Pope 146, January–March 1045. He is also considered an anti-pope.

17. Pope 147, A.D. 1045–1046.

18. All the following details are derived from William of Malmesbury, *De gestis regum Anglorum* II.13.

flee. Once those areas were freed from the predators, he regained many possessions, including the castles that he had lost. For this reason he was not called a pope but bloodthirsty, that is to say, he delighted in blood.

Not long afterwards, he fell so ill that it clearly showed a sudden death was about to overcome him, which led him to beg the cardinals that he be buried in the church of St. Peter. The cardinals replied that since he had caused so many deaths, he was unworthy of such a burial. In his reply he showed the many ways he had done a great deal of good and finally added, "At least place my body in front of the church; then let God's will be done." After his death, the cardinals did so. Whereupon the church doors that were of iron were struck by such a strong wind that they suddenly opened, a sign that greatly affected the cardinals, and consequently they gave him an honorable burial in the church.

CLEMENT II (POPE 155[19]), A.D. 1050

Clemens II [Clement II][20] held the pontificate for nine months. Previously bishop of Bamberg, he gained the office at the insistence of Henry [III], whom he then crowned emperor.

HENRY III (EMPEROR 97[21]), A.D. 1050

Henry [III],[22] the son-in-law [son] of Emperor Conrad, succeeded him and ruled for four years. When he went to Italy he captured and imprisoned Prince Pandolfo of Capua,[23] substituting for him as prince another Pandolfo, count of Rieti. In his day there was found in Rome a giant's body of unusual size, still uncorrupted, that emitted a terrible stench. Near the corpse was an epitaph saying, "Here lies Pallas, son of Evander, who was killed by the lance of the knight Turnus."[24] Also at

---

19. Text reads "XCVII."
20. Pope 148, A.D. 1046–1047.
21. The text reads "CLV."
22. Emperor A.D. 1039–1056.
23. Pandulf IV, d.1049/50.
24. From William of Malmesbury, *De gestis regum Anglorum* II.13, under A.D. 1065. The classical reference is to Virgil's *Aenead* XII.33.

this time the Normans went to Rome and captured it.[25] The churches of Gaul were likewise attacked during Henry's reign by someone called Berengar del Corso[26] who maintained that the sacrament on the altar that we receive was not the true body and blood of Christ.

DAMASUS II (POPE 156), A.D. 1050

The Roman Damasus II[27] held the pontificate for twenty-five days. The Church was without a leader for eleven days. Having gained the papacy by force, he died suddenly, shortly afterward.

LEO IX (POPE 157), A.D. 1051

Leo IX,[28] born in Germany, held the pontificate for six years, two months and six days. He led a holy and pious life, and dying in everyone's good graces, he was buried in the church of St. Peter.

HENRY IV (EMPEROR 98), A.D. 1054

Henry [IV],[29] called the second son of Henry the Elder, succeeded his father and reigned for forty-eight years. He waged many and various battles and ruled successfully. In his day Cardinal Hildebrand, who later became pope with the name of Gregory [VII], was sent as an ambassador to France to take measures against many simoniac bishops. Also at this time a great number of rodents attacked a very powerful man who was avaricious and hoarding food; he fled to a ship at sea, but they followed him and viciously killed him.[30] This Henry [IV]

---

25. The Normans sacked Rome in 1084. The author may have confused events from the pontificates of Gregory VI and VII.

26. Berengar of Tours, c.999–6 January 1088, in Rome in 1059 to debate the Eucharist.

27. Pope 149, July–August 1048.

28. Pope 150, A.D. 1049–1054.

29. Emperor A.D. 1050–1106.

30. Possibly an incorrect dating of the folk legend of Hatto II, the archbishop of Mainz, (d.970), a greedy ruler who restored a tower on the Rhine (the Mouse Tower, near Bingen am Rhein), used it to demand tribute from passing ships, accumulated great wealth and resources and, during a famine, deprived the population of the grain stored up in his barns by selling it at a very high price. Legend recounts that Hatto trapped Mainz's peasants in a barn with the promise of food, then burned the barn and described the peasants, in their

THE ELEVENTH CENTURY

was the father of Countess Matilda who was married to the Marquis Bonifazio; for this reason Henry allowed them to rule a large part of the empire in Italy.

VICTOR II (POPE 158), A.D. 1057

Victor II,[31] born in Germany, held the pontificate for two years, three months and fourteen days. The Church was without a leader for three days. Because of the political situation, Emperor Henry [III] appointed him pope; he proceeded to convene a council in Tuscany in the city of Florence[32] where he removed many bishops for fornication and simony. Later he went to Gaul where he was received graciously, and there he died.

STEPHEN IX (POPE 159), A.D. 1059

Stephanus X [Stephen IX],[33] born in Lorraine, held the pontificate for nine months and twenty-six days. He was first the abbot of Monte Cassino and later was raised to the papacy. He died in the noble city of Florence and was buried there.

BENEDICT X [ANTIPOPE] (POPE 160), A.D. 1060

Benedictus [Benedict] X [antipope] held the pontificate for nine months. Having been made pope by force, he later voluntarily left the

---

dying moment, as "squeaking mice." He was welcomed back to his castle by an army of mice who followed him as he fled to his tower across the river and ate him alive there. See: *Bloudy news from Germany, or the peoples misery by famine, being an example of God's just jugement on one Harto a nobleman of Germany of the town of Ments, who … was sore beset and beat with rats, that his Castles top was never after free of them, and at last devoured by them, a ballad* (London: 1675?); Sabine Baring-Gould, *Curious Myths of the Middle Ages: The Sangreal, Pope Joan, the Wandering Jew and Others* (Newburyport: Dover Publications, 2012), 154–64. Hatto is pictured in *The Nuremberg Chronicle* fol. CLXXXII verso with mice running up and down his body.

31. Pope 151, A.D. 1055–1057.

32. June 1055.

33. Pope 152, A.D. 1057–1058. The line of Stephen popes contains two numberings dating back to Stephen II (III).

papacy. In his day Lanfranc of Bec[34] became well known as Anselm's teacher.

NICHOLAS II (POPE 161), A.D. 1061

Nicolaus [Nicholas] II,[35] born in Burgundy, held the pontificate two years, six months and twenty-six days. While bishop of Florence, he was elected pope in Siena with great approval. He then convened a council of many bishops against Berengar[36] who maintained that the sacrament on the altar was not the true body of Christ. For this reason Berengar, being in every other respect a true Christian and having learned the subtle truth involved, rejected such an error.

ALEXANDER II (POPE 162), A.D. 1063

Alexander II,[37] of Milanese descent, held the pontificate for eleven years and three months. The Church was without a leader for twenty-five days. As bishop of Lucca, he was unanimously elected pope by a general agreement of cardinals. But there rose against him Bishop Churrado [Cadalus] of Parma who, after being elected pope [as Honorius II] by all the bishops of Lombardy, twice[38] went to Rome with a large army with the hope of seizing Alexander by force. Whereupon, at Emperor Henry's request, the pope went into Lombardy to Mantua[39] where he convened a solemn council. After resolving all disagreements, he returned to Rome where not much later he died and was buried in the church of St. John Lateran. At this time the Normans, who had occupied and held the kingdom of Apulia against the pope's wishes, sacked all of Campania and evicted

---

34. Lanfranc of Bec and Canterbury, c.1005/1010 Pavia–24 May 1089 Canterbury. Archbishop of Canterbury, abbot and theologian, teacher of both Anselm of Badagio, later Pope Alexander II, and the theologian Anselm of Canterbury.

35. Pope 153, A.D. 1059–1061.

36. Berengar of Tours, see above n. 26.

37. Pope 154, A.D. 1061–1073.

38. In April 1062 and May 1063.

39. In May 1064.

from power Duke Gotofredo of Spoleto and Countess Matilda, a very powerful and devout lady.

GREGORY VII (POPE 163), A.D. 1074

Gregorius [Gregory] VII,[40] born in the city of Sovana, held the pontificate for twelve years, one month and three days. Because of his holy life, he was elected pope by the cardinals, but then on Christmas Eve as the first Mass was being sung the pope was seized in Sta. Maria ad Praesepe by a certain powerful man named Cencius[41] and imprisoned. Angered by this action, the Romans exiled Cencius from the city and freed the pope from prison.

Then at a council[42] the pope excommunicated Emperor Henry [IV] because he threatened the unity of the Church; whereupon the emperor went to Lombardy and humbly asked the pope's pardon, begging him with much difficulty.[43] Later when the German princes were in Italy, they elected Duke Rudolf of Saxony as emperor. Because the pope would not excommunicate Rudolf at Henry's request without understanding his justification, the emperor marched against Rudolf and defeated him. He assembled his court in Brescia, and to the best of his ability he did what he could to unseat Pope Gregory and nullify all his orders. He then had many cardinals elect Bishop Guibert of Ravenna as pope, giving him the name of Clement III.

And so once again Pope Gregory excommunicated him. Whereupon, after assembling a great army, Henry went to Rome with the pope and bishops who had elected him and besieged Pope Gregory in Castel Sant'Angelo.[44] But Robert Guiscard, king of Apulia, came to the pope's aid while the emperor fled with his pope to Siena. Whereupon Robert, after freeing Gregory from the siege,

---

40. Pope 155, A.D. 1073–1085.

41. Cencio I Frangipane, Roman patrician and consul, kidnapped the pope on 25 December 1075 at Sta. Maria Maggiore and released him the next day.

42. The Lateran Lenten synod of 1076.

43. At Canossa in 1077.

44. In March 1084.

severely punished the many Romans who had been found guilty. Pope Gregory then went to Apulia with Robert and died in Salerno,[45] and after his death God performed many miracles in his honor.

As time passed, the city of Siracusa in Sicily was struck by a very strong earthquake that caused its main church to crumble. Also at that time Emperor Henry encamped in Florence on 21 July but had to leave as though in defeat.

Victor III (Pope 164), A.D. 1086

Victor III[46] held the pontificate for three years, four months and seven days. As abbot of Monte Cassino he had been known as Desiderius.[47] He eventually died from poison put into his chalice.[48] In his day the Carthusian order was founded.

Urban II (Pope 165), A.D. 1089

Urbanus [Urban] II[49] held the pontificate for eleven years, eleven months and one day. The Church was without a leader for fifteen days. In his day Raymond, son of Duke Guiscard of the Normans who held Apulia, assembled a very large army of Christians overseas and entered Constantinople, which later was captured from the Christians in A.D. 1093[50] Similarly Antioch was recaptured by the Christians in the following year, as was Jerusalem and the sepulcher of Christ, all of which the barbarians had occupied. Also in this year someone who

45. On 25 May 1085.

46. Pope 156, 9 May–16 September 1087.

47. Abbot since 1058.

48. Victor III is more commonly thought to have died of illness.

49. Pope 157, A.D. 1088–1099. Urban II is best known as the pope who launched the crusade movement with his speech at Clermont 27 November 1095. It is curious that here and in the next passage the *Lives* displays little knowledge of these events.

50. The chronology here is mistaken. The author may have mistaken the Norman attack against the Byzantine army in the campaign of Dyrrhachium (Durazzo) in 1081 in which Robert Guiscard defeated Emperor Alexius I Comnenus. The campaign ended in 1084 after the Byzantine victory over the Normans at Larissa. The Raymond referred to here may be Raymond IV of Toulouse, one of the leaders of the First Crusade, which took Jerusalem on 15 July 1099.

THE ELEVENTH CENTURY

was identified as a religious man named Andrew found the lance that pierced Christ's side.[51] At this time began the custom of saying hourly on Saturdays the Office of the Virgin Mary. In England Anselm,[52] a man outstanding in learning and sanctity, became famous, having been at first an abbot and then bishop of Canterbury. Duke Godfrey [de Bouillon] of Burgundy died in Jerusalem[53] and was succeeded by his brother Baldwin.

*

---

51. The Holy Lance of Longinus. In June 1098, during the crusaders' siege of Antioch, a monk named Peter Bartholomew had a vision of St. Andrew, who informed him where the lance was buried.
52. Anselm of Canterbury, c.1033–21 April 1109.
53. On 18 July 1100.

THE TWELFTH CENTURY

Paschalis ij.

PASCHAL II (POPE 166), A.D. 1100

Paschalis [Paschal] II,[1] born in Tuscany, held the pontificate for eighteen years and five months. The Church was without a leader for twelve days. He was arrested and imprisoned with all his court by Emperor Henry [V],[2] but after he had been there for some time, he was set free once the investiture of bishops, abbots and other clerics was conceded to the emperor,[3] something that the popes had contested at other times. In his day Countess Matilda[4] ruled over the city of Ferrara and died not long afterward. Also a monk, Robert of Colan,[5] along with twelve others founded the order of Citeaux.

HENRY V (EMPEROR 99), A.D. 1102

Henry II [V][6] succeeded his father Henry whom he kept in prison so long that he died there; he thus took over the empire by deception and ruled for twenty-five years. In his day lived Robert Guiscard, as well as Alessio[7] and Ariano,[8] the emperors in Constantinople. With a large army Robert went from France to Rome and attempted to capture the

1. Pope 158, A.D. 1099–1118.

2. On 12 February 1099.

3. In the Privilege of Ponte Mammolo. On this conflict see William of Malmesbury, *De gestis regum Anglorum* V.13, under A.D. 1112.

4. Of Canossa or Tuscany, 1046–24 July 1115.

5. Robert of Molesme, c.1029–17 April 1111. Robert was a hermit in the forest of Colan when he was asked to establish a monastery in 1075. Robert and his companions founded Citeaux in 1098.

6. Emperor A.D. 1099–1125.

7. Alexius I Comnenus, emperor A.D. 1081–1118.

8. Most likely John II Comnenus, emperor A.D. 1118–1143.

THE TWELFTH CENTURY

city, but he was driven out and then proceeded to attack Apulia, gradually occupying that kingdom.[9]

He had one son who was king of Sicily,[10] and a daughter named Constance who later became the mother of Frederick [II], the emperor. He was succeeded in the office by his son, a gentle and gracious man. In his day Apulia exceeded every other kingdom in wealth. At this time, after Pope Paschal [II] had been freed from prison three [anti]popes rose up against him, that is Albert, Theoderic and Arnolf [Maginulf]. Since each had a large following, this gave him trouble at first, but in the end they were all overcome and defeated.

Also at this time St. Bernard[11] entered the order of Citeaux at the age of twenty-two. The abbot of the monastery with about thirty monks at the time was Stephen.[12] In the same year Clairvaux was founded, St. Bernard was sent there by Pope Paschal as abbot. It was then that, after the pope had been freed from prison, he crowned Henry with whom he had reconciled with much ceremony. Paschal later died and was buried in the church of San Salvatore in the presence of all the clergy. He was succeeded by Giovanni [Caetani], a Roman knight, who took the name of Gelasius [II]. But since this was done without imperial consent, the emperor raised another pope named Bordino from Spain who, however, does not appear in the chronicle of the popes.[13]

9. The Norman Hauteville, c.1015–17 July 1085, count of Apulia and Calabria (1057–1059), duke of Apulia and Calabria and duke of Sicily (1059–1085). The author again shows a blurring of details of southern Italian events and the Hautevilles' (Altavilla) rise to prominence from Norman mercenaries and adventurers to papal allies against Henry IV and their gradual conquest of Sicily and the kingdom of Naples, then known as the kingdom of Apulia.

10. Again the *Lives* mistakes details of southern history here: it was Roger I, count of Sicily (1071–1101) whose son was Roger II, king of Sicily (1130–1154). Constance (1154–1198), queen of Sicily 1194–1198), was the daughter of Roger II of Sicily and mother of the future Emperor Frederick II.

11. Bernard of Clairvaux, 1090–20 August 1153.

12. Stephen Harding, d.28 March 1134.

13. According to William of Malmesbury, *De gestis regum Anglorum* V, under 1119, this was Burdinus, archbishiop of Braga in Portugal, consecrated as Gregory VIII. See also

Because of that action, the emperor and all his followers were excommunicated. During this period, around the year 1016 in May, there occurred in Florence a fire in the section known as Borgo Sant'Apostolo which caused much damage with many buildings burned.

GELASIUS II (POPE 167), A.D. 1118[14]

Gelasius II,[15] born in the city of Gaeta, held the pontificate for one year and five days. The papacy was without a leader for twenty-four days. Because he feared Emperor Henry [V], he went to France by sea and there fell ill and died.[16] At this time, a sow miraculously gave birth to a piglet that had a human face.[17] St. Bernard (as we said above) became a monk. In Jerusalem the order of Hospitallers was formed to aid ill pilgrims.

CALLIXTUS II (POPE 168), A.D. 1119

Callistus [Callixtus] II,[18] born in Burgundy, held the pontificate for five years, ten months and thirteen days. The Church was without leadership for five days. While archbishop of Vienne, he was made pope after Gelasius' death with the cardinals' consent in the city of Innacho.[19] En route to Rome later, he was happily received by the people all along the way. Burdinus who had been made pope by Emperor Henry learned of his coming and departed from Rome to go to Sutri. There, besieged by the Romans and by the army, he was captured and put on a camel with his face to the rear[20] and, after giving him the

---

Landolf Junior, *Historia Mediolensis* 32.

14. Text reads "1018."

15. Pope 159, A.D. 1118–1119.

16. At Cluny on 28/29 January 1119.

17. Of uncertain origin, but widely disseminated; the allusion to a piglet with a human face also appears in Gilles d'Orval's *Gesta episcoporum Leodiensium*, ed. I. Heller, MGH SS 25 (Hannover, 1880); and *Albertus Milolus notarius Regini, Liber de temporibus et aetatibus* (1286), ed. O. Holder-Egger, MGH SS 31 (Hannover, 1903), as cited in Irven M. Resnick, *Marks of Distinctions: Christian Perceptions of Jews in the High Middle Ages* (Washington, DC: The Catholic University of America Press, 2012), 149.

18. Pope 160, A.D. 1119–1124.

19. At Cluny on 2 February 1119.

20. From the *Vita Calixti* ex Cardinale Aragonense.

THE TWELFTH CENTURY

camel's tail in place of a bridle, he was taken back to Rome and imprisoned in a fortress.[21]

Not long afterward, Emperor Henry, who was feeling guilty, restored the investiture of bishops and other prelates to Pope Callixtus.[22] He had argued at length about this with Paschal [II] and insisted that in all the churches of the empire the pope be responsible for distributing benefices. Besides this, he had all possessions, whether castles or other places, seized because of disagreements he had had with the Church, returned to the pope. Moreover, every other possession that he had gained through the war that had been fought was to be returned to the Church or to clerics or to laypeople. Having reconciled with the pope, they agreed to a peace.

At this time, Lucca was honored with a banner through the good graces of the pope who died sometime later and was buried in the church of St. John Lateran. One also reads that, under Callixtus's pontificate, the Pisans encamped in Maiolica, leaving the city of Pisa guarded by the Florentines and, having easily seized Maiolica, stripped it of valuable ornaments and returned to Pisa.

HONORIUS II (POPE 169), A.D. 1125

The Bolognese Honorius II[23] held the pontificate for five years, two months and three days. After he had made peace with Count Roger [II] of Sicily who occupied Aquileia,[24] he ceded to him the duchy of Apulia.[25] He also deposed through one of his cardinal legates two patriarchs, namely the one in Aquileia and the one in Venice. In his day, the Phoenician city of Tyre was taken by the Christians,[26] and

---

21. William of Malmesbury, *De gestis regum Anglorum* V, under 1119, calls this fortress the "Den," the monastery of Cava dei Tirreni just north of Salerno.
22. With the Concordat of Worms in 1122, ending the Investiture Conflict.
23. Pope 161, A.D. 1124–1130.
24. This may be a misreading of L'Aquila, a major strategic center in the Abruzzi, commanding access from the north to Rome, Naples and the South.
25. On 22 August 1128.
26. In 1124.

THE LIVES OF THE POPES AND EMPERORS

King Baldwin of Jerusalem was captured by the Saracens.[27] Hugh of St. Victor[28] who was regarded as a prophet became famous in Paris, and the order of the Knights of St. Mary was founded in Jerusalem.[29] Emperor Henry [V] died without sons, which people believed had happened because he had behaved badly toward his father. He was succeeded as emperor by Lothair.

LOTHAIR II (EMPEROR 100), A.D. 1127

Lottieri [Lothair] II,[30] duke of Saxony, reigned as emperor for thirteen years. In his day throughout Italy there was great famine and in France so severe a drought that rivers, fountains and lakes all dried up, and for two years neither cold nor rain could overcome such a drought. In Spain was born a monster with two bodies, which in the front had the complete form of a man and in the rear that of a dog.[31]

INNOCENT II (POPE 170), A.D. 1130

Innocentius [Innocent] II,[32] born in Rome and the son of Giovanni di Trastevere,[33] held the pontificate for eight years, seven months and eight days. The papacy was vacant for two days. He condemned all the supporters of Pietro Leone[34] who, having been elected pope by a few cardinals, plotted to attack him. Unable to do so, Pierleoni attacked the church of San Pietro in Vincoli and despoiled it of gold, silver and all its ornaments. Finally he did the same to the church of

27. Near Castle Gargar in 1123.

28. Theologian, c.1096–11 February 1141.

29. The Knights Templar were founded in 1120. The Knights of St. Mary were the Teutonic Knights, founded c.1190.

30. Emperor A.D. 1133–1137.

31. *The Nuremberg Chronicle*, fol. CXCVIII recto also shows an image of this prodigy. Remote sources for this story do back to the Black Shuck of the British Isles, a hairy black dog and a likeness of the devil, described for the first time under the year 1127 in *The Peterborough Chronicle* (a version of the *Anglo-Saxon Chronicles*). The Black Shuck is also reminiscent of the Catalan mythical Dip.

32. Pope 162, A.D. 1130–1142.

33. Papareschi.

34. Pierleoni, antipope Anacletus II.

Sta. Maria Maggiore and many other churches he thought contained much wealth. With this wealth he held the papacy by force, corrupting many Romans.

For this reason, Innocent could find no help in Rome, so with his cardinals he boarded a ship to go to France where he was received with honor by the king and then convened a council on the Rhine.[35] But Lothair, who had been elected emperor, went to Italy with a large army, bringing with him Innocent and his court.[36] He then deposed Pierleoni and victoriously returned the papacy to Innocent from whom he then received the imperial crown with much honor. Whereupon, inspired by the Catholic faith and wishing to be a good defender of the Church of Christ, Lothair assembled a large army with the pope and together they attacked Count Roger [of Sicily] who had rebelled against the Church. Having driven him from Apulia to Sicily, he appointed another duke for Apulia.[37] After this Lothair returned to Germany.

Because the Pisans and Genoese had supported him, the pope named a bishop for the Genoese, who previously were under the bishopric of Milan, and an archbishop for Pisa and made him the head of the Sardinian bishoprics. At this time a council was held in Rome; and Master Arnold, who had severely reproached clerical excesses, was crucified, something which even today would be done to a preacher who did a similar thing.[38] The cathedral of Ferrara was also begun at this time.

---

35. At Liège on the Meuse or at Würzburg on the Main.

36. In 1133.

37. In fact, Roger inflicted a decisive defeat on Anacletus, forcing him to recognize him as king of Sicily on 27 September 1130.

38. The episode of Arnold of Brescia, c.1090–1155, who revived the Roman commune and criticized clerical abuses. He was hung by order of Emperor Frederick I Barbarossa and his body burnt. The reference to the author's contemporary practice reflects growing conflicts over Church authority from the later fifteenth century onward.

THE LIVES OF THE POPES AND EMPERORS

CONRAD III (EMPEROR 101), A.D. 1140
Conrad II [III],[39] born in Serbia, ruled the empire for twelve years. In his day died Ioannes, Charlemagne's squire, having lived (as the ecclesiastics write) more than 360 years.[40] There also passed from this life Hugh of St. Victor, while Master Richard[41] became famous in Paris.

CELESTINE II (POPE 171), A.D. 1141
Coelestinus [Celestine] II,[42] born in Tuscany in Castello di Santa Felicità, held the pontificate for five months and thirteen days. After his death he was buried in St. John Lateran.

LUCIUS II (POPE 172), A.D. 1144
Lucius II,[43] a Bolognese and the son of Alberto, held the pontificate for eleven months and four days. He was the first cardinal of Santa Croce,[44] which he repaired and completely restored.

EUGENIUS III (POPE 173), A.D. 1145
Eugenius [Eugene] III,[45] from Pisa, held the pontificate for seven years, three months and twenty days. As abbot of St. Anastasius,[46] he was elected pope by general agreement of the cardinals, but since the senators disliked him, he was ousted by them and went to Gaul. Later, upon his return to Rome, he was given a polite reception. Shortly thereafter at the request of the French king Louis,[47] he went to France, sending St. Bernard on ahead. He joined Emperor Conrad [III] who organized a large army, gathering together a great number of Germans, English

---

39. Emperor A.D. 1138–15 February 1152.
40. We have not been able to identify the source for this story.
41. Hugh (c.1096–11 February 1141) and Richard (prior, 1162–1173) of St. Victor, Parisian theologians.
42. Pope 163, October 1143–March 1144.
43. Pope 164, A.D. 1144–1145.
44. In Gerusalemme, one of the major Roman basilicas.
45. Pope 165, A.D. 1145–1153.
46. The Cistercian house of SS. Vincenzio e Anastasio outside Rome.
47. Louis VII, 1137–1180.

and French, and along with many others marked by the Cross, they went overseas, many in large ships and others going through Pannonia and Hungary. Finally they arrived in Constantinople. There, despite great difficulties because of the deceit and fraud of the Greeks, they nevertheless were able to enter the Holy Land and fought many battles victoriously.[48]

At this time Gilbert,[49] an eminent master of science, became well known. The book by John Damascene was translated from Greek into Latin. Blessed Thomas, archbishop of Canterbury, by order of the king of England, was killed in church.[50] The monk Gratian, born in Tuscany, composed a book of *Decretals* at the monastery of San Felice in Bologna.[51]

FREDERICK I (EMPEROR 102), A.D. 1152

Frederick I,[52] the eldest son of Conrad's brother and a descendant of the Swabians, known as Barbarossa, ruled the empire for thirty-seven years. He was invited to Rome by Eugenius [III], the above-mentioned pope, and crowned by him. But then, during the first year of his reign, he had Spoleto destroyed as he was returning home. He was a magnificently liberal emperor, good and creative, and successful in all his undertakings. In his day the city of Dissa, which is called Arat in the Bible, was captured by the Saracens, and the archbishop, rector of the town, was killed along with those who would not deny Christ. And thus that city — which had earlier converted to the Catholic faith — was bathed in the blood of Christian martyrs.

---

48. This is the Second Crusade.
49. Gilbert de la Porrée, c.1075–4 September 1154.
50. In the cathedral of Canterbury, on 29 December 1170.
51. The *Concordia discordantium canonum,* by Gratian of Bologna, c.1150.
52. Frederick I, Barbarossa, emperor A.D. 1155–1190.

ANASTASIUS IV (POPE 174), A.D. 1154

The Roman Anastasius IV,[53] son of Benedetto, held the pontificate for one year, four months and twenty-seven days. The papacy was vacant for twenty days. He embellished Sta. Maria Rotonda[54] and donated many gifts to St. John Lateran.

ADRIAN IV (POPE 175), A.D. 1154

Hadrianus [Adrian] IV,[55] born in England, held the pontificate for three years. The papacy was unoccupied for twenty days. First as bishop of Albano, he was sent as an envoy to Norway to preach the faith of Christ, and there he converted many nonbelievers. Later after his return he was elected pope following Anastasius's death. Because of a seditious cardinal, he placed the entire city of Rome under interdiction until he was given full satisfaction. He also excommunicated King William of Sicily as a rebel against the Church, but upon meeting the pope's demands the king was absolved.[56] One reads that he was the first to hold court in Orvieto.

At this time the emperor [Frederick] captured Cremona with his army with which not much later he built the fortress of Lodi. Also during Adrian's pontificate, there flourished the abbot Joachim of Fiore,[57] who wrote many books on the Apocalypse[58] and on Jeremiah[59] and other prophets, and went from Calabria to Pope Urban III in Verona. Master Peter Lombard[60] also became famous as the writer of the *Sententiae*. Likewise, in this period the relics of the three Magi that

---

53. Pope 166, A.D. 1153–1154.
54. The Pantheon in Rome.
55. Pope 167, A.D. 1154–1159.
56. William I was confirmed as king of Sicily in the treaty of Benevento of 1156.
57. Calabrian abbot and writer, c.1135–30 March 1202.
58. *Expositio in Apocalipsim* and others.
59. *Super Hieremiam*, incorrectly attributed to Joachim.
60. Theologian, 1096–21/22 August 1164.

had been brought from Persia to Constantinople and later to Milan were then moved by the emperor to Cologne.[61]

ALEXANDER III (POPE 176), A.D. 1159

The Sienese Alexander III[62] held the pontificate for twenty-one years, eleven months and nine days. In opposition to him were elected four schismatics in succession; the first was named Victor [IV], the second Paschal [III], the third Callixtus [III], the fourth Innocent [III].

At that time the emperor [Frederick I] defeated the Romans in a great rout near Tusculum.[63] But Pope Alexander, seeing that the emperor was providing assistance in order to harass him, fled to France and was received with acclaim by the king.[64] Upset by this, the emperor and a large army went to France with the intent of seizing the kingdom, but the king of France, with the aid of the king of England, defended himself vigorously.[65] Not much later, the emperor realized that many people were rebelling against him because of his persecution of the pope, and he tried to reach an accord with him through ambassadors. Thus they reached a mutual agreement after a schism that had lasted some eighteen years.[66]

Alexander convened two councils, one at Torso[67] and the other in Rome,[68] and brought about peace and accord between Frederick, the emperor in the West, and Manuel [Comnenus], at that time emperor in Constantinople, as well as between King William of Sicily and the Lombards. But Manuel died shortly thereafter.

---

61. In 1164 Frederick took them as loot from the basilica di Sant'Eustorgio in Milan to the cathedral of Cologne.

62. Pope 168, A.D. 1159–1181.

63. On 29 May 1167.

64. The chronology is confused here. Alexander fled to France in April 1162.

65. There is no factual basis for this statement.

66. At the Peace of Venice in 1177 Frederick ended his war with Alexander and the Lombard League and its allies.

67. At Toulouse in October 1160.

68. The Third Lateran Council of 5–19 March 1179.

THE LIVES OF THE POPES AND EMPERORS

At this time there were many terrible earthquakes in various places. In Syria they devastated Antioch, Damascus, Tripoli and many other cities, while in Sicily the city of Chaina[69] was completely destroyed. According to records, more than twenty thousand people perished under its ruins while the nearby sea was so rough that five thousand people drowned. Also at this time, because of the hatred the inhabitants of Milan, Piacenza and Brescia bore against the inhabitants of Pavia, they built a city in Liguria that they wanted to make more famous, naming it Alessandria[70] in honor of Alexander who was the pope. The pope then gave it a bishop, thereby taking away from the bishop of Pavia the dignity of the crozier and the pallium because he feared what Emperor Frederick's men might do against the Church. Also at this time the city of Milan was captured and pillaged by the emperor, resulting in the death of several thousand people.[71] King Roger of Sicily died,[72] and Argenta[73] was captured by the Ferrarese. Vicenza was nearly burned to the ground after widespread fires swept through most of the city. One also reads that at this time three moons were seen together with a cross at their center, and not much later three suns appeared miraculously at the same time.[74]

One must believe that this work was in some way corrupted at this point since Petrarch would not have omitted the Venetian victory over the emperor and their restoration of the pontiff, something all the great writers of this period have treated and commemorated.[75]

---

69. Perhaps Catania is meant.
70. In 1168.
71. 6 March 1162.
72. Roger II died on 26 February 1154.
73. In the province of Ferrara, Emilia-Romagna.
74. These are depicted for these years in the *Nuremberg Chronicle*, fol. CCIII verso.
75. At this point the author begins emending the text.

THE TWELFTH CENTURY

LUCIUS III (POPE 177), A.D. 1180

Lucius II [III],[76] born in Tuscany, occupied the pontificate for four years, six months and eighteen days. In his day flourished Pietro who gathered into a single volume some histories with useful analyses of the Old and New Testaments; the book is entitled *Scholastic Histories*.[77] St. Bernard died, and the relics of St. Nicholas were also at this time transferred from Myra to Bari. Marquis Conrad of Monferrato[78] was killed because of envy by King Richard of England.

URBAN III (POPE 178), A.D. 1185

Urbanus [Urban] III,[79] born in Lombardy, occupied the pontificate for one year, ten months and twenty-five days. In his day Emperor Frederick went to Florence, and after seizing the territory of almost all the cities in Tuscany except Pisa and Pistoia, he besieged Siena for some time. Also during this period, in 1186, Jerusalem was occupied and the Holy Land captured by Saladin of Babylon.[80] When Urban heard this news, he became very upset and died of melancholy in Ferrara where he was buried with honor.

When Emperor Frederick also heard of this loss, he organized a very large number of troops to retake the Holy Land.[81] He passed through Thrace on his way to Asia, and not long after that, while washing in a polluted river in Antioch, which today is called the Ferro, he choked and drowned.[82] For this reason his son, whom he had taken with him, took his body to Tyre and there buried him, while nearly all

---

76. Pope 169, A.D. 1181–1185.

77. The author's identity is not clear, perhaps Peter Lombard (1096–21/22 August 1164) and his *Libri Quatuor Sententiarum*.

78. Elected king of Jerusalem against the objections of Richard I and assassinated on 28 April 1192.

79. Pope 170, A.D. 1185–1187.

80. That is, Babylon of Egypt.

81. This is the Third Crusade.

82. Frederick drowned riding across a swollen river in Cilician Armenia on 10 June 1190.

the noblemen and barons who had accompanied him in this crossing perished, making the undertaking unsuccessful.

Gregory VIII (Pope 179), A.D. 1187

Gregorius [Gregory] VIII,[83] born in Benevento, occupied the pontificate for one year and twenty-seven days. In his attempt to help retake the Holy Land he sent ambassadors and messengers to various parts of the world to rally the people. Exhausted by his attempt to make peace between Pisa and Genoa, which were then enemies, he died in Pisa during that trip and was buried there. At this time a territory ten miles from Florence was returned to that city.

Clement III (Pope 180[84]), A.D. 1188

Clemens [Clement] III,[85] born in Rome, occupied the pontificate for three years and sixteen days. He established the cloister of San Lorenzo fuori le Mura [in Rome] and built the palace of the Lateran, decorating it with various paintings. He also had a bronze horse with rider made and placed there.[86]

Henry VI (Emperor 103), A.D. 1189

Henry V [VI],[87] son of the elder Frederick [I, Barbarossa], emperor of the Swabian people, ruled the empire for eighteen years. In the month of April he was crowned by Pope Celestine [III]. After invading Apulia with a large army he went on to besiege Naples and continued the siege for several months. Since little progress was made, he departed, but returned four years later and subjected the entire kingdom of Apulia,[88] taking back with him to Germany the son of King Tancred of Sicily with his mother Margherita and several others. At

---

83. Pope 171, 25 October–17 December 1187.

84. Text reads "CXXX."

85. Pope 172, A.D. 1187–1191.

86. This is the bronze statue of Marcus Aurelius, now atop the Capitoline, long thought to be of Constantine.

87. Emperor A.D. 1191–1197.

88. Henry took Naples in 1194.

THE TWELFTH CENTURY

this time the area around San Miniato was destroyed by the Germans from Terzanni, and there was peace throughout Italy. Saladin the sultan of Babylon died.[89]

CELESTINE III (POPE 181), A.D. 1191

The Roman Coelestinus [Celestine III],[90] installed as pope on the day of Christ's Resurrection, held the pontificate for six years, nine months and two days. He crowned Henry [VI] as emperor on the second day after his election as pope. In this year, on the kalends of July the sun darkened and remained so from terce to nones. Huguccio of Pisa, bishop of Ferrara,[91] became famous, and King Richard of England died after being wounded in the siege of a castle fortress.[92]

INNOCENT III (POPE 182), A.D. 1197

Innocentius [Innocent] III,[93] born in Campania, held the pontificate for eighteen years, four months and twenty-four days. He was installed on the feast of the Chair of St. Peter. How extraordinary he was can be seen by such works as restoring the hospital of Sto. Spirito[94] and the church of San Sisto [Vecchio], composing the *Decretals*,[95] many sermons and the treatise on *The Condition and Misery of Humankind*,[96] as well as by many other beautiful works, even the elaborate decoration of the churches in Rome. At this time, in 1200, Constantinople was captured by the French and the Venetians whose army was led by a man called Baldwin [IX], count of Flanders, who was later crowned emperor following the emperors Alesso [Alexius IV] and Marzusto [Murzuphius or Alexius V].[97] In this way Baldwin took over the

89. On 4 March 1193.
90. Pope 173, A.D. 1191–1198.
91. Canon lawyer, d.1210.
92. Wounded on 25 March 1199 at Châlus-Chabrol, d.6 April 1199.
93. Pope 174, A.D. 1198–1216.
94. On the Vatican bank of the Tiber near St. Peter's.
95. The *Compilatio secunda*, 8 January 1198–7 January 1210.
96. *De miseria humanae conditionis*.
97. These are events of the Fourth Crusade, between 1202 and 1204.

empire in the East. Also at this time Henry [VI], emperor in the West, died in Palermo. After his death there was great discord among rulers deciding who was to be emperor, with some voting for Philip [of Swabia] and others for Otto [IV] who was finally crowned and later excommunicated (as we shall discuss below).

During Innocent's pontificate began the power and rule of the Tartars who lived in the mountains of India. After losing David, their king and the son of a priest named John, they began to do battle and acquired cities, fortresses and many other places.[98] Under this pope there also began the order of Preachers under the venerable patriarch, St. Dominic of Spain,[99] and not much later the order of Friars Minor, begun by St. Francis who was known as a venerable religious.[100] The castle fortress of Bragantino was built by the Ferrarese near the Po River. John, count of Brienne, was named king of Jerusalem, and took as wife King Conrad's daughter, by whom he had a daughter who was later married to Emperor Frederick II.

*

---

98. This story originated in letter 7 of 1221 by Jacobus de Vitry, bishop of Acre, in which he states that King David of India, the son or grandson of Prester John, would ally with the Christians against the Saracens.

99. The Dominican Order was formally approved by Honorius III on on 22 December 1216.

100. Francis and his companions first petitioned Innocent III in 1209.

THE THIRTEENTH CENTURY

Otto iiij.

OTTO IV (EMPEROR 104), A.D. 1207

Otto IV,[1] born in Saxony and crowned emperor of the West by Innocent III because he swore to defend the Church of St. Peter, ruled the empire for four years. However, not long afterwards he initiated a war with the Romans, entered Apulia against the pope's wishes, and even stole from those who were going to Rome. He thus broke the oath he had previously taken, was excommunicated by the pope and deprived of the empire. This was the reason that the rulers of Germany, with the Church's assistance, elected Frederick [II] as emperor (as we will show below).

Otto declared war against King Philip [II, Augustus] of France, but was routed and defeated by him with serious loss of men.[2] In his day, the son of King Philip of France was sent by his father with a large army against the king of Hungary, who had declared war on them, and defeated him in a great victory.[3] While Otto still ruled, Azzo, marquis of Este,[4] after defeating his adversary Salinguerra,[5] entered Ferrara, whereupon Archbishop Ubaldo of Ravenna seized Argenta from Otto's vicar who held it.

---

1. Emperor A.D. 1209–1215.
2. At battle of Bouvines, 27 July 1214.
3. The reference here is unclear.
4. Azzolino, 1170–November 1212. The author begins to focus attention here on the Romagna and the northern districts of the Papal States.
5. Salinguerra Torelli.

FREDERICK II (EMPEROR 105), A.D. 1211

Frederick [II],[6] Emperor Henry [VI]'s son, who was elected emperor by the German princes with the Church's approval, ruled for eight years.[7] When he went to Rome, he was kindly received by the pope and the Roman people. Later, after going to Germany, he successfully fought Otto, the previous emperor who had been excommunicated. At this time Pope Innocent [III] held a council[8] in Rome to aid the Holy Land and for the welfare of the universal Church that numbered around 1215 patriarchs, bishops, archbishops and other orders of prelates. At that council many decrees were passed, and it was then that the church of Sta. Maria in Trastevere was consecrated. Also at this council the treatise written by Joachim against Peter Lombard[9] was condemned. In addition Amalric[10] was condemned for saying that the forms located in the mind of God, through which everything is made, were and are created, whereas St. Augustine says that in the mind of God there are only eternal and immutable things. Amalric also said that God is the end of all things, since all things must return to him, and that in God they rest without changing and will remain with him. He also affirmed that God is the essence of all creatures and the being of all things, and he argued falsely about many other things, because of which he and all his books were burned in Paris.

During this time too Pope Innocent wished to make peace among the Pisans, the Genovese and the Lombards in order to aid the Holy Land, so he made great preparations to go there, but died in Perugia where he was buried in the church of San Lorenzo. Azzo, marquis d'Este, also died. Elizabeth,[11] a daughter of the king of Hungary, became famous who, after losing her husband Langrave Lewis [IV] of Thuringia,

6. 26 December 1194–13 December 1250, elected emperor September 1211 at the diet of Nuremberg.

7. That is, according to pro-papal calculations.

8. The Fourth Lateran Council opened on 15 November 1215.

9. *Liber contra Lombardum*.

10. Amaury de Bène or Amaury de Chartres, d. c.1205.

11. St. Elizabeth of Hungary, 7 July 1207–17 November 1231.

THE THIRTEENTH CENTURY

lived a very holy life. In addition, the Cremonese in their battle with the Milanese overcame and defeated them near [Castel] Leone.[12]

HONORIUS III (POPE 183[13]), A.D. 1216

The Roman Honorius III[14] held the pontificate for ten years, seven months and twenty-three days, and was elected pope in Perugia. He crowned in Constantinople Count Artisio,[15] who was named Pietro, as emperor of the East.[16] Pope Honorius also renovated the church of San Lorenzo and another named Sancta Sanctorum.[17] Besides this, in the first year of his pontificate he approved the order of Friars Preachers,[18] founded by St. Dominic, the glorious patriarch born in Spain. At this time the city of Damietta was besieged by the Christians,[19] and after two years' siege they destroyed the city, and all the Saracens who were there were either captured or killed.

FREDERICK II (EMPEROR 106), A.D. 1220

Emperor Frederick II[20] ruled the empire for twenty-four years. Previously he was duke of Swabia, and his mother, Constance, was the daughter of King Roger of Sicily. He was crowned emperor by Pope Honorius at Rome in the church of St. Peter, yet he was unfriendly to the Church and tried to diminish its authority and dignity. At this time the Saracens recaptured Damietta, and the king of Jerusalem,[21] who

---

12. At Castelleone in 1213.
13. Text reads "CXXXIII."
14. Pope 175, A.D. 1216–1227.
15. Perhaps a misreading of the Latin for Auxerre, one of the Courtenay holdings.
16. Peter II of Courtenay, crowned Latin emperor of Constantinople in April 1217.
17. The chapel of San Lorenzo in Palatio ad Sancta Sanctorum at the Lateran in Rome. Again, later sections of the *Lives* begin to display less knowledge of the city of Rome.
18. On 22 December 1216.
19. During the Fifth Crusade, from 1218 to 1219.
20. This is the same Frederick II as above, p. 189. The pro-papal writer of the *Lives* counts only the years when Frederick was not declared excommunicated or deposed by the papacy.
21. It is unclear who is meant here. Isabella II (1212–25 April 1228), also known as Yolande of Brienne, was queen of Jerusalem at the time of the Damietta campaign.

had reigned for thirty years, died on the feast of St. Lucia, the same day he had been crowned. In addition, St. Dominic died in Bologna in 1223, and in 1226 St. Francis passed away. King Philip II of France also died,[22] followed not much later by Louis[23] who was then canonized. At this time too, there were terrible earthquakes throughout Italy, and a comet appeared. Pope Honorius also died and was buried in the church of Sta. Maria Maggiore.

GREGORY IX (POPE 184), A.D. 1226

Gregorius [Gregory] IX,[24] born in Campania, held the pontificate for thirteen years and ten days. His given name was Ugolino [di Conti], and he was the cardinal bishop of Ostia. He canonized St. Elizabeth as well as St. Dominic, the founder of the Friars Preachers. Having differences with Emperor Frederick [II], he wished to convene a council, but because the emperor had closed the passes, he sent by sea two cardinals, Bishop Iacopo of Palestrina and Otto, along with many other prelates, to seek aid for the Church.[25] At the emperor's command, these were captured by the Pisans at sea and drowned. Because of his continuing persecution of the Church, the emperor was excommunicated by the pope.

Gregory had the many volumes of the *Decretals* condensed into a single volume by Fra Raimondo of the order of Friars Preachers, his confessor and chaplain.[26] At this time the king of Castile drove out the Saracens who had entered Spain, and the king of Aragon with a large army captured the islands of Majorca and Minorca[27] as well as Valencia. Count Riccardo of Verona was captured in his palace and

22. Philip Augustus died on 14 July 1223.

23. Philip's successor was Louis VIII the Lion, 5 September 1187–8 November 1226. His son, Louis IX reigned from 1226 to 1270 and was later canonized.

24. Pope 176, A.D. 1227–1241.

25. Jacopo [Colonna?], bishop of Palestrina, and Otto, bishop of Porto, called the White Cardinal. These details appear in Giovanni Villani, *Nuova Cronica* VII.19.

26. Raymond of Peñafort published the *Liber extra* of Canon Law in 1234.

27. In the autumn of 1229.

THE THIRTEENTH CENTURY

his party driven out. Also at this time when Emperor Frederick discovered that his eldest son, Henry, was causing trouble against him in favor of the Church, he had him placed in prison where he later died.

St. Anthony of the order of Friars Minor likewise died in 1233 under Gregory's pontificate, after having lived a saintly life in Padua. Michael Scotus,[28] the outstanding astrologist, became famous. One also reads that there was a man in Sicily named Nicolao Pesce who lived in the sea like a fish and could not stay for long out of the water; he revealed to the public many things about the secrets of the sea.[29] In addition, at this time Bishop Guidotto of Mantua was killed in the church of Sant'Andrea following an argument with partisan noblemen.

In his battles with the Milanese, Emperor Frederick overcame and defeated them,[30] captured the son of the doge of Venice, their rector, and had him decapitated. A church emissary, the Venetians and the Bolognese, after battling with exiles from Ferrara, besieged that city and some time later were allowed inside where Salinguerra, leader of the party that had been besieged, was taken. He was sent to Venice where he was kept under guard and died, while his followers were dispersed. At this time too, with the death of Paolo, his adversary in Ravenna, and the capture of Ravenna, the emperor took two columns from the church of San Vitale and sent them to his kingdom. Brother Giordano, a teacher in the order of Friars Preachers who was a man highly praised for his life and knowledge, died at sea while traveling to preach to the Saracens.

---

28. 1175–c.1232, mathematician and scholar.

29. The myth of Nicolao Pesce, often thought to be from Messina, has a long history. He first appears in a Byzantine bestiary and, over time, developed into a Peter Pan–like figure for Italian boys. On the legacy of Nicolao Pesce, see Sergio Palumbo, "Dalla mitologia alla favola popolare: L'ibrido pesce-uomo nello Stretto di Messina," in *È c'è di mezzo il mare: Lingua, letteratura e civiltà marina* (Florence: F. Cesati, 2002), 213–23.

30. The battle of Cortenuova in November 1237. For these decades the *Lives* focuses attention on Lombardy and the Romagna.

THE LIVES OF THE POPES AND EMPERORS

CELESTINE IV (POPE 185), A.D. 1239

Coelestinus [Celestine] IV,[31] born in Milan, held the pontificate for seventeen days. The Church was without a leader for one year, eight months and fourteen days. While bishop of Sabina he was elected pope, but being old and infirm he suddenly died. In that year on the first Friday of June, the sun darkened nearly at nones and remained darkened for a long period.[32] Also at this time the Tartars [Mongols], who were expanding into various areas, waged very difficult and cruel battles in Pannonia and in Hungary.

INNOCENT IV (POPE 186), A.D. 1241

The Genoese Innocentius [Innocent] IV[33] occupied the pontificate for eleven years, six months and twelve days. He filled cardinal seats that had been vacant for some time by holding elections in various parts of the world. After many attempts at peace between himself and Emperor Frederick [II], who was a contumacious adversary, Innocent went to Gaul with Genoese aid and convened a general council in Lyons[34] that proclaimed Frederick an enemy of the Church; he excommunicated him once again and stripped him of the empire. For this reason, after the barons and the princes had reached an agreement, and with the Church's approval, they elected in the second year the landgrave of Lotharingia[35] who died after organizing an army to march against Conrad, Frederick's son. After his death William [II], count of Holland, was elected emperor, but he was killed shortly thereafter while battling the Frisians.

Meanwhile, after assembling a large army, Frederick besieged Parma where he had begun building a city nearby that he wished to call Vittorie. As a result the Parmesans confronted him with the aid of the

---

31. Pope 177, 25 October–10 November 1241.

32. Also illustrated in the *Nuremberg Chronicle*, fol. CCIX recto, facing the discussion of Celestine IV.

33. Pope 178, A.D. 1243–1254.

34. The first council of Lyons, 26 June–17 July 1245.

35. Heinrich Raspe, landgrave of Thuringia.

THE THIRTEENTH CENTURY

pope's emissary, defeated him and made him flee in shame, evicting him from that city in which he had established order.[36] Shortly thereafter, his son Enzo, king of Sardinia,[37] while fighting the Bolognese in the town of Modena, was captured by them and imprisoned in Bologna where he lived for a while and died a wretched death. Not long after that, Emperor Frederick was deposed and, still an excommunicated unrepentant, fell seriously ill in Florence[38] on the feast of St. Lucia and was strangled (according to hearsay) by his son at the age of fifty-seven. He left Conrad as his legitimate son as well as Enzo, who was imprisoned in Bologna, and Prince Manfred of Taranto, who went on to rule fraudulently. He also left many other children, both male and female. After Frederick, no one was elected to the imperial office until the time of Pope Gregory X.

During this period, Cardinal Hugo,[39] a brother in the order of Friars Preachers, who was highly praised for his life and knowledge, became well known. In the same period King Louis [IX] of France went abroad to regain the Holy Land, set up camp in Damietta and captured it, but he was soon taken prisoner by the Saracens.[40] In order to gain his release, the Christians left Damietta and thus Louis was saved. And finally, on his way to Apulia, Innocent died in Naples and was buried there. During his pontificate, King Amerigo of Dacia[41] was strangled by his younger brother who, after seizing the kingdom, was only able to enjoy it for a short time since the following year he was killed in a battle with the Frisians.

---

36. On 18 February 1248. See Giovanni Villani, *Nuova Cronica* VII.34.

37. At the battle of Fossalta, in May of 1249.

38. At Firenzuola. See Giovanni Villani, *Nuova Cronica* VII.41.

39. This may be Hugh of St. Cher, O.P., c.1200–19 March 1263, cardinal and noted biblical scholar.

40. At the battle of Fariskur, on 6 April 1250.

41. Perhaps Emeric of Hungary, king 1196–30 November 1204, whose brother Andrew defied him early in his reign.

THE LIVES OF THE POPES AND EMPERORS

ALEXANDER IV (POPE 187), A.D. 1252

Alexander IV,[42] born in Campania, held the pontificate for nine years and six months. He canonized St. Clare of the order of St. Damian.[43] At this time King Conrad of Sicily,[44] Emperor Frederick's son, was poisoned through the deception of his brother Manfred who, after seizing the kingdom, crowned himself king of Sicily.[45] Because he was on bad terms with the Church, the pope excommunicated him and sent a large army against him that was unable to defeat him. Also, during Alexander's pontificate, after King William of Germany[46] was killed by the Frisians, because of disagreements among themselves some elected King Alfonso [X][47] of Spain, while others elected Richard,[48] the king of England's brother; and this disagreement lasted a long time.

Azzolino, lord of Verona, Vicenza and Padua, besieged Mantua but was unable to capture it, while Archbishop Filippo of Ravenna, a church legate, organized and blessed a large army, and, upon hearing that the Paduans were with Azzolino at the siege of Mantua, went to Padua, which was emptied of men, and soon destroyed it. Not much later Azzolino was wounded and died while fighting with the Cremonese. His brother named Alberisio,[49] the tyrant at Treviso, was defeated by the Paduans, the Trevigians and the Vicenzians at Castello San Zeno. Later on, he was betrayed by his men and captured. His children were killed in his presence and his wife burned with her daughters, and after beholding this cruelty he was cut to pieces by his men.

42. Pope 179, A.D. 1254–1261.
43. St. Claire of Assisi, 16 July 1194–11 August 1253.
44. Conrad IV of Germany (25 April 1228–21 May 1254), king of Sicily, 1250–1254.
45. 1258–1266.
46. William of Holland, anti-king, 1247–28 January 1256.
47. King of Castile, León and Galicia, 1252–4 April 1284.
48. Richard of Cornwall, 5 January 1209–2 April 1272.
49. Alberico da Romano, 1196–26 August 1260. The following details are taken from the *Cronica* of Salimbene da Adam, under 1250, who claims "*Vidi ista oculis meis*" ("I saw these things with my own eyes"). Salimbene borrowed many details of much earlier events from the *Cronica* of Sicard of Cremona.

THE THIRTEENTH CENTURY

Also at this time the Venetians, while battling the Genoese at sea and being the more powerful, destroyed a Genoese tower that was located in Ancona and later built a fortress near the Po in a place called San Alberto. At the same time there became famous a Tuscan, Accorso,[50] and a Bolognese, Odofredus,[51] both skilled in civil law, who wrote commentaries and analyses of the law. After their deaths they were both buried in Bologna in the church of the Friars Minor. And eventually Alexander died in Viterbo.

URBAN IV (POPE 188), A.D. 1261

The French Urbanus [Urban] IV[52] held the pontificate for three years, one month and four days. After convening a council of cardinals, he summoned Count Charles of Provence, the brother of King Louis [IX] of France, and gave him the kingdom of Sicily and Apulia,[53] with the understanding that he had to earn it inasmuch as Manfred, Emperor Frederick [II]'s son, held it against the wishes of the Church.[54] This led to much fighting between them. At this time, the Florentines and the Lucchesi fought near Siena against the Sienese, but they were soundly routed due to the deceit of many in the Florentine army. Emperor Baldwin[55] was driven from Constantinople by the Greeks and Venetians. In his battles with the Saracens, King Alfonso [X] of Spain overcame and conquered them. Finally, Urban died in Perugia.

---

50. Accorso di Bagnolo, c.1182–1263.

51. Odofredus, d.3 December 1265.

52. Pope 180, A.D. 1261–1264.

53. As the kingdom of Naples, or Regno, was variably called.

54. This is the investiture of Charles of Anjou (Charles I of Naples) with the kingdom of Naples, approving his subsequent conquest from the Hohenstaufen heirs of Frederick II, in 1265.

55. Baldwin II, emperor A.D. 1228–October 1273.

CLEMENT IV (POPE 189), A.D. 1264

Clemens [Clement] IV,[56] from Saint-Gilles in Provence, held the pontificate for four years and eight months. The papacy was without a leader for three years, two months and ten days. Earlier he had a wife and children and was a good and clever man and an advisor to the king of France. But after his wife died, he was made bishop because of his outstanding life, then archbishop of Narbonne and finally cardinal when he was sent as an envoy to Hungary by Pope Urban IV. Sometime later, after the pope's death, Clement was elected in Perugia, although he was absent.

At this time, Count Charles of Provence went secretly by sea to Rome in order to take possession of the kingdom of Sicily that Urban IV had given him. There on the feast of the Epiphany he was crowned king by two cardinals as mandated by the pope. Later upon his army's arrival he went through Italy to Apulia and daringly captured many castle-fortresses and cities. Finally, after meeting with Manfred in the town of Benevento and having defeated and overcome his people, he deprived him of their lives and of the kingdom that he had occupied by force. In the battle many people were killed and captured, among whom were Count Giordano and Messer Piero,[57] a Florentine dolt. These men were sent to Provence where they died a wretched death. It was in this way that Count Charles obtained Apulia and most of Sicily. Later that same year, having been made vicar of the empire by the Church of Rome, he went to Tuscany and stayed in Florence eight days where he was received with great ceremony.[58]

At this time also Conradin, King Conrad's son, went with a large army from Germany to Verona in order to deprive Charles of the kingdom of Sicily. Charles was then encamped at the fortress of Poggibonsi, which, following a brief siege, he had stormed

---

56. Pope 181, A.D. 1265–1268.

57. Piero Asini degli Uberti.

58. These and the following details on Conradin can be found in Giovanni Villani, *Nuova Cronica* VIII.

THE THIRTEENTH CENTURY

and captured and then set free all the Ghibelline prisoners. But after learning of Conrad's advance, Charles returned with his army into Apulia, leaving in Tuscany a senior official to help Conradin's trip into Apulia. Whereupon Conradin, who also had been excommunicated by the pope, left Verona and together with Genoese forces went through Pavia to Pisa where he was kindly received by the Pisans and the Tuscan Ghibellines. He then set up camp in Lucca where Charles's senior official had met with the pope's emissary and, seeing that there was nothing to be gained there, had gone on to Siena. The top official or seneschal likewise left for Florence, but later, on his way to Arezzo, he encountered Conradin and his men near the Avalle Bridge where, provoked by certain gentlemen called Ubertini, he was captured and many of his men killed.

Because of this victory, Conradin became arrogant and, together with his troops as well as the Ghibellines of Tuscany and Lombardy and rebels from Charles's men, he left Siena and went to Rome. There he entered as a victor and, after despoiling many churches of their treasures, he departed in 1268, accompanied by Arrigo[59], the Spanish king's brother, who was at that time a Roman senator. Then, accompanied by the Romans, the Tuscans and the Lombards, he clashed with Charles on the plain of San Valentino[60] in order to gain the kingdom of Sicily, but Charles defeated him with great loss of troops. In that battle, Senator Arrigo was captured, but Conradin escaped and went to Asturi with the son of the duke of Sterlicchi, Count Calvano and Count Gherardo of Pisa. But then, as he was setting sail, he was captured by one of the Lanfranchi and handed over to Charles. Conradin was taken to Naples where Charles had him beheaded, together with the duke of Sterlicchi and several other nobles. Charles had Senator Arrigo imprisoned and then, having regained the lands that had rebelled against him, took great vengeance on them.

---

59. Henry of Castile.
60. At the battle of Tagliacozzo on 23 August 1268.

At this time, the Tartars were fighting in their homeland with the Saracens and captured the city of Baldalch[61] as well as their great pontifex; they drowned him in gold since he possessed an immense amount of it, but never wanted to use or spend it for the necessities of war. Also at this time King Louis [IX] of France, a very Christian and holy king, together with his brother King Charles of Sicily, King Edward [I] of England and the king of Navarre raised a great army in order to retake the Holy Land; they went overseas and encamped near Carthage.[62] There, many died because of illness, as did King Louis, the pope's emissary, many other barons and his oldest son, as well as the king of Navarre who also passed from this life because of illness. With the departure of King Edward of England, the remainder of the army, very numerous but leaderless, received a considerable amount of gold from the Saracens and likewise departed, with each member returning to his own country.

Meanwhile Philip [III], son of King Louis of France, left Carthage and went to Sicily where he unfortunately suffered substantial losses because of the rough sea in the port of Trapani. Later on, he went to Viterbo where Count Guy de Monfort killed Henry, a son of Richard who was the king of England's brother, while he was at Mass.[63] After remaining there for some time Philip returned to France, taking with him the remains of his father, Louis, and there he was crowned as king.[64] At this time the Guelphs drove the Ghibellines from Florence. Albigeo de Fontana was poisoned through the deception of a man he had made marquis, and Albigeo's brother and sons, who wished to make innovations in Ferrara, were thrown out of the city with some nobles. The Bolognese wanted to build a fortress near their main port,

---

61. I.e., Baghdad. These are the Mongol incursions.

62. At Tunis in the Eight Crusade in July 1270. Navarre played no significant role.

63. This is Guy de Montfort, count of Nola (1244–c.1288), who murdered Henry of Almain (son of Richard, earl of Cornwall) in Viterbo at the church of San Silvestro in revenge for his father's and brother's deaths at the battle of Evesham. See Villani, *Nuova Cronica* VIII.39. Dante discusses the incident in *Inferno* 12.111–12.

64. Philip III reigned 30 August 1271 to 5 October 1285.

THE THIRTEENTH CENTURY

but the Venetians did not allow them to do so because they were on the opposite bank of the Po River, and thus were able to stop them. Also during Clement's pontificate thrived the German Albertus Magnus, St. Thomas Aquinas, the angelic doctor of the order of Preachers, and Brother Bonaventure from Bagnareto [Bagnorea] of the Friars Minor who later became cardinal.

GREGORY X (POPE 190), A.D. 1272

Gregorius [Gregory] X,[65] born in Piacenza, held the pontificate for four years. While he was overseas, he was elected pope by the cardinals at Viterbo. As soon as he was installed, he convened a council at Lyons in France.[66] On his way to the council with the cardinals he went to Florence and there tried to bring an accord between the Guelphs and Ghibellines. After assembling many people at a square on the River Arno, he achieved the desired peace; later on it was not honored, but on that very place he built a church in honor of St. Gregory and then left Florence.

Once in Lyons, he opened the council in 1274 in the month of June during which Paleologus,[67] emperor of the Greeks, together with the patriarch of Constantinople, were reconciled with the pope by promising to abandon their previous errors. For this reason, the pope upheld the emperor's status in the Eastern Empire. At the council too, it was decided to go overseas to preach the Cross and to collect tithes from all the churches. This enabled him to give the cardinalate to many outstanding men without including relatives or friends, as many popes are accustomed to do.

---

65. Pope 182, A.D. 1272–1276.
66. Second council of Lyons in 1274.
67. Michael VIII.

The order of Friars Preachers was also accepted as was the order of Friars Minor,[68] but the order of Hermit Friars,[69] the order of the Carmine[70] and all the other orders that live by begging were terminated. On his return to Rome Gregory fell ill at Arezzo, died and was buried there. At this time with the pope's approval, the German princes elected as emperor Count Rudolf, king of the Germans.

RUDOLF (EMPEROR 107), A.D. 1274

Ridolpho [Rudolf],[71] king of the Germans, was elected emperor by the German princes and ruled about twenty years. A just man, he was skilled in the use of arms. In battling the king of Bohemia, he overcame and defeated him, and after the victory he did not persecute the king's son but in fact received him peacefully and made him his son-in-law. At this time, the Bolognese crossed the bridge of San Proculo with a large army and sacked the town of Faenza.

INNOCENT V (POPE 191), A.D. 1276

Innocentius [Innocent] V,[72] born in Burgundy, held the pontificate for five months and eleven days. He was a friar in the Order of Preachers. Because of his persistence Pope Gregory [X] made him a cardinal. Eventually, following the pope's death at Arezzo, he assumed the papacy and then five months later died in Viterbo where he was buried.

ADRIAN V (POPE 192), A.D. 1276.

The Genoese Hadrianus [Adrian] V[73] held the pontificate for thirty-nine days.

---

68. The Dominicans and Franciscans were approved by Honorius III in 1216 and 1223 respectively.

69. It is unclear what group is meant here. The Order of Hermits of St. Augustine was approved by Innocent IV in 1243.

70. The Carmelites were approved by Honorius III in 1226.

71. Rudolf I, emperor A.D. 1273–1291.

72. Pope 183, 21 January–22 June 1276.

73. Pope 184, 11 July–18 August 1276.

JOHN XXI (POPE 193), (N.D.)

Ioannes [John] XXI[74] held the pontificate for eight months. The papacy had remained vacant for six months and sixteen days. In that year in the month of January, the Della Torre lords of Milan were overcome, driven from the city and killed or captured by those whom they had exiled, many by the marquis of Monserrat. Whereupon, the archbishop and others who had been exiled from the city returned and dispersed all of Pope John's adversaries. Finally, by divine judgment, a building collapsed on the pope and killed him, there being no one else present.[75] At this time King Philip [III] of France strongly persecuted the usurers throughout his kingdom.

NICHOLAS III (POPE 194), A.D. 1277

Nicolaus [Nicholas] III,[76] of Roman descent from the house of Orsini, held the pontificate for three years, nine months and fifteen days. The papacy was without a leader for six months and six days. He took the tithing funds[77] that had been collected for his installation and spent them as he pleased, building beautiful palaces and gardens. One reads that at this time a woman from Modena named Antonia gave birth before the end of her 40th year to some forty-two children by her husband. She was so fertile that she gave birth at times to three children and at other times five children. Eventually she died while giving birth.[78]

---

74. Pope 185, A.D. 1276–1277.

75. In his study in the papal palace at Viterbo.

76. Pope 186, A.D. 1277–1280.

77. Dante places him in Hell for his simony: *Inferno* 19.61–84.

78. Many ancient historiographers and medieval chroniclers mention similar phenomena in their collections. It is possible that the figure here, mistakenly identified as Antonia from Modena, actually refers to Margaret, the wife of Polish Count Virboslaus, who gave birth to thirty-six children, as recounted by the sixteenth-century Polish historian Martin Cromerus. See George M. Gould and Walter L. Pyle, *Anomalies and Curiosities of Medicine* (London: W. B. Saunders and Co., 1901), chapter 4.

In Nicholas's day, the Lambertaci of Bologna[79] who were in exile thanks to Bertoldo of the Orsini, the foremost count of Romagna,[80] returned to Bologna during a shaky peace. In that same year, on Christmas Eve, after learning that their adversaries were plotting to drive them from the city, they took up arms and occupied the square, but later fled when they were abandoned by certain Germans who had given them hope of assistance. Also at this time the Venetians caused much havoc in Ancona with their navy.

MARTIN IV (POPE 195), A.D. 1280

Martinus [Martin] IV,[81] of French descent, held the pontificate for four years, four months and twenty-seven days. The papacy was vacant for eleven days. He fought against the Ghibellines in Romagna. In his time, Palermo rebelled against King Charles [I],[82] killing anyone who was French; not long after, Messina and eventually all the cities of Sicily rebelled, killing all the French who were religious or laymen.[83] At this time King Pedro [III] of Aragon, who had advanced a little into the kingdom of Tunisia, battling and acquiring lands, withdrew after suffering a major defeat, and as he sailed he learned that the Sicilians had rebelled against Charles. This led him to send ambassadors to offer his assistance, and as a result, the Sicilians willingly elected him their king. Pedro went to Sicily with his troops, but without clerics and religious who refused to go because of the papal excommunication. There he was received cordially. But Charles, who had organized a large army of French, Provençals and Tuscans, had gone in September by ship to encamp at Messina. There he remained for some time without making progress, but when winter arrived, he left.

---

79. Reported in the *Chronicon Estense*, under 1274.
80. The nephew of Nicholas III.
81. Pope 187, A.D. 1281–1285.
82. Charles I of Naples, 1265–1285.
83. This is the Sicilian Vespers, of 30 March 1282.

THE THIRTEENTH CENTURY

Not long afterwards, his son Charles,[84] after assembling a large number of ships near Naples, was defeated and captured by Roger Lauria[85] who had come to aid King Pedro of Aragon. All his troops were killed, but he escaped with a few chosen ones. Later when Charles heard that his son had been captured, he tried to go to Sicily, but as he was unable to do so, he returned to Capua where he passed from this life, and his remains were taken to Naples. This Charles [I] was the foremost leader, the most skilled in arms and planning than of any other king since Charlemagne as well as the greatest supporter of the Church's authority.

At this time, in the month of March, Count Giovanni of Romagna[86] and his followers engaged in battle near Forlì with townspeople who had as their leader Guido da Montefeltro.[87] There were great losses on both sides, and they were finally defeated and overcome with the Forlese being victorious.[88] Nevertheless Forlì was later subjected to Count Giovanni, and its walls were torn down. Also at this time the Genoese navy defeated the Pisan navy in the port of Pisa with many thousands killed and captured.

HONORIUS IV (POPE 196), A.D. 1285
Honorius IV,[89] of German descent, held the pontificate for two years. The papacy was vacant for ten months. In his day King Philip [III] of France, after assembling a large army with Cardinal Gervais and the papal legate, went to the kingdom of Raona,[90] and there captured the city of Girona. Then because of the high casualties and hunger following the deaths of large numbers of men and animals, he too

---

84. Charles II of Anjou, king of Naples, 1285–1309.
85. In the battle of the Bay of Naples in 1284.
86. Giovanni Malatesta, d.1304.
87. Guido I, 1223–29 September 1298.
88. At Ponte di San Proculo, on 15 June 1275.
89. Pope 188, A.D. 1285–1287.
90. That is, Aragona, as used by Villani, *Nuova Cronica* VIII.102–3. Philip's war (1284–1285) against the Aragonese was deemed a papally sanctioned crusade.

died there. While there King Pedro of Aragon[91] recaptured the city of Girona and likewise passed from this life. After his death, Alfonso,[92] his first-born son, acquired the kingdom of Aragon while his other son, Jayme,[93] gained possession of the kingdom of Sicily.

Also at this time Bishop Guglielmo of Arezzo,[94] who was skilled in arms, had his troops seize the fortress of Poggio di Santa Cecilia from the Sienese, which led to the Sienese raising an army and, with the help of Florentines and other Tuscans, encamping at the fortress. Consequently, the bishop summoned a large number of Ghibellines to remove them, but failed, and so, his followers abandoned the fortress, and the Sienese then recaptured it.[95] At this time too Rudolf, the current emperor, named as his vicar in Tuscany Prezzivalle dal Fiesco in order to regain those regions of the empire. Because Prezzivalle wished the Florentines, the Sienese and many others to swear obedience to the imperial laws, and they refused to do so, he sentenced them to pay a sum of money and returned to Germany after scattering some of them.[96]

Also under Honorius's pontificate, the bishop of Arezzo once again assembled his troops (among whom were the Ubertini, the Pazzi of Valdarno and the good count of Montefeltro as well as those banished from Florence and Tuscany) and one night secretly entered Arezzo from which he had been driven and took over the city, driving out all the Guelphs who were there. They went to a fortress called Monte a Sansavino where they joined the Florentines and other Tuscan troops to wage war against Arezzo. But at that time Prezzivalle returned from Germany to Arezzo, raised a large force there and did battle for some time against the Florentines, the Sienese and the Guelphs.

91. Pedro III, 1239–2 November 1285.
92. Alfonso III, 4 November 1265–18 June 1291.
93. Jayme II of Aragon, king of Sicily 1285–1296.
94. Guglielmino degli Ubertini.
95. For these events see Villani, *Nuova Cronica* VIII.131.
96. Villani, *Nuova Cronica* VIII.112

THE THIRTEENTH CENTURY

NICHOLAS IV (POPE 197), A.D. 1287

Nicolaus [Nicholas] IV,[97] from Ascoli, held the pontificate for four years. The papacy was vacant for two years. When he was superior general of the Friars Minor, he was made cardinal and later elected to the papacy. At this time the Florentines and the Sienese set up camp in Arezzo and drew many fortresses to their side. But the Sienese advanced first, and with the support of Lucignano attacked and defeated the Aretines who had been driven out. They took many prisoners and killed a great number among whom was Rinuccio di Pepo from Maremma, a noble and vigorous man.

Also at this time, Count Ugolino [della Gherardesca], lord of Pisa, was arrested by the people and imprisoned with his five sons and grandsons. All the viscounts were driven out, together with many other Pisan Guelphs who had joined forces with the Florentines and the Luccans who had long waged war against Pisa. Not long afterward, Guido da Montefeltro, who had been exiled by the pope, came out of exile with his son to Pisa where he was made lord. Whereupon, the pope excommunicated him and the Pisans, proclaiming him an enemy of the Church; but Guido nevertheless accepted the lordship. The people who had imprisoned Count Ugolino let him slowly starve to death, together with his children and grandchildren.[98] At this time too, in 1290, the Saracens with a large army encamped near the city of Tripoli in Syria, captured and burned it to the ground, killing all the inhabitants except women and children.

In the same year Prince Charles, King Charles' son, went to the pope after leaving prison, was cordially received by him and the cardinals, and on the following Pentecost was crowned king of Sicily and Apulia, and called King Charles,[99] a holy and Catholic man. Also during Nicholas's pontificate the Florentine army went on foot to battle the Aretines near the River Arno where they fought and defeated

---

97. Pope 189, A.D. 1288–1292.
98. For which see Villani, *Nuova Cronica* VIII.121; Dante, *Inferno* 33.1–93.
99. Charles II of Naples.

them and the Ghibellines. Many brave men were killed and captured, among whom was Bishop Gugielmo of Arezzo who fought courageously and was killed in the fray. The victorious Florentines destroyed Bibbiena and many other fortresses; they then went to Arezzo and besieged it for a long time.[100]

At this time Jayme, who was occupying Sicily, tried to capture with his cavalry Count Artese[101] at his campground, but he was defeated, and then, on his way to encamp at Gaeta, he met up with King Charles who had ridden there. But since they wanted to avoid a conflict, they declared a truce for some months. The king of Hungary[102] died without heirs, and as a result Andreasso,[103] who was of Hungarian descent, invaded the kingdom and in a short while gained a large portion of it.[104] Also during this period the Florentines, the Lucchesi and other Tuscans joined the Genoese in order to confront the Pisans, and arriving at port, they captured Livorno and destroyed many of its towers and sacked many other Pisan lands.[105] The marquis of Monserrat had gone to the Lombard city of Alessandria, which he possessed, where he was treacherously captured and poisoned by the Alessandrians, whereupon the Milanese occupied much of the area.[106] Also in this year Stefano di Ginazano, count of Romagna, was captured in Ravenna, along with all his cavalry of Polentese who controlled the town, and was killed. This caused all of Romagna to prepare for war. Shortly thereafter, Bishop Bandino of Ravenna was made count of Romagna, which he took over completely.

---

100. See Villani, *Nuova Cronica* VIII.131–32.

101. This is a reference to the invasion of Sicily in 1287 by Robert II, count of Artois and Charles I's leading lieutenant. See Villani, *Nuova Cronica* VIII.134.

102. Ladislas IV, 1272–10 July 1290.

103. Andrew III, the Venetian, 1290–1301.

104. See Villani, *Nuova Cronica* VIII.135.

105. See Villani, *Nuova Cronica* VIII.141.

106. *Chronichon Estense*, under 1290.

THE THIRTEENTH CENTURY

In 1291, the Saracens encamped at Ancona, and for forty days they fought and captured the city, burning and leveling it to the ground. This prompted the pope to give an indulgence of the Cross for prayers against them throughout all Christian lands. Obizzo, lord of Ferrara, Modena and Reggio [Emilia], was strangled in his bed by his sons in an attempt to have the control of Ferrara left to his third son. Likewise at this time died Rudolf, king of Germany and emperor,[107] without ever receiving the imperial benediction. Thereupon, the princes of Germany elected Adolf [I] as king of Germany, who refused to yield Albert [I], duke of Austria; this led them to engage in battle, resulting in the king's death and the duke's victory.

CELESTINE V (POPE 198), A.D. 1293

Clemens [Coelestinus or Celestine] V[108] held the pontificate for nine months. Being a religious and holy man of deep conviction, he absented himself from the cardinals in Perugia and was elected pope by general consensus. After naming a number of cardinals, he went to the court of Naples where Charles [II] cordially received him, and there a decree was proposed that the pope should renounce the papacy to save his soul. Later in a consistory with the cardinals at Sta. Lucia he removed his crown and mantle and abdicated the papacy.

BONIFACE VIII (POPE 199), A.D. 1294

Bonifacius [Boniface] VIII,[109] born in Anagni, held the pontificate for eight years, eight months, and seventeen days. While he was cardinal with the given name of Benedetto, he was elected pope in Naples; whereupon he quickly went with his court to Rome where he was crowned in mid-January. Later on, he decreed that the feasts of the Apostles, the evangelists and the four doctors of the Church be celebrated no differently than Easter. He also composed the sixth book of

---

107. On 15 July 1291.
108. Pope 190, 29 August–13 December 1294.
109. Pope 191, A.D. 1295–1303.

the *Decretals* and in Orvieto canonized King Louis [IX] of France, who had died in Tunis during a campaign with his army.

At this time, King Charles [II] of Sicily had reconciled with King Jayme of Aragon and gave him his daughter[110] as wife, thus denying to Charles [of Valois], the French king's son, the kingdom of Aragon that the pope had conceded to him if he wanted it. Whereupon, not long afterward, Jayme went to Rome, accompanied by Constance [of Sicily], his queen mother, Roger Lauria, who had been an enemy of the Church, and his sister Violante [Yolande], all of whom the pope kindly pardoned and asked Jayme to give his sister Violante to Robert, King Charles' son.[111] In addition, the pope removed two cardinals from office because of errors they had committed; they were Iacopo and Pietro Colonna whose palaces and other property he tore down.[112]

King Philip of France made peace with King Edward [I] of England, who had been at war because of the count of Flanders. Having accepted with papal dispensation his sister as wife so as to be related, he gave him his daughter as wife. At this time, Master Taddeo da Imola, distinguished in the field of medicine, died in Bologna. While fighting on the feast of St. John the Baptist against Albert [I], duke of Austria, King Adolf [I] of Germany was killed in battle. Whereupon Duke Albert of Austria seized the kingdom of Germany, succeeded him and ruled for about ten years.

During Boniface's pontificate, the Genoese and Venetians, while battling on the Adriatic Sea at a place called Curzola[113] inflicted many deaths on both sides. The Genoese were finally victorious and took many Venetian prisoners and ships to Genoa; the prisoners were treated so well that they agreed to a truce, and the following year all returned home.

---

110. Blanche of Anjou, on 29 October or 1 November 1295.
111. See Villani, *Nuova Cronica* IX.18.
112. Villani, *Nuova Cronica* IX.21.
113. On 9 September 1298.

THE THIRTEENTH CENTURY

At this time too, also in 1300, Pope Boniface proclaimed a jubilee of pardons for one year, that is, anyone who was truly repentant and went to confession, went to Rome and visited the churches of St. Peter and San Paolo for fifteen days would have all his sins pardoned and enjoy the same indulgence as though he had visited the Holy Land. This then resulted in an infinite multitude from various nations going to Rome for pardon.[114] In the same year, Guido de Bonarosi drove his uncles from Mantua and took over the principality, and the Tartars and the king of Armenia occupied Syria, taking many cities and conquering the Saracens many times with numerous casualties.

Likewise in this period the city of Pistoia was divided between two parties, the Whites and the Blacks, which fought many times between themselves with considerable bloodshed. When many Florentines became involved to try to resolve the disagreements, the city of Pistoia began to look with suspicion upon the Florentine Republic. After several years, when Florence itself became divided into two parties, the Cerchi and the Donati, with each side having the support of important citizens, the Cerchi party began to favor the Whites of Pistoia and to persecute the Blacks with which the Donati sided. Since the Cerchi were more powerful than the Donati, they sent many Blacks from Pistoia into exile, seriously damaging the party and driving out many, thereby breaking their promises, agreements and pacts, which had been drawn up between them and the commune of Pistoia.[115]

While such fighting was going on, Boniface wished to resolve their differences and sent Cardinal Matteo with a full legation to Florence with orders that all dissensions cease, but the Cerchi party that was ruling Florence did not wish to participate and paid little attention to the legate. The cardinal departed, leaving Florence under interdict.[116] The pope tried to achieve peace in other ways, but was unsuccessful. But

---

114. The brevity of the account matches that in the *Chronicon Estense*, under 1300. See also Villani, *Nuova Cronica* IX.36.

115. Villani, *Nuova Cronica* IX.38–39.

116. Villani, *Nuova Cronica* IX.40. The cardinal is Matteo d'Acquasparta of Porto.

when Charles [of Valois], the French king's brother, went to Rome, the pope commissioned him to be peacemaker in Tuscany. Charles arrived in Florence accompanied by Corso Donati and his troops (after Corso had been expelled from the Cerchi party), but he failed to achieve peace and departed; whereupon the Donati party, the Blacks, expelled all the Whites. The pope once again sent Cardinal Matteo to Florence who did succeed in establishing peace among the Cerchi, the Donati and the Pazzi [at] Dimari. Shortly thereafter, upon his return to Florence, Charles noted that the Whites were behaving badly, so he condemned them and sent them into exile. As a result, after all had departed from Florence, with the help of the Pisans, the Bolognese and other Italian Ghibellines they mounted many attacks against the Florentines.[117]

Also during this pontificate, King Philip [IV] of France with a large army engaged Flanders in battle, but the Flemish, with astuteness rather than force, defeated them in a great rout in which many of his knights were killed.[118] Later, in 1303, when a rift occurred between Boniface and King Philip of France, the pope was captured in Anagni, his birthplace, with Philip's consent by his enemy Sciarra de' Colonna of Rome, whom he had excommunicated. Freed not long afterward, he left Anagni and came to Rome with his court, where he died of depression because of the insult he had received, and was buried in a sumptuous tomb that he had had prepared for himself.[119]

*

---

117. Villani, *Nuova Cronica* IX.41–43.
118. At the battle of the Golden Spurs, 11 July 1302. Villani, *Nuova Cronica* IX.55–56.
119. See Villani, *Nuova Cronica* IX.63.

THE FOURTEENTH CENTURY

Benedictus ři.

BENEDICT XI (POPE 200), A.D. 1303

Benedictus [Benedict] XI,[1] born in Treviso, held the pontificate for eight months and fifteen days. The papacy was vacant for thirteen months. After becoming pope, he reaffirmed what Boniface [VIII], his predecessor, had done. Later, having made peace with the king of France, he removed the ban of excommunication and blessed him.[2] He also sent Brother Nicolo, bishop and primate of Ostia,[3] to Tuscany to bring about peace in its ongoing war. When the cardinal came to Florence to act as leader of the region, he nearly achieved peace and then went on to Prato, his birthplace, and from there, after settling some affairs, he went to Pistoia where he remained several days, taking control of the region. He made a count of Messer Galasso, a cleric and his chaplain, and placed him in charge.

Cardinal Nicolo returned to Prato where the inhabitants, mistrusting him and the Whites, who had become quite bold throughout the region because of him, began to rebel; whereupon the cardinal, mistrusting them, returned to Florence as a refugee. But the Florentines were very angry over this and marched against the Pratese with their army, stopping near Prato. After remaining there for some time, the Pratesi won the good will of the cardinal and the Florentines. Then

1. Pope 192, A.D. 1303–1304.

2. Boniface VIII had excommunicated King Philip IV in 1303 over issues of spiritual and secular authority. The conflict led to Philip's ordering a personal attack on the pope at Anagni on 7 September 1303. Benedict published a papal bull exonerating Philip on 25 March 1304.

3. Niccolaio da Prato. See Villani, *Nuova Cronica* IX.66.

the cardinal had some important men come to work out the details for peace, but the Florentines became suspicious and renewed the battle in which many men died. Consequently the envoy fled Florence and went to Siena, leaving in Florence widespread discord that resulted in many fires, many citizens evicted and many Florentine towns in revolt.[4]

Not long afterward, the Whites, together with the Ghibellines, Florentines, Pisans and Bolognese, went to Florence where the land had been wasted by fires and killings. After stopping on a road not far from Florence, the following morning they arrived in the city, captured the Spadai Gate and entered by a route named Via Nuova. For this reason, in Piazza San Giovanni and Piazza San Lorenzo the Florentines vigorously attacked them, ousted and pursued them, killing a large number.

Also during this time the Florentines encamped at a castle called Le Stinche, after capturing it, and took some of the men to Florence and put them in a new prison that, because the first prisoners came from a fortress called Le Stinche, they called the same thing.[5] Somewhat later, the Florentines together with the Guelph troops, elected as their leader and commander Robert, King Charles' son, and went to fight in Pistoia, which they relentlessly besieged. Finally Pope Benedict died, having had a diamond that he valued put in his scrotum.[6]

CLEMENT V (POPE 201), A.D. 1305

Clemens [Clement] V,[7] born in Gascony, held the pontificate for eight years and ten months. The Church was without a leader for two years, three months and nineteen days. While archbishop of Bordeaux, he was made cardinal and pope, and once elected he convened the cardinals and went with his court to Lyons where on the next feast day, that

4. These details are recorded in Villani, *Nuova Cronica* IX.68–69, 71–72.

5. Villani, *Nuova Cronica* IX.75.

6. The source for this story is unidentified. Villani, *Nuova Cronica* IX.80 states that the pope was killed by a man posing as a woman servant who served him what Villani implies were poisoned figs.

7. Pope 193, A.D. 1305–1314.

of St. Martin, he was installed in the presence of King Philip [IV] of France.[8] Later on, after naming a number of cardinals, he restored to the pristine dignity of the cardinalate Pietro and Iacopo della Colonna who had been deposed. He then sent two envoys to Florence to remove the troops at Pistoia, and when he was not obeyed, he excommunicated all those involved. Whereupon Duke Robert[9] departed and went to Lyons.

Soon after, when the siege of Pistoia had lasted about eleven months, because of famine the citizens surrendered to the Florentines and the Lucchesi who destroyed the walls, filled in the moats and destroyed towers and other defenses, assuming control over the city. They divided the region between them and destroyed the stronghold of Carmignano.[10] The pope summoned a council to Vienne,[11] and among many deliberations he had the order of Knights Templar disbanded and Henry [VII] crowned and elected emperor by some of his cardinals.

At this time an outstanding painter, Giotto Fiorentino,[12] became famous. When Maffeo [Visconti], the ruler of Milan, became intolerable, his princely power was taken away, which caused the Della Torre family to come to Milan in order to drive Matteo from the city and occupy it. Meanwhile the people of Modena, who had a strong hatred for the cruel tyranny of Azzo d'Este, freed themselves from their slavery; upon seeing this, the people of Reggio did likewise. As a result, all the strongholds that had been built to defend tyranny were destroyed by the people, hungry for freedom. In Bologna there was a large uprising, and many who had been Azzo's supporters were driven out.[13] Also at

---

8. On 15 November 1305.
9. Robert of Anjou, then duke of Calabria, son and heir of Charles II of Naples.
10. Villani, *Nuova Cronica* IX.82.
11. The council of Vienne, October 1311–May 1312.
12. Giotto di Bondone, 1266/7–8 January 1337.
13. These events are discussed at length in the *Chronicon Estense*, under 1308. Villani, *Nuova Cronica* IX.88 narrates them with the same brevity as here.

this time the church of [St. John] Lateran caught fire, which spread to some nearby houses, but was quickly brought under control with the aid of men and women and rebuilt with the help of volunteers and money.[14] There was a strong earthquake in Rimini that destroyed many buildings.

Azzo d'Este, the tyrant of Ferrara, died in January.[15] Fresco, who was considered a concubine's son, took over the lordship with the aid of supporters and held it until October when he departed out of fear.[16] Thus, the people of Ferrara, following the advice of their bishop named Guido, freed themselves from the marquis' control. King Albert of Germany was killed by his brother's sons. Also during Clement's pontificate, many friars from the order of St. Mary of the Temple [Templars], after being reported to King Philip [IV] of France for living dishonestly, were arrested on Clement's command and had all their belongings confiscated.[17]

Furthermore, in July there was great discord and divisiveness in Ferrara between one party who sought freedom and another who favored the marquis; consequently, the people's party burned the palace belonging to the marquis. Finally, when some church envoys became involved, the scandals were resolved and the disagreements settled. Clement died while traveling from Vienne to Bordeaux, and because he had his court in Gaul, all of his successors down to Gregory XI continued to keep it there.

HENRY VII (EMPEROR 108), A.D. 1308
Henry [VII], count of Luxembourg, was made emperor[18] by the princes of Germany and ruled for fifty-four years[19] and seven months.

14. Recounted in Villani, *Nuova Cronica* IX.97.
15. Azzo VIII d'Este, d.31 January 1308.
16. Francesco d'Este, 1308–1309.
17. In the bull *Pastoralis praeeminentiae* of 22 November 1307.
18. Ruled as emperor 1312–24 August 1313.
19. The text here is corrupt.

THE FOURTEENTH CENTURY

Before him King Albert of Germany had been elected emperor, but he was killed by his nephew for having taken over the duchy of Austria that belonged to him.

Henry entered Italy, went to Pavia and then to Milan where he peacefully recalled all who had been banished. Later he besieged Brescia and conquered it in a few days. Shortly thereafter, Count Filippo who ruled Pavia rebelled against him, but in 1312 Henry went to Rome, which he entered by force, fighting fiercely against those who opposed him and taking control of everything except Castel Sant'Angelo. Finally, at Christmas he was crowned emperor by some cardinals whom the pope had commissioned to do so. When daily fighting continued in the city, the pope ordered both sides to leave; whereupon, the emperor departed and went to Tuscany, and after causing much damage in Perugia he went on to Rimini.[20] Later on, in Florentine territory, he captured Monte Varchi and went to Ancisa where he banished all whom he had conquered. Finally, he encamped not far from the city near the monastery of the Friars of San Salvi. Remaining there for eleven days he suffered many losses with no gains and departed.[21]

He went to a fortress named San Casciano about eight miles from Florence where he wintered, causing much damage to the Florentine and Sienese countryside. Unable to capture the stronghold, he went to the fortress of Poggibonsi which he restored to its original condition. King Charles I of Sicily had built it originally on a hill, but later its inhabitants moved it to the bottom of the hill. Finally Henry departed and went to Buonconvento [in Tuscany] when he began to feel ill; the illness worsened and he died.[22] At this time there was serious war between the Paduans, the emperor's adversaries and the Vicentini. In the same period throughout Italy there was great famine with much loss of life that struck men more than women, and the wealthy more than the poor.

20. See Villani, *Nuova Cronica* X.43.
21. Villani, *Nuova Cronica* X.46–48 relates these events in great detail.
22. Villani, *Nuova Cronica* X.52.

JOHN XXII (POPE 202), A.D. 1317

With the papacy unoccupied for around two years, Ioannes [John] XXII[23] became pope when the cardinals who had been convoked in Avignon could not agree. He held the papacy for nineteen years. He was an excellent and praiseworthy pastor who sent all the decisions rendered by Pope Clement to all the appropriate offices. He did much good and condemned many heretics for excessive zeal in the faith. He canonized many saints among whom were the angelic doctor, St. Thomas Aquinas, of the order of Friars Preachers, and St. Louis of Toulouse, the king of Sicily's son and a Friar Minor. He also approved the order of New Knights and incited Gaul against the Saracens.

At this time, some Poor [Men] of Lyons,[24] who were thought to be in the Third Order of St. Francis, were burned as heretics in many places and towns with their false articles of faith, one of which held that the Church was wrong in its interpretation of scripture. Pope John had judged this as heretical and proclaimed by decree that this was not to be believed. Also at this time there was a schism when Lewis [IV], whom the pope had stripped of the empire, had a man named Pietro of the order of Friars Minor named pope.[25] But shortly thereafter, this Pietro repented and, kneeling before Pope John, asked for pardon. But even after having done this, he remained an enemy of the Church.

In this period flourished John of Anglia,[26] a medical doctor and outstanding soldier who had traveled almost the entire world. Following this journey, which he wrote about in three languages, he died and was buried in Lodi. Oderico,[27] a saintly man of the order of Friars Minor, also became well known because of his travels through Asia and India, evangelizing and performing many miracles. He transported

---

23. Pope 194, A.D. 1316–1334.

24. The Poor Men of Lyons, or the Waldensians.

25. Pietro Rainalducci da Corbaro as antipope Nicholas V in 1328.

26. Unidentified, perhaps confused with John of Montecorvino O.F.M. (1247–1328) who did travel on a mission to China.

27. Oderico of Pordenone, O.F.M., c.1286–May 1330.

THE FOURTEENTH CENTURY

the remains of four holy martyrs from a city called Hermes[28] to the Indian city of Carrhae.[29] Likewise at this time there was a serious war between King Philip [VI] of France and King Edward [III] of England, in which there were a great many casualties on both sides.[30] There was also a great plague.

Lewis IV, of Bavaria (Emperor 109), a.d. 1323

Lewis [IV],[31] duke of Bavaria, was elected emperor and lived for thirty years, but at the same time Frederick, duke of Austria,[32] was elected emperor, so they battled one another in Germany at the end of September, each believing that he was the true emperor. In this terrible and frightening battle, Frederick was overcome and defeated while Lewis remained emperor. Lewis then went to Rome in 1328, and since the pope and his court were in France, he had himself crowned emperor by Sciarra di Colonna, but the crowning was done without proper protocol and without papal authority. As a result of his scorning the pope and attempting to break the unity of the Church, he was denied the empire and Charles, son of King John of Bohemia, was elected emperor.

Benedict XII (Pope 203), a.d. 1335

Benedictus [Benedict] XII[33] of Toulouse held the pontificate for seven years, three months and seventeen days. Previously he was a monk in the order of Citeaux[34] with the name Jacques Fournier. In his adolescence he led a good, clean life and later taught theology. Upon becoming pope, he reformed the order of St. Benedict and Citeaux. He was demanding in granting benefices, taking great care that they not be

---

28. Most likely present-day Ephesus, Turkey.
29. Modern Harran in Turkey.
30. That is, the Hundred Years' War, 1337–1453.
31. Emperor a.d. 1328–1347.
32. Frederick the Handsome, of Hapsburg, 1314–13 January 1330.
33. Pope 195, a.d. 1335–1342.
34. The Cistercian Order.

given to unworthy candidates. He was not well-liked by many since he was so rigid and harsh that he feigned not to recognize his parents, saying the pope has no parents. He declared that holy souls do not need purging since, as soon as they leave the body, they see God face to face. He maintained that holding any other opinion was heretical and against the Catholic faith.[35]

Clement VI (Pope 204), A.D. 1342

Clemens [Clement] VI from Lyons[36] held the pontificate for ten years, six months and sixteen days. Through his reputation and actions he displayed many virtues and mitigated many of the harsh things that Pope Benedict had done, and although Benedict's rigidity and severity were appreciated, Clement's kindness was much more so. He was likable and affable in conversation, and all who went to speak with him departed contented. He canonized St. Ivo of Brittany, a doctor and martyr who was an advocate of the poor.[37]

Charles IV (Emperor 110), A.D. 1347

Charles IV,[38] son of King John of Bohemia, was elected to rule the imperial kingdom soon after Emperor Lewis was deposed by Pope Clement. He was a prudent and wise man and a great lover of the Christian religion. In 1353 he established many excellent laws in favor of religious people. He went to Italy to receive the imperial crown, and upon his arrival in Rome he was crowned in 1355 by some people whom Pope Innocent had authorized to do so because his court was in France. During this period, in 1348, there was a very serious plague in Florence that resulted in more than sixty thousand men dying, and the same happened in Venice.[39]

---

35. This is the great controversy of the Beatific Vision, which arose during the pontificate of John XXII.
36. Pope 196, A.D. 1342–1352 was from Gascony.
37. Ivo of Kermartin, canonized by Clement VI in June 1347.
38. Emperor 5 April 1355–29 November 1378.
39. This is, the Black Death.

Innocent VI (Pope 205), A.D. 1353

Innocentius [Innocent] VI[40] from Lyons held the pontificate for ten years. He was a great admirer of the religious orders. In the kingdom of France near St. André he built a monastery for the Carthusian Order and granted it many great privileges. He excelled in canonical reasoning, and at the end, after leading a holy life, he died and was buried in the monastery he had built.[41]

Urban V (Pope 206), A.D. 1363

Urbanus [Urban] V[42] held the pontificate for eight years. Previously he was the abbot of the order of St. Benedict in Marseilles, very learned in sacred scripture, and lived a very holy life. He preached a crusade against the Turks and raised the troops for the undertaking. Eventually he was killed by poisoning.[43] At this time flourished St. Bridget of the kingdom of Sweden[44] who founded the order of which she was patroness. There also flourished the seraphic Catherine of Siena, a virgin incomparable in sanctity, who was in the Third Order of the Friars Preachers; Maestro Raimondo of that order wrote her biography.[45]

Gregory XI (Pope 207), A.D. 1371

Gregorius [Gregory] XI,[46] elected in Avignon, held the pontificate for [seven] years. His original name was Piero del Forte.[47] He returned the Curia to Rome.

40. Pope 197, A.D. 1352–1362.

41. At Villeneuve-lès-Avignon.

42. Pope 198, A.D. 1362–1370.

43. Of uncertain attribution. Saint Brigitta [Bridget] of Sweden had prophesied Urban V's death upon his return to Avignon. See *The Revelations of St. Brigitta of Sweden* 2: *Liber Caelestis*, books IV–V, ed. Denis Searby and Bridget Morris (Oxford: Oxford University Press, 2006), 248–49.

44. 1303–23 July 1373.

45. 25 March 1347–29 April 1380. Raymond della Vigna of Capua, O.P., c.1330–5 October 1399, was minister general of the Dominican Order and Catherine's spiritual advisor.

46. Pope 199, A.D. 1371–1378.

47. Pierre Roger.

THE LIVES OF THE POPES AND EMPERORS

***

Here end *The Lives of Roman Pontiffs and Emperors* composed by Messer Francesco Petrarch.[48]

There follow the lives briefly and carefully collected until the year 1534.

***

URBAN VI (POPE 208), A.D. 1378

The Neapolitan Urban V[I][49] was elected Roman pontiff by a conclave of cardinals convened in Rome upon the death of Gregory XI, who had held the pontificate for seven years. Urban occupied the papacy for eleven years. Originally named Bartolomeo [Prignano], he was archbishop of Bari. But that same year, the cardinals declared that they had elected him pope out of fear and then fled to the city of Fondi. Having declared that Gregory was an invalid pope, they elected Robert of Geneva, who was then named Clement VII. As a result, a schism occurred and the clergy were divided, and finally Christians became so divided that some gave allegiance to one and many to the other. Italy, Germany and Hungary gave allegiance to Urban, while France, Spain and Catalonia gave allegiance to Clement.[50]

This division lasted until the time of Martin V. Until that time, with dukes creating popes who were chosen from their sides, it was difficult to decide who administered what, and the schism became so confusing that even learned men of good conscience did not know whom to favor or obey. There resulted a great scandal within the Church and many heresies arose; whereupon to foster union and accord Pope Urban instituted the feast of the Visitation. We therefore intend to describe briefly when each pope was elected and who was replaced. We come first to Clement VII who was made pope in the same year as Urban.

---

48. See Introduction, XXV–XXVI.
49. Pope 200, A.D. 1378–1389.
50. This is the Great Western Schism of 1378–1417.

THE FOURTEENTH CENTURY

CLEMENT VII [ANTI-POPE] (POPE 209), A.D. 1379

Clemens [Clement] VII[51] [anti-pope], born in Geneva and previously named Messer Robert, was elected pope by some cardinals at Fondi. Since the Curia was in Avignon, he established his papacy there, which caused a great schism in Christianity, with some regions preferring Urban who had his Curia in Rome and others preferring Clement who had his in Avignon. Nevertheless, as we noted above, France, Spain and Catalonia with their large populations obeyed Clement. But in 1391 Clement finally died in Avignon and was replaced by Benedict VIII as we shall see below.

BONIFACE IX (POPE 210), A.D. 1389

Bonifacius [Boniface] IX,[52] following the death of Urban VI, was elected his successor in Rome while Clement was still alive in Avignon and considered himself the legitimate Roman pontiff. Of Neapolitan descent, he was named Pietro belonging to the noble and ancient family of the Tomacelli. Thus the schism continued with the clergy divided. Finally, in 1404 Boniface, who had his own curia in Rome, died from stones and was replaced by Innocent VII as we shall discuss below.

WENCESLAUS (EMPEROR III), A.D. 1393

Wenceslaus [IV],[53] king of Bohemia, after ruling the empire for some years, was deposed by his father because of his corrupt and lustful life. His father, Charles [IV], king of Bohemia and emperor, had two sons, Wenceslaus and Sigismund.[54] Because Wenceslaus was the elder, Charles declared him his successor in the kingdom and in the empire, but he scorned the imperial crown, led a lustful life and did nothing extraordinary, and so was deprived of the crown in great shame. Subsequently, Rupert, duke of Bavaria,[55] was elected his successor, and

---

51. Robert of Geneva, antipope 20 September 1378–16 September 1394.
52. Pope 201, A.D. 1389–1404.
53. King 1363–16 August 1419.
54. Emperor A.D. 1433–1437.
55. Rupert was count of the Palatinate, an imperial elector, king 1400–18 May 1410.

after his death (as we shall see below), Charles's son and Wenceslaus' brother Sigismund was elected his successor.

BENEDICT XIII [ANTI-POPE] (POPE 211), A.D. 1399
Benedictus [Benedict] XIII[56] [anti-pope] gained the pontificate after being elected by cardinals gathered in Avignon. He replaced the deceased Clement VII who had his Curia in Gaul. His given name was Pedro de Luna, and he was a close relative of the king of Aragon.[57] He occupied the papacy until the council of Constance where he and John XXIII were deposed (as we shall see below), and Martin V was elected. But Benedict refused to surrender the papacy in order to unify the Church and refused to obey even after being deposed by the council. He continued being stubborn, and on his deathbed ordered his cardinals to meet and elect another pontiff as his successor. Upon his death the cardinals did so, electing a pope given the name of Clement VIII, but they accomplished little since they did not swear fealty to him. Instead Christendom turned to Martin V as the legitimate and unquestionable vicar of Peter.

*

---

56. Pedro Martínez de Luna y Pérez de Gotor, antipope 28 September 1394–23 May 1423.
57. Alfonso V.

THE FIFTEENTH CENTURY

Ruprecht

RUPERT OF BAVARIA (EMPEROR 112), A.D. 1401

Rupert,[1] duke of Bavaria, following the imperial electors' removal of Wenceslaus as emperor, was elected emperor and ruled for nine years as a just and Catholic emperor. When he went to Italy, he was crowned by Pope Boniface IX, who had his curia in Rome. He organized a large army of Germans and attacked the Visconti,[2] but after being seriously defeated in Italy, he returned to his kingdom without honor. In his day many heretics arose in Bohemia with the help of Jerome of Prague,[3] and in an attempt to destroy ecclesiastical rule they inflicted much harm on the Christian faith. This all happened because of the terrible division caused by the schismatics.

INNOCENT VII (POPE 212), A.D. 1404

Innocentius [Innocent] VII[4] was elected pope by the cardinals in Rome, following the death of Boniface IX, and held the papacy for two years. Originally named Messer Cosimo da Sulmona,[5] he was cardinal of Bologna. Upon his death the cardinals elected as his successor Gregory XII.

---

1. Rupert III, emperor A.D. 1398–1410.
2. Text reads "Iuliani." His campaign against Milan ended in April 1402.
3. 1379–30 May 1416. One of Jan Hus's major disciples.
4. Pope 202, A.D. 1404–1406.
5. Cosimo de' Migliorati.

THE LIVES OF THE POPES AND EMPERORS

GREGORY XII (POPE 213), A.D. 1406

Gregorius [Gregory] XII,[6] who succeeded Innocent, held the pontificate for nine years until the election of Martin V. Originally known as Angelo [Correr], he was from Venice and the patriarch of Constantinople. At this time, in 1409, since he wished to have Christianity be in accord with Benedict XIII, who was then reigning as pope in France, he tried to reach an understanding with him that would confirm one as pope and would have the other withdraw so that the harmful schism and division within the Christian religion would not continue forever. When the meeting could not be arranged, the cardinals who were meeting in Pisa[7] condemned them as schismatics, dividers of the vicariate of St. Peter, and forbade all Christians to obey either one. They then elected a third pontiff named Pietro di Candia,[8] a Milanese cardinal who after his election took the name of Alexander V. Thus, the papacy that had been divided between two popes had another one added, with the result that there were now three who were considered Roman pontiffs and vicars of St. Peter, namely Benedict XIII, Gregory XII and Alexander V.

ALEXANDER V [ANTIPOPE] (POPE 214), A.D. 1409

Alexander V[9] [antipope] held the pontificate for one year. Originally named Pietro di Candia, he was cardinal of Milan and was elected pope (as we said above) at the council of Pisa. He later died in Bologna and was succeeded by John XXIII [antipope], as will be shown below.

SIGISMUND (EMPEROR 113), A.D. 1410

Sigismund,[10] king of Hungary and Emperor Charles [IV's] son, was amicably elected emperor after his brother King Wenceslaus of Bohemia had been stripped of the empire and after Duke Rupert

6. Pope 203, A.D. 1406–1415.
7. The council of Pisa in 1409.
8. Peter Phillarges, c.1339–3 May 1410.
9. Antipope 26 June 1409–3 May 1410.
10. Emperor A.D. 1433–1437.

THE FIFTEENTH CENTURY

of Bavaria, who had been elected emperor following Wenceslaus' removal, had died. He was such a strong Christian and a humble and devoted emperor that, according to general opinion, he deserved to be canonized after his death. He gave his full support to the Church that was badly distressed following the papal schisms and was able to help it with his marvelous wisdom. Nor did he ever cease exerting every care and attention by promoting unity and harmony in the Church, one vicariate and one pastor.

He also excelled in war, successfully battling the Turks about nine times, and managed the empire so well that he can be rightly compared to Constantine, Charlemagne and other outstanding emperors. He went to Rome and was crowned by Eugenius III, the pontiff at the time. He then went to Germany and, upon his return to Hungary, after having successfully ruled the empire for three years following his coronation, died in 1438 A.D. After his death Duke Albert of Austria was elected.

JOHN XXIII [ANTIPOPE] (POPE 215), A.D. 1410

Ioannes [John] XXIII[11] [antipope] held the pontificate for about five years. Originally named Messer Baldassare [Cossa], he was cardinal of the Order of Sant'Eustacio from the kingdom of Apulia.[12] He replaced Alexander V who had died in Bologna, and as soon as he was elected went with his curia to Rome. Shortly thereafter, in an attempt to restore the unity of the Church and reduce the vicariate of Peter to one Roman pontiff, it was decided to hold a council in the city of Constance[13] so that Benedict XIII and Gregory XII might retain some papal power. While the council was being held with Pope John's approval, in the presence of Gregory's and Benedict's cardinals, there arose a disagreement between Pope John and Emperor Sigismund who was working hard to unite the Church.

---

11. Antipope A.D. 1410–1415.
12. That is, the kingdom of Naples.
13. The council of Constance, 1414–1418.

John was deposed from the papacy, whereupon he secretly fled from the council, but to no avail since Martin V was elected pope. John was captured and the papacy taken away from him later in the city of Florence in order to avoid any suspicion of schism in the papacy, but at the Florentines' request Martin made him a cardinal. He did not live long and died shortly thereafter in Florence where he was buried with honors in a beautiful tomb at the Oratorio di San Giovanni.[14] At that council too, Gregory XII renounced the papacy to eliminate any suspicion of schism, but when Benedict XIII[15] refused to renounce the position and continued to hold on to it, the cardinals stripped him of it and raised Martin V as pope. And so the schism was brought to an end as well as the split in the Church that had lasted for many years to the great dishonor and damage of our religion.

Martin V (Pope 216), A.D. 1415

The Roman Martinus [Martin] V[16] held the pontificate about fifteen years. He was elected by the council held in the city of Constance after all three men who held papal territory had been stripped of it (as we indicated above). Originally named Oddone and a descendent of the Colonna family, he was a very powerful pope, wealthy and just above all others. The roads and the areas along them had become dangerous because of robbers and killers, but he made them all so safe that one could travel without fear. He sentenced many wicked and corrupt heretics who had sprung up because of the split in the pontificate. By aiding that illustrious and most noble prince, Emperor Sigismund, he accumulated many riches to re-purchase the Holy Land. But death prevented him from bringing this noble and great undertaking to fruition.

Eugenius IV (Pope 217), A.D. 1430

Eugenius IV[17] held the pontificate for sixteen years. Originally named Messer Gabriele [Condulmaro] of Venetian descent and the cardinal

14. San Giovanni Battista della Calza, at Piazza della Calza (Porta Romana).
15. Text reads "XVII."
16. Pope 204, A.D. 1417–1431.
17. Pope 205, A.D. 1431–1447.

THE FIFTEENTH CENTURY

of Siena, he was peacefully elected to the papacy in the city of Rome upon the death of Martin V. He took the name Eugenius and was unquestionably a true shepherd, yet not long afterwards he was driven out by the Romans in such a manner that he had to flee nearly naked and in great peril.[18] He boarded a galley that the Florentines had obtained for him and went to Florence where he was received kindly and held court for many years.

In the meantime certain people who had been refused bishoprics because of their shortcomings organized a council in Basel[19] and summoned Eugenius to it. When he did not come, they deposed him and selected as Roman pontiff Duke Amadeus of Savoy, who was a hermit, and gave him the name Felix V [antipope] after the election. In this manner the schism occurred once again, as did the division within the Church. But Eugenius paid no attention to this since Felix did not enjoy support in the papal territories. He still continued administering the Church from Florence and excommunicated Felix. Eugenius was actually a good man and led a good life, and ultimately with the aid of many, including the Venetians, he reoccupied the see of Rome and enjoyed greater support than before.

ALBERT II (EMPEROR[20] 114), A.D. 1438

Upon Emperor Sigismund's death, Albert [II],[21] duke of Austria, succeeded him and ruled for one year. He was Sigismund's son-in-law, and for this reason, in addition to the imperial dignity conferred upon him after the emperor's death, he was made king of Bohemia and Hungary since Sigismund had no sons. He was certainly a man of great virtue and so pious that all the common people said that never had there been anyone like him. He was elected king of Germany but soon after was poisoned. Thus because of his short reign he never

---

18. In May 1434 during an uprising inspired by the Colonna family of his predecessor, whose encroachments on the Papal States he sought to reverse.

19. The council of Basel, 23 July–18 December 1431.

20. Text reads "Pope."

21. Elected king of the Romans on 18 March 1438.

received the imperial crown. His young son and two daughters were similarly poisoned.

FELIX V [ANTIPOPE] (POPE 218), A.D. 1439
Felix V [antipope][22] held the pontificate for nine years. Originally named Amadeus, duke of Savoy, he was elected, as we said above, at the council of Basel following the removal of Eugenius [IV], which caused a schism for a long time. Nevertheless he did not have much support and, although he outlived Eugenius, Nicholas V became pope after Eugenius's death.

FREDERICK III (EMPEROR 115), A.D. 1439
Frederick III,[23] elected after Emperor Albert's death, ruled for forty-nine years. Originally known as the duke of Austria, he was made king of Germany after being elected emperor. Upon becoming emperor, he did not wish to receive the imperial crown from the pope because of the schism and division within the Roman pontificate and since there were then two pontifical territories, namely that of Felix and that of Eugenius.

Felix had little following, but when unity was finally achieved within the Church, Frederick went to Rome with his wife Leonora,[24] the Portuguese king's daughter, and was given the imperial crown with great pomp by Nicholas V. As he was returning, he was besieged by the Austrians and the Bohemians in Città Nova and forced to leave behind Ladislaus, the young king of Bohemia, who had accompanied him. He was a peaceful and quiet emperor of outstanding patience, and especially a caring supporter of the clergy.

Not long after his crowning, the city of Constantinople was captured by Turks[25] following its betrayal by a Genoese who was made king in keeping with the promises made by the Turks. After four days he

22. Antipope November 1439–April 1449.
23. Emperor A.D. 1452–1493.
24. Eleanor of Portugal, 18 September 1434–3 September 1467.
25. On 29 May 1453.

THE FIFTEENTH CENTURY

was decapitated, and following the city's capture many Christians were killed or sold. After that ruler's ignominious death, his head was separated from his body and the Christian faith almost entirely perished. At this time died Brother Bernardino of the order of Friars Minor, a venerable religious responsible for many miracles.[26] Finally in 1413 [1493] the emperor died; he lived peacefully to nearly ninety, after having first made his son Maximilian a partner in the kingdom.

NICHOLAS V (POPE 219), A.D. 1447

Nicolaus [Nicholas] V[27] held the pontificate for eight years. Originally named Messer Tommaso [Parentucelli] and the cardinal from Bologna, he was born in Sarzana from lowly and disreputable stock. He was elected in the city of Rome to replace Eugenius, thereby continuing the schism since the antipope Felix was still living. After his election, he slowly gained support to everyone's surprise, seeing that he was of such lowly birth, and yet he enjoyed more support than Felix who was duke of Savoy. Not long after Felix's death, he alone retained the papacy, causing the schism to cease completely.

Nicholas excelled in theology and was especially fond of men of letters and learned men, supporting and helping with honors and awards whoever he knew had a great mind. As a result, in his day the study of the fine arts that had been long dormant gradually started to return, thanks to his doing. He was wealthy and rebuilt many buildings that had fallen in ruins, and also built a great wall around the palace and repaired the walls encircling the city.[28] He canonized San Bernardino, and finally having lived out his life in praiseworthy fashion he died and was buried with honorary ceremonies. A jubilee occurred in his time.[29]

---

26. Bernardino da Siena, 8 September 1380–20 May 1444.

27. Pope 206, A.D. 1447–1455.

28. Nicholas was known for his patronage of Renaissance humanists and for his role in the creation of the Vatican Library.

29. The jubilee of 1450.

THE LIVES OF THE POPES AND EMPERORS

CALLIXTUS III (POPE 220), A.D. 1455

Callistus [Callixtus] III[30] held the pontificate for three years and five months. Originally named Messer Alfonso [Borgia], he was the cardinal of Aragon, and upon assuming the papacy he took the name of Callixtus. Of Catalan descent, he became pope when old and infirm, but he was still a constant almsgiver and assister to the poor. His attempt to attack the Turks was cut short by his death. He canonized St. Vincent[31] of the order of Friars Preachers.

At this time died the most serene King Alfonso [II] of Aragon and Sicily,[32] a man truly worthy of the kingdom and endowed with worthy virtues, a lover of learned men, showing himself liberal with honors and awards, highly human and affable. He was succeeded by his most excellent son Ferrante[33] who imitated his father's virtues in every way.

PIUS II (POPE 221), A.D. 1458

Pius II[34] held the pontificate for five years, eleven months and twenty-five days. Originally named Messer Aeneas, the son of Silvio of the noble family of the Piccolomini of Siena, he was an eloquent man, an outstanding orator, a poet laureate, bishop of Siena and cardinal of Sta. Sabina. He was unanimously elected in Rome on the kalends of September.[35] Not long after, he called a meeting of Christian princes in order to consult on declaring war against the Turks, enemies of the name of Christ. He left Rome in the month of January to go, despite some difficulties, to Mantua where with consent of the Christians it was unanimously decided to declare war against the Turks.[36] It was further determined that to wage this war the clergy should pay the pope a tenth of their salary, the Jews a twentieth and the public officials a

30. Pope 207, A.D. 1455–1458.
31. Vincent Ferrer, O.P., 23 January 1350–5 April 1419, canonized on 3 June 1455.
32. King of Naples 25 January 1494–22 February 1495.
33. Ferdinand I, king of Naples 1495 to 7 September 1496.
34. Pope 208, A.D. 1458–1464.
35. September 1, a day of public administration.
36. He issued the bull in October 1458.

THE FIFTEENTH CENTURY

thirtieth. Subsequently, he ordered Cardinal Bishop Bessarion of Tuscany,[37] who was of Nicaean descent, to go as legate to Germany, where people were fighting each other, to settle their differences and to lead them against the Turks.

After bringing the situation under control, the pope returned to Rome, stopping first in his homeland, Siena, to settle some discords that had risen among the inhabitants. There, in the month of March, he created five cardinals, among whom was Messer Francesco Piccolomini, his nephew. Finally, in order to increase the effectiveness of his campaign against Mehmed, king of the Turks,[38] he decided to go in person to attack him, but soon after setting forth, he died in Ancona.[39] Paul [II] was elected to take his place, as we will show below.

This pontiff [Pius II] crowned the most serene King Ferdinand, son of Alfonso, king of Aragon, as king of Naples and received from him annually a certain amount as tribute. He canonized St. Catherine of Siena, who was in the Third Order of Friars Preachers. He also stripped Sigismund, duke of Austria, of the duchy since he had besieged and taken into custody Nicola, bishop of Brescia and cardinal of San Pietro in Vincoli. Furthermore, he excommunicated Sigismondo di Pandolfo dei Malatesta,[40] vicar of Rimini, a city of the Roman church, because he did not pay tribute to the Church and later continued to scorn the Church's power. As a result he was stripped of all his offices and power and condemned to the eternal flames as happens to heretics. Then the forces of the Church seized from him certain cities under his control, such as Senigallia,[41] that then returned to the Church. At this time Messer Antonio de' Piccolomini, Pius's

---

37. Basilios Bessarion of Trebizond, 2 January 1403–18 November 1472.
38. Mehmed the Conqueror, sultan August 1444–September 1446, February 1451–May 1481.
39. He issued the next call in October 1463 and travelled to Ancona in June 1464.
40. The "Wolf of Rimini," 19 June 1417–7 October 1468.
41. On 12 August 1462.

nephew, married King Ferdinand's daughter, which prompted the king to make him duke of Amalfi.

In the year 1461 the Genoese shook off their yoke of slavery to the French to whom they had been subject and attained freedom. As their leader they chose Messer Prospero of the noble family of the Adorni,[42] but soon after they removed him to replace him with Messer Lodovico di Campofregoso.[43] Also at this time King Charles[44] of France died and was succeeded by his son, Louis. Queen Charlotte of Cyprus,[45] who was stripped of her position by her brother James, went to Rome, was welcomed by the pontiff and asked that the Church's forces help restore her kingdom. Also at this time Tommaso, who had been ousted from the house of the Porphyrogenitus, took the head of St. Andrew the Apostle to Ancona as he fled from the Turkish siege.[46] Since he was a faithful Christian he was sent to Rome through the assistance of Alexander, cardinal of Sta. Susanna and envoy of the Apostolic see, where he was received kindly with the utmost respect by the pope and with great honor by the people. In the year 1462 Messer Paolo di Campofregoso, archbishop of Genoa and a bold man, seized control of the republic[47] after Messer Lodovico, who was duke at that time and who belonged to the same family, had been removed. But after a year of doubt whether he could sustain such eminence, he handed Genoa over to Francesco Sforza, duke of Milan.[48]

42. Prospero Adorno, 1428–1486.

43. Succeeded first by Spinetta di Campofregoso, 8 July 1461–11 July 1461, and then by Lodovico di Campofregoso, July 1461–March 1462.

44. Charles VII, king 1422–22 July 1461.

45. Queen 7 October 1458–16 July 1487. Her brother James usurped the throne in 1463.

46. Thomas Palaeologus, 1409–12 May 1465, despot in Morea from 1428 until the Ottoman conquest, fled to Italy in 1461 and gave the purported head to Pius II. It is encased in one of central piers of St. Peter's Basilica.

47. In March 1462, and 9 June 1462–late 1463.

48. 1463–1477.

THE FIFTEENTH CENTURY

PAUL II (POPE 222), A.D. 1464

Paulus [Paul] II[49] occupied the pontificate for six years and eleven months. Originally named Messer Pietro Barba of Venetian descent and titular cardinal of San Marco, he took the name of Paul II following his election. In his day, not long after his election, Count Iacobo from Castelnuovo,[50] son of the magnanimous Capitano Niccolò Piccinino,[51] an illustrious and famous duke of the knightly order whom all the Italians considered formidable,[52] was cordially summoned by King Ferdinand of Naples; he was arrested, detained and died within a few months. Also at this time Deifobo degli Anguillara, a prince of considerable power, who with his father[53] had always been inimical to the pope, was driven from his principality by Church forces, causing him to flee Italy. In 1466 died Francesco Sforza, the renowned duke of Milan, and Galeazzo Maria, his first-born, succeeded him in the duchy.

In 1467 the Roman pontiff, Paul, who had arranged a truce among all the Italian powers that were at odds, succeeded in gaining the peace and promulgating it. In that year Mehmed [II], Amoranto's[54] son, the powerful Turkish ruler whom all Christians feared, besieged the island of Euboea, today called Negroponte, and after a long siege captured it from the Venetians who controlled it and hacked all the inhabitants to pieces.[55] Also at this time, the condemnation for heresy previously imposed on George, king of Bohemia,[56] by the Roman pontiff Pius II,

---

49. Pope 209, A.D. 1464–1471.
50. Jacopo Piccinino, 1423–July 1465.
51. The condotttiere, 1386–15 October 1444.
52. That is, mercenaries or *condottieri*.
53. Everso II, d.1464.
54. Murad II.
55. In 1470.
56. George of Podebrady, king 1458–1471.

was upheld by Paul II,[57] his successor in the papacy. Shortly after, his son, Victor,[58] was defeated by Mattias, king of Hungary.[59]

Furthermore, in considering the brevity of human life, Pope Paul decreed that every twenty-five years a jubilee be declared in which a plenary remission of sins is granted. Initially Pope Boniface VIII had declared such a jubilee every hundred years. Later Clement VI reduced it to fifty years and Urban VI to every thirty-three years, while Paul [II] recently reduced it to twenty-five years. Moreover, Paul had the palace of San Marco[60] rebuilt at his own expense, since it was falling into ruins, and adorned it with very beautiful decoration. In 1469, when Emperor Frederick III came to worship in Rome, he entered the city dressed in black and was cordially received by the pope. Finally, having gloriously ruled over the Apostolic See,[61] Paul died from choking[62] in 1471. Following his death Sixtus IV was elected pontiff.

SIXTUS IV (POPE 223), A.D. 1471

Pope Xystus [Sixtus] IV[63] occupied the pontificate for twelve years. The Church was without a pontiff for nine days. He was elected pope with the full consent of the cardinals on the ninth of August. Originally named Francesco della Rovere from the city of Savona, he was a friar in the order of Friars Minor of which he was superior general, and later on, he was made titular cardinal of San Pietro in Vincoli. Very bright and outstanding in theology, he wrote many fine works, among which were *De sanguine Christi, De potentia Dei* and *De futuris contingentibus*. Once he assumed the papacy, he ruled with the utmost goodness and liberality toward his people, promoting many of

57. In December 1466.

58. Duke of Münsterberg, 29 May 1443–30 August 1500.

59. Matthias Corvinus (I), king 1458–6 April 1490.

60. That is, Palazzo di Venezia in Rome.

61. The positive assessment of Paul II here contrasts vividly with Platina's negative portrait, arguing against any direct borrowing or influence.

62. Of a stroke.

63. Pope 210, A.D. 1471–1484.

THE FIFTEENTH CENTURY

his relatives to the position of cardinal and others to secular principalities according to their abilities.

He was a pope of such liberality that, during a war with the Florentines when he was summoned to a council by princes favorable to the Florentines, he did not become upset but replied that he willingly accepted the summons since he hoped to reveal many of their faults. In addition, he undertook other wars, one against King Ferdinand of Naples, in which with Roberto Malatesta[64] as his leader he defeated the duke of Calabria along with the entire army of the Neapolitan king[65]; the second against the Venetians because Ercole d'Este of Ferrara, who was angered that things were not going his way, died of anguish, according to what some say.[66] He was the first pope to begin selling offices of the Roman Curia and consequently to establish new ones.

INNOCENT VIII (POPE 224), A.D. 1484

Innocentius [Innocent] VIII,[67] who succeeded Sixtus, occupied the pontificate for seven years minus one month and seven days. The Church was without a pontiff for twenty-two days. He was of Genoese descent and originally named Giovanni Battista Cibò. While in Rome he had stayed for a long time with the household family of the cardinal of Bologna, later becoming auxiliary bishop of Savona and then of Amalfi. He was made cardinal by Sixtus from whom he had also received the position of bestower of benefices. He was a very human pontiff to the point of being accused of being too secular, and yet he was not praised for liberality. At the beginning of his pontificate he declared war on King Ferdinand [I] of Naples[68] and his barons, but later, upon seeing that he was not winning and was being deceived by his supporters,

---

64. Condottiere leader, 1441/42–10 September 1482.
65. At Campo Morto, 21 August 1482.
66. The War of Ferrara, 1482–1484, between Ercole I d'Este, duke of Ferrara, and papal forces, which ended with the treaty of Bagnolo on 7 August 1484.
67. Pope 211, A.D. 1484–1492.
68. King 1458–25 January 1494.

he made peace with Ferdinand[69] with the understanding that he would pay the tribute owed the Church and would pardon the barons who had rebelled against him, neither of which Ferdinand honored.

Innocent then turned to the pursuit of peace, something that proved extremely beneficial to the public welfare since he administered justice with severity and pacified his subjects by providing abundant food. Nevertheless, he did harm to posterity and subsequent popes with the terrible example of being the first to dare recognize publicly his illegitimate children, giving them riches and stature and having his daughter[70] as well as his son[71] marry with great pomp, including giving them castles near Rome.

During this pontiff's time, the Medici family flourished in Florence, especially in the person of Lorenzo[72] who was a great patron of letters and the formal arts. Equally famous were Giovanni Pico de' Conti della Mirandola[73] and Ermolao Barbaro,[74] a Venetian nobleman, who was later patriarch of Aquileia and outstanding in learning. Also at this time in the church of the Sto. Spirito in Rome[75] was discovered the inscription on the Cross of our Lord Jesus Christ; it was found within the walls and was written in three languages as follows: JESU CHRISTO NAZZARENUS REX ...with the rest missing.[76] Likewise, the Turkish emperor sent as a gift to Pope Innocent the iron lance that opened the

---

69. In 1486.

70. Teodorina Cibò, who married Gerardo Usodimare.

71. Franceschetto Cibò (d.1519) married Maddalena de' Medici (1473–1528), the daughter of Lorenzo de' Medici.

72. Lorenzo de' Medici, 1 January 1449–9 April 1492.

73. Giovanni Pico della Mirandola, 24 February 1463–17 November 1494.

74. Ermolao Barbaro, 21 May 1454–14 June 1493.

75. Santo Spirito in Sassia.

76. "Jesus of Nazareth, King ...." On the church of Sto. Spirito in Sassia and its art, see Louise Smith Bross, "The Church of Santo Spirito in Sassia: A Study in the Development of Art, Architecture and Patronage in Counter Reformation Rome" (Ph.D. diss. University of Chicago, 1994).

THE FIFTEENTH CENTURY

Lord's side. As we said elsewhere, it had been found in Antioch and later taken to Constantinople.[77]

Also during his era, Ferdinand and Isabella, exemplary rulers of the kingdom of Spain, fought at great length with the Moors who occupied Granada, finally defeating and driving them out, and converted all of Spain to the Christian faith.[78] They even drove out the very numerous Jews who refused to convert. It is believed that this gave rise to that wicked sect that in the vernacular is called Maronite and that, while openly espousing the Christian faith, secretly practiced Jewish rites.[79] Ferdinand and Isabella also sent to sea in search of new lands the privateer, Christopher Columbus of Genovese descent, who in his journeys discovered many lands unknown to the ancients.[80] The king of Portugal had done a similar thing many years previously when his men, sailing to the left [i.e., south] outside of the strait of Spain [Gibraltar], went so far beyond the coast of Africa that in our day they reached the Indian Ocean; from there they brought back to Spain many spices and many other things to show us that were unknown to us. This pontiff with whom we are dealing [Innocent VIII] died at the age of sixty, having raised several cardinals. He was buried in the church of St. Peter.

ALEXANDER VI (POPE 225), A.D. 1492[81]

Alexander VI,[82] who succeeded Innocent, occupied the pontificate for eleven years and eleven days. The Church was without a pontiff for twenty-three days. Formerly he was a cardinal and vice-chancellor named Rodrigo Borgia, nephew of Callixtus III through his sister

77. One of the gifts sent to the pope — along with 40,000 ducats as the price to keep in Rome Mehmed's brother and rival.

78. On 2 January 1492.

79. The Syriac Maronite Church of Antioch, founded in the fourth century by Marun, a Syriac monk and, later, saint. It remains a prominent religious group in Lebanon today.

80. One of the earliest references to Columbus's life and voyages.

81. Text reads "1392."

82. Pope 212, A.D. 1492–1503. Rodrigo Borgia.

who, like him, was of Valentian descent. He was a pontiff of whom it might be said that his virtues were equal to serious vices since he was magnanimous and creative, eloquent and able to adjust to any person. He was very diligent in his work, and although he had not paid much attention to learning, he seemed to give considerable weight to it. So careful was he in maintaining the morale of the troops in all circumstances that he always seemed to have a well-trained and contented army, but he stifled all these virtues with vices that cannot be mentioned now.

Alexander had an excessive desire to make his illegitimate children famous, making one of them the duke of Gandía in Spain.[83] When he died, he had him thrown one night into the Tiber and started concentrating on another one named Cesare,[84] a cardinal whom he had renounce his office and wed in France. He then made him supreme magistrate of the Church, gave him an army with the pretext of recovering the lost property of the Church, and made him a very important prince in Italy. Having a powerful army and an apparently justifiable reason, in a short time Cesare subdued all of Romagna that had been under different rulers, except for Ravenna and Cervia, and exiled and killed the previous rulers.

In addition, Cesare seized Piombino in Tuscany, Senigallia in the Marches, and above all the territory of the duke of Urbino, which, unlike all the others, he occupied through deceit rather than by force of arms. Shortly thereafter, he had Paolo Orsini together with Vitellozzo and Levoroto da Fermo killed. Previously they had conspired against him and seized a large part of his holdings, but he had been reconciled with them. He captured Città di Castello, which had been ruled by Vittelozzo, as well as Perugia, governed by the Baglioni, driving out both families from both these cities. But while he was more concerned about winning, the pope's death intervened and confusion reigned

---

83. Giovanni Borgia (c.1476–1497), second duke of Gandía.

84. Cesare Borgia, 13 September 1475–April 1476. One might compare this account with that of Machiavelli in *The Prince*.

THE FIFTEENTH CENTURY

during which Cesare too became seriously ill, giving rise to the suspicion that both had been poisoned. As a result, he allowed all the princes who were still alive to return peacefully to their realms. Among them was Guidobaldo, duke of Urbino, a prince prudent, learned and well-mannered, who had been living all that time in Venice with his wife, Elisabetta da Gonzaga, a lady who will be well remembered for her virtues in the centuries to come. Upon being recalled by his followers, he peacefully returned to his principality.

During this pontiff's [Alexander's] time, in 1495, King Charles [VIII] of France went to Italy under the pretext of having rights to Naples and occupied all of it within a very short period of time.[85] Later, having quarreled with the Venetians and with the duke of Milan, he was attacked by them in Parma[86] on his way back to France and, following a very hard-fought battle, many on both sides were killed. Shortly thereafter, Ferandino [Ferdinand II], Alfonso [II]'s son, who had been driven out with Venetian aid and approval, recovered all the paternal kingdom of which the Venetians then acquired some cities of Apulia. But upon the deaths of King Ferdinand of Naples and King Charles of France, Charles was succeeded by the duke of Orleans Lodovico [Louis XII]; Frederick[87] who succeeded Ferdinand as king was stripped of the kingdom by Louis and taken to France where he died shortly thereafter. With Venetian aid, this king of France also drove Ludovico, duke of Milan,[88] from his principality, which as his nephew's guardian he had usurped; he was imprisoned in France where he is at present.[89] The state remained under the king

---

85. Charles began his invasion in September 1494.

86. At Fornovo, near Parma, on 6 July 1495.

87. King 1496–1501.

88. Ludovico Maria Sforza (il Moro), 27 July 1452–27 May 1508, duke of Milan 1489–1500.

89. He was handed to the French in 1500 and sent to the dungeon at Loches. He died there on 17 May 1508. The writing of this section of the *Lives* was therefore completed between those dates, which coincides with the appearance of the 1507 edition. See Introduction, XI–XVI.

THE LIVES OF THE POPES AND EMPERORS

of France, except for Cremona and the Castelle di Geradada that the Venetians had acquired. And with the coming of the French to Italy began the disease that is named after them; it had never been known by the ancients to be so horrible-looking or painful.[90]

This pontiff [Alexander VI] celebrated a jubilee year that drew a very large turnout of all Christian nations to Rome. Although the situation in Italy was very confused, the Venetians still waged terrible wars with the Turks, which eventually after many losses and victories finally ended in peace. With the death of their leader, Agostino Barbadico, under this pontiff's reign, they chose with the utmost accord and agreement as his replacement Leonardo Loredan, a truly just and modest man.

Nor must we pass over in silence what happened in the city of Florence during this pope's time. Since the Medici family resided in that principality and no longer governed it, a friar in the order of Preachers known as Friar Geronimo [Savonarola] da Ferrara[91] was so learned and eloquent that he controlled the city to the point where nothing could be done without his permission. But later on, reluctant to follow the pope's orders, he was arrested and burned together with two brother friars.[92] And finally, Pope Alexander, after having raised more than ten cardinals, died in the eleventh year of his pontificate, as we said, and was suspected of being poisoned. His remains were buried behind the church of St. Peter in the chapel dedicated to Sta. Maria delle Febbre.

---

90. Syphilis. The first written records of its outbreak in Europe are from Naples in 1494/95 during the French invasion, where, one theory holds, it was brought by mariners returning from the Americas. It was spread by returning French troops, hence the "French disease." An alternative theory holds that is was long endemic in Europe and only recognized after the first encounters with the Americas.

91. Girolamo Savonarola, O.P., 1452–1498.

92. On 23 May 1498.

THE FIFTEENTH CENTURY

MAXIMILIAN (EMPEROR 116[93]), A.D. 1494[94]

Maximilian,[95] the son of Frederick [III], was the third emperor with this name and the twenty-sixth emperor of Germany. After his father died in 1494, he was elected emperor of the Christians. He ruled in that position for twenty-six years, declared wars and did other things all worthy of honor and praise, both in his youth and later when elected emperor. A very wise and humane man, he reflected in his appearance a truly imperial majesty. In the first year of his rule, he took as his wife the most virtuous Diana Maria di Visconti,[96] daughter of Duke Galeazzo of Milan.

Around the fourth year of his reign he defeated the Swiss[97] and the Agnelines[98] who had rebelled against the empire. By nature he was very compassionate and humble, and for this reason did not get involved in warfare — in fact he disliked it. When he went into Italy in 1509 he never allowed much killing by his troops while fighting against the most illustrious Venetian lords, something that was clearly seen in the siege of Padua.[99] There, neither out of excessive anger nor scorn, nor indeed out of ambition to conquer, did he show any desire to be cruel to the people, nor did the city itself fight him as they usually did. In fact, he returned to Germany, giving thanks to God for what he pleased to do in his divinity. Finally, in the year 1520, he died quietly and peacefully in his domain.

*

93. The text reads "XXVIII."

94. This entry has been placed into correct chronological order

95. Emperor A.D. 1508–1519.

96. Bianca Maria Sforza (5 April 1472–31 December 1510), his second wife.

97. The Swiss Confederation defeated Maximilian at the battle of Dornach on 22 July 1499 and confirmed its independence through treaty in Basel on 22 September 1499.

98. The French term for wool or lamb. This may be a reference to the Netherlands, which at the time took the lamb as one of its chief symbols of its wealth and religious devotion. The Netherlands remained rebellious from 1482 to 1492 but were kept part of Maximilian's Hapsburg lands.

99. In September 1509.

THE SIXTEENTH CENTURY

PIUS III (POPE 226), A.D. 1503

Pius III,[1] nephew of Pius II, was elected pontiff after Alexander [VI] and occupied the pontificate for only thirty days. In such a brief period of time he was unable to accomplish any of the things he intended, since it is said that he meant to call a council to reaffirm Church positions and to organize an expedition against the infidels similar to what his uncle had also planned. He was a fine person of considerable learning. For the Christian faithful he gave great promise of being an excellent pontiff. He died of a sore that he had had for a long time on his leg[2] as a result of medication. He was succeeded by Julius II.

JULIUS II (POPE 227), A.D. 1503

Julius II,[3] from Savona, who succeeded Pius III, was elected pontiff on 1 November in the year 1503. He was worthily raised to such dignity and occupied the papacy for ten years, two months and twenty days. The nephew of Sixtus IV, he was a just, prudent and wise man and a hater of tyrants; for this reason, he ousted many important people who enjoyed ecclesiastical privileges. At the beginning of his pontificate, he was submissive and silent and thus began building the marvelous church of St. Peter in Rome. And to support the undertaking, he was the first to increase indulgences and jubilees.

He was very prone to and impetuous in starting wars. After his papacy had enjoyed years of widespread peace and had raised large

1. Pope 213, 1–18 October 1503.
2. He suffered from gout.
3. Pope 214, A.D. 1503–1513. Giuliano della Rovere.

amounts of money, he began waging war, which caused so much harm that very few failed to feel the consequences, especially the most illustrious lords of the Venetian Senate and the Christian King Louis [XII] of France. Some of his adherents followed in his footsteps because they considered it shameful to remain idle, while he suffered serious persecution from several cardinals prompted by King Louis of France.[4] This resulted in the creation of an anti-pope, causing a great schism, against which Julius skillfully defended himself by reaching a favorable peace with the noble Venetian senators and winning over the Catholic King Ferdinand of Spain.[5] Subsequently, he peacefully enjoyed the papacy until his death.

Leo X (Pope 228), A.D. 1513

Leo X[6] was of Florentine descent from the noble family of the Medici.[7] Following the death of Julius II, he was elected pope on 1 March 1513. A man truly devoted to virtue, he enjoyed this reputation at the beginning of his papacy, although later on he did not live up to this general opinion. He occupied the papacy for eight years, eight months and twenty-five days. Since he especially wished to promote the Medici family, he made one of his nephews[8] a cardinal (he later became Clement VII) and his brother Giuliano the duke of Urbino after he had captured the duchy from Francesco Maria [I della Rovere], nephew of Julius II, and destroyed Urbino's city walls. After Giuliano's death, he made his nephew Lorenzo the duke of Urbino.

He governed the city of Rome with great liberality and justice and also created a large number of cardinals, more than any of his predecessors. In his day, a cloistered friar named Martin Luther caused within the church in Germany and Saxony a great schism based on

---

4. Louis summoned a council at Pisa on 11 October 1511 and then in Milan, where it deposed the pope.
5. The Holy League against the French invasion of Italy.
6. Pope 215, A.D. 1513–1521.
7. Giovanni de' Medici, the son of Lorenzo de' Medici.
8. Giulio di Giuliano de' Medici.

the rite and teaching of Jan Hus who had earlier been condemned for heresy and false teaching against the faith of Jesus Christ.[9] The schism did much harm to the Roman Catholic Church and lasted for many years during the reigns of many pontiffs. Leo also declared war against the most Christian king of France, François [I], but death prevented him from attaining his goal of victory.

CHARLES V (EMPEROR 129[10]), A.D. 1521

Charles V[11] known as the emperor of Germany, the son of King Philip [I of Castile] and archduke of Burgundy, was crowned king of Spain after Ferdinand's death. Later, upon Emperor Maximilian's death, he was crowned king of the Romans in the city of Aachen in June 1521. He was badly treated and pestered at the beginning of his reign, but was nevertheless always victorious and successful.

When he became king of Spain, the country rose up in protest because he lived in Germany, whereupon he was forced to go to Spain, which he won over through cunning and false modesty. Later on, the French king, François [I], yielded to his election as emperor. And after being elected with the help of Leo X, he returned the duchy of Milan to the Sforzas and drove out King François of France, who then went in person to Italy in order to recapture the duchy of Milan, but he was taken prisoner near Pavia[12] by Emperor Charles's army and sent to Spain where Charles resided. The emperor kept him prisoner for many months[13] and eventually sent him back to France, keeping two of his sons as hostages and reaching many agreements and conditions with them.[14] His army remained in Lombardy and finally took

9. Martin Luther, 10 November 1483–18 February 1546, was a German Augustinian friar who began the Protestant Reformation with the posting of his Ninety-Five Theses on 31 October 1517. The connection to Hus is not strictly correct theologically, but it demonstrates the conflation of "heretical" ideas coming to Italy from the North.

10. The text reads "XXIX."

11. Emperor A.D. 1519–21 September 1558.

12. At the battle of Pavia on 24 February 1525.

13. In Madrid.

14. Under the terms of the treaty of Madrid of 14 January 1526.

THE SIXTEENTH CENTURY

control of Milan from the duke whom he had appointed. Why he did so and what will follow, only God knows.[15] He was a young man of the times, Catholic and faithful.

ADRIAN VI (POPE 229), A.D. 1522

Adrianus [Adrian] VI[16] was of Flemish descent. Following the death of Leo X, he was elected pontiff on 7 January 1522. Being absent, without knowing or even thinking about such an innovation because of the serious disagreement among the cardinals, he did not go to Rome until the end of the following August. He was a mild, just and Catholic man. At the beginning of September 1523 he died, but during that short period of his papacy he proved to be very productive for the ecclesiastical state, even though modern times consider him unsuited for the position because of the gross injustice among Christians.

In his day there was great upheaval among the people in the cities of Romagna, and the same occurred in the fortress of Forlì and in Ravenna where many nobles and citizens were killed. The powerful citadel of Rhodes was captured because of Christian negligence and wickedness by the Turks on 26 June of his first year. Adrian's intention was to make peace among Christians. Following Lorenzo's[17] death, he returned Francesco Maria[18] to the duchy of Urbino and established unity among nearly all the Christian rulers.

CLEMENT VII (POPE 230), A.D. 1523

Clemens [Clement] VII[19] of Florentine descent, from the Medici family of Leo X and his nephew, was elected pontiff after the death of

---

15. This section was therefore written between the battle of Pavia and treaty of Madrid in January 1526, while the imperial army remained in Lombardy, and before the sack of Rome in 1527.

16. Pope 216, A.D. 1522–1523.

17. Lorenzo di Piero de' Medici (Lorenzo II), de facto ruler of Florence from 1513–4 May 1519, was also duke of Urbino 1516–1519.

18. Francesco Maria I della Rovere, duke of Urbino 1508–1516, and from 1521, when he retook the city from Lorenzo II de' Medici, until his death on 20 October 1538.

19. Pope 217, A.D. 1523–1534.

Adrian VI in the month of November. The see remained vacant for two months because of disagreement among the cardinals, but finally, through his skill and persistence, he was elected pontiff. His pontificate was as troubled by Martin Luther as was his predecessor's. Clement was quiet and much more modest than anyone might expect.

He accomplished many good works for the Roman Catholic Church, and in 1524 declared a universal jubilee throughout Christendom so that every Christian might do penance to placate the divine anger that seemed to be directed against Christians. The jubilee was very holy and resulted in a great deal of good. For many years he has not wished to create any cardinals, and this has continued to the present day; what will ensue only God knows. In 1526, a treaty and alliance[20] was declared between the Christian king François [I] of France and [Henry VIII] the king of England, and between the most illustrious lords of Venice and the duke of Milan. May God preserve this in perpetuity.[21]

* * *

---

20. The League of Cognac. Henry VIII eventually withdrew from the alliance.

21. This appears to be a final dating element of the complete version of the *Lives*, as the author does not include any mention of the most disastrous event of Clement VII's reign, the sack of Rome by imperial forces under Charles V, on 6 May 1527.

SELECT BIBLIOGRAPHY

Primary Sources

Ammianus Marcellinus. *Res Gestae*. Charles Upson Clark and John Carew Rolfe, ed. 3 vols. Loeb Classical Library 300, 315, 331. Cambridge, MA: Harvard University Press, 1935–1939.

Bruni, Leonardo. *History of the Florentine People*. James Hankins, ed and trans. Cambridge, MA: Harvard University Press, I Tatti Renaissance Library, 2001.

Chronicon Estense. Rerum Italicarum Scriptores 15.3. Giulio Bertoni and Emilio Paolo Vicini, ed. Città di Castello: Casa Editrice S. Lapi, 1907.

Da Bisticci, Vespasiano. *The Vespasiano Memoirs*. William George and Emily Waters, trans. Toronto: University of Toronto Press, 1997.

Einhard. "Life of Charlemagne." In *Charlemagne and Louis the Pious: The Lives by Einhard, Notker, Ermoldus, Thegan, and the Astronomer*. Thomas F.X. Noble, trans. University Park: Pennsylvania State University Press, 2009.

Geoffrey of Monmouth. *The History of the Kings of Britain: An Edition and Translation of* De gestis Britonum (Historia regum Britanniae). Michael D. Reeve, ed. Neil Wright, trans. Woodbridge: Boydell Press, 2007.

Historia Augusta. David Magie, trans. 3 vols. Loeb Classical Library. Cambridge, MA: Harvard University Press, 1960.

Jacobus de Voragine. *The Golden Legend: Readings on the Saints*. William Granger Ryan, trans. 2 vols. Princeton, NJ: Princeton University Press, 1993.

Liber Pontificalis. Raymond Davis, trans. and ed. 3 vols. Liverpool: Liverpool University Press, 1989–1995.

Map, Walter. *De nugis curialium*. M.R. James, Christopher Nugent, Lawrence Brooke and R.A.B. Mynors, ed and trans. Oxford Medieval Texts. Oxford: Clarendon Press, 1983.

Paul the Deacon. *History of the Lombards*. William Dudley Foulke, trans. Edward Peters, ed. Philadelphia: University of Pennsylvania Press, 1974.

Petrarca, Francesco. *De viris illustribus*. Silvano Ferrone, ed. Florence: Le Lettere, 2006.

—. *Liber Sine Nomine*. Laura Casarsa, ed. Turin: N. Aragno, 2010.

—. *Petrarch's Book without a Name*. Norman P. Zaccour, trans. Toronto: The Pontifical Institute of Mediaeval Studies, 1973.

Platina, Bartolomeo. *Lives of the Popes*. Anthony F. D'Elia, ed and trans. I Tatti Renaissance Library. Cambridge, MA: Harvard University Press, 2008.

Pseudo-Petrarch, *Chronica delle vite de Pontefici et Imperatori Romani....* Jacomo Pintorni, ed. Venice: Bindoni and Pasini, 1507. MS Chicago, Newberry Library, Case E 436.65.

—. Venice: Iacomo de pinci da Lecco, 1507. MS Rome, Biblioteca Nazionale Centrale 71.2.C.4.

—. Venice: Melchiorre Sessa, 1534. MS Florence, Biblioteca Nazionale Centrale, Magl. 4.6.92.

Schedel, Hartmann. *Nuremberg Chronicle*. Nuremberg: Anton Koberger, 1493.

Suetonius. *Lives of the Caesars*. John Carew Rolfe and K.R. Bradley, eds. Loeb Classical Library 31, 38. Cambridge, MA: Harvard University Press, 1998.

Villani, Giovanni. *Nuova Cronica*. Giuseppe Porta, ed. 3 vols. Milan: Fondazione Pietro Bembo, 1990–1991.

William of Malmesbury. *De gestis regum Anglorum libri quinque: Historiae Novellae Libri Tres*. Cambridge: Cambridge University Press, 2012.

SECONDARY WORKS:

Brown, Alison. *Bartolomeo Scala, 1430–1497. Chancellor of Florence: The Humanist as Bureaucrat*. Princeton, NJ: Princeton University Press, 1979.

Brand, Peter, and Lino Pertile, ed. *The Cambridge History of Italian Literature*. Cambridge: Cambridge University Press, 2001.

Celenza, Christopher. "Late Antiquity and the Florentine Renaissance: Historiographical Parallels." *Journal of the History of Ideas* 62.1 (2001): 17–35.

Cochrane, Eric. *Historians and Historiography in the Italian Renaissance*. Chicago: University of Chicago Press, 1981.

BIBLIOGRAPHY

Crevatin, Giuliana. "Leggere Tito Livio: Nicola Trevet, Landolfo Colonna, Francesco Petrarca." *Incontri triestini di filologia classica* 6 (2006–2007): 67–79.

Dale, Sharon, Allison Williams Lewin and Duane J. Osheim, ed. *Chronicling History: Chroniclers and Historians in Medieval and Renaissance Italy*. University Park: Pennsylvania State University Press, 2007.

Deliyannis, Deborah Mauskopf, ed. *Historiography in the Middle Ages*. Leiden: Brill, 2003.

Dotti, Ugo. "Introduzione." *Gli Uomini Illustri: Vita di Giulio Cesare di Francesco Petrarca*. Ugo Dotti, ed. Turin: Einaudi, 2007, 5–38.

Duffy, Eamon. *Saints and Sinners: A History of the Popes*. New Haven: Yale University Press, 2001.

Grafton, Anthony. *Commerce with the Classics: Ancient Books and Renaissance Readers*. Ann Arbor: University of Michigan Press, 1997.

Green, Louis. *Chronicle into History: An Essay on the Interpretation of History in Fourteenth-Century Chronicles*. Cambridge: Cambridge University Press, 1972.

Gregorovius, Ferdinand. *History of the City of the Rome in the Middle Ages*. Annie Hamilton, trans. 8 vols. London: George Bell & Sons, 1909–1912; rev. ed., with intro. by D.S. Chambers. New York: Italica Press, 2000–2004.

Joost-Gaugier, Christiane L. "The Early Beginnings of the Notion of 'Uomini Famosi' and the 'De viris illustribus' in the Greco-Roman Literary Tradition." *Artibus et Historiae* 3.6 (1982): 97–115.

Kallendorf, Craig. "The Historical Petrarch." *The American Historical Review* 101.1 (1996): 130–41.

Kirkham, Victoria, and Armando Maggi, ed. *Petrarch: A Critical Guide to the Complete Works*. Chicago: University of Chicago Press, 2009.

Kohl, Benjamin G. "Petrarch's Prefaces to *De viris illustribus*." *History and Theory* 13.2 (1974): 132–44.

Marchesi, Simone. "Petrarch's Philological Epic *(Africa)*." In Kirkham and Maggi, *Petrarch*, 113–30.

Marsh, David. "Petrarch and Jerome." *Memoirs of the American Academy in Rome* 49 (2004): 85–98.

McBrien, Richard P. *Lives of the Popes: The Pontiffs from St. Peter to John Paul II.* San Francisco: HarperCollins, 1997.

Mommsen, Theodor E. "Petrarch and the Decoration of the Sala Virorum Illustrium in Padua." *The Art Bulletin* 34.2 (1952): 95–116.

Regn, Gerhard, and Bernhard Huss. "The History of the *Africa* and the Renaissance Project." *Modern Language Notes* 124.1 (2009): 86–102.

Ross, W. Braxton, Jr. "Giovanni Colonna, Historian at Avignon." *Speculum* 45.4 (1970): 533–63.

Sage, Michael M. "The *De Viris Illustribus:* Chronology and Structure." *Transactions of the American Philological Association* 108 (1978): 217–41.

Spencer, John R. "Filarete, the Medallist of the Roman Emperors." *The Art Bulletin* 61.4 (1979): 550–61.

Spiegel, Gabrielle M. *The Past as Text: The Theory and Practice of Medieval Historiography.* Baltimore, MD: Johns Hopkins University Press, 1997.

Stone, Harold S. "Review of *Commerce with the Classics.*" *Libraries and Culture* 35.3 (2000): 475–76.

Vasina, Augusto. "Medieval Urban Historiography in Western Europe (1100–1500)." In Delyannis, *Historiography*, 317–52.

Witt, Ronald G. "The Rebirth of the Romans as Models of Character: *De viris illustribus.*" In Kirkham and Maggi, *Petrarch*, 103–11.

*

INDEX

A
Aachen 135, 137, 246
Abd al-Malik, caliph 111
Abindius of Nicopolis 32
Abruzzi Mountains 177
Abu-Bakr 105
Acacius, bishop 81, 83, 85
Acciaiuoli, Donato XXXIII
Accius of Constantinople 79
Accorso di Bagnolo 197
Acephalian heresy 78, 86
Achab, prophet 68
Achillas 3
Achyron 57
Actium 6
Acts of the Apostles 14
Adalbero of Eppenstein 165
Adalbert of Italy 155
Adalbert of Prague, bishop, St. 158, 163
Adalmatius, Byzantine general 94
Adam XXVII, 8
Adelaid, wife of Lothair II 155
Adelchis, king of Lombards 135
Adeodatus II, pope 113
Adolf I, king of Germany 209, 210
Adorno, Prospero 234
Adriana Augusta 80
Adrian I, pope 132
Adrian II, pope 145
Adrian III, pope 147
Adrian IV, pope 182
Adrian V, pope 202
Adrian VI, pope 247, 248
Adriatic Sea 210
Aelia. *See* Jerusalem.
Aelii family 22
Aelius Donatus, grammarian 58
Aelius Galenus. *See* Galen.
Aeneas XXXV, 2
Africa; Muslim conquest 115, 116; Portugese navigations 239; Roman 22, 35; Vandal 71, 76, 81, 88
Agapitus I, pope 44, 89, 92
Agapitus II, pope XXI, 155
Agatha, St. 50
Agatho, pope 113–14
Agilulf, king of Lombards 100
Agnelines. *See* Netherlands revolt.
Agnellus of Ravenna 95
Agnes, St. 50
Agrippina, virgin 39
Agrippina, wife of Claudius 12, 13
Aistulf, king of Lombards 124, 125, 140
Alamanni 122
Alans 65, 68, 71, 73
Alaric, king of Goths 68, 70, 71, 88
Albano 69, 182
Albanzani, Donato degli XXVIII
Alberic I, duke of Spoleto 153
Alberic II, duke of Spoleto 156
Alberic III Theophylact 157
Alberico da Romano 196
Albert, antipope 175
Albert I, duke of Austria 209, 210
Albert II, emperor 227, 229
Alberti, Olivier XVI
Albert, king of Germany 216, 217
Alberto, father of Lucius II 180
Albert of Poland, bishop 164
Albertus Magnus 201
Albigeo de Fontana 200
Albinus, emperor 40
Alboin, king of Lombards 95
Alcuin of York 121, 137
Alemanni 44, 64
Alessandria 184, 208
Alexander, cardinal of Sta. Susanna 234
Alexander of Cappadocia 36
Alexander I, pope 25–26
Alexander II, pope 170
Alexander III, pope 183
Alexander IV, pope 196
Alexander V, antipope 226, 227
Alexander VI, pope 239, 244
Alexander Severus, emperor 38
Alexander the Great 2
Alexandria 3, 4, 6, 7, 10, 12, 33, 34, 35; church of St. John the Baptist 88;

demonic possession 82
Alexius I Comnenus, emperor 172, 174
Alexius IV, emperor 187
Alexius V, emperor 187
Alexius, St. 70
Alfonso III, king of Aragon 206
Alfonso V, king of Aragon 224
Alfonso X, king of Leon and Castile 196, 197
Alfonso I, king of Naples 224, 232, 233
Alfonso II, king of Naples 241
Alpaida, mother of Charles Martel 121
Alps 66, 132, 146
Altinus, St. 10
Amadeus, duke of Savoy. *See* Felix V, antipope.
Amalasuntha, queen of Goths 88, 89
Amalfi 234, 237
Amaury de Bène 190
Ambrose, St. 55, 62, 63, 64, 66; hymns 83
Amelianus 19
Amelius and Amicus, Sts. 128
Amerii 147
Anacletus I, pope 24
Anacletus II, antipope 178
Anagni 149, 209, 212, 213
Anastasia, St. 50, 106
Anastasius, father of Felix II 62
Anastasius, father of John III 94
Anastasius I Dicorus, emperor 62, 69, 80, 82, 83, 85, 86
Anastasius II, emperor 120, 122
Anastasius, patriarch of Constantinople 124
Anastasius I, pope 69
Anastasius II, pope 83
Anastasius III, pope 152
Anastasius IV, pope 182
Anastasius the Persian, St. 104
Anchises 2
Ancisa 217
Ancona 197; Pius II 233; Saracen sack 209; St. Andrew's relics 234; Venetian attack 204
Ancus Marcius 2

Andrea, bishop of Ostia 93, 114
Andrew III, the Venetian 208
Andrew the Apostle, St. 10, 173, 234
Angles 12
Anguillara, Deifobo degli 235; Everso II, degli 235
Anicetus, pope 31
Anicius Auchenius Bassus, consul 431 75
annals xxx
Anselm, Lombard duke 124
Anselm of Badagio 170. *See also* Alexander II, pope.
Anselm of Canterbury 170, 173
Anterus, pope 39, 40, 41
Anthimus, heretic 89–92
Anthony of Padua, St. 193
Antioch 10, 16, 23, 27, 37, 46; earthquakes 87, 184; First Crusade 172; Holy Lance 239; Muslim conquest 107; Third Crusade 185
Antoninus Pius, emperor 28–29, 30–35
Antonius, consul 5
Antonius, father of Damasus I 62
Antony of Egypt, St. 42, 56, 58; relics 88
Apollinaris of Antioch 63, 64
Apollinaris, St. 10
Apollonaris, bishop 33
Apulia 71, 175; Norman 147, 172, 175, 177, 179; Saracen raids 141, 152. *See also* Naples, kingdom of.
Aquila, scholar 27
Aquileia 10, 29, 39, 40, 45, 65, 67; battle of 80; capture by Huns 77; patriarch 177, 238; schism 117
Aquinas, Thomas 201, 218
Aquitania 6, 122, 131, 139, 143
Arabs 34; conquest of Damascus 112; rise of Islam 105. *See also* Muslims, Saracens.
Aragon 192
Arat 181
Arator, poet 88
Arbogastes 65
Arcadius, emperor 66, 67, 68, 70, 73
Arcolanus of Perugia, bishop 91

INDEX

Arelate. *See* Arles.
Arezzo 199, 202; Florentine siege 208; Guelph/Ghibelline conflict 206, 207
Argenta 184, 189
Argentoratum. *See* Strasbourg.
Arians and Arianism 53, 55, 57, 58, 59, 64, 65, 66, 73, 81, 82, 86, 87, 98; and Goths 80; and Vandals 85
Arichis, duke of Benevento 134
Arius of Alexandria 55, 57, 59, 65
Arles 53, 71
Armenia 25; Cilician 211; conversion to Christianity 96
Arnold of Brescia 179
Arnolf, antipope 175
Arno River, battle of 207
Arnulf, duke of Aquitania 144
Arnulf, emperor 144, 148
Arnulfus, St. 85
Arrius Aper 48
Arsenius, hermit 66, 70
Arthur, king 78
Ascanius 2
Ascoli 207
Asinarius, king of Goths 91
Assyrians 28
Astolf, king of Lombards 96
Asturi 199
Atawulf 71
Athanasius of Alexandria 57, 58
Athens 24, 29, 63, 144
Atia 5
Attalus, emperor 71
Attila the Hun 74, 77, 147
Audianism 58
Audius, theologian 58
Augustine of Canterbury 99, 100
Augustine of Hippo, St. 64, 71, 73, 109; relics 122; theology 190
Augustus, emperor 5, 6, 7, 8, 9
Aurelia, city in Gaul 46
Aurelian, emperor 45, 46, 61
Aurelius, co-emperor 28
Ausonius, poet 65
Austria, duchy of 217

Auxentius, bishop of Milan 62
Auxerre 191
Avalle Bridge, battle of 199
Avignon XVI, XXIV, XXX, 216; papal conclave 218, 224; papal court 218, 221, 223

B
Babylon 22
Baghdad 200
Bagnolo, treaty of 237
Baia 25
Baldalch. *See* Baghdad.
Baldini, Vittorio XXXVI
Baldwin II, Latin emperor of Constantinople 197
Baldwin IX, count of Flanders 187
Baldwin, king of Jerusalem 173, 178
Bamberg 167
Bandino, bishop of Ravenna 208
Barba, Arian heretic 82, 86
Barbadico, Agostino 242
Barbanus, abbot of Fondi 141
Barba, Pietro. *See* Paul II, pope.
Barbara, St. 50
Barbaro, Ermolao 238
Barbarus, St. 96
Bari 185
Barlaam 63
Barnabas, St. 81
Bartholomew the Apostle, St. 96, 158
Basel, treaty of 243
Basilide, heretic 25
Basiliscus, usurper 80
Basil of Caesarea, St. 60, 63
Bassianus. *See* Caracalla, emperor.
Bavaria 134, 139, 164, 219, 223
Beatific Vision 220
Bede, the Venerable 33, 118, 121, 125; *Ecclesiastical History of the English People* 115
Belisarius, general 88-93
Benedict I, pope 96
Benedict II, pope 114
Benedict III, pope 145
Benedict IV, pope 150

255

THE LIVES OF THE POPES AND EMPERORS

Benedict V, pope 157
Benedict VI, pope 158
Benedict VII, pope 159, 161
Benedict VIII, pope 164, 223
Benedict IX, pope 166
Benedict X, pope 169
Benedict XI, pope 213
Benedict XII, pope 219
Benedict XIII, antipope 224, 226, 227, 228
Benedict of Nursia, St. 88, 89, 94, 113
Benedictine Order 219, 221
Benedictus, father of pope Marcellus 51
Benedictus, father of Sergius III 151
Benevento 95, 111, 118, 127, 134, 182, 186; and Charlemagne 133; battle of 1266 198; Lombard 96; Otto II 158; San Bartolomeo Church 96; St. Bartholomew, relics 158
Berengar I, king of Italy 151, 154, 155
Berengar II, emperor 152
Berengar III, emperor 154
Berengar IV, emperor 155
Berengar of Tours 151, 152, 154, 155, 168, 170
Bergamo XXXV, 23, 77, 95
Berhtwald, archbishop of Canterbury, 116
Bernardino da Siena 231
Bernard of Clairvaux, St. 175, 176, 180, 185
Bernhard, king of Lombards 137, 141
Bertrada, daughter of Charlemagne 137
Bertrada, mother of Charlemagne 137
Bessarion, Basilios, of Trebizond 233
Bethlehem 8, 24, 28
Bethsaida 10
Bibbiena 208
Bible: Ecclesiastes 39; interpretation 218, 221; Matthew in Hebrew 81; New Testament 185; Old Testament 185; Psalter 63
Bibulus, consul 3
Bindoni, Francesco XI
Biondo, Flavio XXXV
Bisticci, Vespasiano da XXXIII, XXXIV, XXXVII; *Lives of Illustrious Men of the Fifteenth Century* XXXIII
Bithynia 9, 23

Black Death. *See* disasters: Black Death.
Blaise, St. 50
Blanche of Anjou 210
Bleda, king of Huns 77
Boccaccio, Giovanni XIII, XXXV, 165; *De mulieribus claris* XXXV
Boethius 81, 85, 87; tomb 85
Bohemia 202; Albert II 229; Hussites 225; Ottonian 153, 158, 164
Boleslav the Cruel 153
Bologna 192, 210, 225; cardinal of 231, 237; conflict with Venice 200; Ghibelline alliance 212; Lambertaci 204; revolt against d'Este 215; San Felice 181; war with Faenza 202; war with Ferrara 193; war with Frederick II 195
Bolsena 124
Bonaventure, St. 201
Boniface I, pope XVIII, 72-73
Boniface II, pope 89
Boniface III, pope 102
Boniface IV, pope 102
Boniface V, pope 104
Boniface VI, pope 149
Boniface VII, antipope 158
Boniface VIII, pope 209, 213, 236
Boniface IX, pope 223, 225
Boniface of Mainz, St. 121
Bonifacius, father of Benedict I 96
Bonifazio, marquis 169
Bonus of Sorrento, bishop 93
Book of Virgins 39
Bordeaux 214, 216
Borgia; Alfonso 232 (*See also* Callixtus III); Cesare XXXVII, 240, 241; Giovanni, duke of Gandía 240; Rodrigo 239
Bragantino 188
Brendan, St. 94
Brescia 144; Henry IV 171; Huns 77; Lombard 95; Lombard League 184; taken by Henry VII 217
Bridget of Sweden, St. 221
Brigid of Kildare, St. 87, 88
Brindisi 7
Brittany 139

256

INDEX

Brown, Alison XXXI
Bruni, Leonardo XXXII; *Historiae florentina populi* XXXII
Bruno of Carinthia 160. *See* Gregory V, pope.
Brutus 5
Bubalia 42
Budapest 166
Buonconvento 127, 217. *See also* Benevento.
Burdinus, archbishiop of Braga 175, 176
Burgundians and Burgundy 62, 85, 115, 122, 170, 176, 202, 246
Byzantium, city 53

C

Cadalus of Parma 170. *See also* Honorius II, pope.
Cadiz 2
Caesarea 39, 56, 35; pogroms against Christians 94
Caesarion 4
Caesonia 11
Caetani, Giovanni 175. *See also* Gelasius II, pope.
Calabria 71, 175, 182
Caligula. *See* Gaius Caligula.
Callixtus, bishop 63
Callixtus I, pope XIX, 37, 38
Callixtus II, pope 176
Callixtus III, antipope 183
Callixtus III, pope 232, 239
Calpurnia 5
Calpurnius 39
Calvano, count 199
Campania 7, 27, 31, 74, 85, 90, 97, 104, 110, 118, 157, 170, 187, 192, 196
Campofregoso: Lodovico di 234; Paolo di 234; Spinetta di 234
Campo Morto, battle of 1482 237
Canossa 171
Cantabria 6
Canterbury 99, 112, 170, 181
Capetians 154, 159
Capita Bubula 5
Capo Colonna, battle of 982 160
Cappadocia 36, 50, 60

Capri 8
Capua 76, 134, 205
Caracalla, emperor 36, 37
cardinals, origins 114
Carinus 48
Carloman, king of France 124, 131, 132, 145
Carlopoli 146
Carmelites 202
Carmignano, fortress 215
Carolingians 124, 154
Carrara, Francesco da XXVI, XXVII
Carrhae 36, 48, 219. *See also* Harran.
Carthage 71, 82, 200; retaken by Belisarius 91. *See also* Tunis.
Carthusian Order XIX, 172, 221
Carus, emperor 48
Cassiodorus 83, 92, 95, 255, 257, 264
Cassius 5
Castelle di Geradada 242
Castelleone, battle of 191
Castello di Santa Felicità 180
Castello San Zeno, battle of 196
Castelnuovo 235
Castle Gargar 178
Castres 50
Catafrigian heretics 32
Catafrigius, heretic 30
Catalonia 222, 223
Catania 184
Catherine of Alexandria, St. 52
Catherine of Siena, St. 221, 233
Cato 3, 4
Cecilia, St. XIX, 38, 140
celestial events 139; blood rain and skies 144, 154; lightning 145; solar eclipse 187, 194; sun flare 165; three moons and suns 184
Celestine I, pope 74
Celestine II, pope 180
Celestine III, pope 186, 187
Celestine IV, pope 194
Celestine V, pope 209
Celestinus, Pelagian 70
Cervia 240
Cesarea, queen of Persia 112
Chalcedon. *See* councils: Chalcedon 451.

Châlus-Chabrol 187
Charlemagne XX, XXXV, 126, 128, 131, 132, 141, 151, 159, 205, 227; and Bretons 134; and Huns 135; Baltic campaign 135; Bavarain campaign 134; Benevento campaign 134; Bohemian campaign 135; death 137; emperor 136; epitaph 138; family 137; Gascony 134; imperial coronation 129; in Jerusalem voyage 136; Lombard campaign 774 127; military campaigns 133; physical description 136; Rome 129, 135; Saxon Wars 133; Spanish campaigns 133; virtues 137; will 138
Charles II, the Bald, emperor 142, 145, 146
Charles III, the Fat, emperor 147
Charles IV, emperor 220, 223, 226
Charles V, emperor 246; sack of Rome 248
Charles IV, king of France 159
Charles VII, king of France 214, 215, 217, 219, 220, 223, 224, 226, 234, 241
Charles VIII, king of France 241
Charles I, king of Naples 197, 200, 217; conquest of Naples 198; Sicilian Vespers 204
Charles II, king of Naples 205, 207, 210, 218; and Celestine V 209
Charles Martel 121, 122, 123-24
Charles of Valois 210, 212
Charles the Younger 129, 137
Charlotte, queen of Cyprus 234
Childeric III, king of the Franks 124, 131
Chonad, Hungary 166
Chosroes II, Persian king 101, 104, 105
Christopher, deposes Leo V 151
chronicles XIII, XIV, XV, XXX
Cibò: Giovanni Battista (*See* Innocent VIII.); Franceschetto 238; Teodorina 238
Ciccarelli, Antonio, *Lives of the Popes* XXXVI
Cicero, Marcus Tullius 5, 7; Letters XII
Cilician Armenia 185
Cinna 4
Cistercian Order 180, 219; Citeaux 174, 175, 219
Città di Castello 240
Città Nova 230
Clare of Assisi, St. 196
Claudianus, poet 68
Claudia, wife of Augustus 7
Claudius I, emperor 10, 12, 13, 18
Claudius II, emperor 45
Claudius, Gothic commander 97
Clement I, pope 10, 17, 20-21, 22
Clement II, pope 167
Clement III, antipope 171
Clement III, pope 186
Clement IV, pope 198
Clement V, pope 214, 218
Clement VI, pope 220, 236
Clement VII, antipope 222, 223, 224
Clement VII, pope XI, XXXVII, 245, 247, 248
Clement VIII, antipope 224
Cleopatra 4, 7
Cleophas 23
Cletus, pope 10, 17, 19, 20, 24
Clovis, king of the Franks 87
Cluny 176
Cochrane, Eric XIII, XV
Colan 174
Cologne XXI, 145, 183
Colonna: Giovanni XVI, XXX; *De viris illustribus* XXX, XXXI; *Mare historiarum* XXX; Iacopo 210, 215; Oddone 228; Pietro 210, 215; Sciarra 212, 219. *See also* John XXIII, antipope; Martin V, pope.
Columba, St. 46
Columbanus, St. 105, 115
Columbus, Christopher 239
Commodus, emperor 30, 32, 33
Concordius 63
Concordius of Fondi 31
Condulmaro, Gabriele. *See* Eugenius IV.
Conon, pope 115
Conrad, Hohenstaufen 180, 181, 185, 188, 194, 195, 196, 198, 199
Conrad I, emperor 152
Conrad II, emperor 164

INDEX

Conrad III, emperor 180
Conrad of Monferrato, king of Jerusalem 185
Conradin, Hohenstaufen 198, 199
Constance, empress 175, 191
Constance of Sicily 210
Constans, co-emperor 57
Constans, father of John I 86
Constantine I, the Great, emperor XX, 48, 52–60. 87, 227
Constantine II, emperor 57–58
Constantine IV, emperor 111, 112, 113, 115
Constantine V, emperor 122, 124
Constantine VI, emperor 128
Constantine, pope 120
Constantine II, antipope 126
Constantinople 46, 53, 54, 55, 57, 58, 63, 65, 66, 67, 68, 70, 73, 74, 75, 76, 78, 80; attacked by Vitalianus 82; Byzantine empire 95; capture by Crusaders 172; capture in Fourth Crusade 187; conquest by Turks 1453 230; Hagia Sophia 95, 114; heresy 85, 89; house of Placidia 109; Iconoclasm 121, 122; Justinianic plague 88, 94; Muslim siege 717/8 122; papal embassy 81, 110; patriarch 88; Persian embassies 113; reconciliation with West 201; relics 106, 183; Second Crusade 181; uses of *Typus* 108, 109
Constantinus, father of Felix I 45
Constantinus, father of Paul I 126
Constantinus, father of Stephen II 125
Constantinus, tyrant 68, 71
Constantius, co-emperor 48, 49, 50, 51–52, 55, 57, 58, 59, 60
Constantius, general 48, 49, 50, 51, 52, 55, 57, 58, 59, 60, 71
Cordoba 14
Cornelia 4
Cornelius, pope 16, 42
Cornell University Library, Catalogue of the Petrarch Collection VII
Correr, Angelo. *See* Gregory XII, pope.
Corsica 119, 127
Cortenuova, battle of 193

Cosimo da Sulmona. *See* Innocent VII.
Cosimo de' Migliorati. *See* Innocent VII.
Cosmas, St. 50
Cossa, Baldassare. *See* John XXIII, antipope.
Costo, Tommaso XXXVI
councils; Aquileia 118; Arles 53; Basel 229; Cadaver Synod 149; Carthage 71; Chalcedon 75–83, 77, 78, 82, 86; Clermont 172; Constance 224, 227, 228; Constantinople 336 57; Constantinople 381 55, 63, 66, 67; Constantinople 448 73; Constantinople 680 112, 114; Ephesus 431 73; Ephesus 449 73; Florence 169; Liège 179; Lyons First 1245 194; Lyons Second 1274 201 Mantua 170; Nicaea 54, 55, 57; Pavia, synod of 118; Pisa 226; Pisa-Milan 245; Ravenna 150; Rome 1155 179; Rome, Third Lateran 183; Rome, Fourth Lateran 190; Sardica 57; Toledo 98–100; Toulouse 183; Trent XXXVI; Trullan 116; Vienne 215; Würzburg 179
Courtenay family 191
Cremona: attacked by Azzolino d'Este 196; capture by Frederick I 182; Lombards 95, 100; Louis XII's invasion 242; war with Milan 191
Crescentii 163; Crescentius, consul of Rome 160, 161
Crete 73
Crusades XIX; First 172; Second 181; Third 185, 186; Fourth 187; Fifth 191; Eighth 200; Second, council of Lyons 201; Innocent III 190; Pius III 244; Urban V 221
Cumae 121
Curzola, battle of 210
Cybele, goddess 102
Cyprian of Carthage, St. 43, 44
Cyril, deacon 60
Cyril of Alexandria 71
Cyril, St. 22, 145
Cyrus, patriarch 120

D

Dacia 25, 46, 78, 148
da Fermo, Vitellozzo and Levoroto 240
Dalmatia and Dalmatians 6, 8, 47, 48, 49, 106
Damascus XXI, 112, 184
Damasus, *Chronicles of Roman Pontiffs* 24
Damasus I, pope 62, 66
Damasus II, pope 168
Damian, archbishop of Ravenna 116
Damian, St. 33, 50, 163
Damietta 191
Danes 147
Dante, *Convivio* XII, 145, 165, 200, 203, 207
Danube River 74, 122
David, king 20
David, king of India 188
Decius, emperor 41, 42
Decretals 112, 181, 187, 192, 210
Demetrius 37
Desiderius, abbot of Monte Cassino 172. *See also* Victor III, pope.
Desiderius, king of Lombards 125, 128, 132, 134, 135
d'Este: Azzolino 189, 190, 196; Azzo VIII 215, 216; Ercole 237; Francesco (Fresco) 216
Deusdedit I, pope 103
diaries XIII
Didius Iulianus, emperor 34
Dignissimus, Roman priest 84
Dimari 212
Diocletian, emperor 47, 48, 49, 50, 51
Dionysius, bishop of Corinth 33
Dionysius of Milan 58
Dionysius, pope 44–45
Dionysius the Areopagite, pseudo 21, 139; *On the Angelic Hierarchies* 144
Dioscorus of Alexandria 73, 74, 75, 89
disasters XII, XVII, XXI, XXIX, XXXIV, 139; Black Death 220; droughts 178; earthquakes 9, 14, 60, 87, 172, 184, 216; famines 12, 90, 96, 168, 169, 178, 215; locusts 144; plagues 219, 220; syphilis 242
Dissa 181

Dolce, Lodovico XVI
Dominican Order 188, 191, 192, 193, 195, 202, 218, 221, 232, 233
Dominic, St. 188, 191, 192
Domitian, emperor 19–20, 21
Domitius 13
Donati, Corso 212
Donation of Constantine 53, 54, 136
Donatist heresy 53
Donatus 53, 58, 68
Donatus of Evorea 64
Donatus the Macedonian 64
Donus I, pope 113
Donus II, pope 158
Dornach, battle of 1499 243
Doryphorus 13
Dotti, Ugo XXIV
droughts. *See* disasters: droughts.
Drusus 11, 12
Dyrrhachium, battle of 172

E

earthquakes. *See* disasters: earthquakes.
Edessa; battle of 260 43
Edmund, king of East Anglia 144
Edradius, bishop, vision 108
Edward I, king of England 200, 210
Edward III, king of England 219
Edward the Martyr, king 160
Egidius, abbot 128
Egidius, St. 121
Egypt 10, 11, 42, 44, 56, 63, 82
Einhard, *Life of Charlemagne* XXXV
Elagabalus, emperor 37, 38
Elbe River 6
Eleanor of Portugal 230
Eleutherius, pope 32–34
eleven thousand virgins of Cologne 76
Elizabeth of Hungary, St. 190, 192
Emeric of Hungary 165, 195
Emous 67
emperors. *See under* individual names.
England and English XXXIV, 33, 34, 35 50, 52, 65, 68, 70, 74, 78; ancient 3, 18; Anglo-Saxons 80, 99, 118; League of Cognac 248; Peter's Pence 143

INDEX

Enzo, king of Sardinia 195
Ephesus 219
Epiphanius of Ticino 76
Epiphanius, St. 57
Eric, Frankish commander 135
Euboea 235
Eudosius 67
Eugenia of Alexandria 33
Eugenius I, pope 110
Eugenius II, pope 140
Eugenius III, pope 180, 227
Eugenius IV, pope 227–31
Eugenius, usurper 33, 66
Eulalius, anti-pope 72
Eunonius 64
Euphrasia, St. 94
Euphrates River 25, 40, 101
Eusebia, empress 70
Eusebius of Caesarea 24, 39, 56
Eusebius of Nicomedia 55
Eusebius, pope 52
Eusebius, Roman priest 59
Eusimia, grandmother of Justin I 86
Eustochium, pilgrim 67
Euthymius of Constantinople 81
Eutropius 43, 48
Eutropius, father of Constantius 51
Eutychian, pope 45, 46
Eutychius, heretic 45, 46, 73, 75, 76, 80, 85
Evaristus, pope 24–25

F
Fabian, St. 39, 41
Faenza 123, 202
Falcondus, abbot of St. Denis 125
famines. *See* disasters: famines.
fate xv
Faustina, wife of Marcus Aurelius 30
Faustinus 20
Faustus, senator 84
Felix, father of Pope Victor I 35
Felix I, pope 45
Felix II, antipope 58, 59, 62
Felix III, pope 81
Felix IV 88
Felix V, antipope 229, 230, 231

Ferdinand I (Ferrante), king of Naples 233, 234, 235, 237, 238
Ferdinand II (Ferandino), king of Naples 241
Ferdinand the Catholic, king of Spain 239, 245, 246
Ferrara 187; and Albigeo de Fontana 200; and d'Este 189, 216, 237; and Urban III 185; captures Argenta 184; captures Bragantino 188; cathedral 179; civil war 193; declared a *civitas* 112; relics 113; under Matilda of Tuscany 174; under Obizzo 209; War of 1482-84 237
Ferrari, Giolito de' xvi
Ferro River 185
Fiesole 70
Filarete (Antonio di Pietro Averlino) xxxi
Filippo, archbishop of Ravenna 196
Filippo, count of Pavia 217
Firenzuola 195
Flanders 78, 210, 212
Flavian, bishop of Constantinople 18, 73, 75
Flavian family 18
Flavius Josephus 15, 147
Flavius Magnus Aurelius Cassiodorus Senator. *See* Cassiodorus.
Flavius Valerius Severus 52
Florence vii, 170; Angevins 198; Bardi di Vernio Chapel of Sta. Croce 55; Black Death 220; Blacks and Whites 211, 214; Borgo Sant'Apostolo fire 176; Carolingian 136, 137; Cerchi 211, 212; chronicles xiv, xv; Confraternity of the Blessed Virgin at Sto. Spirito xxxvi; Council of Constance 228; Donati 211, 212; editions of *Lives* xi; Eugenius IV 229; Frederick I 185; Gothic siege 70; Guelph alliance 206, 207, 208; Guelph-Ghibelline conflict 200, 201; Henry IV 172; Henry VII 217; internal strife xxii; Le Stinche 214; Medici 238; papal interdict 211; papal legate 213, 215; Piazza San Giovanni 214; Piazza San Lorenzo 214; San Giovanni

Battista della Calza 228; San Salvi 217; Savanarola 242; Spadai Gate 214; territory 186; Via Nuova 214; war with Arezzo 207; war with Pistoia 215; war with Prato 213; war with Siena 197; war with Sixtus IV 237
Florianus, emperor 47
Fondi 40, 222, 223
Foresti da Bergamo, Jacopo Filippo, *Supplementum chronicarum* XXXV
Forlì 205, 247
Formosus, pope 148, 149, 150, 151
Fornovo, battle of 1495 241
Fortius of Lyons, St. 30
Fossalta, battle of 1249 195
Fournier, Jacques. *See* Benedict XII, pope.
France: XIX; Carolingian 151; disasters XXI, 178; early church 93; Great Schism 222, 223; League of Cognac 248; Lothair's division of empire 142; Normans 148; papal relations 168, 176, 179, 180, 183, 219, 220, 226; relics 125
Francesco Bindoni VI
Franciscan Order 188, 193, 197, 201, 202, 207, 231, 236; missions to Asia 218
Francis of Assisi, St. 188
Franciscus, father of Pope Agatho 113
François I, king of France 246, 248
Frangipane, Cencio I 171
Frederick, duke of Austria 219
Frederick I Barbarossa, emperor XX, 179, 181, 186–88; Third Crusade 185; Tuscan campaign 185; Tusculum 183
Frederick II, emperor 175, 188, 189, 190, 191; and Gregory IX 192; and Innocent IV 194; conquest of Milan 193; deposition 195; excommunicated at Lyons 194; journey to Rome 190; *stupor mundi* 160
Frederick III, emperor 230, 236, 243
Frederick, king of Naples 219, 230, 236, 241
Frederick the Handsome, duke of Austria 219
French disease. *See* disasters: syphilis.
Friars Minor. *See* Franciscan Order.
Friars Preachers. *See* Dominican Order.
Fridian, missionary 33
Frigia 32
Frigidus, battle of, 394 66
Frisia and Frisians 116, 122, 135, 194–95, 196
Friuli 140
Frosinone 85
Fulgentius, bishop 77, 81, 82

G
Gades. *See* Cadiz.
Gaeta 176, 208
Gaius Caligula 11
Gaius, nephew of Augustus 7
Gaius Octavius. *See* Augustus, emperor.
Gaius, pope 2, 5, 7, 11, 23, 47
Galasso, papal legate 213
Galba, emperor 17
Galen 23, 28
Galerius, co-emperor 48, 51–52
Galganus, St. 116
Galilee 10
Galla Placidia 74
Galla, sister of Henry II 164
Gallienus, emperor 43, 44, 45
Gall, St. 105
Gallus Hostilianus, emperor 42
Garanta, Nicolo XVII
Garigliano, battle of 915 153
Garonne River 131
Gascony and Gascons 133, 134, 214, 214, 220, 224; prodigies 155
Gaul: ancient 4; early Christian 3, 6, 7, 8, 10, 21, 26, 30, 38, 46, 47, 51, 53, 57, 58, 60, 64, 65, 66, 68, 94; in Arthurian romance 78; under Vandals 71
Gelasius I, pope 15, 83
Gelasius II, pope 175, 176
Geneva 223
Geneviève, St. 76
Gennadius XXXV
Genoa: alliance with Innocent II 179; alliance with Innocent IV 194; chronicles XIII; fall of Constantinople 230; Hohenstaufen 199; rebellion against French 234; under Campofregoso 234;

INDEX

under Sforza 234; war with Pisa 186, 190, 205; war with Venice 210
Genseric, king of Vandals 73, 76, 81, 85
George of Cappadocia, St. 50
George of Podebrady, king of Bohemia 235
Gerard, count of Burgundy 124
Gerard Sagredo, St. 166
Gerbert d'Aurillac 159, 161
Gergani 32
Germani 3, 6, 8, 40. *See also* Germany.
Germanicus 11
Germanos, patriarch of Constantinople 124
Germanus, bishop of Capua 86
Germanus of Auxerre, St. 74, 81
Germanus of Paris, St. 95
Germany: Carolingian 133, 135, 139, 147, 151, 152; Great Schism 222; Hapsburg 209, 210, 216 17, 219, 227, 229 30, 243, 246; Hohenstaufen 190, 196, 198; Ottonian 153, 156, 164, 179; papacy 233; Protestant Reformation 245; Salian 186, 189; Treaty of Verdun 142
Gerold, Frankish commander 135
Gerontius 71
Gervais, cardinal 205
Gervaise, St. 50, 100
Gherardo of Pisa, count 199
Ghibellines 200, 201, 204, 206, 208, 212; Florence 214; Lombardy 199; Tuscany 199, 214
Gibraltar 239
Gilbert de la Porrée 181
Giordano, count of Caserta 198
Giordano, OP, missionary 193
Giotto xxxi, 215
Giovanni, archpriest 166. *See also* Gregory VI, pope.
Giovanni, duke of Naples 121
Giovio, Paolo xxxvi
Girona 205, 206
Gisila, daughter of Charlemagne 137
Gisulf, duke of Benevento 118
Godfrey de Bouillon 173
Golden Legend 22, 33, 54, 55, 98, 100, 102
Golden Spurs, battle of 212

Gonzaga, Elisabetta da 241
Gordian, usurper 40
Gordian III, emperor 40–41
Gordianus, father of Gregory I 98
Gordianus, Roman priest 84
Goths 43, 45, 46; conversion to Catholicism 97; in Italy 70, 132; in Thrace 64; invasion of East 43; sack of Florence 136
Gotofredo of Spoleto, duke 171
Granada 239
Gratian, co-emperor 62, 64
Gratian of Bologna 181
Great Western Schism 222
Greece 9, 16, 24, 43, 44
Gregorio di Gregorii xi
Gregorio, father of Benedict VIII 164
Gregoriopolis. *See* Ostia.
Gregory, bishop of Ostia 17
Gregory, father of John VII 119
Gregory, father of John XIX 165
Gregory I, the Great, pope 55, 98, 98–100, 145; criticism of 101; destroys pagan idols 99; *Dialogues* 76, 98; Greek translation 123; liturgy 99; Maurice plots against 99; mission to Constantinople 97; *Moralia in Job* 98, 108; on Ezekiel 98; relics 141; visions of 101, 109
Gregory II, pope 121, 123
Gregory III, pope 123
Gregory IV, pope 141
Gregory V, pope 160, 161
Gregory VI, pope 166, 168
Gregory VII, pope 168, 171
Gregory VIII, antipope 175. *See also* Burdinus, archbishiop of Braga.
Gregory VIII, pope 175, 186
Gregory IX, pope 192
Gregory X, pope 195, 201, 202
Gregory XI, pope 216, 221, 222
Gregory XII, pope 225, 226, 227, 228
Gregory Nazianzen 63
Gregory of Antioch, bishop 99
Griffio, Alessandro xvi
Grimwald, king of Lombards 95, 111, 112

Gudfred, king of Vikings 135
Guelphs 200, 201; Arezzo 206; Pisa 207; Tuscany 214
Guerre horrende de Italia XII
Gugielmo, bishop of Arezzo 208
Guibert of Ravenna. *See* Clement III, antipope.
Guido, bishop of Ferrara 216
Guido, count 141
Guido de Bonarosi 211
Guidobaldo, duke of Urbino 241
Guidotto, bishop of Mantua 193
Guiscards: 147; Robert 171, 172, 174, 175
Guy de Monfort 200

H

Hadrian, emperor 25, 26, 27, 28, 61
Hadrian I, pope 127
Hadrianus, father of Stephen V 148
Hannibal 132
Hapsburgs 219, 243
Harding, Stephen 175
Harran 219
Hasa River 133
Hatto II, archbishop of Mainz XXXIV, 168
Heclide, hermit 63
Hegesippus, historian 31
Heinrich Raspe, landgrave of Thuringia 194
Helena, St. 52, 55, 56; relics 142
Henry Claude, duke of Bavaria 164
Henry I, of Saxony, emperor 152, 153, 156
Henry II, emperor 164
Henry III, emperor 166–67, 169
Henry IV, emperor 168, 170, 175; at Canossa 171; excommunication 171; Roman campaign 171
Henry V, emperor 174, 176, 177, 178
Henry VI, emperor 186, 187, 188, 190
Henry VII, emperor 215, 216; coronation in Rome 217; Italy campaign 217; revolt against Frederick II 193
Henry I, king of France 164
Henry VIII, king of England 248
Henry of Almain 200
Henry of Castile 199
Henry of Tusculum, father of Benedict IX 166
Heraclea 46
Heraclianus, rebel 71
Heraclitus, assassin of Valentinian III 76
Heraclius, emperor 101, 103, 104, 105, 106, 107, 108, 112
Hercules XXVII, 2
heresy. *See* Acephalian, Arian, Donatist, Eutychian, Hussite, Manichaean, Nestorian, Pelagian, Sebellian, Waldenian.
Hermes of Lyons 32
Hermes, prefect of Rome 26
Hermes, St. 29, 30
Hermit Friars 202
Herod, king 9
Heruli 80. *See also* Ostrogoths.
Hidalgari, Lombard queen 127
Hilarius I, pope XVIII, 78
Hilary of Poitiers, St. 58, 62
Hildebrand, cardinal 168
Hildelgarde, wife of Charlemagne 137
Hildeprand, king of Lombards 123
Hilderic, king of Vandals 87
Hippo 66
Hippolytus, St. 39, 44
Historia de la guerra del Piamonte XII
Holy Land 190, 195, 200; crusades 181, 186; Muslim 164, 185; negotiations over 228; pilgrimage to 67, 211
Holy League 245
Honorius, co-emperor 66, 67, 70–72
Honorius I, pope 104
Honorius II, pope 170, 177
Honorius III, pope 188, 191, 202, 204
Honorius IV, pope 205
Honorius, king of Vandals 81
Honorius, St. 66
Horace 7
Hormisdas, pope 85, 86
Hormuzd IV, king of Persia 107
Hospitallers 176
Hrotrud, daughter of Charlemagne 137
Hugh Capet 154, 159
Hugh of St. Cher, OP 195

INDEX

Hugh of St. Victor 178, 180
Huguccio of Pisa 187
Hugues the Great of Burgundy 150, 154
humanism and humanists XII, XVI; civic XXXII; German XXXIV; historiography XV
Humilianus, St. 50
Hundred Years' War 219
Hungarians 153; Albert II 229; and Great Schism 222; papal relations 198; Second Crusade 181; Tartars 194; under Sigismund 227
Hunoldus of Aquitania 131
Huns 65, 76, 77; in Italy 133
Hus, Jan 246
Hyginus, pope 29

I

Iacopo of Palestrina, bishop 192
Iconoclasm 78
Ignatius of Antioch, St. 23
Ilium. *See* Troy.
Illyria 6, 8, 48
India 56, 63, 96, 188, 258
Indian Ocean 239
Innocent I, pope 69, 72
Innocent II, pope 178
Innocent III, antipope 183
Innocent III, pope 190; *The Condition and Misery of Humankind* 187
Innocent IV, pope 194
Innocent V, pope 202
Innocent VI, pope XIX, 221
Innocent VII, pope 223, 225
Innocent VIII, pope 237
Innocentius, father of Innocent I 69
Ioannes, bishop of Porto 114
Ioannes, deacon, papal candidate 142
Ioannes, doctor 52
Ioannes, father of Boniface IV 102
Ioannes, father of Lando 152
Ioannes of Constantinople, bishop 68
Ioannes of Perugia, bishop 93
Ioannes the Anchorite 66
Ioannes Vicus 31
Ireland 74

Irene Sarantapechaina, empress 128, 129
Isabella, queen of Spain 239
Isabella II, queen of Jerusalem 191
Isacius, Roman patrician 106
Isauria 80
Isidore, hermit 63
Isidore of Seville XXXV, 105
Istria 106
Italy: Angevins 198; Byzantine 80, 93, 109, 111; Carolingian 133–35, 139, 142, 146, 151; Catholicism XVIII, XXII; famine 178; Franks 97, 127; French 241–43, 246; Goths 68, 85–88; Great Schism 222; Henry II 164; Huns 74, 77; late Roman 58, 63, 65; literary culture VIII, XIII, XVI, XXXVI, 78; Lombards 95–96, 118, 124–25; Ottonians 155–56, 160; Salians 167–69; Saracens 141, 146, 152. *See also* Ghibellines, Guelphs.
Iuba, king 4
Iucundus, father of Boniface I 72
Iulia, daughter of Augustus 7
Iulia, daughter of Julius Caesar 3
Iulia, sister of Gaius Caesar 5
Iulianus, father of Stephen I 44
Iulianus, Pelagian 70
Iulius, father of Stephen IV 139
Iustinus 28
Iustus, father of Hormisdas 85
Ivo of Brittany, St. 220

J

Jacobus de Vitry, bishop of Acre 188
Jacomo de Pinci XI
James, king of Cyprus 234
James, St. 15, 20, 107
Jarrow 115
Jayme II, king of Sicily 206, 208
Jerome of Prague 225
Jerome, St. 24, 39, 58, 62, 64, 105; *De viris illustribus* XII, XXX, XXXV; Latin Vulgate 67; *Life of the Holy Fathers* 56; Old Testament 66; Psalter 63
Jerusalem 12, 17, 18; Aelia Capitolina 25, 27; Byzantine 99, 104; Dome of the Rock 111; early Christian 23; First Crusade 172;

265

Holy Sepulcher 172; in legend of Gerbert d'Aurillac 161; Muslim conquest 106, 107; Persian wars 101, 104; pilgrimage to 36, 67; Saladin's capture of 185; temple rebuilt under Julian 60

Jesus Christ: birth 8; crucifixion 9; relics of 99; Holy Lance of Longinus 173, 238; True Cross 104, 105, 106, 107

Jews: baptism of 29; Caesarea 94; Christ 9; crusade tax 232; Domitian 20; Hadrian 25; Jerusalem 12; Innocent I 69; Julian 60; Mosaic law 27; Passover 35; Spain, expulsion from 239; St. Helena 55, 56

Joan, pope XXXIV, 144
Joachim of Fiore XXXVI, 182; *Liber contra Lombardum* 190
John II Comnenus, emperor 174
John I, pope 86
John II, pope 89
John III, pope 94, 96
John IV, pope 106
John V, pope 115
John VI, pope 118
John VII, pope 119
John VIII, pope 146, 147, 148
John IX, pope 150
John X, pope 152
John XI, pope 154
John XII, pope 156, 157
John XIII, pope 157
John XIV, pope 159
John XV, pope 159
John XVI, antipope 159
John XVII, pope 161
John XVIII, pope 163
John XIX, pope 165
John XXI, pope 203
John XXII, pope 218
John XXIII, antipope 224, 226, 227
John Chrysostom, St. 57, 70
John Damascene 63, 181
John, king of Bohemia 219, 220
John of Anglia 218
John of Brienne, king of Jerusalem 188
John of England XXXIV. *See* Joan, pope.

John of Montecorvino, OFM 218
John Scotus 144
John, St., martyr 60
John the Baptist, St. 9, 66
John the Deacon 146
John the Evangelist, St. 20, 23, 30
John the Greek of Piacenza, antipope 160
Joost-Gaugier, Christiane L. XXXI, XXXII
Jordan 9
Josephat 63
Josephat, town in Holy Land 99
Joseph, St. 8
Jovian, emperor 61, 62
Jubilee; 1300 211; 1450 231; 1525 248; Alexander VI, of 1500 242; Boniface VIII, 100-year 236; Clement VI, 50-year 236; Julius II 244; Paul II, 25-year 236
Judea 9, 14, 88
Julian, emperor VII, 58, 59–61, 62, 73
Julianus, assassin 34
Julianus, jurist 34
Julius Caesar XI, XVIII, XX, XXVII, XXVIII, 2–8, 29
Julius I, pope 56–57, 61
Julius II, pope 244–45
Justin I, emperor 29, 30, 80, 86, 87, 88, 96
Justin II, emperor 95–96, 96
Justin of Vienne, St. 30
Justinian I, emperor 86, 89, 91, 93, 94, 95, 117, 259; *Digest* 88; Gothic War 90
Justinian II, emperor 115, 116, 117, 119, 120

K

Kherson 22, 110, 117, 119, 145
Knights of St. Mary (Teutonic Knights) 178
Kunigunde, St. 164

L

Ladislas, king of Bohemia 230
Ladislas IV, king of Hungary 208
Lake of St. Cristina. *See* Bolsena.
Lambert, St. 116
Lambertaci family 204
Lando, pope 152

INDEX

Lanfranc of Bec 170
Lanfranchi 199
Lapondo, count 164–65
L'Aquila 177
Larissa, battle of 172
Laurentius, papal candidate 84
Lauria, Roger 205, 210
Lawrence, St. 44, 54, 81, 94, 259
League of Cognac, 1526 248
Leander, St. 105
Leandro of Campania, bishop 97
Lech River 134
Leguscus [Augustus], father of Pope Liberius 58
Lemieux, Simon XXXVI
Lenna, bishop 90
Leo, antipope 116
Leo I, emperor 78
Leo II, emperor 78, 80
Leo III, the Isaurian, emperor 78, 121, 122, 123, 124, 128
Leo IV, the Khazar, emperor 127, 138
Leo I, pope XXXVI, 73, 74, 76, 77, 78, 80; and Huns 77
Leo II, pope 78, 114, 115
Leo III, pope 78, 121, 122, 123, 124, 126, 128, 131, 136, 138, 140; Charlemagne 129; conflict with Romans 135
Leo IV, pope 127, 129, 143
Leo V, pope 151
Leo VI, pope 153
Leo VII, pope 154
Leo VIII, pope 157
Leo IX, pope 168
Leo X, pope 245, 246, 247
Leonidas, martyr 35
Leontius II, emperor 115, 117, 118, 119
Leptis 34
Le Stinche 214
Levites 36
Lewis I, king of Germany 139, 142
Lewis II, king of Germany 146
Lewis IV, emperor 190, 218, 219, 220
Lewis IV of Thuringia 190
Liber extra of Canon Law 192

Liberius, pope 58–59
Liber Pontificalis X, XV, XVIII, XX, XXIX, XXXV, 39
Libius Severus, emperor in the West 78
libraries: Biblioteca Laurenziana XXXIII; Bibliothèque Nationale de France XXVII; Cornell University VII; Indiana University VII; Newberry XI; New York Public VII; Princeton University VII; University of Chicago VII; University of Miami VII; Vatican XXXIII; Washington University, Seattle VII; Yale University VII
Licinius 52, 53
Liguria 45, 184
Linus, pope 10, 16, 17, 20
Lipari 96
liturgy: *Agnus Dei* 114, 116, 163; All Saints 141; All Souls 141; Antiphon 63; Ascension 79, 130; Blessed Sacrament 55; Confirmation 41; Consecration 74, 77, 116; Credo 64; *Deus cuius dextera beatum Petrum* 143; *Dies que nostros in tua pace disponat* 99; Easter 209; Exaltation of the Cross 105; exclusion of women 72; Feast of Evangelists 209; Feast of the Chair of St. Peter. 187; Feast of the Visitation 222; feasts of the Apostles 209; four doctors of the Church 209; Gallic 63; *Gloria in excelsis Deo* 27, 85; *Gloria, laus, et honor tibi fit rex Christe* 140; *Glory be to the Father* 62, 63; kiss of peace 70; Latin rite 64; Lent 121, 126; Lesser Doxology 62; litanies 104, 129; Masses for martyrs 45; Office 101, 103; Office of the Virgin Mary 173; papal processions 130; pascal candle 72; Passion 103; processions of relics 104; reading of scripture 69; Roman 63; *Sanctus, sanctus, sanctus, Dominus Deus Sabaoth* 26; Secret of Mass 123; Seven Forms 99; sign of peace 114; *Uere dignum et iustum est* 83; *Ut in conspectum divinae maiestatis tuae* 123

THE LIVES OF THE POPES AND EMPERORS

Liutprand, king of the Lombards 122, 123, 149
Lives of the Popes and Emperors: 1478 edition XI, XXV, XXIX, XXXV; 1507 edition XI, XVII, XXIII; 1526 edition VII, XI, XVII, XXII, XXVI, XXXVI; 1534 edition VII, VIII, XI, XII, XVII, XXII, XXIV, XXVI, XXXVII; as artifact and its history XVII–XXIII; authorship XXIV; *Liber pontificalis* and *De viris illustribus* traditions XXVIII–XXXIV; Petrarch's *De viris illustribus* XXV–XXVIII; print copies in libraries VII, XI; public and purpose XXII; Roman events XVIII; sources XII–XVI
Livia Drusilla, wife of Augustus 7, 8
Livorno 208
Livy; *Decades or Roman History* XII, XVI
Lo assedio [et] impresa de Firenze XII
Loches 241
locusts. *See* disasters: locusts.
Lodi 182
Lodogonius, St. 85
Lombard League 183, 190
Lombards: Byzantines 97–100, 111, 118; Christianity 96; dress 95; Franks 111, 127; Italy 95, 96; Naples 121; Papal States 121; Rome 100, 121, 123, 125
Lombardy: Charles V 246; Frederick II 193; Ottonian 155, 170
Longres 49
Loredan, Leonardo 242
Lorraine 142, 148
Lothair I, emperor 139, 142, 143, 146
Lothair II, emperor 154, 155, 178, 179
Lotharingia 142
Louis I, the Pious, emperor XXI, 138, 139, 145, 146; death 141; Italian campaign 141
Louis II, Balba, emperor 143
Louis III, emperor 150
Louis VII, king of France 180
Louis IX, St., king of France 106, 192, 197; canonization 210; Damietta (Seventh) Crusade 195; Tunisian (Eighth) Crusade 200
Louis XII, king of France 241, 245

Louis, king of the Lombards 142
Louis of Toulouse, St. 218
Loup, duke of Gascony 132
Lucan 12, 14
Lucca 170, 177; Guelph alliance 207, 208; Hohenstaufen 199; war with Pistoia 215; war with Siena 197
Lucia, St. 50, 51, 192, 195
Lucignano 207
Lucina, St. 42
Lucius Aurelius, co-emperor 30
Lucius, co-emperor 28
Lucius, king of England 33
Lucius, nephew of Augustus 7
Lucius I, pope 43, 140
Lucius II, pope 180
Lucius III, pope 185
Lucius Piso 5
Lucius, St. 21
Lugdunum. *See* Lyons.
Lupus, bishop 77
Luther, Martin XXXVI, XXXVII, 245, 248
Luxembourg dynasty 216
Lyons 7, 30, 32, 65, 194, 201, 218, 220, 221; papal court 214, 215

M
Macarius 63
Macarius, bishop of Antioch 114
Maccius Balbus 5
Macedomus 67
Macedonia 2, 3, 43
Machiavelli, Niccolò XXXVII
Macrinus, prefect 36, 37
Madrid 246, 247
Maeotine Marshes 135
Mainz 38
Maiolica 177
Maiorca 192
Majorian, co-emperor 78
Malatesta; Giovanni 205; Roberto 237; Sigismondo di Pandolfo 233
Mamaea, mother of Alexander Severus 38
Mamertus of Vienne 79
Manes. *See* Mani, prophet.
Manfred of Taranto, Hohenstaufen 195,

INDEX

196, 197
Mani, prophet 47, 69
Manicheans 48, 66, 67, 69, 83, 85, 107, 112; in Rome 85
Manichaeus. *See* Mani, prophet.
Mantua 74; Azzolino d'Este 196; Bonarosi 211; Lombard war 100; Pius II's crusade bull 232; Sant'Andrea 193
Manuel Comnenus, emperor 183
manuscripts XXXV; Florence, BNC, Magl. 4.6.92 XVIII; Munich, Bayerische Staatsbibliothek, MS Clm 131 XXXV; Paris, BnF, MS Lat. 6069 XXVII; Rome, BNC, 71.2.C.4 XVIII
Marcellinus, pope 49, 50
Marcellus, pope 50, 51
Marches, of Ancona 240
Marcian, co-emperor 75–76
Marcus Agrippa 6, 102
Marcus Aurelius, emperor 30, 32
Marcus Crassus 3
Marcus Lepidus 6
Marcus, pope 56
Marcus, usurper 80
Maremma 207
Margaret, wife of Virboslaus 203
Margherita, queen of Sicily 186
Marineto, bishop of Vienne 129
Marinus I, pope 146, 147, 148
Marinus II, pope 155
Mark Antony 6, 7
Mark, St. XVIII 10, 12, 15, 78
Maronites 239
Marseilles 125, 221
Marsi 102
Martial, St. 10
Martianus Augustus 77
Martin I, pope 109
Martin IV, pope 204
Martin V, pope 222, 224, 226, 228, 229
Martin of Tours, St. 61, 65, 68; biography 94; feast 215; relics 148
Martinus, bishop of Ferrara 112
Martinus of Luna 45
Martionus, heretic 29, 30

Mary Magdalen, St. 124
Mary, Virgin 8, 60, 92, 93, 94, 103, 136; as Mother of God 118
Masinus, father of Anastasius I 69
Maso del Banco 55
Matilda of Tuscany 169, 171, 174
Matteo d'Acquasparta 211, 212
Matthew, St. 11
Mattias, king of Hungary 236
Maurice I, emperor 85, 97–100, 101
Mauritius, cartularius 55, 106, 107
Maurus, St. 89, 94, 261
Maxentius, emperor 51, 52, 53
Maxentius, usurper 111
Maximian, emperor 48, 49, 52
Maximilian I, emperor 231, 243, 243
Maximin, emperor 38, 39, 40
Maximin, St. 58
Maximinus, St. 57–68
Maximinus Thrax, emperor 39–40
Maximus, usurper 65, 76
Medici: Cosimo de' XXXIII; Giovanni de' 245 (*See also* Leo X, pope); Giuliano, duke of Urbino 245; Giulio di Giuliano de' 245 (*See also* Clement VII, pope); Lorenzo de' XXXVII, 238, 245; Lorenzo di Piero (Lorenzo II) 247; Lorenzo, duke of Urbino 245; Maddalena de' 238; ousted from Florence 242
Mehmed I, the Conqueror, sultan 233, 239
Mehmed II, sultan 235
Melantia of Alexandria 33
mercenaries, German 204
Mercurius. *See* John II, pope.
Meridiana, demon 161
Merlin 79
Merovingians 124
Mesenus, bishop, papal envoy 81, 83
Mesopotamia 25
Messalina 12
Messina 204
Mexia, Pedro; *Spanish Lives of all the Emperors* XVI
Michaeas, prophet 68
Michael I Rhangabe, emperor 138

269

Michael VIII Paleologus, emperor 201
Michael Scotus 193
Milan: XIV, XXII, XXII, 34, 44, 48, 58, 62, 64, 66, 67, 72; Alessandria campaign 208; cardinal of 226; Carolingian 137; Charles V 247; Charles VIII 241; chronicles XIII; Cremona 191; Delle Torre 203, 215; ecclesiastical jurisdictions 179; Frederick I 184; Frederick II 193 Henry VII 217; Huns 77; internal strife XXII; League of Cognac 248; Lombards 95; Lombard League 184; Sant'Eustorgio 183; Sforzas 234, 246; Visconti 215, 225, 243
Miltiades, pope 53
Minorca 192
Mirabilia Urbis Romae II.8. 54
Misenum 9
Misitheus 40
Mithridates 3
Modena 6; Antonia, legend of 203; d'Este 215; Frederick II 195; Obizzo 209; San Giovanni Battista 100
Modestus, St. 50
Moesia 79
Mongols 194, 200
Monserrat, marquis of 203, 208
Mont Cenis 146
Monte a Sansavino 206
Monte Cassino 88, 113, 124, 169, 172; Saracen sack of 883 140
Montefeltro: counts of 205, 206; Federico da XXXIII; Guido I da 205, 207
Monte Varchi 217
Morea 234
Mortara, battle of 128
Moses, hermit 63
Moses of Crete 73
Mouse Tower at Bingen 168
Muhammad, the prophet 105
Murad II, sultan 235
Murzuphius. *See* Alexius V, emperor.
Muslims: Africa 108; early conquests 104; Persia 107; rise of 101
Myra 185

N

Naples, city and kingdom XIV, XX, 7, 8, 175, 177, 186, 197, 227, 241; Angevins XX; Belisarius 91; Charles VIII 241; chronicles XIV; Conradin 199; internal strife XXII; Henry VI 186; Innocent IV tomb 195; Lombards 118; naval battle 1284 205; Normans 175; papal conclave 209; Sta. Lucia 209; syphilis theory 242 villa of Lucullus 9
Narbonne 48, 198
Narcissus, patriarch of Jerusalem 34, 35
Narius Avibus Bassianus. *See* Elagabalus, emperor.
Narni 21, 157
Narses, general 93, 95, 96
Navarre 200
Negroponte 235. *See also* Euboea.
Nero, emperor 11, 12, 13–16, 19, 20
Nerva, emperor 21
Nestorians 75
Nestorius of Constantinople 73, 75
Netherlands revolt 243
New Knights 218
Nicaea, battle of 122. *See also* councils, Nicaea.
Nicephorus I, emperor 129, 130, 138
Nicholas I, pope XXI, 22, 145
Nicholas II, pope 170
Nicholas III, pope 203
Nicholas IV, pope 207
Nicholas V, antipope 218
Nicholas V, pope XXXIII, 218, 230, 231
Nicholas of Myra (Bari), St. 56, 185
Nicola, bishop of Brescia 233
Nicolao Pesce 193
Nicolaus, father of Leo, antipope 116
Nicolo, cardinal of Ostia 213
Nicomedia 55, 57
Nicopoli 37
Ninus, king 28
Nocho (Antiochus) 24
Nola 7, 76, 200
Nolhac, Pierre de XXVII
Noricum 44

INDEX

Normandy 139, 147
Normans 32; Apulia 147, 170; sack of Rome 1084 168; war with Byzantium 172. *See also* Northmen.
Northmen 135. *See also* Vikings.
Norway 182
Novatian, heretic 41, 42, 43
Nuceria 84
Numacius Plancus 5
Numerian, orator 48

O

Obizzo, lord of Ferrara 209
Obrotrites 134, 135
Ocean 62
Octavian Augustus 61, 102
Octavia, wife of Nero 13
Oderico of Pordenone, OFM 218
Odoacer, king of Goths 80, 136
Odofredus of Bologna 197
Odo I, abbot of Cluny 156
Olinia. *See* Sabina, St.
Olympius, Arian heretic 82
Olympius, exarch of Italy 109, 110
Onesimus, St. 15
Opusculo de trenta documenti del reuerendo padre Don Pietro da Luca canonico regulare XII
Order of Preachers. *See* Dominican Order.
Order of Sant'Eustacio 227
Origen 34, 35
Orkneys 12
Orléans 46
Orsini 203; Bertoldo 204; Giovanni Gaetano 203; Paolo 240
Orte 153
Orvieto 182, 210
Osneng Hill, battle of 133
Ostia 15, 141; battle of 143; cardinal bishop 56, 192, 213
Ostrogoths 80. *See also* Goths.
Otho, emperor 17
Ottaviano Theophylact 156. *See also* John XII, pope.
Otto, bishop of Porto 192
Otto I, emperor 151, 155, 156, 157, 158
Otto II, emperor 157, 158, 160, 162; Calabrian campaign 159
Otto III, emperor 158, 160, 161, 162, 163; Roman campaign 160
Otto IV, emperor 188, 189; Apulia 189
Otto of Saxony 153
Ovidius Naso (Ovid) 7, 9

P

Pachomius 63
Padua XI, XXVI, XXXIV; Baglioni 240; Este 196; Lombard sack 100; Filippo of Ravenna 196; Maximilian 243; Sala dei Giganti XXVI; university XXXIV; war with Vicenza 217
Palaeologus, Thomas 231, 234
Palermo 188; Sicilian Vespers 204
Palestine 67, 94
Palestrina 192
Palladius, missionary 74
Pamplona 133
Pandataria 91
Pandolfo, count of Rieti 167
Pandolfo IV of Capua 167
Pannonia 6, 8, 30, 32, 42, 47, 48, 61, 135, 147, 153; Huns 77; rebellion against Rome 44; Second Crusade 181; Tartars 194
Paolo of Ravenna 193
Papal States XX, XXXVII; Carolingians 133; Lombards 121, 123; origins 118; Romagna 189
Papareschi, Giovanni di Trastevere 178
Paphnutius, St. 57
Papinianus, jurist 36
Parentucelli, Tommaso. *See* Nicholas V, pope.
Paris: barbarian invasions 76; early Christian 94—95; relics 106; Saint-Germain-des-Prés 148; theologians 178, 180; university 137, 190
Parma: Charles VIII 241; Frederick II 194
Parthia and Parthians 30, 34, 36, 40, 48, 58
Paschal I, pope XIX, 140
Paschal II, pope 174, 177
Paschal III, antipope 183
Pasini, Maffeo XI
Patmos 20

THE LIVES OF THE POPES AND EMPERORS

Patricius, missionary 74
Paul, hermit 63
Paul I, pope 126, 129
Paul II, pope XXX, 233, 235, 236
Paul, St. 9, 11, 14, 15, 42, 109; tomb 105
Paul, St., martyr 60
Paul the Hermit, St. 43
Paula, pilgrim XIV, 67
Paulinus of Nola, St. 58, 76
Paulinus of Trier, St. 58
Paulus, father of Leo II 114
Paulus II, patriarch of Constantinople 108, 109
Pavia 10, 85; battle of 246, 247; Charlemagne 128, 132, 135; ecclesiastical jurisdiction 184; Franks 125; Henry VII 217; Hohenstaufen 199; Lombard 124; Lombard League 184; San Pietro in Ciel d'Oro 122
Pazzi family 206, 212
Peace of Venice 183
Pedro de Luna. *See* Benedict XIII, antipope.
Pedro III, king of Aragon 204, 205, 206
Pelagianism 74, 81
Pelagius, bishop 70, 71
Pelagius I, pope 93–94
Pelagius II, pope 97
Pepin I, king of Franks 96, 124
Pepin II, of Herstal 96, 121, 122, 123, 124, 125, 127, 128, 131, 137, 139
Pepin, king of Aquitania 139, 141
Pergamum 28
Persia and Persians 22, 25, 30, 40, 43, 47, 53, 57, 60, 61, 98; Chosroes II 101; conquest of Middle East 103; Romans 38; Sasanian Empire 82, 107;
Persius of Luna 14
Pertinax Helvius, emperor 34, 35
Perugia 6; Cesare Borgia 240; Henry VII 217; Lombard siege 123; papal conclaves 191, 198, 209; Papal States 197; San Lorenzo 190
Peter Bartholomew 173
Peter Damian 162
Peter of Alexandria, heretic 79, 81, 83, 85

Peter II of Courtenay, Latin emperor of Constantinople 191
Peter Lombard 182, 185
Peter, St. 10–11, 12, 14, 15, 16, 17, 19, 20, 21, 24, 26, 42, 50, 109
Petrarch (Petrarca), Francesco XXXV, XXXVI, XXXVII, 2, 256, 262; *Africa* XXVI; authorship of *Lives* XI, XXIV–XXXVIII, 159, 184, 222; death VIII; *De viris illustribus* VII, XV, XVI, XX, XXIV, XXV, XXVIII–XXXVIII, XXX, XXXI, XXXV; humanism XIII; Avignon XXX; Livy XXX; Padua XXVI; reputation as historian VII; Vaucluse XXVI
Petrinus, bishop 26
Petronius Maximus 76
Petrus, bishop of Altinum 84
Petrus, bishop of Ravenna 75
Petrus, deacon 100
Petrus, papal candidate 686 115
Pharnaces 3
Pharsalia 3
Philadelphia, in Asia Minor 30
Philip I, the Handsome, king of Castile 246
Philip II, Augustus, king of France 189, 192
Philip III, king of France 200, 203; war with Aragon 205
Philip IV, king of France 212, 213, 215, 216
Philip VI, king of France 219
Philip of Swabia 188
Philippi 6
Philippicus Bardanes, emperor 120
Philippus, prefect of Alexandria 33
Phillarges, Peter. *See* Alexander V, antipope.
Phillip of Arabia, emperor 40, 41
Phocas, emperor 98, 100, 101, 102, 103
Photinus 64
Phrygia 50
Piacenza 184, 201
Piccinino: Jacopo 235; Niccolò 235
Piccolomini: Aeneas Silvius XXXV, 232 (*See also* Pius II); Antonio de' 233; Francesco 233
Pico della Mirandola, Giovanni 238
Pierleoni, Pietro Leon 178, 179
Piero, prefect of Rome 157

INDEX

Pietro di Candia. *See* Alexander V, antipope.
Pietro Rainalducci da Corbaro 218
Piombino 240
Pio, Theodoro XVII
Pisa 180; Frederick I 185; Frederick II 192; Guelphs 207; Hohenstaufen 199; Innocent II 179; Maiolica campaign 177; Roman 2; Ugolino della Gherardesca 207; war with Genoa 186, 190, 205; war with Guelph alliance 208
Pistoia 185, 211, 213, 214, 215
Pius I, pope 29, 30
Pius II, pope 232, 233, 234, 235, 244
Pius III, pope 244
Placentinus, bishop 114
Placidia Augusta 72
Placidus 23
plagues. *See* disasters: plagues.
Plancus Munatius 7
Platina, Bartolomeo XXIX, XXXV, XXXVI, 236; *Vitæ Pontificum (Lives of the Popes)* XXVIII, XXX
Pliny the Younger 23
Poggibonsi 198, 217
Poggio di Santa Cecilia 206
Poitiers 58, 62, 94, 258
Poland 158
Polemon, grammarian 12
Polenta 208
Poliziano (Angelo Ambrogini) XXXI
Pollentia 68
Polycarp of Ephesus, St. 30
Pompeia 4
Pompeius Trogus 28, 29
Pompey the Great 3; sons 4
Pontian, pope 39
Pontianus, father of Urban I 38
Pontius Pilate 9
Pontus 3, 4, 27, 43
Poor Men of Lyons 218
popes. *See under* individual names.
Popilius, Cicero's assasin 7
Poppaea Sabina, wife of Nero 13
Po River XII, 77, 132, 188, 197, 201

Porphyrius 43
Porphyrogenitus. *See* Palaeologus, Thomas.
Porto 39, 148, 192
Portugal 230, 239
Potentiana, St. 31
Potentianus, St. 10
Pothinus 3
Prasians 82
Prato 213
Prester John 188
Prezzivalle dal Fiesco 206
Prignano, Bartolomeo. *See* Urban VI, pope.
Priscian, grammarian 88
Priscilian 65, 66
Priscus 103
Priscus, father of Marcus 56
Priscus, father of Sixtus III 74
Probinus, senator 84
Probus, emperor 47–48
prodigies 98; Antonia of Modena 203; Black Shuck 178; co-joined twins 155–162; Dip 178; Ioannes, Charlemagne's squire 180; man and dog's body 178; piglet with human face 176; Roman giant 167; unnatural births XXI
Projectus, father of Marcellinus 49
Prosper of Aquitaine 79
Prossedia, St. 31
Protasius, St. 50, 100
Protestant Reformation 246
Provence 50; Angevin 197, 198; Frankish 111; Muslim conquest 122
Prüm 142
Ptolemy, king of Egypt 3
Publius Clodius Pulcher 4
Pulcheria Augusta 77
Pupienus, emperor 40
Pyrenees 131, 133
Pyrrhus I, patriarch of Constantinople 107, 108, 109

Q

Quintianus, father of Leo I 76
Quintilis, month 5
Quintillus, emperor 45

273

Quirentius, St. 85

R
Radagaisus 68, 70
Raphael, angel VII, XVII
Ratchis, king of Lombards 123, 124
Ravenna 10, 72, 78, 83, 161; Adrian VI 247; Cesare Borgia 240; church jurisdiction 113, 114; election of bishops 152; Frederick II 193; Goths 44, 84, 87; Lombard siege 123; Lombard war 100; mausoleum of Galla Placidia 74; Papal States 127; Romagna wars 208; San Severo 96; Sant'Apollinare 95; San Vitale 95, 193
Raymond della Vigna of Capua, OP 221
Raymond IV of Toulouse 172
Raymond of Peñafort 192
Recared, king of Goths 97
Reformation XXXV, XXXVI
Reggio Emilia 209, 215
relics: of Jesus Christ (*See* Jesus Christ, relics); of Magi 182; of saints 146
Remigius, St. 85, 87, 88, 93
Reticius of Lyon 35
Rhaetia 6, 8, 44
Rheims 139, 161
Rhine River 3, 6, 8, 62, 68, 122, 137, 168, 179
Rhodes 247
Riccardo, count of Verona 192
Richard, earl of Cornwall 196, 200
Richard I, king of England 185, 187
Richard of St. Victor 180
Ricimer 81
ricordanze XIII. *See also* diaries.
Rimini 216, 217, 233
Rinuccio di Pepo 207
Robert II, count of Artois 208
Robert II, king of France 159, 161, 163, 164, 172
Robert of Anjou, king of Naples 208, 210; Guelph leader 214, 215
Robert of Geneva. *See* Clement VII, antipope.
Robert of Molesme 174

Roger I, count of Sicily 175
Roger II, king of Sicily 175, 177, 179, 184, 191
Roger, Pierre. *See* Gregory XI, pope.
Roland 134
Rollo, king of Normans 147
Romagna XX, XXXVII, XXXVIII, 189, 204; Adrian VI 247; Cesare Borgia 240; Frederick II 193; Ghibellines 204; Malatesta 205
Roman Empire XX, XXVIII
Romania 18
Romanus, pope 150
Rome: Appian Gate 26; Arnold of Brescia 179; Augustan 6; Aventine hill 110; basilica of Constantine (*See* Rome: St. Peter's); basilisk legend 143; Byzantine imperial visits 111; Cadaver Synod 149; Caelian Hill 20, 41, 74, 89; Campus Martius 76; Capitoline 6, 19, 25, 32, 45, 49, 186; Castel Sant'Angelo 140, 158, 159, 160, 171, 217; catacomb of Callixtus 36, 37, 39, 40, 41, 46, 61; catacomb of St. Sebastian 118; chronicles XIV; Curia 5, 45; Domine Quo Vadis 26; Domitii family 13; episcopal councils 128; floods 98, 122; Forum 6, 17; Golden Age XXVIII; Gothic Wars 90, 93; Great Schism 223; Henry VII 217; Hohenstaufen 199; interdict of Adrian IV 182; internal strife XXII; Julian's Palace 163; kingship 2; Lateran Palace 54; equestrian statue of Marcus Aurelius 186; legend of giant's body 167; Leonine City 143; Leonine Walls 129; Lombard sieges 96, 97, 123, 125, 127; Ludi Saeculares 41; Milvian Bridge 53; Nero's fire 14; Nero's Palace 15, 42; Nicholas V restorations 231; Orsini 203; Otto I 157; Palazzo di Venezia 236 (*See also* Rome: San Marco); Pantheon 6, 23, 102, 182 (*See also* Rome: Sta. Maria Rotonda); pilgrimage 211; relics 106, 136; return of papacy 221; revolt of Decius 41; sack by Visigoths 70; sack of 1527 247, 248; San Bartolomeo

INDEX

all'Isola 158, 163; San Clemente 145; San Germano 144; San Giovanni a Porta Latina 166; San Lorenzo fuori le Mura XIX, 17, 54, 59, 78, 79, 130, 186, portico of 145; San Lorenzo in Fonte 81; San Lorenzo in Palatio ad Sancta Sanctorum 191; San Lorenzo in Panisperna 81; San Marco 235, 236; San Paolo fuori le Mura XIX, 59, 71, 79, 105, 130, 211, portico of 145; San Pellegrino 140; San Pietro in Vincoli 178, 233, 236; San Salvatore 54, 130, 175 (*See also* Rome: St. Peter's); San Silvestro 129; San Sisto Vecchio 187; Santa Croce in Gerusalemme 180; Sant'Agapito 81; Sant'Agata dei Goti, 81; Sant'Agnese fuori le Mura 105; Sant'Anastasio ad Aquas Salvias 128; Sant'Angelo in Pescheria 144; Santi Dodici Apostoli 96; San Valentino 61; Saxon borgo 140, 143; Senate 3, 5, 7, 18, 19, 21, 32, 34, 38, 39, 40, 42, 43, 44, 45, 52, 84; SS. Vincenzio e Anastasio 180; Sta. Cecilia 92; Sta. Croce in Gerusalemme 130, 161; Sta. Lucia 143; Sta. Maria ad Praesepe 110, 130, 171. (*See also* Rome: Sta. Maria Maggiore); Sta. Maria in Trastevere XIX, 37, consecration of 190; Sta. Maria Maggiore 75, 79, 83, 84, Honorius III and 192, papal tomb 192; Sta. Maria Rotonda 6, 103, 182 (*See also* Rome: Pantheon); Sta. Sabina 26, 130, 140, 232; Sta. Susanna 234; St. John Lateran 79, 106, 107, 170, 177, 180, 182, fire at 216, Sergius III's renovations of 151; Sto. Spirito in Sassia 187, 238; Sto. Stefano Rotondo 79; St. Peter's XIX, 59, 71, 72, 79, 93, 104, 108, 111; atrium of 113, bronze doors of 128, frescoes of 148, imperial coronations at 191, new building of 244, oratory of St. Mary 119, pilgrimage to 132, 211, portico of 129, portico frescos of 120, relics in 138, 234, Saracen sack of 141, 143, Sta. Maria delle Febbre chapel 242, St. Peter's tomb in 140; temple of Apollo 42; temple of Jupiter 6; temple of Mars 6; temple of the Sun 46; Tiber Island 158, 163; Tiburtine district 56; tomb of Augustus 7; Tower of Maecenas 14; Tre Fontane 128; Vandal sack 71, 87; Vatican cemetery (and crypt) 16, 17, 19, 25, 26, 27, 30, 32, 34, 79, 86, 96, 106, 107, 112, 116, 123, 141, 145, 150, 151, 167, 168, 239; Vatican Hill 15, 42; Vatican Library 231; Vatican palaces and gardens 203; Via Appia XIX, 26, 36, 37, 46; Via Aurelia 15, 45, 105; Via del Corso 51; Via Flaminia 7, 51, 61; Via Lata 26, 38, 51, 58, 127, 148, 156; via Mazzarino 81; Via Nomentana 26, 105; Via Ostia 42; Via Ostiense 128; Via Salaria 51; Via Tiburtina XIX, 54; Vicus Patricius 19; walls rebuilt under Hadrian I 128

Romuald, Lombard duke of Benevento 95, 96, 111

Romulus 28.

Romulus Augustulus, emperor 80, 136

Roncesvalles 134

Ross, W. Braxton, Jr. XVI, XXX

Rotumnius, king of Lombards 95

Rovere: Francesco della 236 (*See also* Sixtus IV, pope); Francesco Maria della 245; Francesco Maria I della 245, 247; Giuliano della 244

Rudolf, emperor 202, 206, 209

Rudolf of Saxony 171

Rudolph, archbishop of Rheims 159

Rufinus, father of Silvester I 53

Rufinus of Aquileia 29, 39, 67

Rupert, count of the Palatinate 223

Rupert III, emperor 223, 225, 226

Rusticus, father of Julius I 56

S

Sabina 166, 194

Sabina, St. 27

Sabinian, pope 101–2

Saint-Clair-sur-Epte, treaty of 911 147

Saint-Gilles in Provence 198

saints. *See under* individual names.

Saladin 185, 187

Salassi 6

Salerno 172

275

THE LIVES OF THE POPES AND EMPERORS

Salimbene da Adam 196
Salinguerra of Ferrara 189, 193
Sallust 7
Salonae 49
Salutati, Coluccio XIII
Samnites and Samnium 88, 95
San Alberto 197
San Casciano 217
San Miniato 187
San Proculo 202
Sansovino, Francesco XVI; Girolamo XVI
Sapor, king of Persia 43
Saracens 50; Byzantines 105; Caesarea 94; Calabria 159; Dominican missions 193; Holy Land 164; Italy 153; Monte Cassino 146; Rome 129, 141; Sicily 152; Tartar invasions 200; Tripoli 207. *See also* Arabs, Muslims.
Sardinia XVIII, 39, 78, 80, 84, 85, 122, 179
Sarmatae 32
Sarzana 231
Sassanian Empire 69
Saturnus 17
Saul. *See* Paul, St.
Savinianus, St. 10
Savona 236, 237, 244
Savonarola, Geronimo, OP 242
Saxons and Saxony: 62, 133, 135, 139, 189; Carolingians 133, 142; England 80; Luther 245; Ottonian 156, 157, 160, 189
Scala, Bartolomeo XXXI; *History of the Florentine People* XXXII
Schedel, Hartmann, *Nuremberg Chronicle* XXXIV–XXXV
Schola Saxonum 140. *See also* Rome: Saxon borgo.
Scipio XXVI, 3, 25
Scipio Africanus XXVI
Scolaius 16
Scolastica, St. 113
Scoti 32
Scotland 74
Scoto, Girolamo XVI
Scribonia, wife of Augustus 7
Scythia 126, 135, 147

Sebastian, St. 50
Sebellian heretics 37
Selinus 22
Semiramia 37
Seneca 14, 15
Senigallia 233, 240
Septimius Severus, emperor 34–35, 36
Serafina, St. 27
Serbia 180
Sergius, bishop 109
Sergius I, pope 116
Sergius II, pope 142, 143
Sergius III, pope 151, 152
Sergius IV, pope 163
Sermona 146
Servilius Caepio 3
Sessa, Marchio XI, XII; Melchiore XVII
Seta, Lombardo de la XXVII, XXVIII
Seur 137
Severinus, pope 106
Severus, emperor in West 34, 35
Sextilis, month 6
Sextus Rufus 61
Sforza: and Charles V 246; Francesco 234, 235; Galeazzo Maria 235; Ludovico Maria (il Moro) 241
Sicard of Cremona, *Cronica* 196
Sicilian Vespers. *See* Sicily: Sicilian Vespers.
Sicily XXI, 6, 91, 92, 93, 115, 126, 160, 177, 182, 184, 196, 198, 210, 232, 265; Angevin 200, 205; Aragonese 204, 206, 208; Belisarius 91; Byzantine 111; kingdom of 197, 198, 199. (*See also* Naples, kingdom of); legends 193; Muslim conquest 110, 112; Normans 172, 175; Saracens 141, 152; Sicilian Vespers 204
Siena 170; Frederick I 185; Henry IV 171; Henry VII 217; Hohenstaufen 199; Piccolomini 232; Pius II 233; war with degli Ubertini 206; war with Florence and Lucca 197
Sigebeht of East Anglia 108
Sigismund, emperor 223, 224, 226, 227, 228, 229, 233

INDEX

Signia 110
Silverius, pope 90, 91, 92, 265
Silvester I, pope xix, 16, 53–56, 87, 125
Silvester II, pope 159, 161. *See also* Gerbert d'Aurillac.
Silvester III, pope 166
Simeon, St. 23, 136
Simon Magus 12, 15
Simon Peter. *See* Peter, St.
Simplicius, pope 79
Siracusa 109, 172
Siricius, pope 67
Sirmium 47, 48
Sisebut, king of Visigoths 103, 107
Sisinnius, pope 119
Sisoes, St. 57
Sixtus I, pope 26–27, 140
Sixtus II, pope 44
Sixtus III, pope 74–75
Sixtus IV, pope xxviii, 236, 244
Smyrna 30, 45
Song of Roland 134
Sophia, empress 95
Soriano Calabro xi
Soter, pope 31, 32
Sovana 171
Spain: Carolingian 133; Charles V 246; Great Schism 222, 223; Hapsburg 246; Muslim 121, 122; prodigies 173; Reconquista 192, 197; Roman 2, 4, 22, 50, 51, 53, 62; united as kingdom 239; Vandalic 71, 73, 74; Visigothic 73, 103, 107
Sparta 82
Spencer, John R. xxxi
Spezia 45
Spoleto 133, 140, 181
Sporus, servant of Nero 13
St. André 221
Statilia Messalina 14
Statius 14
Staurakios, emperor 129
St. Cornelius monastery 146. *See also* Carlopoli.
Stefano di Ginazano, count of Romagna 208

Stephanus, father of Deusdedit I 103
Stephen, archdeacon 43
Stephen I, king of Hungary, St. 158, 164
Stephen I, pope 44
Stephen II, pope 125, 126
Stephen III, pope 126
Stephen IV, pope 139
Stephen V, pope 148
Stephen VI, pope 149, 150
Stephen VII, pope 153
Stephen VIII, pope 155
Stephen IX, pope 169
Stephen of Vercellae 58
Stephen, St., protomartyr 9; relics 94
Sterlicchi, duke of 199
Stilicho, Roman commander 68
Strasbourg 64
Suebi 6
Suetonius xxxv
Sugambri 6
Suintila, king of Visigoths 103
Sulmona 7, 9
Sulpitii family 17
Sutri 176
Swabia and Swabians 181, 186, 191
Swiss Confederation 243
Symmachus, Boethius' father-in-law 87
Symmachus IV, the interpreter 34–35
Symmachus, pope 84
Symphorosa, St. 144. *See also* Tiburtine martyrs.
syphilis. *See* disasters: syphilis.
Syria: xxi, 3, 22, 25, 31; Christian 115, 119, 120; disasters xxi, 184; Muslim 207; Persian 103; Roman 3, 22, 25, 44, 46; Tartars 211
Syriacus, pope 39
Syrus, St. 10

T
Tacitus, emperor 12, 46, 47
Taddeo da Imola 210
Tagaste 71
Tagliacozzo, battle of 1268 199
Tancred, king of Sicily 186
Tartars 65, 188, 194, 200, 211. *See*

277

also Mongols.
Tassilo, duke of Bavaria 134
Tauritius, emperor 129, 130. *See also* Staurakios, emperor.
Taurus 14
Telesphore XVIII
Telesphorus, pope 27–28
Templars XXIII, 178, 215, 216
Tertullian 34
Theodahad, king of Goths 88, 89, 90
Theoderic, antipope 175
Theodo of Bavaria 134
Theodolus, deacon 26
Theodora, empress 48, 265
Theodora Augusta, empress 90, 92
Theodora, Herculeus' stepdaughter 48
Theodore, archbishop of Ravenna 114
Theodore I, pope 75
Theodore II, pope 150
Theodore of Tarsus 112
Theodore, papal candiate 686 115
Theodore, theologian 118
Theodoric, king of Goths 76, 80, 84, 85, 86, 87
Theodorus, father of Hadrian I 127
Theodorus of Nicaea, bishop 93
Theodosius I, emperor 65, 67, 73
Theodosius II, co-emperor 68
Theodosius III, co-emperor 73
Theodosius III, emperor 121, 122
Theodosius of Ephesus 32
Theodotto of Naples 121
Theophanu, wife of Otto II 162
Theophilas, archdeacon 126
Theophilus, archdeacon 92
Theophilus of Alexandria, bishop 68
Theophilus of Caesarea 35
Theophilus of Orléans 140
Theophonius, bishop of Antioch 114
Theophylact counts of Tusculum 151, 156
Theotmel. *See* Osneng Hill, battle of.
Theudelinda, queen of Lombards 100
Third Order of St. Francis 218
Thomas of Canterbury, St. 181
Thomas of Jerusalem, bishop 99

Thrace 39, 64, 185
Thrasamund, king of Vandals 85, 87
Thurinus. *See* Augustus.
Tiberius, father of Sergius I 116
Tiberius I, emperor 8–10, 9, 11, 12
Tiberius II, emperor 96, 97
Tiberius III Apsimar, emperor 117, 118, 119
Tiberius Nero 7, 8
Tiber River 7, 53, 58, 76, 98, 122, 149, 151, 187, 240
Tiburtine martyrs 144
Tiburtius, father of Siricius 67
Tiburtius, St. 140
Tigris River 48
Timothy, St. 15
Titus, emperor 17–19, 20
Titus, St. 15
Tivoli 144
Tobit VII, XVII
Tomacelli, Pietro. *See* Boniface IX, pope.
Torelli, Salinguerra 189
Totila, king of Goths 93
Totona (Ottone), duke of Nepi 126
Toulouse 218, 219
Tours, or Poitiers, battle of 122
Trajan, emperor XXVII, 21, 22–23, 25, 66
translatio imperii; to Franks 126
Trapani 200
Treviso 196, 213
Tripoli 184, 207
Tripolis 34
Trophimus, St. 15
Troy 2, 14
True Cross. *See* Jesus Christ: relic of True Cross.
Tunis 200, 210
Turin XI, XXIV, XXV, 132
Turks, war with 227
Tuscany: Angevins 198–99; Cesare Borgia 240; chronicles XIV; Frederick II 185; Hapsburgs 206; Henry VII 217; papal peacemaking 212–13; Roman 16; Saracen raids 141
Tuscia 68, 70, 149
Tusculum 76, 156; battle of 1167 183

INDEX

Tyre 177, 185

U
Ubaldo of Ravenna, archbishop 189
Ubertini 199, 206; Guglielmino degli 206
Uberti, Piero Asini degli 198
Ugolino della Gherardesca 207
Ugolino di Conti. *See* Gregory IX, pope.
Ulfilas 71
Urban I, pope 38, 140; relics 144
Urban II, pope XVIII, 172
Urban III, pope 182, 185
Urban IV, pope 197, 198
Urban V, pope 221
Urban VI, pope 222, 223, 236
Urbino 247
Ursatius, Arian priest 58, 59
Usodimare, Gerardo 238

V
Valencia 50
Valens, Arian priest 58, 59
Valens, emperor 58, 59, 61, 62, 64
Valentinian I, emperor 61–62, 63, 64
Valentinian II, co-emperor 65
Valentinian III, emperor 72, 73, 75, 87
Valentinus, heretic 29, 30
Valentinus, pope 141
Valeria, Diocletian's daughter 48
Valerian, emperor 43
Valerianus, father of Gelasius I 83
Valerianus, husband of St. Cecilia 38, 140
Valla, Lorenzo 53, 55
Valois dynasty 159
Vandals: 68; Arianism 73; Carthage 73; Italy 133; Rome 76; Spain 71, 73
Varchi, Benedetto, *Storia Fiorentina* XIV
Varius, father of Alexander Severus 38
Vaucluse XXVI
Vecchi, Alessandro de' XVI
Veletrae 5
Venantius Fortunatus 94
Venice: Ancona 204; Black Death 220; Bologna 201; Byzantine alliance against Latin empire 197; Charles VIII invasion 241; chronicles XIII; Cortenuova 193; Eugenius IV 229; editions of *Lives* XI; Frederick I 184; Fourth Crusade 187; internal strife XXII; Julius II 245; League of Cognac 248; Louis XII 242; Maximilian 243; patriarch of 177; publishing in XVI; San Paolo diocese XVII; Senate 245; Turkish wars 242; wars in East 101; war with Genoa 197, 210
Venus 2
Vercelli 132
Verdun, treaty of 142
Verona: 41; Carolingian 151; Conradin 198, 199; d'Este 196; Huns 77; Urban III 182
Vespasian, emperor 14–16, 18, 19, 20, 111
Vicenza 77, 184, 196, 217
Victor, duke of Münsterberg 236
Victor I, pope 35
Victor II, pope 169
Victor III, pope 172
Victor IV, antipope 183
Vienne 9, 30, 65, 115, 123, 176, 215, 216
Vigilantia, mother of Justin II 95
Vigilius, pope 90, 91, 92, 93, 94, 117
Vikings 135, 139, 143, 147, 148; invade Carolingian empire 142
Villani: *Chronicle* XIV, XV; family XIV; Giovanni, *Nuova Cronica* XXXV, 192, 195, 198, 200, 205, 206, 208, 210–17
Vincent Ferrer, OP, St. 232
Vincent of Saragossa, St. 50
Vincentius, St. 106
Vindelici 6, 8
Violante of Aragon. *See* Yolande of Aragon.
Vipianus 38
Virgil 7
Visconti: Diana Maria 243; Galeazzo 243; Maffeo 215
Vision of Charles the Fat 145
Vitalian, pope 110–12
Vitalis, bishop, papal envoy 81
Vitellii family 18
Vitellius, emperor 17, 18
Viterbo 197, 200, 202, 203; papal conclaves

201; papal palace 203; Papal States 197;
  San Silvestro 200
Vittorie 194
Vitus, St. 50, 125; relics 139
Volusian, emperor 42
Vratislaus I, duke of Bohemia 153

W

Waifar, duke of Aquitania 131
Waldensians 218. *See also* Poor Men of
  Lyons.
Wenceslaus, duke of Bohemia 153
Wenceslaus IV, king of Bohemia, emperor
  223, 224, 225, 226, 227
wheel of fortune xv
White Cardinal. *See* Otto, bishop of Porto.
William I, duke of Aquitaine 152
William I, king of Sicily 182, 183
William II, count of Holland 194, 196
Willibrord, bishop of Utrecht 116
Witiges, king of Goths 90, 91, 92
Wolf of Rimini 233. *See also* Malatesta,
  Sigismondo di Pandolfo dei.
Wynfrith. *See* Boniface of Mainz, St.

Y

Yolande (Violante) of Aragon 210
Yolande of Brienne. *See* Isabella II, queen
  of Jerusalem.

Z

Zachariah, patriarch of Jerusalem 104, 105
Zachary, pope 123
Zaragoza 133
Zedekiah the Jew 146
Zela 124
Zenobia, queen of Palmyra 46
Zeno I, emperor 80, 81, 82–83, 136
Zephyrinus, bishop 68
Zephyrinus, pope 36, 41
Zimus 26
Zizanus, heretic 30
Zosimus, pope 65, 72

This Book Was Completed on February 15, 2015
At Italica Press in New York, NY. It Was Set
in Monotype Poliphilus and Garamond Italics.
This Print Edition Was Produced
On 60-lb White Paper
in the USA and
Worldwide

* * *
* *
*

www.ingramcontent.com/pod-product-compliance
Lightning Source LLC
Chambersburg PA
CBHW030102170426
43198CB00009B/465